A New Religious America

A NEW
RELIGIOUS
AMERICA

★

How a "Christian Country" Has Now Become
the World's Most Religiously Diverse Nation

DIANA L. ECK

HarperSanFrancisco
A Division of HarperCollinsPublishers

A NEW RELIGIOUS AMERICA: *How a "Christian Country" Has Now Become the World's Most Religiously Diverse Nation.* Copyright © 2001 by Diana L. Eck. All rights reserved. Printed in the United States of America. No part of this book may be used or reproduced in any manner whatsoever without written permission except in the case of brief quotations embodied in critical articles and reviews. For information address HarperCollins Publishers, Inc., 10 East 53rd Street, New York, NY 10022.

HarperCollins books may be purchased for educational, business, or sales promotional use. For information please write: Special Markets Department, HarperCollins Publishers, Inc., 10 East 53rd Street, New York, NY 10022.

HarperCollins Web site: http://www.harpercollins.com
HarperCollins®, ▉ ®, and HarperSanFrancisco™ are trademarks of HarperCollins Publishers, Inc.

FIRST EDITION

Designed by C. Linda Dingler

Library of Congress Cataloging-in-Publication Data
Eck, Diana L.
    A new religious America : how a "Christian country" has now become the world's most religiously diverse nation / Diana L. Eck.
        p. cm.
    ISBN 0-06-062158-3 (cloth)
    ISBN 0-06-062159-1 (paperback)
    1. United States—Religion. I. Title

BL2525 .E35 2001
200′.92—dc21   2001016884

01 02 03 04 05 RRD(H) 10 9 8 7 6 5 4 3

For Dorothy Austin

Contents

★

ACKNOWLEDGMENTS

★

This study began with my interest in the religious life of India and my gradual discovery of just how extensively India's religious traditions have now been transplanted to America by a new generation of immigrants. It began with my international work in interreligious relations with the World Council of Churches and the World Conference on Religion and Peace, and my gradual realization that the challenge of creating a multireligious society is now our own. This is a book about the religious energies of a new America. It has taken shape over many years and it is a pleasure to thank all who have richly contributed to it.

My first debt is to my students, many of whom are the children of the post–1965 immigration whose complex questions of identity pose in a new key some of the perennial questions of American immigration and identity. More than eighty of these students became researchers in the Pluralism Project at Harvard University, beginning in 1991. They spent summers energetically engaged in fieldwork all over the country. They have made the Pluralism Project what it is, and I am grateful to them, one and all. Their groundbreaking research has contributed to this portrait of a new America and their enthusiasm for their work constantly invigorated my own.

Many graduate students who worked on the Pluralism Project have now become colleagues in the academic and professional world. I would like to acknowledge especially the contributions of Patrice Brodeur (Connecticut College), Julie Ann Canniff (Harvard Graduate School of Education), Stuart Chandler (Indiana University in Pennsylvania), Christopher Coble (Lilly Endowment), Rebecca Kneale Gould (Middlebury College), Maria Hibbets (California State University in Long Beach), Douglas Hicks (University of Richmond), Tracey Hucks (Haverford College), R. Scott Hanson (University of Chicago), Steve Jenkins (Humboldt State University), Lance Laird (Evergreen College), Sara McClintock (Carleton College), Michael McNally (Eastern Michigan University), Sharon Suh (Seattle University), Duncan Williams (Trinity College), and Neelima Shukla-Bhatt, Qin Wen-Jie, and Jenny Juyun Song (Harvard University).

I have benefited at every step from the inspiration of colleagues who have served as advisers to the Pluralism Project. Thank you to Richard Seager at Hamilton College, Charles Haynes and Marcia Beauchamp of the Freedom Forum First Amendment Center, Karen McCarthy Brown and Karen Prentiss of Drew University, Gurinder Singh Mann of the University of California at Santa Barbara, Jack Hawley at Barnard College, Azizah al-Hibri at the University of Richmond, Vasudha Narayanan at the University of Florida in Gainesville, Paul Numrich of the University of Illinois in Chicago, E. Allen Richardson of Cedar Crest College in Pennsylvania, Donald Swearer of Swarthmore College, Muzammil Siddiqi of California State University in Fullerton, and Vivodh Anand at Montclair State University. Here at Harvard Ali Asani, Leila Ahmed, Nathan Glazer, Charles Hallisey, and Christopher Queen have been immensely generous with their support. Colleagues at other colleges and universities from Alaska to Florida have made this work their own as affiliates of the Pluralism Project, enabling me to learn from them and from their students, and I thank them one and all.

Thank you to the core of dedicated colleagues at the home-base of the Pluralism Project at Harvard. First and foremost, thanks to Ellie Pierce, the research director of the Pluralism Project. She has brought to our work a keen eye for American developments in religion, the skills of a seasoned researcher, and the ability to build relationships of trust with religious leaders across the country. Her perfectionist eye for detail was a great gift in the final stages of writing, and I am deeply grateful for her prodigious and generous help. Our project manager, Grove Harris, has been a steady hand at the helm over many years. Susan Shumaker was there at the beginning and created good will for the project wherever she went. Susan and Than Saffel, produced our CD-ROM, *On Common Ground: World Religions in America* (Columbia University Press, 1997). In the course of this work, Susan completed a formidable set of interviews with Americans of many religious traditions and the transcript of these interviews has enriched my text here. Rachel Antell was one of our most enthusiastic researchers and organizers, and her cheer and humor made the office hum. Annie Astley, Amy Moulton, Colleen Rost, and many other students worked hard behind the scenes, and Alan Wagner, our webmaster, created our public presence on the Internet at *www.pluralism.org*. In the past year Victoria Purvis and Joe Lydon have helped immeasurably to keep chaos at bay while I worked. To all in this circle of closest associates, I owe a great debt of gratitude.

This research has been generously supported by grants from many foundations. I would especially like to thank Dr. Craig Dykstra at the Lilly Endowment, who entrusted the Pluralism Project with our first grant ten years ago, with the promise that I would produce a general readership book to make known what we were discovering about America. Our CD-ROM, *On Common Ground: World*

Religions in America, intervened in that trajectory, and Lilly enabled us, through an additional grant, to produce that work. Now, finally, the general readership book is done, and I thank Craig and the Lilly Endowment for their patience. I would also like to thank Susan V. Berresford, Alison R. Bernstein, and Constance H. Buchanan for the encouragement and the funding of the Ford Foundation for the research of the Pluralism Project and my own research and writing. Lynn A. Szwaja at the Rockefeller Foundation has also been a great help in supporting the Pluralism Project and encouraging my own work; the Rockefeller Foundation made possible my first stint of full-time writing on this book during an altogether perfect month at the Bellagio Study and Conference Center. The Henry Luce Fellowship in Theology supported a sabbatical leave and provided a collegial context for the presentation of my work in its first phase.

In the summer of 2000 as my writing was nearing completion, I was fortunate to have the stimulating company of a group of fifteen secondary school teachers who came to Harvard for an NEH summer seminar on World Religions in America. This was one of the most rewarding teaching experiences I have ever had, and it gave me a burst of energy in my final months of work. Thanks to all of them, who have now become a corps of teacher-affiliates of the Pluralism Project and have given me a sense of the promising future of the study of religion in American education.

Initial versions of several parts of this book had a trial run in the *Harvard Magazine*, the *Nieman Reports*, *The Papers of the Henry Luce III Fellows in Theology*, and *On Common Ground: World Religions in America*. Conference papers appeared in *One Nation Under God?* (Routledge, 1999) and *The South Asian Religious Diaspora in Britain, Canada, and the United States* (State University of New York Press, 2000). In the early 1990s, I worked with the gifted film maker Michael Camerini and Producer Terry Rockefeller on "Becoming the Buddha in L.A.,"(Boston: WGBH, 1994), a venture for which I served as primary academic adviser and from which I learned a great deal, as is amply evident here. Thank you!

Above all, I am grateful to the many people in religious communities throughout the country who have opened their doors and hearts to us, welcomed us into their temples and mosques, told us their stories, shared with us their hopes and concerns, and given us a glimpse of their religious lives in America. The hospitality, especially of those who have come to America as newcomers and strangers, has set a new standard of hospitality for us all. Special thanks to Mian Ashraf, Talal Eid, Mary Lahaj, Shabbir Mansuri, Pravin Shah, Premananda dasa, Rajshri Gopal, Uma Mysorekar, Ranjini Ramaswamy, T.A. and Lata Venkataraman and their son Aneesh, Bernard Tetsugen Glassman, Jakusho Kwong Roshi, Ma Jaya Sati Bhagavati, Joseph Goldstein, the late Havanpola Ratanasara, Sharon Salzberg, Larry Rosenberg, Sylvia Boorstin, Rohinton Rivetna, and Victor Kazanjian.

This project would never have come to fruition without the critical eye and the firm, yet merciful, deadlines of those who think professionally about publication, namely Jill Kneerim of the Palmer & Dodge Agency and John Louden and his entire team at Harper San Francisco. Thank you!

My brother Laury, a brilliant lawyer, died just about the time I was beginning this work. Our wonderful conversations about church-state issues made me miss the exchange he and I would have had at every step of the way. In a sense, this work is his as well as mine. My mother, Dorothy Eck, joined me on many temple visits. I am so grateful for her energetic company and for her considerable help in the final reading of the manuscript. Many dear friends have cheered me on during this work, especially Kathryn Walker, Laura Shapiro, Jack Hawley, Nell Hawley, and our beloved Willie.

Most of all, I want to thank Dorothy Austin, with whom I have shared my life for the past twenty-five years and whose company I have enjoyed in this journey into the religious cultures of America. As a professor of psychology and religion and a minister with a genius for making friends, Dorothy was an immensely helpful co-worker. She kicked off her shoes with me at many temples, mosques, and gurdwaras. I remember especially a spring vacation in Washington, D.C. when Dorothy joined me at Baisakhi festivities in a local Sikh gurdwara. We arrived as strangers at about 6:00 P.M. and by the time we left well after midnight, we were exchanging hugs and addresses with people we felt we had known a lifetime. It just would not have happened without Dorothy. She has shared my enthusiasm for this project, and whenever I was flagging in energy, she renewed my spirits. This book is dedicated, heart and soul, to her.

This book has been slowed down and also enriched by the past three years in which Dorothy and I have been co-masters of Lowell House at Harvard. This community gives visible testimony to the new religious America that is ours. Thanks to the entire Lowell House community and especially to Gene McAfee, Adrienne McLaughlin, and Tracy Marshall who have taken up the slack in the months in which my energies were consumed with writing. Finally, thanks, too, to the four young Kosovar Albanians—Amella, Aida, Kreshnik and Sokol—who have joined us in the masters' residence as our extended family, and who have patiently inquired about the progress of the book that never seemed to be done. Now it is. Thanks be to God.

CHAPTER ONE

INTRODUCTION
TO A NEW AMERICA

★

The huge white dome of a mosque with its minarets rises from the cornfields just outside Toledo, Ohio. You can see it as you drive by on the interstate highway. A great Hindu temple with elephants carved in relief at the doorway stands on a hillside in the western suburbs of Nashville, Tennessee. A Cambodian Buddhist temple and monastery with a hint of a Southeast Asian roofline is set in the farmlands south of Minneapolis, Minnesota. In suburban Fremont, California, flags fly from the golden domes of a new Sikh gurdwara on Hillside Terrace, now renamed Gurdwara Road. The religious landscape of America has changed radically in the past thirty years, but most of us have not yet begun to see the dimensions and scope of that change, so gradual has it been and yet so colossal. It began with the "new immigration," spurred by the 1965 Immigration and Naturalization Act, as people from all over the world came to America and have become citizens. With them have come the religious traditions of the world—Islamic, Hindu, Buddhist, Jain, Sikh, Zoroastrian, African, and Afro-Caribbean. The people of these living traditions of faith have moved into American neighborhoods, tentatively at first, their altars and prayer rooms in storefronts and office buildings, basements and garages, recreation rooms and coat closets, nearly invisible to the rest of us. But in the past decade, we have begun to see their visible presence. Not all of us have seen the Toledo mosque or the Nashville temple, but we will see places like them, if we keep our eyes open, even in our own communities. They are the architectural signs of a new religious America.

For ten years I have gone out looking for the religious neighbors of a new America. As a scholar, I have done the social equivalent of calling up and inviting myself, a stranger, to dinner. I have celebrated the Sikh New Year's festival of Baisakhi with a community in Fairfax County, Virginia. I have feasted at the Vietnamese Buddhist "Mother's Day" in a temple in Olympia, Washington, and I have delivered an impromptu speech on the occasion of Lord Ram's Birthday at a new Hindu temple in Troy, Michigan. I have been received with hospitality, invited to dinner, welcomed into homes, shown scrapbooks of family weddings, and asked to return for a sacred thread ceremony or a feast day. In the early 1990s I mapped out an ambitious plan of research that I called the Pluralism Project, enlisting my students as hometown researchers in an effort to document these remarkable changes, to investigate the striking new religious landscape of our cities, and to think about what this change will mean for all of us, now faced with the challenge of creating a cohesive society out of all this diversity.

Our first challenge in America today is simply to open our eyes to these changes, to discover America anew, and to explore the many ways in which the new immigration has changed the religious landscape of our cities and towns, our neighborhoods and schools. For many of us, this is real news. We know, of course, that immigration has been a contentious issue in the past few decades. Today the percentage of foreign-born Americans is greater than ever before, even than during the peak of immigration one hundred years ago. The fastest growing groups are Hispanics and Asians. Between 1990 and 1999 the Asian population grew 43 percent nationwide to some 10.8 million, and the Hispanic population grew 38.8 percent to 31.3 million, making it almost as large as the black population. The questions posed by immigration are now on the front burner of virtually every civic institution from schools and zoning boards to hospitals and the workplace. How many customs and languages can we accommodate? How much diversity is simply too much? And for whom? We know that the term *multiculturalism* has crept into our vocabulary and that this term has created such a blaze of controversy that some people mistake it for a political platform rather than a social reality. But for all this discussion about immigration, language, and culture, we Americans have not yet really thought about it in terms of religion. We are surprised to discover the religious changes America has been undergoing.

We are surprised to find that there are more Muslim Americans than Episcopalians, more Muslims than members of the Presbyterian Church

USA, and as many Muslims as there are Jews—that is, about six million. We are astonished to learn that Los Angeles is the most complex Buddhist city in the world, with a Buddhist population spanning the whole range of the Asian Buddhist world from Sri Lanka to Korea, along with a multitude of native-born American Buddhists. Nationwide, this whole spectrum of Buddhists may number about four million. We know that many of our internists, surgeons, and nurses are of Indian origin, but we have not stopped to consider that they too have a religious life, that they might pause in the morning for few minutes' prayer at an altar in the family room of their home, that they might bring fruits and flowers to the local Shiva-Vishnu temple on the weekend and be part of a diverse Hindu population of more than a million. We are well aware of Latino immigration from Mexico and Central America and of the large Spanish-speaking population of our cities, and yet we may not recognize what a profound impact this is having on American Christianity, both Catholic and Protestant, from hymnody to festivals.

Historians tell us that America has always been a land of many religions, and this is true. A vast, textured pluralism was already present in the lifeways of the Native peoples—even before the European settlers came to these shores. The wide diversity of Native religious practices continues today, from the Piscataway of Maryland to the Blackfeet of Montana. The people who came across the Atlantic from Europe also had diverse religious traditions—Spanish and French Catholics, British Anglicans and Quakers, Sephardic Jews and Dutch Reform Christians. As we shall see, this diversity broadened over the course of three hundred years of settlement. Many of the Africans brought to these shores with the slave trade were Muslims. The Chinese and Japanese who came to seek their fortune in the mines and fields of the West brought with them a mixture of Buddhist, Taoist, and Confucian traditions. Eastern European Jews and Irish and Italian Catholics also arrived in force in the nineteenth century. Both Christian and Muslim immigrants came from the Middle East. Punjabis from northwest India came in the first decade of the twentieth century. Most of them were Sikhs who settled in the Central and Imperial Valleys of California, built America's first gurdwaras, and intermarried with Mexican women, creating a rich Sikh-Spanish subculture. The stories of all these peoples are an important part of America's immigration history.

The immigrants of the last three decades, however, have expanded the diversity of our religious life dramatically, exponentially. Buddhists have come from Thailand, Vietnam, Cambodia, China, and Korea; Hindus from India, East Africa, and Trinidad; Muslims from Indonesia, Bangladesh, Pakistan, the Middle East, and Nigeria; Sikhs and Jains from India; and Zoroastrians from both India and Iran. Immigrants from Haiti and Cuba have brought Afro-Caribbean traditions, blending both African and Catholic symbols and images. New Jewish immigrants have come from Russia and the Ukraine, and the internal diversity of American Judaism is greater than ever before. The face of American Christianity has also changed with large Latino, Filipino, and Vietnamese Catholic communities; Chinese, Haitian, and Brazilian Pentecostal communities; Korean Presbyterians, Indian Mar Thomas, and Egyptian Copts. In every city in the land church signboards display the meeting times of Korean or Latino congregations that nest within the walls of old urban Protestant and Catholic churches. While the central chapters of this book focus on the Hindu, Buddhist, and Muslim streams of America's religious life, old and new, it is important to hold in mind that these are but part of a far more complex religious reality of encyclopedic dimensions.

Through these same decades since the liberalization of immigration policy in 1965, the Moral Majority and the Christian Coalition have raised the public profile of fundamentalist Christianity. The language of a "Christian America" has been voluminously invoked in the public square. However, I sense in some of the most strident Christian communities little awareness of this new religious America, the one Christians now share with Muslims, Buddhists, and Zoroastrians. They display a confident, unselfconscious assumption that *religion* basically means Christianity, with traditional space made for the Jews. But make no mistake: in the past thirty years, as Christianity has become more publicly vocal, something else of enormous importance has happened. The United States has become the most religiously diverse nation on earth.

In the past thirty years massive movements of people both as migrants and refugees have reshaped the demography of our world. Immigrants around the world number over 130 million, with about 30 million in the United States, a million arriving each year. The dynamic global image of our times is not the so-called clash of civilizations but the marbling of civilizations and peoples. Just as the end of the Cold War brought about a new geopolitical situation, the global movements of people have brought about a new georeligious reality. Hindus, Sikhs, and Muslims are now part of the religious landscape of Britain, mosques appear in Paris and Lyons, Buddhist temples in Toronto, and Sikh gurdwaras in Vancouver. But nowhere, even in today's world of mass migrations, is the sheer range of religious faith as wide as it is today in the United States. Add to India's wide range of religions those of China, Latin America, and Africa. Take the diversity of Britain or Canada, and add to it the crescendo of Latino immigration along with the Vietnamese, Cambodians, and Filipinos. This is an astonishing new reality. We have never been here before.

The new era of immigration is different from previous eras not only in magnitude and complexity but also in its very dynamics. Many of the migrants who come to the United States today maintain strong ties with their homelands, linked by travel and transnational communications networks, e-mails and faxes, satellite phone lines and cable television news. They manage to live both here and there in all the ways that modern communications and telecommunications have made possible. When my own grandparents and great-grandparents left Sweden, they did not return every few years and never again heard the voices of those they had left behind. Indeed, only my paternal grandmother ever returned at all. But today's globalization enables an immigrant from India to read the *Times of India* every morning on the Internet, to subscribe to Indian cable news on the satellite dish, to bring artisans from rural India to work on Hindu temples in suburban America, and to return home for a family wedding. As our own identities become increasingly multilocal, the formation of complex national identities becomes increasingly challenging.

What will the idea and vision of America become as citizens, new and old, embrace all this diversity? The questions that emerge today from the encounter of people of so many religious and cultural traditions go to the very heart of who we see ourselves to be as a people. They are not trivial questions, for they force us to ask in one way or another: Who do we mean when we invoke the first words of our Constitution, "We the people of the United States of America"? Who do we mean when we say "we"? This is a challenge of citizenship, to be sure, for it has to do with the imagined community of which we consider ourselves a part. It is also a challenge of faith, for people of every religious tradition live today with communities of faith other than their own, not only around the world but also across the street.

"We the people of the United States" now form the most profusely religious nation on earth. But many, if not most, Christian, Jewish, or secular Americans have never visited a mosque or a Hindu or Buddhist temple. Many Americans are not so sure what Sikhs or Muslims believe, let alone Jains and Zoroastrians. Similarly, Muslim or Hindu Americans may have sketchy and stereotypical views of Christians and Jews. So where do we go from here? It's one thing to be unconcerned about or ignorant of Muslim or Buddhist neighbors on the other side of the world, but when Buddhists are our next-door neighbors, when our children are best friends with Muslim classmates, when a Hindu is running for a seat on the school committee, all of us have a new vested interest in our neighbors, both as citizens and as people of faith.

As the new century dawns, we Americans are challenged to make good on the promise of religious freedom so basic to the very idea and image of America. Religious freedom has always given rise to religious diversity, and never has our diversity been more dramatic than it is today. This will require us to reclaim the deepest meaning of the very principles we cherish and to create a truly pluralist American society in which this great diversity is not simply tolerated but becomes the very source of our strength. But to do this, we will all need to know more than we do about one another and to listen for the new ways in which new Americans articulate the "we" and contribute to the sound and spirit of America.

ENVISIONING THE NEW AMERICA

President Lyndon Baines Johnson signed the new immigration act into law on July 4, 1965, at the base of the Statue of Liberty. America's doors were opened once again to immigrants from all over the world. Since 1924 an extremely restrictive quota system had virtually cut off all immigration. Entry from Asia had always been extremely limited, beginning with the 1882 Chinese Exclusion Act. The scope of Asian exclusion expanded decade after decade to exclude Japanese, Koreans, and other "Asiatics" as well. Asian-born immigrants could not become citizens, argued the Supreme Court in the case of Bhagat Singh Thind. Thind was a Sikh, a naturalized citizen, who had served in World War I. Drawing on a 1790 statute, the court declared Asians to be outside the range of "free white men" who could become citizens. In 1923 he was stripped of his citizenship. The 1924 immigration law then barred from immigration anyone ineligible for citizenship, and that meant all Asians.

The 1965 Immigration and Naturalization Act was linked in spirit to the Civil Rights Act passed just a year earlier. As Americans became critically aware of our nation's deep structures of racism, we also saw that race discrimination continued to shape immigration law, excluding people from what was then called the Asia-Pacific triangle. Early in his term President John F. Kennedy prepared legislation to "eliminate discrimination between peoples and nations on a basis that is unrelated to any contribution immigrants can make and is inconsistent with our traditions of welcome."[1] Robert Kennedy, the attorney general, observed, "As we are working to remove the vestiges of racism from our public life, we cannot maintain racism as the cornerstone of our immigration laws." And so began a new era of immigration and a new, complex, and vivid chapter in America's religious life.

The framers of the Constitution and the Bill of Rights could not possibly have envisioned the scope of religious diversity in America at the beginning of the twenty-first century. When they wrote the sixteen words of the First Amendment, "Congress shall make no law respecting an establishment of religion or prohibiting the free exercise thereof," they unquestionably did not have Buddhism or the Santería tradition in mind. But the principles they articulated—the "nonestablishment" of religion and the "free exercise" of religion—have provided a sturdy rudder through the past two centuries as our religious diversity has expanded. After all, religious freedom is the fountainhead of religious diversity. The two go inextricably together. Step by step, we are beginning to claim and affirm what the framers of the Constitution did not imagine but equipped us to embrace. Even so, the road is rocky.

In November of 1998, President Clinton sent a letter to the Sikh communities of America on the occasion of the 529th birthday of the teacher who launched the Sikh movement in the sixteenth century, Guru Nanak. The president wrote, "We are grateful for the teachings of Guru Nanak, which celebrate the equality of all in the eyes of God, a message that strengthens our efforts to build one America. Religious pluralism in our nation is bringing us together in new and powerful ways."[2] I am certainly among those who agree with him, for I believe that our society becomes stronger as each group's religious freedom is exercised and as people like the Sikhs articulate principles like equality and freedom in their own voice and in their own key.

For many Americans, however, religious pluralism is not a vision that brings us together but one that tears us apart. The controversies of the public square are just beginning. "Screw the Buddhists and kill the Muslims" was the response of one public official to the issue of religious diversity in May of 1997. The context was a discussion in South Carolina on whether the Ten Commandments should be posted in the public schools. The official, a member of the state board of education, was also quoted as having spoken of Islam as a "cult," worshipers of "Lucifer." The

Council on American Islamic Relations (CAIR), an Islamic advocacy group, called for his resignation from the state board of education, saying,

> American Muslims, and particularly Muslim parents in South Carolina, view these remarks with great alarm. The remarks demonstrate a level of bigotry and intolerance that is entirely inappropriate for a person charged with formulating public policy. As you may recall, when a South Carolina mosque was the target of an arson attack in October of 1995, the suspect in the case was quoted as saying he set the fire to "rid the world of evil." [His] comments can only serve to incite further acts of violence.[3]

No doubt this is an extreme case. It was widely publicized and widely repudiated, although the official did not lose his job on the state board of education. Most incidents of bigotry and hatred are not so widely publicized, from the 1990 arson attack on the old Islamic center here in Quincy, Massachusetts, to the destruction of a Minneapolis mosque by arson in 1999. The final decade of the twentieth century saw dozens of attacks on Muslims and their places of worship. In June of 2000, a Memphis man opened fire with his shotgun as worshipers approached the mosque next door for prayers. A few weeks later in Boston, vandals vaulted a fence into a Vietnamese temple compound and smashed to smithereens the white image of the bodhisattva of compassion. Difference can all too easily become a license for violence, and watchdog groups have been formed by Muslims, Sikhs, and Hindus to monitor and record assaults on the rights and dignity of their members. There are also more muted controversies, like the new issues that have landed on the agenda of the armed services, the public schools, the zoning board, and the workplace. Can a Sikh wear his turban on a hard-hat job or as part of his uniform in the U.S. Army? Can a practitioner of Wicca exercise his or her religion on a Texas army base? Can a Sikh high school student carry the symbolic dagger of Sikh religious initiation to school? Will the Whirlpool Corporation in Nashville find a way for Muslim employees to meet their obligations for prayer? Does a Hindu temple have to look more "Spanish" to meet the planning board standards of Norwalk, California? Will a young Jain, an observant vegetarian, find the contents of the meals in her school cafeteria clearly marked?

As we think through the challenges of a new multireligious America, we will need to take stock of the many difficult questions "we the people" encounter today, questions not fully anticipated by the framers of our

Constitution. And we will need to face squarely the fact that many of our newest immigrants have experienced some of the same kinds of prejudice and hatred that greeted Irish and Italian Catholics and Russian and Polish Jews a century ago. They have been attacked for wearing a red dot on the forehead, for observing Islamic dress with a head scarf, or for wearing a turban.

Religion is never a finished product, packaged, delivered, and passed intact from generation to generation. There are some in every religious tradition who think of their religion that way, insisting it is all contained in the sacred texts, doctrines, and rituals they themselves know and cherish. But even the most modest journey through history proves them wrong. Our religious traditions are dynamic not static, changing not fixed, more like rivers than monuments. The history of religion is an ongoing process. America today is an exciting place to study the dynamic history of living faiths, as Buddhism becomes a distinctively American religion and as Christians and Jews encounter Buddhists and articulate their faith anew in the light of that encounter or perhaps come to understand themselves part of both traditions. Even humanists, even secularists, even atheists have to rethink their worldviews in the context of a more complex religious reality. With multitheistic Hindus and nontheistic Buddhists in the picture, atheists may have to be more specific about what kind of "god" they do not believe in.

Just as our religious traditions are dynamic, so is the very idea of America. The motto of the republic, *E Pluribus Unum,* "From Many, One," is not an accomplished fact but an ideal that Americans must continue to claim. The story of America's many peoples and the creation of one nation is an unfinished story in which the ideals articulated in the Declaration of Independence and the Constitution are continually brought into being. Our *pluribus* is more striking than ever—our races and faces, our jazz and *qawwali* music, our Haitian drums and Bengali tablas, our hip-hop and *bhangra* dances, our mariachis and gamelans, our Islamic minarets and Hindu temple towers, our Mormon temple spires and golden gurdwara domes. Amid this plurality, the expression of our *unum,* our oneness, will require many new voices, each contributing in its own way—like the voices of Sikhs who will stand up for the "self-evident truth" of human equality not only because it is written in the Declaration of Independence but also because it is part of the teachings of Guru Nanak and a principle of their faith as Sikhs. Hearing new ways of giving expression to the idea of America is the challenge we face today.

As we enter a new millennium, Americans are in the process of discovering who "we" are anew. Each part of the composite picture of a new religious America may seem small, but each contributes to a new self-portrait of America. One word may signal a shift in consciousness. For example, as Muslims become more numerous and visible in American society, public officials have begun to shift from speaking of "churches and synagogues" to "churches, synagogues, and mosques." The annual observance of the Ramadan month of Muslim fasting now receives public notice and becomes the occasion for portraits of the Muslims next door in the *Dallas Morning News* or the *Minneapolis Star Tribune*. The fast-breaking meals called *iftar* at the close of each day have become moments of recognition. In the late 1990s there were *iftar* observances by Muslim staffers on Capitol Hill, in the Pentagon, and in the State Department. In 1996 the White House hosted the first observance of the celebration of Eid al-Fitr at the end of the month of Ramadan, a practice that has continued. The same year also saw the U.S. Navy commission its first Muslim chaplain, Lieutenant M. Malak Abd al-Muta' Ali Noel, and in 1998 the U.S. Navy's first mosque was opened on Norfolk Naval Base in Virginia, where Lieutenant Noel was stationed. When fifty sailors attend Friday prayers at this facility, they signal to all of us a new era of American religious life.

Hindus have begun to signal their American presence as well. For instance, on September 14, 2000, Shri Venkatachalapathi Samudrala, a priest of the Shiva Vishnu Temple of Greater Cleveland in Parma, Ohio, opened a session of the U.S. House of Representatives with the chaplain's prayer of the day. He prayed in Hindi and English and closed with a Sanskirt hymn, all recorded on the temple's Web site. The occasion was the visit of the prime minister of India to the United States, but the wider message was clearly that Ohio too has its Hindus, as does every state in the union. As Americans, we need to see these signs of a new religious America and begin to think about ourselves anew in terms of them.

As we shall see at the very end of the book, America's burgeoning interfaith movement gives us another set of signals about what is happening in America today as people of different faith traditions begin to cooperate in concrete ways. One example is of interest because it was led by Buddhists. In the spring of 1998, from the dazzling white Peace Pagoda, which sits on a hilltop of maples in the rural countryside of Leverett, Massachusetts, a community of Buddhist pilgrims launched the Interfaith Pilgrimage of the Middle Passage. Bringing together American "pilgrims" of all races and religions, they walked fifteen to twenty miles a day for seven months, visiting sites associated with slavery all along the coast from Boston to New Orleans. From there, some of them continued the journey by sea to the west coast of Africa. The Buddhist community sponsoring the walk, a group called the Nipponzan Myohoji, was small in size, but, like the Quakers, this group extends leadership far beyond its numbers. It was not the first time this group had walked for racial and religious harmony. It had also journeyed from Auschwitz to Hiroshima to remind the world of the atrocities of the concentration camps and the atomic bomb. On a local level, every year this group walks for three days from its hilltop pagoda to downtown Springfield, Massachusetts, to observe Juneteenth, the annual celebration of black liberation from slavery. In each case, members walk to remind the rest of us of our deepest commitments.

Envisioning the new America in the twenty-first century requires an imaginative leap. It means seeing the religious landscape of America, from sea to shining sea, in all its beautiful complexity. Between the white New England churches and the Crystal Cathedral of southern California, we see the sacred mountains and the homelands of the Native peoples, the Peace Pagoda amid maples in Massachusetts, the mosque in the cornfields outside Toledo, the Hindu temples pitched atop the hills of Pittsburgh and Chicago, the old and new Buddhist temples of Minneapolis. Most of us have seen too little of this new religious America. But having seen what I have seen, with my own eyes and through the eyes of my students and colleagues, this is the landscape I now call home. This is the America I find rich and full of promise precisely because of all it embraces.

"Let's go for the gold!" said a city councilwoman in San Diego in the fall of 1998. The issue before them was whether the Sikhs could build a temple with three gold domes along the West Valley Parkway in Escondido. The planning commission wanted the new building to have a red tile roof in order to fit in with the Mediterranean style of the area, but the city council overturned their recommendations, allowing the Sikhs to proceed with their traditional design—and the gold domes. Here, in the language of architecture, is the issue we Americans face. Do we, whoever "we" are, demand conformity, or do we "go for the gold" and open our eyes and hearts to the new differences that are ours?

PASSAGE TO AMERICA

Let me tell the story of the new religious America another way, beginning here at Harvard University, where I have taught for more than twenty years. I first came to Harvard as a graduate student at the end of the 1960s. I studied comparative religion, focusing on India, where the texture of religious life is so complex that a comparative approach is essential. I had already spent a year in India as a college student, in the days before satellite telecommunications and e-mail, when it took a whole afternoon to place a phone call and more than a month to send a letter home and receive a response. I was fascinated by India's many religious communities and their interrelations, tensions, and movements over many centuries. India became a kind of second home for me as I moved back and forth between Boston and Banaras, doing my fieldwork on the other side of the world and then returning to Harvard Square, which seemed by comparison a quiet village, moving at a leisurely pace.

When I began teaching comparative religion at Harvard in the mid-1970s, the challenge was to get my students to take seriously what we then called the "other," to begin to glimpse what the world might look like from the perspective of a Hindu, Muslim, or Sikh, those people whose lives and families I had come to know on the other side of the world. My students held all the usual preconceptions and misconceptions afloat in mainstream American culture; these religions were seen as exotic, deeply spiritual, perhaps seductive, even dangerous. In any case, they were far away, at least until the gurus of the "new age" brought them to America. But never did I imagine as I started teaching at Harvard in the 1970s that by the 1990s there would be scores of Hindu, Muslim, and Sikh students in my classes—not just international students from India, but second-generation Americans, the children of what we have come to call the new immigration. Never did I imagine that by the 1990s I would be taking my students to Hindu temples, Islamic centers, and Sikh gurdwaras right here in Boston. Or that by the 1990s the very interest that had drawn me to India—the study of a complex, multireligious society—would lead me to study the world's religions in my own country.

My return passage from India to America started right here at Harvard. I remember the moment it began in the spring of 1990. A bright young freshman named Mukesh showed up at my office door. He had enrolled in my class called Hindu Myth and Image and had a thousand questions for me, trying to relate what he was learning in class to what the swami had taught him at a Hindu summer camp in Pennsylvania. I had no idea there was a Hindu summer camp in the Poconos, and I had never had a Hindu student engaged in the tumultuous searching I had known so often among Christian or Jewish students, trying to relate the critical study of religion to their own faith. In fact, it had never occurred to me that one of my roles as a professor would be to teach American-born Hindus about their own religious tradition.

I had always had a few students from India in my classes, but that year marked the beginning of a new era of students like Mukesh. They were Indian Americans, born and raised in San Antonio, Baltimore, or Cleveland. They were the children of the first generation of immigrants who had settled in America after 1965. From the perspective of India, I knew all about the effects of the new immigration. We called it the "brain drain," as thousands of Indian engineers, doctors, and scientists left India for the United States. But I had never stopped to think what the new immigration would mean for the United States, at least not until Mukesh and his classmates reached college age and enrolled in my classes. Some of them came from secular families and had learned little of their Indian heritage; their parents were professionals who had gained their own cultural and religious knowledge by osmosis in India or Pakistan but could pass it on in only a very dilute form to their children. Others had grown up in the new Hindu or Muslim institutions their parents had begun to create here in the U.S. Some had been to a Muslim youth leadership camp organized by the Islamic Society of North America or to a Hindu family camp at Arsha Vidya Gurukulam in Saylorsberg, Pennsylvania. There were young Jains who had been founding members of the Jain Youth of North America. Straddling two worlds, critically appropriating two cultures, they lived in perpetual tension between the distinctive cultures of their parents and grandparents and the forceful assimilative currents of American culture. In their own struggles with identity lay the very issues that were beginning to torment the soul of a newly multicultural America.

The questions that emerged in my classes were not only those that underlay the foreign cultures requirement of Harvard's core curriculum, such as, How might we understand some "other" civilization so different from our own? New questions pushed themselves to the front of the agenda: What does it mean to speak of "our own" culture? What does it mean to find different streams of culture within ourselves? How are *difference* and *otherness* defined, and by whom? The word *multicultural* found a new place in our vocabulary, signaling the fact that every dimension of American culture had become more complex as a result of immigration and increasing globalization. Racial issues took on many sides, with Hispanic and Latino, Korean and Filipino, Chinese and Indian perspectives. Religious diversity was greater than ever before. In the 1950s the sociologist Will Herberg had confidently described America as a "three religion country"—Protestant, Catholic, and Jewish. By the 1990s it was Protestant, Catholic, Jewish, Muslim, Buddhist, Hindu, and Sikh, and our collective consciousness of the wide and deep presence of America's Native peoples was greater than ever before.

During the first few years of the 1990s, the sons and daughters of the first generation from South Asia alone grew in numbers to become about 5 percent of the Harvard undergraduate population. In the spring of 1993, during the graduation ceremonies for Mukesh's class, I happily discovered in the balcony of The Memorial Church the families of both Mukesh and his classmate Moitri. Mukesh's family had immigrated to the U.S. from Bihar and Moitri's family from the neighboring state of Bengal. Mukesh and Moitri were the first marshals of the Harvard and Radcliffe graduating classes that year, meaning their classmates had elected them to lead in the commencement activities. Both were Hindus. In the baccalaureate ceremonies Moitri recited a hymn from the Rig Veda in ancient Sanskrit, while Mukesh told a devotional story from his family tradition. Other members of the graduating class read from the sources of their own traditions—the Qur'an, the Hebrew Bible, and the New Testament. A year or two earlier, the ceremonies enacted beneath the white steeple were carefully constructed in the Catholic-Protestant-Jewish framework, but this was a new Harvard. It had happened in four years, and it had changed the university forever.

Harvard is hardly a bellwether of American culture. Having myself come east from the Rocky Mountains in Montana with an eye trained in the vastness of the West, I know how easy it is to lose perspective among the bricks, maples, and hills of New England. Nonetheless, Harvard *is* old, and its history as a place of higher education spans the history of our nation, from the time of the first European settlement to today. Like many of America's private colleges, Harvard College began as a religious school with a normative, Christian vision of itself. In 1636 the Puritans of New England founded it to educate Christian clergy. In their own words, so often quoted from *New England's First Fruits,* published in 1643, "After God had carried us safe to New England, and we had builded our houses, provided necessaries for our livelihood, reared convenient places for God's worship, and settled the civil government, one of the next things we longed for and looked after was to advance learning and perpetuate it to posterity; dreading to leave an illiterate ministry to the churches, when our present ministers shall lie in the dust."

Harvard was a Christian college, as exclusively and unapologetically as Massachusetts was a Christian commonwealth. In 1649 a Sephardic Jewish merchant named Solomon Franco was "warned out" of the town of Boston, which is to say he was invited to leave. In 1720, however, another Sephardic Jew, an Italian named Judah Monis, managed to get an M.A. from Harvard and eventually published A Grammar of the Hebrew Tongue, a text for the young would-be clerics who were then required to learn Hebrew, Greek, and Latin. But before Monis was hired to teach Hebrew in 1722, he publicly converted to Christianity. Over three and a half centuries, the small homogeneous college of young men faced the struggles of our wider culture. In the late nineteenth century, as the numbers of Catholics grew, so did prejudice against them. As the numbers of Jews mushroomed in the first two decades of the twentieth century, from 7 percent in 1900 to 21.5 percent in 1922, some voiced concern, including President Abbott Lawrence Lowell, who suggested a quota for Jewish students. The faculty wisely rejected the idea but began to cast a new and wider net for admissions in urban centers beyond the East Coast.[4]

Both the Puritan founders of Harvard and our first Jewish instructor, Judah Monis, would be astounded at the Harvard of today. Harvard's Christians now flock to a vibrant Catholic student center, to ecumenical, evangelical, and mainline Christian groups, and to energetic Chinese and Korean Christian fellowships. The new Rosovsky Center for the Jewish community is named after a beloved dean, Henry Rosovsky, often referred to as the "rabbi" of the Faculty of Arts and Sciences. It is already bursting at the seams with Reform, Conservative, and Orthodox congregations. The building has a glass exterior, making its busy life of study, mealtime fellowship, and prayer completely transparent to the passing motorist or pedestrian, signaling the visible presence Jews now have at the university.

The Harvard Islamic Society, launched in the 1950s, has moved time and again to larger, but still temporary, quarters as the numbers of Islamic students in the university has grown. While the organization has a designated prayer room in the basement of one of the freshman dormitories, Friday prayers need a larger space and are held in the Lowell Lecture Hall. Symbolically, the Islamic presence gained public recognition when, in June of 1997, Imam Talal Eid stood on the platform of The Memorial Church before twenty-five thousand people assembled for commencement and opened the ceremonies with prayer. This was the first time in Harvard's history that the preacher of the day had been Muslim. One Friday in the fall of 1998, I climbed the steps of Widener Library to hear a young African American from the Harvard Islamic Society recite the call to noontime prayer. It was the conclusion of the annual Islam Awareness Week, and those who heard the lilting Arabic broadcast across Harvard Yard were hearing a call sounded for the first time in this space at the heart of America's oldest university.

In December of 1994, I attended the ceremony of the Buddha's Enlightenment Day. It was the first public event of the newly founded Harvard Buddhist Community. In a stately, wood-paneled room at the Divinity School, beneath august portraits of a long lineage of Divinity deans, some fifty Harvard students from a dozen Buddhist lineages sat on rows of square *zabutons,* listening to Pali, Tibetan, and Vietnamese chanting. One by one, they rose to bow to the Buddha and to make offerings of incense. The Divinity School eventually purchased a dozen *zafus* and *zabutons* for sitting meditation, and by the Buddha's Enlightenment Day of 1998 there were six Buddhist sitting groups. The fixed pews of the Divinity School chapel had been removed in favor of chairs to accommodate Buddhist meditators.

For most of the 1990s, there was no specifically Hindu organization at Harvard. Swami Sarvagatananda of Boston's old Ramakrishna Vedanta Society in the Back Bay had a place on Harvard's United Ministry, but Harvard Hindus did not gravitate to the downtown center or to Vedanta. In 1997 they organized a Hindu student group called Dharma—the first in Harvard's 360 years. One Sunday afternoon a month, they now gather in a common room to sing devotional songs called *bhajans* and study the Bhagavad Gita together. They also organize observances of Hindu festivals. That first year the Festival of Lights, or Diwali, a domestic celebration of the goddess Lakshmi, took place in the suite of a Harvard senior named Kavita and her roommates. There was a makeshift altar to which everyone contributed the images of the gods they had brought from home; there were strings of electric lights, flowers, fruits, sweets, incense, and candles. "When I came to college," said Kavita, "I didn't realize how much I would miss Diwali. At home, Diwali was our favorite holiday, but I never had to *do* anything for Diwali to happen at home. It just happened. But here at Harvard I realized that Diwali would not just happen. There would be no Diwali celebration unless I made one. So I called home and found out what to do."

In the fall of 1998 my partner, Dorothy Austin, and I moved onto campus to be house masters in one of the student houses. It had not been an easy decision. On the plus side, it meant having the opportunity to help create a pluralist community in a living context. On the downside, it meant giving up my planned sabbatical leave in India and missing the festival of the Goddess, called Navaratri, which I had not been able to attend for over twenty years. But the first week in October, I received an invitation to a Navaratri festival organized by Dharma. The group had booked the common room in the house for a worship service, called a *puja,* to be followed by a *ras garbha* dance, the traditional stick dance now all the rage in the South Asian American subculture, across the way in the dining hall.

That night, I put on my black-mirrored *selvar kamiz* and went to the common room. There at the far end of the room, under the stern portraits of Harvard dignitaries, they had arranged an altar. Students were swirling about the room in their holiday best—the young women in a rainbow of silk saris and *selvar kamizes* and the young men in pressed *kurtas.* They had brought a range of deities for the altar, the ones they ordinarily kept on their dorm room bureaus or bookshelves in the makeshift altars of college life. Manish and Monica, the chief organizers, sat at the altar and began the ceremonies. Manish led the *puja,* reciting Sanskrit verses and explaining the steps of worship as he performed them. Monica encouraged the assembled students to share in singing their favorite *bhajans,* and they did, occasionally apologizing for the parts they could not remember. Finally, they stood for the lamp offering called *arati* and sang the traditional Hindi verses, which many of the students knew by heart. It was a simple celebration, but in the life of an American institution like Harvard, even such a simple celebration is truly a revolution. With a happy heart, I stayed for the *ras garbha* and danced till I dropped.

What has happened here has also happened at colleges and universities throughout the country. Our campuses have became the laboratories of a new multicultural and multireligious America. The interreligious issues we face here are not just Harvard's issues or America's issues. They have become our own distinctive recasting of the world's issues—the issues of India and South Africa, Bosnia and Sierra Leone, China and Indonesia. Will all these differences of race, culture, ethnicity, and religion fracture our communities, or will they lead us toward the common purpose of an informed, energetic, and even joyous pluralism?

THE PLURALISM PROJECT

When I first met these new students—Muslims from Providence, Hindus from Baltimore, Sikhs from Chicago, Jains from New Jersey—they signaled to me the emergence in America of a new cultural and religious reality about which I knew next to nothing. At that point I had not been to an American mosque, I had never visited a Sikh community in my own country, and I could imagine a Hindu summer camp only by analogy with my Methodist camp experience. I felt the very ground under my feet as a teacher and scholar begin to shift. My researcher's eye began to refocus—from Banaras to Detroit, from Delhi to Boston.

It became clear to me that the very shape of our traditional fields of study was inadequate to this new world. In the field of religious studies, those of us who study Buddhism, Islam, or Hinduism traditionally earn our academic stripes by intensive study in Japan, Egypt, or India, doing language studies, textual editions and translations, and fieldwork. Now it became clear that to teach a course on Hinduism, I would also have to know something about Hinduism in America. Something similar was happening to my colleagues in the field of American religion. For decades they had focused largely on the Protestant mainstream, or perhaps on American Catholicism or Judaism. But what about the many submerged histories—the old Islamic traditions of the African slaves, the old Chinese temple communities in Montana and Idaho, or the early Sikh communities in California's Imperial Valley? And what about the immigrant religious histories just now unfolding—the Korean Buddhists and Christians, the Tamil Hindus, the Indian and Pakistani Muslims? Didn't these also belong in a course on American religion? Other colleagues were on the front lines of the developing fields of multicultural studies or ethnic studies. Reading their works, I was astonished to find a strong normative, ideological secularism that seemed studiously to avoid thinking about religion at all. For them, the religious traditions of America's ethnic minorities were simply not on the screen. Their lively discussions of Asian immigrants, for example, proceeded as if Asian Americans had no religious lives, built no religious institutions, gathered in no religious communities.

I scarcely had time to undertake new research, so I decided on a makeshift strategy: teaching a class on a subject I knew nothing about. I announced a research seminar called World Religions in New England. In the company of twenty-five students, I set out to study multireligious America, beginning here in Boston. I had lived in the city for twenty-five years, and I was amazed. Yes, the imagined New England landscape of white steeples and colonial town greens was still here, almost picture perfect, but what a range of other communities had settled right next door!

We visited the spectacular new Sri Lakshmi temple in Ashland, not far from the starting point of the Boston marathon, a temple designed by

Hindu ritual architects, its ornate tall towers decorated with images of Hindu deities and consecrated with the waters of the Ganges mingled with the waters of the Mississippi, Colorado, and Merrimac Rivers. We joined weekend worshipers for the weekly Saturday morning liturgies as the tall granite image of Lord Vishnu was bathed in gallons of milk and royally dressed to receive the offerings of the faithful and dispense his gifts of grace—sanctified fruits and water. The next week we split into teams to visit half a dozen other Hindu communities in the Boston area—from the older Vedanta Society and the Hare Krishna temple to the Swaminarayan temples of Lowell and Stow.

One Friday we took the subway down to Quincy, where New England's first mosque was built in the 1950s in the shadow of the great cranes of the Quincy shipyards. Back then, the community consisted of Lebanese who immigrated early in the century, but the hundreds of Muslims who come today for Friday prayers are from all over the world. We discovered that some twenty other mosques and Islamic centers are members of the Islamic Council of New England. On a quiet residential street in Norwood, we visited the Jain community gathered in what was formerly a Swedish Lutheran church. The Jains of New England are heirs of an ancient religious tradition going back to the beginning of the first millennium B.C.E. in India. Now, halfway around the world, they were celebrating the end of their yearly season of fasting with songs, dancing, and feasting. We found Boston's Sikhs, also from India, gathered in what was formerly a Kingdom Hall of the Jehovah's Witnesses in the town of Milford, and in nearby Millis was a community of American-born Sikhs of the Sikh Dharma movement.

There were more Buddhist communities than we could readily visit, even in teams. Down the street from the university we all spent an hour sitting in silence at the Cambridge Insight Meditation Center. Then we heard about the history of Insight meditation in the West from the resident teacher, Larry Rosenberg, who had taught psychology before heading for Southeast Asia to study Buddhist meditation practice. The next week we fanned out to see the Korean Kwan Um Zen Center and the old Cambridge Zen Center, the Dharmadhatu Tibetan center, and the Korean Zen Martial Arts Center. North of Boston, in the old industrial city of Lynn, one of our seminar members attended the monastic ordination of a young Cambodian man who had come to the U.S. as a refugee. He kneeled, his head shaved, to receive his robes, amid a Cambodian community that by then had three temples in the northern outskirts of Boston. Some of us visited the Vietnamese temple in Roslindale, the

Chinese Buddhist temple in Lexington, and the new Thousand Buddha Temple built by Chinese nuns in Quincy. The variety was breathtaking. While some, like the Insight Meditation Center, were exclusively devoted to meditation practice, others, like those in the Chinese communities, practiced the chanting and recitations of Pure Land Buddhism. One fine day, the Thousand Buddha Temple community chartered a harbor cruise boat and took hundreds of live lobsters out into Boston Harbor to release them into the sea as an act of compassion.

This is Boston today, a city that would astonish its Puritan founders—as it astonished us. That semester the reading list took a backseat to our citywide forays, which resulted in animated and serious discussion like I had never before experienced in a seminar. Eventually we published *World Religions in Boston*, a documentary guide to a city whose Asian population had doubled in ten years, a city that gave us our first glimpse of the new religious America.

This was the genesis of the Pluralism Project. I was sure that what had happened here in Boston was happening also in many other American cities. What about Houston, Denver, Detroit? With foundation funding, I hired students to spend the summer in their own hometowns and find out what changes were under way there. For three summers students fanned out across the United States, staying with parents, grandparents, and roommates, visiting mosques, Sikh gurdwaras, and Hindu, Buddhist, and Jain temples. It was a fascinating summer job and not always easy. All these students—no matter what race or religion—had to become strangers in their own homes. As Jonathan, a religion major from Minneapolis, put it, "I grew up in the Twin Cities, so I have lived here all my life. But the city I discovered this summer was something I had never imagined." Minneapolis and St. Paul, traditionally 34 percent Lutheran, are now home to more than 80,000 Asians and Pacific Islanders, approximately half of whom are refugees, including 14,000 Hmong, 10,000 Vietnamese, 8,000 Lao Buddhists, and 7,000 Cambodians. Their temples are an important part of the religious texture of the cities today—along with Islamic Centers, Baha'i communities, and the temples of Minnesota Hindus and Jains.

Like Jonathan, all of our Pluralism Project researchers found a religious landscape they had not known before. Of course, this new religious reality is most visible in the sprawling cosmopolitan cities of America, in world cities like Los Angeles, New York, and Houston. But even in the heartland of America, the new multireligious reality is becoming a Main

Street phenomenon. Muslims, Hindus, and Buddhists live in the heavily Mormon neighborhoods of Salt Lake City and in the Bible Belt of Dallas. One of America's most spectacular new mosques is in the suburbs of Cleveland. One of the most beautiful Hindu temples sits on a hilltop south of Chicago. There are Cambodian and Vietnamese Buddhist communities in Iowa and Oklahoma, Tibetan Buddhist retreat centers in the mountains of Vermont and Colorado, and Sikh gurdwaras in the wooded suburban countryside of Fairfax County, Virginia.

These changes to the American landscape have only recently become visible at least architecturally. The first generation of American mosques could be found in places like a former watch factory in Queens, a U Haul dealership in Pawtucket, Rhode Island, a gymnasium in Oklahoma City, and a former mattress showroom in Northridge, California. You could easily drive right on by the warehouse, the storefront, or gymnasium and not notice anything new at all. Because the meeting places were invisible, many Americans, understandably, remained unaware of the new communities. The 1980s and 1990s, however, saw a crescendo of construction. Dozens of new mosques were built, such as the mosque on 96th Street and Third Avenue in New York, the Bridgeview and Villa Park mosques in Chicago, or the Southwest Zone mosque in Houston, to name but a few. There are now multimillion-dollar Hindu temples, like the Bharatiya Temple, in the wealthy northern suburbs of Detroit and the spectacular Sri Meenakshi Temple rising from the flats south of Houston. The Buddhists have also made a striking architectural imprint, with the huge Hsi Lai temple in Hacienda Heights, California, a construction project resisted at every step by the community and now so beautiful that "temple view" real estate is coveted—and expensive. In the western Chicago suburb of Bartlett, the Jains have built a large new temple, and to the north in Palatine lies the visually striking hexagonal gurdwara of the Sikhs.

Driving out New Hampshire Avenue, one of the great spokes of the nation's capital, just beyond the Beltway is a stretch of road only a few miles long where one can glimpse in brief compass the new landscape of religious America. Set back from the road on a grassy slope is a new Cambodian Buddhist temple with its graceful, sloping tiled roof. Then one sees the new copper-domed mosque of the Muslim Community Center, set between an onion-domed Ukrainian Orthodox Church and a Disciples of Christ church. Farther along is a new brick Gujarati Hindu temple called Mangal Mandir, and just off New Hampshire Avenue is a Jain temple. The many churches along the way also reveal the new dimensions of America's Christian landscape, with Hispanic Pentecostal, Vietnamese Catholic, and Korean evangelical congregations sharing facilities with more traditional English-speaking mainline churches.

We must be clear about the fact that this diversity alone does not constitute pluralism. It is plain evidence of the new religious America, but whether we are able to work together across the lines of religious difference to create a society in which we actually know one another remains to be seen. On New Hampshire Avenue, that process is just beginning. Schoolchildren come for visits to the mosque and the Cambodian temple; the two churches that flank the Islamic center lend their parking lots for the two large Eid prayers; and all these communities have a growing awareness of the InterFaith Conference of Metropolitan Washington.

Beyond the changing landscape of our cities, the Pluralism Project is interested in how these religious traditions are changing as they take root in American soil. When Tristan, one of our summer researchers, interviewed a Vietnamese monk in Phoenix, the monk said, "We have to take the plant of Buddhism out of its Asian pot and plant it in the soil of Arizona." The monk's observation could apply to any of the new religious communities. What does Buddhism look like as it begins to grow in its new soil? What will Islam become as it spreads into the suburban life of Houston? What will Hinduism look like as it takes root in central Minneapolis, where Hindu young people take ski trips together and celebrate their high school graduation at the temple with a *puja*? Religions are not like stones passed from hand to hand through the ages. They are dynamic movements, more like rivers—flowing, raging, creative, splitting, converging. The history of religions is unfolding before our eyes. Perhaps nowhere in the world is it more interesting to study the process of dynamic religious change in this new century than in America.

Not only is America changing these religions, but these religions are also changing America. This too is an important question for ongoing study. What does this new religious diversity mean for American electoral politics, for the continuing interpretation of church-state issues by the Supreme Court? What does it mean for American public education and the controversies of school boards? What will it mean for colleges and universities with an increasingly multireligious student body? What about hospitals and health care programs with an increasingly diverse patient population? While many people are just beginning to become aware of the changing religious landscape, the issues it has begun to raise for the American pluralist experiment are already on the agenda of virtually every public institution.

Our new questions are not only civic, however, but also spiritual and theological. How will Christians and Jews, long dominant in America, respond to this new diversity? Churches, synagogues, and theological schools have barely begun to take notice of this new religious reality. Yet, with the changing landscape, the entire context of ministry has begun to change. Adherents of other faiths are no longer distant metaphorical neighbors in some other part of the world but next-door neighbors. A block down the street from a United Church of Christ congregation in Garden Grove, California, is the Lien Hoa Buddhist temple, the home of several Vietnamese Buddhist monks. Next door to the Atonement Lutheran Church in San Diego is San Diego's largest Islamic Center. In Flushing, New York, a synagogue stands next door to a storefront Sikh gurdwara, across the street from Swaminarayan Hindu temple, and down the street from the Ganesha Hindu Temple. And yet few theological schools are able to equip Christian or Jewish clergy for their changing educational roles in this new ministerial context. The issue of living in a pluralist society and thinking theologically about the questions it poses is important today for every community of faith. How do we think about our own faith as we come into deeper relationship with people of other faiths and as we gain a clearer understanding of their religious lives?

As a Christian, a Montana-born, lifelong Methodist who has lived and studied in India, I too have asked this question. How do I articulate my faith in a world in which neighbors, colleagues, and students live deeply religious lives in other communities of faith? When I began my studies of the Hindu tradition, living in the sacred city of Banaras, I tried to articulate, in *Banaras, City of Light,* what this holy city and all it represents means for Hindus. Further along life's journey, I wrote *Encountering God: A Spiritual Journey from Bozeman to Banaras,* which tackled another equally difficult question: What does Banaras and all it represents mean for me, as a Christian? Through the years I have found my own faith not threatened, but broadened and deepened by the study of Hindu, Buddhist, Muslim, and Sikh traditions of faith. And I have found that only as a Christian pluralist could I be faithful to the mystery and the presence of the one I call God. Being a Christian pluralist means daring to encounter people of very different faith traditions and defining my faith not by its borders, but by its roots.

Many Christians would not agree with me. In the fall of 1999 the Southern Baptist Convention published a prayer guide to enable

Christians to pray for Hindus during Diwali, their fall festival of lights. It spoke of the 900 million Hindus who are "lost in the hopeless darkness of Hinduism . . . who worship gods which are not God."[5] Many Christians have no trouble at all speaking of "our God" in exclusivist terms as if God had no dealings with Hindus. The problem with such a response, however, is that it misunderstands both Hindu worship and Hindu experience of God. The American Hindus who carried placards protesting the Southern Baptist prayer guide before Second Baptist Church in Houston did so not because they were averse to being the focus of Christian prayers, but because the characterization of their religious tradition was so ill-informed and ignorant. As I would put it in the language of my own tradition, it is fine for Baptists to witness to their faith; indeed, it is incumbent upon Christians to do so. But it is not fine for us to bear false witness against neighbors of other faiths.

Articulating one's own faith anew in a world of many faiths is a task for people of every religious tradition today, and in every tradition there are thinkers and movements taking up this task. We cannot live in a world in which our economies and markets are global, our political awareness is global, our business relationships take us to every continent, and the Internet connects us with colleagues half a world away and yet live on Friday, or Saturday, or Sunday with ideas of God that are essentially provincial, imagining that somehow the one we call God has been primarily concerned with us and our tribe. No one would dream of operating in the business or political world with ideas about Russia, India, or China that were formed fifty, a hundred, or five hundred years ago. I might sing "Give me that old-time religion! It's good enough for me!" with as much gusto as anyone, but in my heart I know that the old-time religion is not "good enough" unless those of us who claim it are able to grapple honestly and faithfully with the new questions, challenges, and knowledge posed to us by the vibrant world of many living faiths. To be good enough, the old-time religion has to be up to the challenges of an intricately interdependent world.

Theological questions and civic questions are different, however. And it is important that we understand the difference. No matter how we evaluate religions that are different from our own, no matter how we think about religion if we are atheists or secularists, the covenants of citizenship to which we adhere place us on common ground. The Southern Baptists who pray for Hindus who are "lost" are perfectly free to do so. Their theological ideas are not governed by our Constitution, but their commitment to the free exercise of religion, even for Hindus, is. For a moment in September of 2000, the conservative Family Research Council became confused about this distinction. When the first-ever Hindu invocation was given at the U.S. House of Representatives, the council denounced it as a move toward "ethical chaos," saying it was "one more indication that our nation is drifting from its Judeo-Christian roots. . . ." On second thought, the council issued a much-needed clarification: "We affirm the truth of Christianity, but it is not our position that America's Constitution forbids representatives of religions other than Christianity from praying before Congress."[6]

Today all of us are challenged to claim for a new age the very principles of religious freedom that shaped our nation. We must find ways to articulate them anew, whether we are Christian, Jewish, Muslim, Buddhist, or secular Americans. We must embrace the religious diversity that comes with our commitment to religious freedom, and as we move into the new millennium we must find ways to make the differences that have divided people the world over the very source of our strength here in the U.S. It will require moving beyond laissez-faire inattention to religion to a vigorous attempt to understand the religions of our neighbors. And it will require the engagement of our religious traditions in the common tasks of our civil society. Today, right here in the U.S., we have an opportunity to create a vibrant and hopeful pluralism, in a world of increasing fragmentation where there are few models for a truly pluralistic, multireligious society.

NOTES

1. John F. Kennedy, *A Nation of Immigrants* (New York: Harper & Row, 1964), 107.

2. *San Diego Union-Tribune,* November 13, 1998.

3. Council on American Islamic Relations press release, "CAIR Calls for Removal of South Carolina Office Who Said 'Kill the Muslims'" (Washington, DC, May 19, 1997).

4. The complexity of these proceedings is recorded in Nitza Rosovsky, *The Jewish Experience at Harvard and Radcliffe* (Cambridge: Harvard University Press, 1986), 8–25.

5. *Divali: Festival of Lights Prayer for Hindus* (Richmond, VA: International Mission Board of the Southern Baptist Convention, 1999); see www.imb.org.

6. Stephen Koff, "Criticism of Hindu Plucked from the Web," *Cleveland Plain Dealer,* September 23, 2000.

CHAPTER TWO

FROM MANY, ONE

★

One March day as the wind blew away the feeble heat of the sun, I boarded a boat in lower Manhattan and set out on a pilgrimage. First stop, the Statue of Liberty. I circumambulated the great lady and admired the crowds of fellow pilgrims posing for photos, skirts and scarves blowing in the wind, but I didn't linger for the films and exhibits. Ellis Island was my real destination. My grandmother and the grandmothers of millions of my generation came this way to America. I had imagined her arrival in New York in 1914 ever since I was old enough to hear the story. Anna Nordquist was no more than twenty when she and her mother, Louisa, and sister, Signe, sailed from Sweden on the *Lusitania*. They were the last in the chain migration of a large family of Nordquists from Sünne, Varmland, to the American West. Eventually, Anna settled in Anaconda, Montana, and married my grandfather, Theodore Eck, also a Swede. He had come in from Ontario via Sault Ste. Marie. That March morning, walking into the great hall at Ellis Island, moving from room to room as the guides directed, sitting on the benches where Anna might have sat, I glimpsed the slow progress Grandma would have made in her first hours in this new world—lines, desks, luggage, health examinations, more lines. Finally, I wound up in the exhibit halls, viewing a perspective on America's immigration saga that Grandma would not have had, so immediate and personal was her own experience.

The most moving parts of the exhibit were the large glass cases displaying the things that other grandmothers, then young women like Anna Nordquist, had brought with them to the new world: a Swedish Bible brought by Larsena Jenson, who came on the Scandinavian-American Line, a Lutheran hymnal belonging to Gertrud Lehnberger from Germany, a Lithuanian prayer book that had come across the Atlantic with

Grucis Visbaras, a cathedral psalter from Trinidad and Tobago, and the sheet music of a Polish cantor. There were Jewish prayer shawls from Russia, hand-painted Easter eggs from Bohemia, a Christmas statue of the Christ child from the Azores, and a baptismal gown from Sicily. All these material objects gave plain testimony to the varieties of religious life that came to the United States with immigrants from Europe.

In the adjacent hall I found a more sobering exhibit: large photographs of the anti-immigrant episodes of American history. First there was a Chinese woman with deep, questioning eyes whose experience was very different from that of Great-Grandma Nordquist, who came to the U.S. to join her sons and her husband. The woman's name was Lam Shi Lin. Her photo had been taken in Canton in 1920. The inscription read: "Her seven sons came to the U.S. with their father, Bing Wang, but the Chinese Exclusion Act barred her from joining them. She died in China before the Law was repealed."

In the next panel a 1902 poster from Tacoma, Washington, caught my eye. I was born in Tacoma General Hospital during World War II when my father worked in the shipyards there, so this was home territory. The large-type headline read: "Anti-Chinese Mass Meeting!" The poster advertised a rally with two featured speakers, both Christian ministers, talking about the threat of Chinese immigrants. The explanatory note informed visitors to Ellis Island that the anti-Chinese movement in Tacoma had begun three decades earlier and that in 1885 three hundred armed residents of Tacoma had forced seven hundred Chinese workers onto wagons, deposited them at the edge of town, and then burned Tacoma's Chinatown to the ground.

A few steps away, I halted before a photo of the Ku Klux Klan marching through the streets of Long Branch, New Jersey, on the Fourth of July, 1924. They were protesting the immigration of Jews and Catholics to the U.S. *The Fiery Cross,* a Klan publication, was cited in the display notes: "Jews dominate the economic life of the nation, while the Catholics are determined to dominate the political and religious life. . . . The vast alien immigration is, at the root, an attack upon Protestant religion with its freedom of conscience, and is therefore a menace to American liberties." The reason for the rise of anti-immigration sentiment after World War I was clearly evident, at least to the Klan: "For forty years the alien, unassimilable masses have been de-Americanizing America. . . . A few more years of our present sentimental, irrational hospitality will reduce the American people to a hopeless minority."

The restriction of immigration eventually won the day in 1924, with the passage of the Johnson-Reed Act, which set strict quotas on immigration until the post–World War II period. The "peak years" exhibit of the period from 1880 to 1924 gave visitors to Ellis Island a chart and map of those decades: 9 million immigrants had come from northern and western Europe, 8.2 million from eastern Europe, 5.3 million from southern Europe, 650,000 from Asia, 475,000 from Mexico, and 50,000 from Australasia.

I had gone to Ellis Island on a family journey, so to speak, but as I moved through these exhibit halls I kept thinking about very public questions. I found myself imagining what a new exhibit of our immigration history might look like, how startlingly different and yet similar it would be. The decades of the post-1965 immigration have given us a different set of statistics: Of the more than 15 million new immigrants who came to the U.S. in the three decades from 1960 to 1990, more than a third were Asian. What would the exhibit of what they brought along look like? In the glass cases there would perhaps be a Bhagavad Gita brought by Mrs. Sharma from New Delhi and a Qur'an that had belonged to Dr. Siddiqi from Lucknow, images of the Buddha and of the elephant-headed Ganesha packed up and brought to America from home altars in Taiwan or Tamil Nadu, vivid polychrome pictures of the Sikh Guru Nanak from the Punjab, gold brocade wedding saris from Banaras, and CD recordings of *qawwali* music from Lahore. Of course there would be all manner of luggage on wheels, for the new immigrants from far corners of the world come and go, returning to their homelands for ceremonies and vacations, remaining in contact with loved ones back home through the Internet and telephone, expressing a bicultural life in ways unimaginable in the peak period a century ago.

Our new exhibit could include compelling photos of the vivid variety of people who have become Americans in this period, amassed at those places where rites of citizenship have an almost iconic visibility—at the base of the Statue of Liberty or in Boston's Fanueil Hall—raising their hands to take the oath of citizenship, born in India, Kenya, Lebanon, Indonesia, all becoming Americans. Our gallery could include glossy color photos of new religious institutions, like the Chinese Buddhist Hsi Lai Temple in Hacienda Heights, California, with a dozen American flags flying in sequence all the way up the grand stairway to the Buddha Hall. And our exhibit could also include today's version of the resistances: the cross burning outside the Dallas suburban home of a Vietnamese

Buddhist monk or the graffiti sprayed on the walls of the old YMCA that New Jersey Hindus were turning into a temple—"Get Out Hindoos!"

FROM MANY, ONE

Printed on the loose change in our pockets is the motto from the Great Seal of the United States: *E Pluribus Unum*—"From Many, One." The words are so familiar to us, we scarcely stop to think what they mean. What is the measure of our manyness? What is the meaning of our oneness? Like any good symbol, these words are capable of stretching in many directions. Their meanings have amplified from the time the motto was first adopted in 1782. It had a political meaning then—from many colonies, one republic; from many states, one nation. On the Great Seal the bald eagle holds a banner emblazoned with *E Pluribus Unum* in its beak; its shield bears thirteen vertical stripes, one for each of the colonies of the new republic. With the booming immigration of the late nineteenth and early twentieth centuries, the motto took on a cultural dimension—from many peoples or nationalities, one people. My own Swedish ancestors were part of the European many. How we became one is a story written out in the successive generations of our families. My mother married another Swede, but my mother's sister Irene married an Italian, Uncle Romeo, whose father had hopped on a Lake Como cruise boat in Bellano, Italy, never to return. Her sister Carolyn married Uncle Roger, whose parents were Polish. Students in my seminar tell their own versions of the story: "On my mother's side, part English and part Irish, and on my father's side, Polish and French, and perhaps some Lithuanian," they will say. These are the *E pluribus unum* stories, and America's family album is filled with them.

Today our cultural differences are magnified with the new immigration. It's not just Swedes and Italians, Lutherans and Catholics, but Russian and Iranian Jews, Pakistani and Bengali Muslims, Trinidadi and Gujarati Hindus, Punjabi Sikhs and Sindhi Jains. Creating the *unum* from the *pluribus* is now more challenging than ever. Skeptics think it can't be done. Peter Brimelow gives voice to this view in his book *Alien Nation*, describing the post-1965 "immigration binge" as a disaster for America. The Immigration Act, he argues, should be repealed so the old Anglo-Saxon core can retain the cultural hegemony that is crucial to a stable nation. But even less alarmist voices wonder whether the *unum* is in danger of disappearing amid the *pluribus*. Arthur Schlesinger Jr. put it succinctly in his book *The Disuniting of America*: there is too much *pluribus* today and not enough *unum*. How we balance the rich particularities of the *pluribus* and the common commitment of the *unum* is today's great cultural argument, and the voices clamoring for a hearing on the issue are many.

Religion is a strong marker of our American manyness in this new era. The exponential growth of cultures and ethnicities in America has dramatically expanded our diversity, including the diversity of our religious traditions. Yet some of the most vocal secular analysts of America's growing multiculturalism leave religion completely out of the discussion, as if this new period of American immigration had no religious dimensions. But to those of us paying attention to the religious currents of America at the beginning of the twenty-first century, it is clear that any analysis of civil and political life will have to include religion along with race, ethnicity, and language. Here, as in multireligious societies throughout the world, difference is often signaled by religious language and symbol. When *Time* wanted to depict the new immigration in its special 1993 edition devoted to "The New Face of America," it began with an image of a tonsured Buddhist monk folding the American flag in the sunset at Hsi Lai temple in Hacienda Heights, California. There were images of African dancing, taken from a distinctive, though small, Yoruba village in South Carolina, a Hindu family at prayer at the Sri Venkateswara temple in Malibu Hills, a Hasidic barber in Brooklyn, and a teacher and student at an Illinois Islamic school. Illustrating difference often means resorting to the visual reference points of religion: a Hindu woman with a red dot on her forehead, a Sikh man in a turban, or a woman in the Islamic head covering called *hijab*. It means referring explicitly to religion even though the most contentious issues may be economic or social. It is not surprising, therefore, that today's incidents of hate crimes and xenophobia are also often aimed at religious markers of identity—mosques or temples, people in distinctive garb. The dot on the forehead of Hindu women became a symbol of the unwelcome difference of the South Asian community in the eyes of the young ruffians in Jersey City who called themselves the "Dot Busters." Religious difference often signals whatever difference we most deeply fear.

Of course there are strong secularizing currents among new immigrants as well. Many who come to the U.S. from traditional Muslim, Hindu, or Buddhist societies breathe a sigh of relief, cherishing not only the freedom to practice religion but also the freedom not to, the freedom to be secular in their life and thought. But being secular does not automatically place one outside the currents of religious ideas, symbolization, and stereotype that move through the heartland of American society.

Grappling with the religious dimensions of America's new diversity is everybody's business—secular and religious alike. The gang that beat Navroze Mody to death in Jersey City crying, "Hindu, Hindu, Hindu!" did not care that he was a Parsi Zoroastrian, not a Hindu at all, or inquire whether he was religiously or only culturally Parsi. The terms *Hindu* or *Dothead* just meant "different." Clearly, the representation and misrepresentation of religion is public business, for it shapes our civic climate whether or not we are religious.

Today we don't form battle lines on the basis of Christian denominational polity as did our seventeenth- and eighteenth-century forebears. Episcopalians, Congregationalists, and Quakers are pretty much at peace today. Our battle lines in the culture wars over issues like homosexuality, the family, education, and moral relativism cut straight across Methodist, Lutheran, and Catholic churches and through Jewish communities as well, attracting partisans to one side or the other. Even with the new cultural wars, America's Protestants, Catholics, and Jews can still affirm "From many, one" given the common historical, civic, and theological ground we already hold. But what happens when Muslims and Hindus, Buddhists and Sikhs jingle the same coins and think about the same motto? The issue of such wide religious difference was one the founders of the republic and even the exponents of cultural pluralism could not have imagined.

One thing *E pluribus unum* clearly does not mean is "From many religions, one religion." Our oneness will not mean the blending of religions into a religious melting pot, all speaking a kind of religious Esperanto. Of course, there will be conversions, intermarriages—probably plenty of them—and forms of public and private syncretism, but there will never be a widespread melting pot of religions or unanimity on matters of religious truth. The *unum* will be civic—a oneness of commitment to the common covenants of our citizenship out of the manyness of religious ways and worlds. Creating and sustaining this civic oneness is a challenge for any nation and a new challenge for ours. Indeed, we have seen nations founder and fracture in the face of such challenges throughout history. The past few decades are no exception and give us little evidence that a multireligious society is easily maintained.

On June 25, 1991, a Muslim imam stood in the chamber of the U.S. House of Representatives and offered a brief prayer as the chaplain of the day. It was the first time in American history a Muslim had done so. The imam was Siraj Wahaj, an African-American Muslim leader from Brooklyn, New York. He had turned a rundown urban corner dominated by drug dealers into a mosque, Masjid al-Taqwa, the home of one of Brooklyn's most vibrant Muslim communities. The landmark Congressional prayer was scheduled as close as possible to the Muslim holy day, Eid al-Adha, the Feast of Sacrifice, when Muslims remember Abraham's faithfulness to God in preparing to sacrifice his son Ishmael. The prayer Siraj Wahaj offered included verses from the Qur'an that spoke to the very question of our *pluribus* and our *unum*.

> In the name of God, Most Gracious, Most Merciful. Praise belongs to Thee alone; O God, Lord and Creator of all the worlds. Praise belongs to Thee Who shaped us and colored us in the wombs of our mothers; colored us black and white, brown, red, and yellow. Praise belongs to Thee who created us from males and females and made us into nations and tribes that we may know each other.[1]

He refers here to a verse of the Qur'an, "Do you not know, O people, that I have made you into tribes and nations that you may know each other." The verse is frequently cited by Muslims to make the powerful point that human diversity of race, gender, tribe, and nation is within the providence of God. After all, God could have made one single people, but as the Qur'an puts it, God made many nations and tribes, not that we may be divided but that we may know one another. It is an instructive first step toward a new religious America: simply to begin to know one another.

BEGINNING WITH THANKSGIVING

On Thanksgiving Day in 1998, I went to "America's Hometown," Plymouth, Massachusetts, to see how the day was observed in the place where it all began. Here, in 1621, the Pilgrims feasted with the Wampanoag peoples among whom they had settled, a celebration of survival and comity that has become part of America's founding story. But for the past thirty years, Plymouth's Thanksgiving Day has been tense with the argument over America's past—and present. As citizens of Plymouth parade through the streets in colonial costume and gather into First Parish Church for the hymns of Harvest Home, the Native peoples gather at Plymouth Rock for a National Day of Mourning. Plymouth on Thanksgiving is surely a good place to begin with an overview of religious encounter in America.

It was an overcast, gray day. I stood on Leyden Street with my colleague and guide, the Reverend Peter J. Gomes, a Plymouth native, to watch the famous Pilgrim Progress, a solemn procession of fifty-one Plymouth residents, the symbolic descendants of the fifty-one survivors who had made it through the brutal winter of 1620–21. They came round the bend right out of the seventeenth century, looking just like the Pilgrims of the imagination, carrying Bibles and muskets, each representing one of those fifty-one people—from Governor William Bradford and Captain Myles Standish to thirteen-year-old Giles Hopkins and fourteen-year-old Elizabeth Tilley. They marched on up Leyden Street, and we fell in after them, trudging up Burial Hill to the site overlooking the sea where there had once been a meeting house. There Elder Brewster led a brief service that included the line chanting of a psalm from the Old Bay Psalter in the style it would have been sung three hundred eighty years ago. At the benediction, we followed the Pilgrims back down the hill, and most of us assembled again inside the First Parish Church for the community service, complete with the hymn that I have associated with this day since childhood, "Come, ye thankful people, come. Raise the song of harvest home."

The National Day of Mourning, which assembled on the hill above Plymouth Rock, was already in full swing when we arrived after the church service. We stood in what was by then a drizzling rain to hear the voices of the Native people who resist this picture-perfect rendition of a history that has remembered by name all the survivors of the colony and forgotten the victims of colonization. "We Indian people do not give thanks just one day a year," said one speaker. "Every day we thank the creator for this beautiful earth and for our survival. But we will not give thanks for the invasion of our country; we will not celebrate the theft of our lands and the genocide of our people; we will not sing and dance to please the tourists who come here seeking a Disneyland version of our history."

The banners that stretched out in the crowd displayed the concerns brought to this gathering by Natives and non-Natives alike. There was a delegation from Cleveland that protests, season after season, the racism inherent in Cleveland Indians team name. A group of Palestinians showed their support for the Native peoples of America. Native gays bore a banner saying "Homophobia is not Native to these shores." There was a message from Leonard Peltier, still imprisoned in South Dakota for his role in the Wounded Knee uprising on the Lakota reservation. Here gathered an assembly of those who have felt marginalized and forgotten by the history, the culture, and the celebrations of the winners.

This National Day of Mourning began in 1970 when the 350th anniversary of the arrival of the Pilgrims was being observed with ceremony and speeches. Frank James, a leader of the Aquinnah Wampanoag, was invited to speak, but when the organizers saw a copy of his prepared remarks, they asked him to change what they viewed as a very critical text. The speech was frank, truthful, and from the heart, and James would not change it. He had written,

> It is with mixed emotion that I stand here to share my thoughts. This is a time of celebration for you—celebrating an anniversary of a beginning for the white man in America. A time of looking back, of reflection. It is with a heavy heart that I look back upon what happened to my people.

He said the Pilgrims had stolen from the Wamponoag their corn and beans and as much of their winter provisions as they could carry. Before long, they had stolen the land and the dignity of his people as well. Massasoit, the chief now memorialized in a statue on Cole's Hill overlooking Plymouth Rock, had befriended the settlers of Plymouth, and this "was perhaps our biggest mistake," said James.

> We forfeited our country. Our lands have fallen into the hands of the aggressor. We have allowed the white man to keep us on our knees. What has happened cannot be changed, but today we must work toward a more humane America, a more Indian America, where men and nature once again are important; where the Indian values of honor, truth, and brotherhood prevail.[2]

The speech was never delivered, at least at that celebratory 350th event. Rather, on Thanksgiving Day hundreds of Native peoples gathered on Cole's Hill for the first National Day of Mourning. James spoke in his own voice and without censorship, and they buried Plymouth Rock in the sand.

The National Day of Mourning became an annual Native American protest event on Thanksgiving Day, organized year after year by the United American Indians of New England (UAINE). In 1996, under new and zealous leadership, the protesters set out on a collision course with the PilgrimProgress parade, blocking the road and forcing the Pilgrims into retreat. The next year, tension was high on Thanksgiving Day. Again the Native protesters and their supporters marched toward the center of Plymouth, aiming to block the Pilgrim Progress. This time, however, forty or fifty city and state police officers were present to keep the roads open, and the confrontation erupted into a melee of shouting, shoving, and pepper spray. Twenty-five protesters were arrested and led away, charged with disorderly conduct and unlawful assembly. Photographs of picture-book Plymouth in disarray on Thanksgiving were published in newspapers all over the country.

Plymouth had done some soul searching and engaged in heated public discussion during the year that had just passed when I visited. The police had been cleared of charges of police brutality, and the town selectmen had tried to persuade the district attorney to drop charges against the protesters. Anger remained on both sides, and bridge builders could be found on both sides too. Could America's hometown find a way both to celebrate its Thanksgiving and embrace the National Day of Mourning? My friend Peter Gomes published a piece in the Thanksgiving edition of the *Boston Globe* counseling the old lessons of civility, honesty, and tolerance, needed now more than ever:

> In 1621 the natives and the newcomers risked each other's company and, according to Governor Bradford, for three days feasted, exercised, and played in friendly fellowship. . . . What the two groups risked in 1621 must now be risked again: the risk of listening to each other and of sharing an ambition for the future. We cannot afford to divide our fragile history into "ours" and "theirs," because it is not all ours, and from it we all have something to learn.[3]

One of the Native leaders affirmed the progress of the past year of pain.

> Finally Plymouth has recognized our right to have National Day of Mourning here and to march in Plymouth without a permit. This settlement marks the first time since 1620 that the Pilgrims have been forced to stop taking and start giving something back to Native people. This victory has been possible only because of the support of people from around the world. Thousands of people have sent letters in support of the twenty-five people arrested last year. People from the four directions have joined us in this struggle.
>
> Today is a powerful demonstration of all people who seek freedom, who want the truth to be told, and want to see an end to the oppressive system brought to these shores by the pilgrims. There are those who feel threatened by us. There are those who would have us be good Indians, and act like a conquered people, and beg for the scraps from the Thanksgiving table. But we are not vanquished. We are not conquered. We are as strong as ever.

Cries of "Ho!" rose from the crowd as he concluded.

The story of the religious diversity of America begins with the vast diversity of America's Native peoples long before European settlers ever arrived: the Wampanoag and Pequot of the Northeast, the Creek and Seminole of the South, the Blackfeet and Lakota of the plains, the Apache and Hopi of the Southeast, the Makah and Klamath of the Northwest. The Christian settlers who encountered the Native peoples of the land, on the whole, thought of this as an encounter, not with people of different spiritual traditions, but with people of no spiritual life at all. Christian missionaries thought of themselves as bringing religion to people who had none. It is a sorry commentary on our history that not until 1968, with the passage of the Native American Religious Freedom Act, was the right of Native peoples to practice their religious lifeways clearly articulated.

THE FIRST ARGUMENT: ESTABLISHMENT OR TOLERANCE

The Pilgrims who sailed the seas to establish communities in a new world wanted to be free to practice their religious faith. But they were not thinking about a wider ethic of religious freedom when they clung to the shores of the Atlantic and built the first cabins in what is now Plymouth. They were thinking about how to survive in the wilderness of a new world. As the decades brought more and more settlers to these shores, our Christian ancestors did not create widely tolerant communities. The Puritans of Boston envisioned a society, a biblical commonwealth, decisively shaped by their own form of Christianity. They were concerned primarily with religious freedom for themselves and did not regard it as a foundation for common life with people who differed from them. In seventeenth-century Puritan Boston, as reported earlier, Solomon Franco, a Sephardic Jewish merchant, was "warned out" of town. An anti-Catholic law was enacted stating "that no Jesuit or ecclesiasticall person ordained by the authoritie of the pope shall henceforth come within our jurisdiction. . . ." Dissenters like Roger Williams and Anne Hutchinson had to flee the Massachusetts Bay Colony because of their nonconformist religious beliefs, settling in what is now Rhode Island. In the period from 1659 to 1661, the Puritan establishment of Boston put four Quakers to death on the gallows on Boston Common.

Religious freedom and what today is called religious pluralism have not always been the American way, even though they have now become an integral part of the story of our country. History reminds us, however, that widespread religious freedom was hard won in this land, and disagreement about how to handle religious difference is as old as the American experiment. At first, religious difference meant various strands of Protestantism, or at most Protestants and Catholics and a small number of Jews. Every student of American history knows that the first colonies developed distinctive patterns of dealing with difference. Here the argument between the one and the many takes a particular historical form. Some colonies had one established or state-supported religion, and others did not. Some were tolerant of what they called dissenters, those who were not of the majority religion, and others were not. As we look back to those controversies more than three centuries ago, it is important to realize that this was not an argument between Christians and secularists, for the twentieth-century notion of secularism was not part of the discourse. This was, rather, an intense religious argument in which both "establishment" and "toleration" were articulated in theological terms. Both the Puritans who argued for an exclusively Christian society, a biblical commonwealth, and Roger Williams, who argued for "soul liberty," did so on biblical grounds.

At his Massachusetts trial in 1635, Roger Williams spoke of this soul liberty as the indispensable condition of faith. It must not be subject to the coercion of the state. The Puritans, he charged, had not gone far enough in separating themselves from the Church of England; the church should have no involvement whatsoever in the affairs of government. He challenged his accusers, saying,

> I do affirm it to be against the testimony of Christ Jesus for the civil state to impose upon the soul of the people a religion, a worship, a ministry. The state should give free and absolute permission of conscience to all men in what is spiritual alone. Ye have lost yourselves! Your breath blows out the candle of liberty in this land.[4]

Unlike Massachusetts, the colony of Rhode Island had no established church and permitted freedom of conscience and worship for everyone, including Jews and Quakers. Again, Roger Williams' arguments were essentially theological arguments: that a state religion with enforced uniformity of religion is against the very principles of God's sovereignty, that blood spilled by states over religion is contrary to the principles of Jesus Christ, that persecuting people because of their religion or their conscience goes against the very grain of Christianity.[5]

This argument between establishment and tolerance resounded in different tones throughout the colonies. In Virginia the Church of England was the established church, and dissidents were not generally welcome. While the Catholic founders of Maryland passed a Toleration Act in 1649, when Protestants came to power in the following decades, Jesuits were banished from the colony and Catholics were denied the right to hold office. Harsh anti-Catholic laws were passed, such as the 1704 law straightforwardly titled An Act to Prevent the Growth of Popery Within This Province. In seventeenth-century New York, the Dutch Reformed Church was recognized as the official church, and both Jews and Quakers were targeted by Peter Stuyvesant's restrictions. The Sephardic Jews who had arrived in New Amsterdam in 1654 were pressured to leave. But these Jewish newcomers appealed to Amsterdam and the Dutch West India Company for reconsideration. They were subsequently permitted to stay, but only because a more tolerant Holland had intervened.

In colonies with established churches, the dilemma was present from the start: How could the settlers who cherished religious freedom for themselves and who had crossed the ocean to secure it not accord it to others? In the mid–seventeenth century in New Amsterdam, the citizens of Flushing raised their voices in what has often been called the first American protest for religious freedom. They opposed a ruling by Peter Stuyvesant banning Quakers from the colony and punishing those who harbored them with a fine of fifty florins. Looking back, we must not misread what they were about in the post-Enlightenment terms of freedom of conscience. The Flushing Remonstrance, drawn up in 1657, was not about freedom of conscience but about hospitality. It is really a theological and ethical document. The residents of Flushing were offended not simply as citizens, but as Christians, that the authorities would impose a ruling that undermined the commandments of love and hospitality at the heart of the Christian message, including hospitality to Quakers.[6] Today, more than 350 years later, Flushing is famous for its cultural and religious diversity and remembers the Flushing Remonstrance with considerable pride.

When I first visited Flushing on a Sunday morning in the early 1990s, I headed for Bowne House, the home of John Bowne, one of the leaders of the Flushing Remonstrance. This modest colonial house has become a "National Shrine to Religious Freedom." Fittingly, the area within half a mile of Bowne House is today one of the most religiously eclectic in all America. Down the street I visited a Congregational church with both English and Chinese congregations, the English service in progress, the Chinese service yet to come. Around the corner, I dropped into a Sikh gurdwara where two hundred people, adults and children, were gathered for a spirited session of singing. Across the street from the gurdwara was a synagogue, quiet now on Sunday morning. On down Bowne Street was a huge Korean Presbyterian Church, a Swaminarayan Hindu Temple, a storefront Sikh gurdwara, and the great Ganesha temple with the formidable name Sri Maha Vallabha Ganapati Devasthanam, one of America's first and most energetic Hindu temples. Flushing today is a living witness to the heritage of this first stand for religious freedom, more precisely the freedom to exercise religious hospitality.

Pennsylvania, like Rhode Island, was a radical colonial experiment, and here religious liberty was, on the whole, cherished and religious difference tolerated. William Penn would certainly have sided with Roger Williams and the citizens of Flushing in the argument. He offered the Pennsylvania colony as a place of refuge for Quakers who had been persecuted in England and Ireland. Writing on freedom of conscience in his essay "The Great Case of Liberty of Conscience," Penn insisted that "imposition, restraint and persecution, for matters relating to conscience, directly invade divine prerogative, and divest the Almighty of a due, proper to none besides himself." We must remember, of course, that in his day this was an argument he also used against the authoritarianism of the Roman Catholic Church as well as against the establishment of state religion and the persecution of minority communities. In Pennsylvania, the Quaker community flourished, while in other colonies Quakers were routinely fined, silenced, or otherwise suppressed. It should also interest us that Penn took a decisive step beyond the climate of toleration for all religions, toward freedom of religious practice. Penn no doubt would be surprised at Pennsylvania today, with one of America's major Hindu temples, the Sri Venkateswara Temple, rising in the Penn Hills near Pittsburgh and with mosques on the Philadelphia mainline and Southeast Asian Buddhist temples in the suburban fringe.

It is impossible to summarize so briefly the different colonial models for dealing with religious difference. These were social and civic arguments carried on within a largely Christian spectrum of belief. But with the birth of a new nation, working through this question among people who disagreed, sometimes intensely, about religious principles became an urgent priority. In Virginia, where the Church of England received the privileges and benefits of an established church, the Presbyterians of Hanover asked, "Why should Presbyterians be taxed to support the

Anglican church?" They went on to reason that establishing any form of the Christian religion is no different from establishing Islam or Roman Catholicism: it arrogates to the civil leader a judgment that would require the authority of infallibility. The text of these rural Virginia Presbyterians is especially interesting to me, for it is one of the few colonial documents that speculate more widely about the consequences of establishing a state religion beyond the bounds of Christianity, mentioning Islam as a hypothetical case.

> In this enlightened age, and in a land where all, of every denomination are united in the most strenuous efforts to be free, we hope and expect that our representatives will cheerfully concur in removing every species of religious, as well as civil bondage. Certain it is, that every argument for civil liberty, gains additional strength when applied to liberty in the concerns of religion; and there is no argument in favour of establishing the Christian religion, but what may be pleaded, with equal propriety, for establishing the tenets of Mahomed by those who believe the Alcoran: or if this be not true, it is at least impossible for the magistrate to adjudge the right of preference among the various sects that profess the Christian faith, without erecting a chair of infallibility, which would lead us back to the church of Rome.[7]

The battle to disestablish the Church of England in Virginia went on for ten years, right through the Revolutionary War. Thomas Jefferson first drafted "An Act for the Establishment of Religious Freedom" in 1777 and argued that freedom of conscience is limited and compromised by the establishment of any religion. In the course of the long civic argument, the eloquent Patrick Henry introduced another proposal: to establish the Christian religion in general in the Commonwealth of Virginia. He argued that the state should actively support Christian education and clergy, because Christianity serves to instill morality and thus helps make good citizens. But James Madison strongly disagreed, insisting that this would take a step back from the vision of freedom for which the American Revolution had struggled. In 1785 he wrote his famous "Memorial and Remonstrance," arguing that the state is not a competent judge of religious truth and has no business interfering in matters of religion. "Whilst we assert for ourselves a freedom to embrace, to profess, and to observe the religion which we believe to be of divine origin, we cannot deny an equal freedom to those whose minds have not yet yielded to the evidence which has convinced us."[8]

Finally, in 1786, the Virginia Statute for Religious Freedom was passed. It was based on a fundamentally religious affirmation: God did not propagate truth by coercion, so why should we? The document began, "Whereas Almighty God hath created the mind free; that all attempts to influence it by temporal punishments or burdens, or by civil incapacitations, tend only to beget habits of hypocrisy and meanness, and are a departure from the plan of the Holy author of our religion, who being Lord both of body and mind, yet chose not to propagate it by coercions on either, as was in his Almighty power to do. . . ." As we can see, the argument for the nonestablishment of religion begins with a theological point: our freedom is grounded in the God-given freedom of the mind to think and to choose. Standing for religious freedom—even freedom from any form of religion—is grounded in the very freedom ordained by God. The statute goes on to insist "that our civil rights have no dependence on our religious opinions" and finally resolves that "no man shall be compelled to frequent or support any religious worship, place or ministry whatsoever . . . nor shall otherwise suffer on account of his religious opinions or belief; but that all men shall be free to profess and by argument to maintain, their opinion in matters of religion."[9]

We know well the next chapter in this story. The Virginia statute became a model for the principles of separation of church and state and the protection of religious freedom that were enshrined in the Bill of Rights in 1791. The very first article consisted of just sixteen powerful words: "Congress shall make no law respecting an establishment of religion or prohibiting the free exercise thereof." The framers of the Constitution could not have imagined the religious diversity of America today. Nonetheless, the sturdy principles of free exercise of religion and the nonestablishment of religion have stood the test of time. America's rich religious pluralism today is a direct result of our commitment to religious freedom. Our secular humanist traditions also are a product of the freedom of conscience built into the Constitution. Freedom of religion is also freedom from religion of any sort.

A CHRISTIAN AMERICA?

In 1992 Governor Kirk Fordice of Arkansas raised a furor when he spoke of America as a "Christian nation." He quickly backpedaled. Of course, he said, the United States is not an officially and legally Christian state. But even under fire, he continued to insist on his meaning in the cultural sense: that this is a nation shaped by Christianity. Many Americans agree, assuming the normative status of Christianity in America. When they envision posting the Ten Commandments in public buildings, teaching the biblical story of creation in school, or having prayer in classrooms or at public school graduations and football games, their underlying presupposition is that America is a Christian country. Christians are the majority and should have their way in setting the public spirit.

The narrative of a Christian America has always had a hold on the collective imagination of Americans. This narrative moves through every chapter in American history, and it is a story deeply embedded in the subsoil of American consciousness. A narrative so deeply held that it is virtually taken for granted is what we in religious studies refer to as a myth. By this we mean not a false story but a deeply true story, so much so that we think of it not as "our" story but as "the" story. The story of America cannot be told without dwelling on the vision of those who sailed the Atlantic on the *Arabella,* their eyes fixed on the western horizon. John Winthrop drafted a vision of the new biblical society they would create: "For we must consider that we shall be as a city upon a hill, the eyes of all people are upon us."[10] Christian scripture shaped the consciousness of those who created colonial communities with an established church and those who dissented and protested in the name of freedom of conscience as well.

Historically, there is no doubt that Christian ideals, along with those of Greek philosophy and the Enlightenment, gave shape to the Declaration of Independence and the Constitution. Those conservative Christians who press today for the proclamation of "America's Christian Heritage Week" cite a litany of founding fathers who acknowledged the significance of their religious principles. They are right, but on the other hand, as we have seen, there was as much debate over what constituted Christian principles then as now. This is one of the reasons the founding fathers wisely wrote what some have called a "godless" Constitution, one that deliberately steered away from the establishment of any sect of Christianity, even Christianity itself, as the basis of the new nation. They intentionally founded a nation in which no form of religious belief would be privileged in the public sphere.

Despite the disestablishment of various Protestant churches in the states of the new republic, Christianity continued to form the dominant ethos of both the public and private spheres of American life. In a sense, it became stronger precisely because the churches no longer had any support from public tax coffers; they had to compete with one another in the free market of Christian ideas in order to thrive, and one of the consequences of this unprecedented approach to religious freedom was the proliferation of churches. When the Frenchman Alexis de Tocqueville traveled around America in the 1820s, he discovered, to his surprise, that severing the ties between church and state seemed to make religion stronger rather than weaker. Unlike in France, where the spirit of religion and the spirit of freedom seemed to march in opposite directions, in America they seemed "intimately united" and "reigned in common over the same country." Churches needed to win the support of parishioners in order to survive, and the spirit of voluntarism inspired a lively and intense competition in religion and the creation of a multitude of "denominations," which have become a distinctive feature of American religion. Tocqueville wrote, "There is no country in the world where the Christian religion retains a greater influence over the souls of men than in America; and there can be no greater proof of its utility and of its conformity to human nature than that its influence is powerfully felt over the most enlightened and free nation of the earth."[11] He called religion the "first of political institutions," astutely discerning that while the churches were not supported by the government and were not directly involved in politics as such, they were nonetheless extremely influential in the political sphere.

Protestant Christians, while supporting the ideal of religious freedom, continued to shape the vision of a Christian America. For a few, like the conservative evangelicals who started the National Reform Association in 1864, this meant working "to secure such an amendment to the Constitution of the United States as will indicate that this is a Christian nation, and will place all the Christian laws, institutions and usages of our government on an undeniable legal basis in the fundamental law of the land."[12] They wanted to make it official. They did not like the fact that there was "not the slightest hint of homage to the God of Heaven" in the Constitution, and they set out to correct it with a new preamble, which read: "We, the people of the United States, humbly acknowledging Almighty God as the source of all authority and power in civil government, The Lord Jesus Christ as the Governor among the Nations, and His revealed will as of supreme authority, in order to constitute a Christian government . . . do ordain and establish this Constitution for the United States of America."[13] Jefferson and Madison would have been appalled at the effort to undo their work, but the drive to insert a Christian amendment went on for eighty-two years until 1945. The National Association of Evangelicals campaigned in 1947 and 1954 for another wording that would add, "This nation divinely recognizes the authority and law of Jesus Christ, Savior and Ruler of Nations, through whom are bestowed the blessings of Almighty God."[14]

Even today some Christians would prefer to amend the Constitution to make sure Christianity gets its due in public life. But on the whole, the vision of a Christian America has been pursued through the voluntary energies of the churches, just as Tocqueville saw in his day. When the Presbyterian minister John Henry Barrows welcomed delegates from all over the world to the World's Parliament of Religions in Chicago in 1893, he explained to the assembly, "There is a true and noble sense in which America is a Christian nation, since Christianity is recognized . . . by general national acceptance and observance as the prevailing religion of our people."[15] The social gospel activist Washington Gladden continued in this vein when he wrote in 1905, "And while we have no desire to see the establishment of any form of religion by law in this land, most of us would be willing to see the nation in its purposes and policies and ruling aims becoming essentially Christian. . . . It must be, in spirit and purpose and character, a Christian nation."[16] Gladden and other proponents of the Protestant social gospel movement had confidence in the ability of the churches to transform and Christianize the social order. This optimism was taken up in the last decades of the twentieth century by the energies and organizing of the Christian evangelical movement, which brought a more conservative vision to creating a Christian nation in spirit, purpose, and character. Insofar as one could speak of a Christian America, it would not be by establishment, but by ethos, by acclamation, by the social and ethical dominance of the majority.

When we look more closely at what all this might mean today, however, the first thing that becomes clear is that Christianity is dynamic and multivocal, and what it means to be Christian "in spirit and purpose" is highly contested among Christians themselves. The mainline churches, who are heirs of the social gospel movement, have continued to speak to issues of social justice and have weighed in on environmental and economic issues. They have argued over gender equality and homosexuality, even within their own denominational bodies. The Roman Catholic Church has brought its own perspectives on ethical issues into public debate through the careful analyses of the National Conference of Catholic Bishops and has found itself embroiled in internal controversies over issues such as women's ordination, abortion rights, and freedom for theological dissent in its colleges and universities. The evangelical churches, which have grown in numbers and influence, have raised a powerful voice in the right-to-life movement against abortion and have found, through the Moral Majority and the Christian Coalition, a significant forum for shaping public discussion. No synopsis could possibly do justice to the controversies of American Christianity at the turn of a new millennium. But one thing is certain: Christians in the new religious America are lined up on every side of every issue.

To make the situation even more complex, the face of American Christianity has also changed with the new immigration. Today there are more than 25 million Hispanic Christians in America. Of course there is a centuries-old Hispanic population in the U.S., but new immigrants have poured into the United States from Mexico and Central America, Puerto Rico and Cuba. Today it is estimated that one of every four American Catholics is Hispanic, to say nothing of the growth of Hispanic Evangelical and Pentecostal churches and the participation of these immigrants in old mainline churches like the United Methodist Church. New Asian churches have also made an impact on the religious landscape. There are new congregations of Vietnamese Catholics, Korean Presbyterians, Samoan Methodists, and Chinese evangelicals. Older Christian communities of Japanese, Chinese, and Filipinos, who have experienced the vulnerability of being small ethnic minorities in the U.S. for nearly a century, have now increased in numbers and have become more vocal, bringing issues like anti-Asian racism into the agenda of major denominations.

Christian America in the late twentieth century began to take stock of its own hypocrisies and own up to some of the ugliest chapters in its history. Apologies began to be issued: a Southern Baptist apology to the African Americans long excluded from its churches, a United Methodist apology to the Native peoples massacred at Sand Creek, an ecumenical apology by church leaders in the Pacific Northwest "for their long-standing participation in the destruction of traditional Native American spiritual practices." The problems of claiming a Christian America, even in spirit and purpose, came home to roost. And racism was paramount among them. In the late 1940s, the Swedish social theorist Gunnar Myrdal had set out to investigate the spirit of American society in the postwar era, and he saw racial discrimination as the central dilemma, the deep contradiction, of American life. In his book *The American Dilemma* he asked the most difficult of questions: How could an idealistic, democratic, egalitarian society contain within it such deep patterns of race discrimination? In post–World War II America, the festering contradiction became a public wound. Black soldiers had fought and died along with whites and then returned home to a segregated society. In Myrdal's analysis, postwar America would have to begin to come to terms with its own hypocrisy. The nineteen fifties and sixties were years when American civic and religious life was torn apart by the contradictions of racism. Christian churches were tumultuously involved—and on both sides.

But beyond the issues of black and white in America, other race issues required serious consideration, among them the long-standing discrimination against people from Asia and the Pacific in America's immigration laws. Even as the Civil Rights Act of 1964 was being debated, a new piece of legislation was working its way through Congress: the Immigration and Naturalization Act of 1965, eliminating for the first time in over a century the systematic exclusion of Asians. Now, after nearly four decades of immigration, a new American dilemma has emerged. Race is, to be sure, still high on the agenda. But in addition, the question of religion has come to the fore. The engine of immigration has plowed up another deep-seated contradiction in the minds of many Americans: the coexistence of commitment to religious liberty with deep structures of Christian entitlement and ideological Christian exclusivism.

The new American dilemma is real religious pluralism, and it poses challenges to America's Christian churches that are as difficult and divisive as those of race. Today, the invocation of a Christian America takes on a new set of tensions as our population of Muslim, Hindu, Sikh, and Buddhist neighbors grows. The ideal of a Christian America stands in contradiction to the spirit, if not the letter, of America's foundational principle of religious freedom. As long as religious diversity meant Methodists, Congregationalists, Southern Baptists, and Catholics, or as long as it meant, at the most, Christians and Jews, the issues were not so troubling and the tension not so palpable. Today, however, America is in the process of coming to terms with this deep contradiction, this very complex form of hypocrisy. As Muslim Americans stand in the halls of Congress, Buddhist Americans ordain monks in temples flying the American flag, Hindu Americans run for local and state office, and Sikh Americans insist on their constitutional right to wear the turban and retain their uncut hair in the military, the presupposition that America is foundationally Christian is being challenged, really for the first time. There is no going back. As we say in Montana, the horses are already out of the barn. Our new religious diversity is not just an idea but a reality, built into our neighborhoods all over

America. Religious pluralism is squarely and forever on the American agenda.

How will we handle the questions of our religious diversity today? If we look at American history through the lens of religious and cultural diversity and the challenges posed by this diversity, we might actually find some models for thinking about the new American dilemma. We have already had some experience and have made some mistakes. In the nineteenth century, both Catholic and Jewish immigrants encountered a strong, normative Protestant culture in America. They were the target of sporadic and very vocal "nativist" movements, which sounded the cry of "America for the Americans." By this they meant America for its "native" inhabitants, which meant not its Native peoples, but those Europeans already here. At each step of the way from the 1850s through the 1920s America's burgeoning cultural diversity sparked intense debates about immigration. The issues of racial and ethnic difference were many, as they are today. And, in addition, religious differences were cast in strong anti-Catholic and anti-Jewish language. Religion was then, as now, one of the ways in which the differences we most disliked were marked and labeled.

The terms *exclusion, assimilation,* and *pluralism* suggest three different ways in which Americans have approached our ever-broader cultural and religious diversity. For exclusionists, the answer to the tumultuous influx of cultural and religious diversity, which seemed to threaten the very core civilization of America, was to close the door, especially against the entry of the truly "alien," whether Asians, Catholics, or Jews. The message, in brief, was stay home, or go home, or in any case be excluded from the table of participation here in America. For assimilationists, the invitation to new immigrants was to come, but leave your differences behind as quickly as possible. In other words, come and be like us. For the pluralist, the American promise was to come as you are, with all your differences, pledged only to the common civic demands of citizenship. In other words, come and be yourselves.

The relation of the *pluribus* and the *unum* can be sounded in all three keys, depending on the emphasis. For the exclusivist, the oneness of the *unum* requires the exclusion of those who are different. The manyness of too much difference poses a threat to oneness. For the assimilationist or inclusivist, the oneness requires the many to shed their differences and become assimilated into the normative culture. For the pluralist, the oneness is shaped by the encounter of the many, the engagement of the many. We hear all three keys sounded in our history, and we can discern all three keys in today's arguments over the new immigration and American multiculturalism.

EXCLUSIVISM: GO HOME!

On August 13, 1993, the cultural affairs officer of the police department in Portland, Maine, called Pirun Sen, one of the leaders of the small Cambodian Buddhist community that had recently settled there. "I am sorry to bother you so early in the morning. . . . Vandals broke into the temple house last night. I think when they discovered all of the Buddhist things in it they decided to mess it up a bit. Can you meet me in twenty minutes?" With a heavy heart, Pirun Sen rushed to the temple and met the police at the small gray house they had dedicated as the Watt Samaki Buddhist Center. The windows of the blue sedan parked in the yard were smashed; the door had been hacked open with an ax; the contents of the Buddha hall were strewn around the yard. When he ventured inside, Pirun Sen saw the worst devastation of all: the words "Dirty Asian, Chink, Go Home" written across the wall. He closed his eyes, frightened and sickened by what he saw.[17]

This is exclusivism, demanding that difference be destroyed, that those who are different go home. Wherever home may be, it's not here. When vandals broke into the newly constructed Hindu-Jain Temple in Pittsburgh and smashed the white marble images of the Hindu deities, they wrote the word "Leave!" across the main altar. That is the simple message of exclusivism: what is foreign should leave. The graffiti and the violence of xenophobia are part of a long history of dealing with difference by excluding it. We recall the Puritans of Massachusetts in the seventeenth century, who told Quakers, Jews, and Catholics in no uncertain terms to leave. The narrative of exclusion has long been part of the American story.

With the new intensity of mid-nineteenth-century immigration, "Leave!" was the cry of what came to be called nativist movements—those who claimed the old Protestant Anglo-Saxon core population as "native" and looked on newcomers, especially Catholics and Jews, with suspicion. Perhaps the most eloquent and virulent expressions of nativist exclusivism came from the pen of the Reverend Josiah Strong, a Congregational minister in Cincinnati who was associated with the American Home Missionary Society. His book, *Our Country: Its Possible Future and Present Crisis,* published in 1886, remained in print for decades. By 1916 it had sold 175,000 copies. Strong clearly touched a nerve as he inveighed against the many "perils" of the day, including immigration, Mormonism, and Catholicism. We can get a senses of the logic of prejudice in his seven points summarizing the great dangers of Catholicism, which he sees as incompatible with "our country."

1. We have seen the supreme sovereignty of the Pope opposed to the sovereignty of the people.
2. We have seen that the commands of the Pope, instead of the constitution and laws of the land, demand the highest allegiance of Roman Catholics in the United States.
3. We have seen that the alien Roman who seeks citizenship swears true obedience to the Pope instead of "renouncing forever all allegiance to any foreign prince, potentate, state or sovereignty," as required by our laws.
4. We have seen that Romanism teaches religious intolerance instead of religious liberty.
5. We have seen that Romanism demands the censorship of ideas and of the press, instead of the freedom of the press and of speech.
6. We have seen that she approves the union of church and state instead of their entire separation.
7. We have seen that she is opposed to our public school system. Our fundamental ideas of society, therefore, are as radically opposed to Vaticanism as to imperialism, and it is as inconsistent with our liberties for Americans to yield allegiance to the Pope as to the Czar.[18]

Even as Strong wrote these words, Catholic immigrants were continuing to arrive from Ireland, Italy, Poland, Germany, and France. Over the next decades, they would struggle with their own internal dynamics and differences as they developed an American church out of all this diversity. Strong's argument, however, is an old one, articulated two centuries earlier by William Penn: a free country requires free minds, and Catholics are not mentally free. The nativist accusation was that it was difficult to be a good American and a good Catholic at the same time because the very freedom of mind and speech on which democracy depends was, in their view, usurped by the Church and the papacy. This characterization took a long time to die. Not really until John F. Kennedy addressed the question specifically during his 1960 campaign, and not really until he was elected president, did it begin to dissipate.

Jews also experienced the exclusions of America, especially social exclusion. In 1877 Joseph Seligman, a successful Jewish banker and a friend of the late Abraham Lincoln, was not permitted to register as a guest at the Grand Union Hotel in Sarasota Springs, New York, a form of exclusion that would be repeated thousands of times for over one hundred years. In these decades of the late nineteenth century, Jews were accused of not assimilating to American culture and keeping themselves separate and aloof but were simultaneously refused admission to schools and universities, clubs, hotels, and resorts. As Leonard Dinnerstein put it in his classic study *Antisemitism in America* "From the end of the Civil War until the beginning of the twentieth century, the United States witnessed the emergence of a full-fledged antisemitic society." During the late nineteenth and early twentieth centuries, Jews streamed into the United States from Eastern Europe and Russia, comprising about a tenth of the total number of immigrants. *McClure's Magazine* called it the "Jewish Invasion." By the 1920s, writers in the popular press could speak of the new Jews as "alienizing America" and as "unassimilatable [*sic*], undesirable, and incapable of grasping American ideals."[19]

The exclusionist agenda had many targets, but Asians were the group most directly and specifically attacked. "Asian exclusion" became embodied in a series of immigration acts, defining in increasingly restrictive terms which immigrants could enter the U.S. and which groups could qualify for citizenship. We know that a sense of identity is often shaped by the categorization of the "other," and in terms of American national identity in the nineteenth century, the clearest "other" apart from the African-American population was Asian.

The Chinese Exclusion Act was passed in 1882. In arguing in favor of the act, John Franklin Miller, a senator from California, insisted that the Chinese culture is wholly "other"—unchanging, wholly immutable. The anti-Chinese movement was cast, not in explicitly religious terms, but in deep cultural terms. The two civilizations of East and West, he argued, have now met on the West Coast of America. They are "radically antagonistic, and as impossible of amalgamation as are the two great races who have produced them. Like the mixing of oil and water, neither will absorb the other."[20] In sum, he argues, since the Chinese will never adapt to American culture, they must be kept out. The exclusionist attitude might be summed up in the words of the editor of the newspaper in Butte, Montana, where a sizable Chinese mining community had settled by the

1870s: "The Chinaman's life is not our life, his religion is not our religion. . . . He belongs not in Butte."[21]

The federal policy of Asian exclusion was renewed every decade over the course of the late nineteenth and early twentieth centuries, gradually expanding to exclude the Japanese and other "Asiatics" as well. "Japs Must Go!" was the San Francisco graffiti that caught the eye of Hirai Ryuge Kinzo, one of the Japanese Buddhist delegates to the World's Parliament of Religions in Chicago in 1893. When he declared to the audience at the parliament how deeply offensive this was to him as a Japanese visitor, cries of "Shame!" resounded through the halls. But many Americans were evidently not ashamed of such sentiments. In the first decade of the twentieth century, the Asiatic Exclusion League was formed to work for a strict exclusionist policy. Its 1911 proceedings included the full text of a piece published in Augusta, Maine, that same year, which spoke of the "impending danger" of the "Yellow Peril from Asia."

> Their ways are not as our ways and their gods are not as our God, and never will be. They bring with them a degraded civilization and debased religion of their own ages older, and to their minds, far superior to ours. We look to the future with hope for improvement and strive to uplift our people; they look to the past, believing that perfection was attained by their ancestors centuries before our civilization began and before Jesus brought us the divine message from the Father. They profane this Christian land by erecting here among us their pagan shrines, set up their idols and practice their shocking heathen religious ceremonies. . . .
>
> We have this day to choose whether we will have for the Pacific coast the civilization of Christ or the civilization of Confucius," said Senator James G. Blaine of Maine in his memorable speech in favor of Chinese exclusion before the U.S. Senate in 1879. But since that day so many Asiatics have come and spread over the country that the yellow peril is not merely a local but a great national danger. Shall we check it in time, now, or wait until it is too strong for us?[22]

In the league proceedings, we find another advocate of exclusion wrestling with the possibility that exclusion legislation might contradict America's foundational commitment to human equality. He mused in his speech to the Asiatic Exclusion League, "I believe also that 'All men are created equal, and endowed by their Creator with certain inalienable rights,' but I do not recognize the right of migration as one of those inalienable rights, because its unlimited exercise may, and frequently is, destructive of the equal rights of others." He went on to argue:

> Must I, in order to comply with this law of equality and fraternity, keep the door of my house standing open for the convenience of such strangers as may desire to use it, nor complain if I find my bed nightly occupied by strangers who happen to reach my house and take possession of the bed before I get there? Certainly not. If not, where shall the line be drawn? We say that our country is the home of our citizens of those people who now inhabit it, and that we have a right to say who else shall come. Without this right, the rearing of our civilizations and of our free institutions as the rearing of families would be without the right to exclude strangers and intruders from our homes.[23]

The record of the proceedings of the Asiatic Exclusion League notes "Loud and prolonged applause" as the response to this impassioned speaker.

As the principle of excluding these "strangers and intruders" was negotiated in ever-new forms of restrictive immigration legislation, the world was gerrymandered into a wider and wider Asia. Jews were sometimes described as Asiatic. Turkey and Syria were said to be part of Asia, and as that matter was debated in Congress, the Syrian consul in New York wrote a petition insisting that under these rules Jesus was an Asiatic and would be ineligible for immigration. This was precisely the point the Nobel Prize–winning Bengali poet Rabindranath Tagore made when he left the U.S. in the 1920s, vowing not to return. He had personally experienced the harassment of Indian immigrants at the hands of American officials, and he chided, "Jesus Christ himself could not get into the United States!"

The racism and Protestant chauvinism inherent in much exclusivist rhetoric found its extreme expression in the Ku Klux Klan, which was resurgent in the anti-immigration climate following World War I. Its slogan summed up the exclusivist vision of America: "Native, white, Protestant supremacy." Most exclusionists don't put it so bluntly, but their more measured voices carry an astonishingly similar message. In the debate on the Immigration and Naturalization Act of 1965, for example, the president of the Republican Committee of One Hundred put it succinctly: "Do we want to build a national population based on the predominantly northern and western European stock which discovered, explored and developed America, and which today so deeply cherishes our freedom and our ways of life? Or, are we willing to permit the American population makeup to be based rather on the makeup of foreign lands whose natives can get in line fastest, in the greatest number, under a first-come, first-served scheme of entry?"[24] His characterization of the process of immigration is rhetorical and hardly accurate, but he clearly positions himself in a hard-core America that is northern and western European. From that standpoint he questions, as have exclusionists for more than a century, whether anyone else can be a good American. This is, of course, the argument of Peter Brimelow in *Alien Nation*: that the hard-core old Anglo-Saxon, Nordic, Protestant America is being compressed between the "pincers" of rising Hispanic immigration on one side and rising Asian immigration on the other.

When I think about the multiple ways in which exclusion operates in the United States, I often see in my mind's eye the big padlock on the gate to the access road into Piscataway National Park in Maryland, with Billy Redwing Tayac standing there, locked out of ancestral lands where his people had gathered for generations. "Our origins are here, our ancestors are buried here. We're so intermingled with the earth here that the earth is part of us," he said. But now that it's a national park, the access of his people to these ancestral lands is limited. They need a permit for a gathering and a key to get into the one vehicular access road. Billy Tayac and his people sometimes find themselves excluded from their own lands. "To worship God, you don't need the permission of God. You need the permission of the Department of Interior,"[25] said Tayac. The padlock could be multiplied a thousand times to indicate the many places where the Native peoples of the United States have been "removed" from their lands in the past three centuries.

Though the scales of exclusion have been practiced in many keys— race, ethnicity, and religion—the deepest exclusions have been race based. Native peoples, blacks, and Asians have often been seen as perpetual strangers, even in the towns they have inhabited for decades. Japanese Americans in their third and fourth generations, who have been here as long as my Swedish family has, report that they are constantly asked where they are from, as if they must be from somewhere other than the United States. The ironies of the exclusivist response to difference are many. For example, an African-American Muslim woman whose family had been here for generations described to the Pluralism Project an incident that is all too common for Muslim women who chose to wear the Islamic head scarf.

I was in a parking lot of one of the grocery stores here. I pulled up and, for some reason, it annoyed a woman who had a van like mine. She got out of her van, and she slammed her door, and she walked up to my car and she shook her finger and she said, "Why don't you go back to Iraq or Iran or wherever you come from!"

And I rolled down the window and I told her, "I am at home."[26]

ASSIMILATION: THE MELTING POT OF DIFFERENCE

A second attitude toward difference in America is summed up in the word *assimilation*. The most vivid image here is the melting pot, the crucible where differences dissolve into the common pot, adding their flavors but losing their form. Newcomers shed difference in order to blend in. This is what we might call an "inclusivist" point of view: people are welcome to come—and be like "us." Taking this perspective on today's issues, the gurdwara should really forego the golden domes of India in favor of the predominant architectural style of southern California, Muslim women should forego distinctive Islamic dress, and the Muslim policeman in Newark should shave his beard to fit in with the rest of the clean-shaven police force. The assimilationist assumes that immigrants will come and blend in, contributing to the cultural mix but ultimately relinquishing the most distinctive aspects of their home culture to take on American culture.

The assimilationist view was voiced early on by John Quincy Adams, who insisted that immigrants "must cast off the European skin, never to resume it. They must look forward to their posterity rather than backward to their ancestors."[27] Adams was not thinking of religion in this remark but rather of racial, cultural, and national identities of Europe. Of course, they had been at war over religion for centuries in Europe, and against this background the assimilationist impulse to leave that tumultuous strife behind was vitally important. When the Jewish writer Israel Zangwill first popularized the "melting pot" image of America in his play *The Melting Pot*, he envisioned the melting away of the "feuds and vendettas" of Europe's religious strife in the crucible of the new world.

The Melting Pot opened in 1908 at the crest of America's greatest wave of immigration. The play's hero, a young Russian Jew named David, recently arrived in New York, utters what became the play's most famous lines as he surveys the crowd at Ellis Island:

> America is God's Crucible, the great Melting-Pot where all the races of Europe are melting and re-forming! Here you stand, good folk, with your fifty languages and histories, and your fifty blood hatreds and rivalries. But you won't be long like that, brothers, for these are the fires of God you've come to—these are the fires of God. A fig for your feuds and vendettas! Germans and Frenchmen, Irishmen and Englishmen, Jews and Russians— into the Crucible with you all! God is making the American![28]

Here the purging flame of the refiner's fire melts not only language and culture but also the religious strife and feuding of the old world. David's faith in this vision of America is tested to the quick when he falls in love with Vera, a Christian girl. As the drama unfolds, it becomes clear to David that she is the daughter of the very Russian army officer who had been in charge of the pogrom in his village back in Russia. Leaving behind those old world feuds and vendettas for the world of the future is as difficult as it could possibly be, but David finally chooses to marry Vera.

When Theodore Roosevelt saw the play on its opening night in Washington, D.C., in 1908, he commented, "We Americans are children of the crucible." There has never been a more popular image of how our *pluribus* and *unum* are related than that of the crucible, the melting pot. But it is a complex image, as historian Philip Gleason has shown.[29] He surveys some of the history and ambiguities of this image, which has been called "a fundamental trait of American nationalism." Zangwill, he notes, was not the first to speak of the melting pot, and Gleason rounds up the various precedents for this image. For instance, the French essayist and traveler Hector St. John de Crevecoeur, astonished at the diversity of America, had written as early as 1782 in his *Letters from an American Farmer,* "Here individuals of all nations are melted into a new race of men whose labours and posterity will one day cause great changes in the world." In the mid–nineteenth century, Emerson spoke of a "smelting pot" and the emergence of a "new race," and in the last decade of the century, the historian Frederick Jackson Turner spoke of the frontier as a crucible that "promoted the formation of a composite nationality for the American people." But, despite these early images of the power of assimilation, it was Israel Zangwill who thrust the image of the melting pot into public view. It caught on, illumining a vision of the American dynamic.

But what kind of melting pot is it? Here is where the confusion lies. Is it basically an Anglo-conformist melting pot in which the races of the rest of Europe are assimilated? Is it more a transmuting pot in which everybody changes in the mix? The melting pot image is used in both ways. The Italians and Irish immigrant became "American," but it is also true that what "American" meant began to change with the addition of the Italians and the Irish. Either way, what melts in the crucible are the boundaries that most constitute difference. Becoming American, in this view, means shedding difference. One of the sites of early-twentieth-century assimilation was American industry, and Henry Ford's plant in Detroit had a "Ford English School Melting Pot." A cartoon of the period displayed its ethos in vivid visual form. Immigrants in their national costumes were depicted on the wheel of change. As the wheel turned, all the costumed Europeans in national dress were dipped into the melting pot and rose again as new Americans, wearing housedresses and business suits and carrying American flags.

The melting pot had its own invisible exclusions. Asian immigrants were not part of the mix. Nor were African Americans or Native Americans. It was a wholly European melting pot, encompassing the Slavic, Anglo-Saxon, and Nordic races of Europe. The exclusion of blacks, Native peoples, and Chinese was so complete they were not even mentioned in the discourse. This did not mean, however, that they were not subject to powerful assimilative forces in America, for they were. One need only view some of the striking images in our American album in the first decades of the twentieth century: Native American school photos in which children, taken from their homes, are dressed in the little suits and dresses of their would-be benefactors; the California-style Sikh-Mexican wedding photo in which the Sikh groom has dispensed with the turban and cut his hair; or the photos of Japanese Buddhists posing in suits and dresses outside their newly constructed Buddhist temples. Dress, of course, is only an indicator of the willingness to dispense with visible difference, either by coercion or choice, and take on a new American image. But it was not enough for the old mainstream cultures of America, and the minorities continued to be marginalized by the melting pot ideology.

PLURALISM: THE SYMPHONY OF DIFFERENCE

Early in the debate over Chinese exclusion, the black abolitionist and orator Frederick Douglass rose to emphasize that the United States is a "composite nation" destined to become "the most perfect national illustration of the unity and dignity of the human family that the world has ever seen."[30] To fulfill this vision, he insisted that the U.S. draw upon the distinctive gifts and energies of people from every nation, including the Chinese. And as for religion, "We should welcome men of every shade of religious opinion, as among the best means of checking the arrogance and intolerance which are the almost inevitable concomitants of general conformity. Religious liberty always flourishes best amid the clash and competition of rival religious creeds." All will be "molded" into Americans, not by uniformity, but by observing the same law, supporting the same government, enjoying the same liberty, and vibrating with the same national enthusiasm. Douglass did not use the term *pluralism,* but his vision of a composite nation strikes me as a pluralist vision in which differences, including religious ones, become constitutive of a new community.

In 1915 a Jewish immigrant, the sociologist Horace Kallen, wrote a much-discussed article in *The Nation* taking issue with the melting pot vision of America. He may well be the first to use the term *pluralism* to describe an alternative vision. The article was titled "Democracy Versus the Melting Pot," and in it he argued that the melting pot ideal is inherently antidemocratic.[31] It collides with America's foundational principles. After all, one of the freedoms cherished in America is the freedom to be oneself, without erasing the distinctive features of one's own culture. Kallen saw America's plurality and its unity in the image of the symphony, not the melting pot. America is a symphony orchestra, sounding not unison, but harmony, with all the distinctive tones of our many cultures. He described this as "cultural pluralism." To those who would see New England and its old Anglo-Saxon core as setting the prototype for what it means to be American, Kallen wrote, "What do we *will* to make of the United States—a unison, singing the old Anglo-Saxon theme 'America,' the America of the New England school, or a harmony, in which that theme shall be dominant, perhaps, among others, but one among many, not the only one?"

In Kallen's view, immigrants can and do change many things—their style of dress, their politics, their religious affiliation, their economic status. But whatever else may change, "they cannot change their grandfathers." Cultural pluralism preserves the inalienable right to the "ancestral endowment" of selfhood imparted by one's parents and grandparents. One has a right to be different, not just in dress and public presentation, but in religion and creed, united only by participation in the common covenants of citizenship. American civilization is "a multiplicity in unity, an orchestration of mankind." In the final paragraphs of his 1915 article, Kallen develops the orchestra image:

> As in an orchestra, every type of instrument has its specific timbre and tonality, founded in its substance and form; as every type has its appropriate theme and melody in the whole symphony, so in society each ethnic group is the natural instrument, its spirit and culture are its theme and melody, and the harmony and dissonances and discords of them all make the symphony of civilization, with this difference: a musical symphony is written before it is played; in the symphony of civilization the playing is the writing, so that there is nothing so fixed and inevitable about its progressions as in music, so that within the limits set by nature they may vary at will, and the range and variety of the harmonies may become wider and richer and more beautiful. But the question is, do the dominant classes in America want such a society?

I find this an appealing image—the symphony of society, each retaining its difference, all sounding together, with an ear to the music of the whole. Of course, many critics and theorists see this as wholly sentimental, and others remind us that Kallen was also not thinking about Asians, blacks, and Native peoples as he envisioned his orchestra of cultural pluralism. But the image itself is promising as we think about how we create a society out of all the diversity that is now ours, a diversity greater than Kallen himself every imagined. We do, after all, "play" some things together: a Constitution, a Bill of Rights, and a way of living with our deepest differences premised on these covenants. Learning how to do that requires our patience with the disharmonies of practice and the dissonance of dissenters.

The symphony image needs some modification, however, as Kallen himself seemed to realize. A symphony is usually written in its entirety before it is played, and no society or nation has such a script. The work of cultural pluralism requires revisiting and reclaiming the energy and vision of democracy in every generation and with every new arrival. Perhaps we need to stretch our imagination to something more akin to jazz, for in jazz the playing is the writing. And because it is not all written out, it requires even more astute attention to the music of each instrument; it requires collaboration and invention among the players. Learning to hear the musical lines of our neighbors, their individual and magnificent interpretations of the themes of America's common covenants, is the test of cultural pluralism. Our challenge today is whether it will be jazz or simply noise, whether it will be a symphony or cacophony, whether we can continue to play together through dissonant moments.

CLOSING THE DOOR

Kallen hoped that "the range and variety of harmonies may become wider and richer and more beautiful." He asked if the dominant classes in America wanted such a society, and America's answer in the 1920s was no. Through decades of ongoing public debate on immigration, all three positions—exclusivist, assimilationist, and pluralist—had been articulated as America struggled to come to terms with the diversity of peoples who streamed through the doors of Ellis Island and Angel Island. By 1910, 14.7 percent of the American population was foreign born, higher than at any period in American history. Antiforeign, nativist sentiment seemed to increase in the period following World War I. After decades of sustained immigration, many Americans experienced so much difference as a threat. Perhaps they saw the disaster of Europe as prognostic of what would happen to America if difference were to flourish unchecked.

The Johnson-Reed Act was passed in 1924, effectively closing the door to new immigration, especially from outside western Europe, establishing quotas for what little immigration would be permitted on the basis of national origins as of the census of 1890. Exclusivism won the day. The 1924 immigration act eliminated what remained of any immigration from Asia, with the exception of the Philippines, not only through its quotas, but also by linking immigration to eligibility for citizenship. A policy of exclusion had also been making its way through the judicial system. America's Supreme Court had made several critical rulings in the early twenties. In the case of Bhagat Singh Thind in 1923, the court ruled, in effect, that Asians were ineligible for citizenship according to the 1790 statute that limited naturalization to "white" races. After the Civil War, people of African descent had been included by exception. But "white" remained the norm. By 1915, courts across the nation were adjudicating numerous cases, with Japanese, Syrians, and Punjabis all pressing claims for "whiteness." A 1917 Naturalization Act established that the term "shall apply to aliens being free white persons and to aliens of African nativity and to persons of African descent."

Bhagat Singh Thind was a Punjabi Sikh who had come to the U.S. in 1913, married an American woman, and served in the armed forces during

World War I. The District Court of Oregon had granted him a certificate of naturalization, but the Oregon Bureau of Naturalization contested the case. It eventually went to the U.S. Supreme Court, which ruled in 1923 against Thind's citizenship on the basis of race, as established by the 1917 Naturalization Act. The justices cited their decision the previous year in the case of Tadeo Ozawa, a "cultivated Japanese," who had been born in Japan but grew up and was educated in the United States. "The intention was to confer the privilege of citizenship upon that class of persons whom the fathers knew as white, and to deny it to all who could not be so classified. It is not enough to say that the framers did not have in mind the brown or yellow races of Asia."[32]

Lawyers argued, perhaps after consulting Indologists of the time, that Indian and European peoples shared a common "Indo-European" racial and language background. Punjabi is, after all, a distant cousin of English, and the heirs of the Indo-Europeans stretched from India to Ireland. Thind's claim to European kinship had some scholarly backing. But the judges nonetheless concluded that the framers of the naturalization law certainly did not have Indians in mind. They wrote, "It may be true that the blond Scandinavian and the brown Hindu have a common ancestor in the dim reaches of antiquity, but the average man knows perfectly well that there are unmistakable and profound differences between them to-day."

The Thind case was clearly about race, not about religion, but this case and others like it deeply affected the Sikh and other Asian communities in the United States. In the wake of the Thind decision, the Justice Department began proceedings to denaturalize some of the sixty-nine Indians, mostly Sikhs, who had already obtained citizenship. New Sikh immigration was stopped. Similarly, the Ozawa decision served to constrict Japanese immigration, especially when the 1924 legislation linked immigration to eligibility for citizenship. We have seen how the 1920s closed the door on immigration from Asia, and how the renewed growth of these communities did not begin again until after World War II and especially after 1965.

The decades between the two wars only increased the resurgence of an exclusivist spirit in America. A new chapter in the life of the Ku Klux Klan brought overt anti-Catholicism to the streets of America, and when Al Smith was nominated by the Democratic Party for president in 1928, cartoons appeared depicting a meeting of his cabinet chaired by the pope. Anti-Jewish groups saw Franklin Roosevelt as favoring Jews in his administration, and they dubbed the New Deal the "Jew Deal." The

1930s saw the rise of hate groups, the Christian Front, and the anti-Jewish rhetoric of Father Coughlin in the Detroit area, whose weekly radio broadcasts were carried on forty-five stations. Finally, in 1939, the *St. Louis* affair set a tragic seal on the very spirit of American liberty. The *St. Louis* was a Hamburg-America Line steamer, filled with nine hundred Jews who had fled Nazi Germany. It sailed for Havana, Cuba, hoping to make it eventually to the United States. En route, the ship received news that even Cuba would not let the ship dock, and despite pleas directly to President Roosevelt, it was not allowed to come into port anywhere in the United States. The sentiment against immigration was so high that Roosevelt apparently feared the consequences showing hospitality would have in the next election. Eventually, the *St. Louis* and its passengers had to return across the Atlantic to Germany and to certain death. There could be no more tragic expression of America's sentiment for exclusion.

PROTESTANT, CATHOLIC, JEW—AND BEYOND

After World War II the mood began to shift, and, as Leonard Dinnerstein put it, the tide of anti-Judaism began to ebb. The full knowledge of Hitler's atrocities made anti-Semitism disreputable and gradually confined to a "lunatic fringe,"[33] although, as we know, anti-Semitism has not disappeared in America, even today. Both Jewish and Catholic communities participated in the growing stability and energy of religious life in the postwar period. As noted earlier, in 1955 the sociologist Will Herberg published a book about the new American religious status quo bearing the simple title *Protestant, Catholic, Jew*. In his view Catholics and Jews now took their place along with Protestants as the bearers of the American experiment. This was the Eisenhower era, and religion was deemed a "good thing," both for the individual and the community. It was consonant with a common overarching "religion" Herberg called the "American Way of Life," whose components, in Herberg's view, were political democracy, economic free enterprise, and social egalitarianism. Herberg wrote that *religion* means "not so much any particular religion, but religion as such, religion-in-general." President Eisenhower had recently declared, "Our government makes no sense unless it is founded in a deeply felt religious faith—and I don't care what it is." Herberg explains that such seemingly heretical indifference was really an affirmation of the common roots of the three faiths, and their common purpose in promoting the American Way of Life.

Herberg argued that postwar America was not at all a single melting pot. Rather, after three decades of sharply reduced immigration, it was a "triple melting pot," in which Protestants tended to marry Protestants, whether Lutheran or Methodist; Catholics tended to marry Catholics, whether Irish or Italian; and Jews tended to marry Jews, whether of Russian or German background. Ethnicity had given way to religion as the "differentiating element" in American life. He argued that while cultural differences tended to fade as European immigrants came to the new world, the main lines of their religious differences, broadly speaking, did not. America was now a "three religion country," and religion had become the primary marker of difference in the America of the 1950s.

> The newcomer is expected to change many things about him as he becomes an American—nationality, language, culture. One thing, however, he is not expected to change—and that is his religion. And so it is religion that with the third generation has become the differentiating element and the context of self-identification and social location."[34]

By the third generation, he argues, people had lost the language and culture of their grandparents but had retained their religion. "By and large, to be an American today means to be either a Protestant, a Catholic, or a Jew."[35]

Religious pluralism, Protestant, Catholic, and Jewish, was to Herberg far more than a statistical fact of American life. It was a deep-seated part of America's mind-set. Everybody is religious in the context and knowledge of the religious other.

> In America religious pluralism is thus not merely a historical and political fact; it is, in the mind of the American, the primordial condition of things, an essential aspect of the American Way of Life, and therefore in itself an aspect of religious belief. Americans, in other words, believe that the plurality of religious groups is a proper and legitimate condition. However much he may be attached to his own church, however dimly he may regard the beliefs and practices of other churches, the American tends to feel rather strongly that total religious uniformity, even with his own church benefiting thereby, would be something undesirable and wrong, scarcely conceivable. Pluralism of religions and churches is something quite axiomatic to the American.[36]

At the time Herberg wrote, the nearly complete dominance of

Protestants on the American scene was approaching its end. Of the 528 members of the 85th Congress in 1957, 416 were Protestant, 95 were Catholic, and 12 were Jewish. One was a Sikh, the first and still the only Sikh to be elected to Congress. Within a few years a Catholic, John F. Kennedy, had been elected president of the United States, and his administration included prominent Jewish appointees. But within a few years it was also clear where Herberg had missed the mark in his assessment of America. He had not even considered the vast and vibrant African-American Protestant churches in his theory of the Protestant melting pot, and Sunday morning worship remained one of the most segregated hours of the week. The variety of Eastern Orthodox communities had escaped his purview altogether, as had the rise of Black Islam. By the time the 1960s were over, Native peoples began to be visibly represented by intertribal organizations, like the American Indian Movement; Hispanic religious life had new Catholic, Protestant, Evangelical, and Pentecostal forms, and the new post-1965 immigration was bringing immigrants to America from all over the world. Never again would an analysis of America's religious life look so simple. The post-1965 immigrants have brought with them their many religious traditions—Hindu, Sikh, Muslim, Buddhist, Jain, and Zoroastrian. They also brought their own perspectives on American society and, increasingly, their own styles of participation. Now the "Protestant, Catholic, Jewish" image of America has been amplified to include many other voices, and a new era of America's religious pluralism has begun.

Following Herberg's model, should we expect Muslim, Hindu, Sikh, or Buddhist communities to continue as distinct and dynamic religious traditions, perhaps developing their own assimilative processes, their own micro–melting pots? Of course, Herberg's theory is based on the fact that for thirty years, from 1924 on, America's immigrant communities were not replenished by new immigrants. Language acquisition and cultural traditions languished by the third generation, leaving religion as the primary marker of identity. Today new immigrants are constantly arriving, and the entire theory of the "second" and "third" generations is questionable. Cultures remain vibrant, with Caribbean and Dominican, Portuguese and Indian festivals and parades. Subcultures have their own neighborhoods and retain their own languages. But elements of his hypothesis will be tested by the new generations of Americans. Perhaps it will not matter in years to come whether a person of Indian origin is a Bengali Hindu or a Tamil Hindu; Hindu parents will be grateful enough if their children marry within the tradition. As one of my Jain students, Vivek, put it, "The circles keep on broadening. My family was from Kutch, a small desert region in Gujarat, one of the regions of India. Two generations ago, it was a scandal to marry somebody whose family wasn't from the same village in Kutch. Now, for me, even to find a Jain woman from Kutch is kind of rare. Do I bump into that every day in North America? Not really. My mom keeps on changing what she tells me: She has to be from Kutch. Well, at least she has to be Gujarati. Well, at least she has to be Jain. The circles just keep on widening."[37]

Extrapolating from Herberg's view of the 1950s, one might well argue that in this new millennium the diversity of religions will be the salient fact of America's civic life, far outweighing in its significance the diversity of ethnic or national origins. From now on, broadening religious pluralism will be an important issue for America. Perhaps there will be many more melting pots within the spectrum of American life—a Jain, a Hindu, a Muslim melting pot. Or we might just find that traditional forms of religion also begin to lose hold here, and the numbers of multireligious families multiply. Just as my students say, "On my mother's side, we were Polish, and on my father's side, we were Irish and Italian," some of them also say, "On my mother's side we were Protestant, and on my father's side, we were Jewish and Hindu," and, "My dad is Muslim, and he's Punjabi, and my mom is a Roman Catholic, born in New Haven. I have three brothers; two are adopted and they are also Roman Catholic, and my biological brother and I have been raised Muslim." Here, the history of the new religious America is still being formed, and as with many things in American life today, we are on new ground.

After three decades of soaring immigration, the argument over who "we" are now is once again on the agenda of national discussion. A 1993 *Newsweek* article posed the question succinctly: "America: Still a Melting Pot?"[38] The authors of the article reported that 60 percent of Americans see the new influx of immigration as too high. They asked, "Is the U.S. still a melting pot, or do immigrants today maintain their national identity more strongly?" Only 20 percent of the respondents felt that American is "still a melting pot," while 66 percent said that new immigrants "maintain their identity." There is clearly a fear that America may be fractured by too much difference, by overemphasizing difference.

In today's immigration debates, we hear echoes from the past as we discuss how America should respond to this broadening diversity. Exclusionists like Peter Brimelow once again call for closing the door, arguing, "The 1965 Immigration Act, and its amplifications in 1986 and 1990, has been a disaster and must be repealed."[39] Modern-day assimila-tionists, like Arthur Schlesinger Jr., call for a renewed emphasis on the common, the *unum,* in the face of the growing *pluribus* he refers to as "the disuniting of America." He writes of "cult of ethnicity" that has arisen to challenge the idea of a melting pot and the concept of "one people." This has shifted the balance from the *unum* to the *pluribus* and amounts to "an attack on the common American identity."[40] Pluralists, like the propo-nents of the Williamsburg Charter, signed at the two hundredth anniver-sary of the Constitution, propose to emphasize that common identity without sacrificing the integrity of the many voices. They brought together a wide and diverse constituency of religious communities, including Muslims and Buddhists, to reaffirm the foundational commit-ments to religious liberty and find ways of living together with "our deep-est differences."

PLURALISM: A WIDER SENSE OF "WE"

In 1991 Imam Abdul-Latif of the Masjid Al-Muminin in Brooklyn and head of the Islamic Leadership Council said, "We are no longer a Judeo-Christian city. We have to deal with a Judeo-Christian-Muslim tradi-tion." The New York City area in the early 1990s held an estimated six hundred thousand Muslims, and now, some ten years later, the number is closer to a million. The Islamic Leadership Council included, at that time, representation from some twenty-five of New York's many mosques. Imam Abdul-Latif deliberately stretched the sense of a civic "we" to include Christians, Jews, and Muslims, but, in fact, he did not stretch it far enough. Today, the "we" of New York City includes a multi-tude of Buddhists, with more than twenty Chinese Buddhist temples alone, to say nothing of the Thai, Cambodian, Vietnamese, Korean, Japanese, and Euro-American Buddhist centers. It includes the Sikhs of the Richmond Hill gurdwara, whose World Sikh Day parade has become a New York tradition, and the Hindus of the Ganesha Temple in Flushing with their annual festival procession of Lord Ganesha down Flushing's Main Street.

The American Constitutions begins, "We the people of the United States . . ." In an era when the "we" is being defined in narrower terms in many parts of the world, when the "we" is the we of ethnic, religious, or national chauvinism, America's "we" has continued, so far, to be elastic and expansive. A November 1993 edition of the *Boston Globe* had a special full-page article on the process of becoming a citizen, under the banner headline, "America's History Is a Story of Immigration." It included photographs of a crowd of new Americans taking the oath of citizenship in Fanueil Hall. That entire page of the paper was published sequentially in Chinese, Spanish, Vietnamese, Khmer, Russian, and French, a testimony to the shape of immigration in Boston. The city's new museum of immigration, called Dreams of Freedom, chronicles the eras and diversities of Boston's immigration history, ending with an exhibit called "Faithful Boston," with photographs and religious displays from the whole range of religious communities, from the Ethiopian Evangelical Church to the Sikh Study Center, from the Thousand Buddha Temple to the Islamic Society of Boston.

America's "we" today includes Buddhist Americans, like the Hawaiian-born Jodo Shinshu Buddhist astronaut who died on the *Challenger.* It includes Muslim Americans, like the mayor of Kuntz, Texas, and the Muslim officer in the Oklahoma City Fire Department who spent two weeks retrieving bodies from the rubble of the Murrah Federal Building. We Americans are Jains, like the Cincinnati businessman who visited us at Harvard when he was president of the Jain Association of North America, and Hindus, like the engineer from Boston Edison who was the first president of the Hindu temple in Ashland. We are also Sikhs, like the woman research scientist in Fairfax, Virginia, and Zoroastrians, like the computer engineer in San Jose who also serves as the *mobed,* or priest, of the Zoroastrian temple.

But beyond the facts of our diversity, appropriating a wider sense of "we" that includes such a range of voices is a significant civic and religious challenge. Who do we mean when we say "we"? America's response to this question is important, perhaps not only for America but also for the world. Building a multireligious society seems to be increasingly difficult in a world in which religious markers of identity are often presumed to be the most divisive of all differences. The evidence of the divisiveness of the "politics of identity" is plainly manifest in the fracturing of complex societies in Lebanon and the former Yugoslavia and in the communal and religious strife of India and Sri Lanka. The continued debate over immigration makes clear that Americans are uncertain about the viability of this wider "we."

As religious difference becomes more visible in America, is it possible to begin to discern some of the ways in which a wider sense of "we" is beginning to be publicly acknowledged and affirmed? Let us survey, for a moment, some of the evidence of a broader "we" in the American public square. We recall, for instance, the first Muslim invocation in the U.S. House by Siraj Wahaj in 1991, followed the next year by Imam W. D. Mohammed, leader of the majority group of orthodox African-American Muslims, giving the first-ever Muslim invocation in the U.S. Senate. The daily invocations of the U.S. Congress are not, on the whole, notable public events. However, after many thousands of Christian and Jewish prayers, decade after decade, the first Islamic prayers before Congress do indeed constitute a landmark in American public life.

The weekly *Muslim Journal,* published by the African-American followers of W. D. Mohammed, reports dozens of other events, many of them local and regional, but all of them significant signals of changes that go almost unrecorded in the popular press: Muslims in Norfolk, Virginia, offer the first-ever Muslim prayers at the Norfolk city council meeting. In Sacramento, California, Muslims open a session of the state legislature with prayer. In Savannah, Georgia, the city council issues a proclamation recognizing Islam as having been "a vital part of the development of the United States of America and the city of Savannah." The proclamation states that "many of the African slaves brought to our country were followers of the religion of Al-Islam" and proclaims that "the Religion of Al-Islam be given equal acknowledgment and recognition as other religious bodies of our great city."

I think that the look and feel of America begins to change if we pay careful attention to the many ways in which Muslims, Buddhists, Hindus, and Sikhs now indicate their own participation in the public square. Among immigrant Buddhist communities, for example, one often sees the visible signals of their new American identity. The American flag is raised every Saturday morning at Wat Thai in North Hollywood, California, as the weekend religious school begins. Inside the temple, the stars and stripes are posted, along with the flag of the state of California, right next to the great golden image of the Buddha. In Santa Monica, the lay-oriented Soka Gakkai International has its headquarters. Though its origins are in Japan, this movement has developed a wide multiethnic and multiracial following in the U.S. and has participated vigorously in displays of American patriotism from the time of the bicentennial to the present. The Buddhist ecumenical group called the Sangha Council of Southern California gathers Buddhists from all over the city for its annual Buddha's Birthday celebrations, and at the head of the procession of monks the American flag is carried along with the international Buddhist flag. In 1990 the Buddhist community of California petitioned to establish the Buddha's Birthday as an official state holiday.

Both individuals and communities negotiate their participation in the public square. In 1993 Dr. Balwant S. Hansra, a Sikh immigrant, now a citizen active in the interfaith movement in Washington, was asked to offer a prayer at the Lincoln Memorial to commemorate the 1963 March on Washington and to remember the "I Have a Dream" speech of Dr. Martin Luther King Jr. Just a week later, I saw him at the Parliament of the World's Religions in Chicago, and Dr. Hansra described the tremendous effect his participation in the Lincoln Memorial event had on him. He said, "When I saw a hundred thousand people there, I could not believe that I had been asked to pray. For the first time, I felt America was my home."

It is also a sign of appropriating America as home that Sikhs as a community have been vigorous in insisting on what they consider to be their religious rights under the U.S. Constitution, such as the right to wear uncut hair wrapped with a turban in the workplace and the right to carry the small knife called a *kirpan,* both of which are emblems of the faith of an initiated Sikh. Litigating for one's right to religious freedom is certainly one historically hallowed way of being an American. While some immigrant groups are reluctant to put themselves in the position of plaintiffs in court, doing so is an important form of engagement within the American system.

Over the past three decades, American Muslims have developed an institutional infrastructure that not only brings them together regionally and nationally but also facilitates Muslim participation in public life. The Islamic Society of North America, based in Plainfield, Indiana, draws as many as twelve thousand Muslims for its annual Labor Day conventions focusing on four-square American themes such as "Building an Islamic Environment in North America" or "Muslims for a Better America."

In terms of political participation, Islam has moved more boldly than any of the other new immigrant traditions to claim a public voice. The American Muslim Council, created in 1990 and based in Washington, D.C., is a forum for Muslim leaders to discuss the many issues of Muslim participation in American public life. It aims to "identify and oppose discrimination against Muslims and other minorities" and to "organize American Muslims to become a powerful political force in mainstream American life." It goes without saying that Muslims, like Christians or

Jews, are not monolithic in their views of either international or domestic issues. Some Muslims were originally hesitant about participating in American politics, but on the whole the tide has turned. At its ninth national convention in June 2000, dozens of speakers explained the ways in which they, or their Islamic center, have become involved. Dr. Riyaz Ahmed, for example, who came thirty years ago as an immigrant from Pakistan, recalled his first uncertain ventures into lobbying in Congress over issues of concern to Pakistan. Now, he urges all Muslims to recognize the critical importance of understanding the American system so that they can be partners in it. "The key point is this: The American political system is accessible, and we must be bold enough to enter it!"

Pluralism is a matter of engaging not only with political institutions but also with Americans of other religious communities, and here too we can look for evidence of changes afoot. Among hundreds of examples, we could look to Cleveland where, in September of 1993, Imam Rahman, representing Cleveland's Muslim community, was invited to say prayers during the Yom Kippur service at Temple Ner Tamid. This was inspired by the September 13, 1993, "handshake" between Israeli Prime Minister Yitzhak Rabin and PLO leader Yasser Arafat. It was said to be the first time ever, anywhere in the world, that a Muslim leader had participated in Yom Kippur prayers. Or we could look to Los Angeles in 1998, when Muslims and Jews worked out a joint code of ethics to govern their civic relations with each other. Or we could look to Milwaukee on Thanksgiving Eve in 2000, when representatives of Christian and Muslim communities signed a covenant affirming their "support and love for one another" and committing themselves and their communities "to the exercise of understanding, cooperation, and growth in unity through faith."

TOWARD A NEW PLURALISM

The language of pluralism is the language not just of difference but of engagement, involvement, and participation. It is the language of traffic, exchange, dialogue, and debate. It is the language of the symphony orchestra and the jazz ensemble. "Couldn't you think of another word than *pluralism?*" The question came to me at a public forum in Louisville from a woman active in the local interfaith council. She explained, "Around here, pluralism has a bad name." What she meant, as we discussed the matter, was the common critique that pluralism means the chaos of "anything goes." It means unprincipled relativism and therefore moral decay. It means giving up on one's own, usually Christian, truth claims in favor of an unconvincing "religious correctness." But I am not ready to give up on the term *pluralism,* because unpacking its meaning, especially with skeptics, steers us into some of the most important issues of our time. Pluralism is not an ideology, not a leftist scheme, and not a free-form relativism. Rather, pluralism is the dynamic process through which we engage with one another in and through our very deepest differences.

First, *pluralism* is not just another word for diversity. It goes beyond mere plurality or diversity to active engagement with that plurality. Religious diversity is an observable fact of American life today, but without any real engagement with one another, neighboring churches, temples, and mosques might prove to be just a striking example of diversity. One can study this diversity, complain about there being too much diversity, or even celebrate diversity. But the diversity alone is not pluralism. Pluralism is not a given but must be created. Pluralism requires participation, and attunement to the life and energies of one another.

Second, pluralism goes beyond mere tolerance to the active attempt to understand the other, like the step taken by Milwaukee's Christians and Muslims when they signed that covenant pledging themselves to the process of mutual understanding. Although tolerance is no doubt a step forward from intolerance, it does not require new neighbors to know anything about one another. Tolerance can create a climate of restraint but not one of understanding. Tolerance alone does little to bridge the chasms of stereotype and fear that may, in fact, dominate the mutual image of the other on a street like New Hampshire Avenue outside our nation's capital. It is far too fragile a foundation for a society that is becoming as religiously complex as ours.

William Penn and, later, the framers of the Constitution wanted to move beyond the tolerance of religious difference to the free exercise of religion. Today, with the free exercise of such a panoply of religious traditions in our nation and in our neighborhoods, a truly pluralist society will need to move beyond tolerance toward constructive understanding. Americans, on the whole, have a high degree of religious identification, according to every indication of the Gallup polls, and yet a very low level of religious literacy. Beginning to root out the stereotypes and prejudices that form the fault lines of fracture is critical for a society that has absorbed so much difference, with so little understanding of our differences. Even today, few school systems have vigorous programs to teach about the world's religions in the context of social studies or history.

While religion departments are flourishing in many colleges and universities, few theological schools training leaders for churches and synagogues require basic literacy in the world religions as part of that training.

Third, pluralism is not simply relativism. It does not displace or eliminate deep religious commitments or secular commitments for that matter. It is, rather, the encounter of commitments. Some critics have persisted in linking pluralism with a kind of valueless relativism, in which all cats are gray, all perspectives equally viable and, as a result, equally uncompelling. Pluralism, they contend, undermines commitment to one's own particular faith with its own particular language, watering down particularity in the interests of universality. I consider that view a distortion of the process of pluralism. I would argue that pluralism is engagement with, not abdication of, differences and particularities. While the encounter with people of other faiths in a pluralist society may lead one to a less myopic view of one's own faith, pluralism is premised not on a reductive relativism but on the significance of and engagement with real differences.

In the late 1950s the Catholic thinker John Courtney Murray described America's civic pluralism as the vigorous engagement of people of different religious beliefs around the "common table" of discussion and debate. He wrote,

> By pluralism here I mean the coexistence within the one political community of groups who hold divergent and incompatible views with regard to religious questions. . . . Pluralism therefore implies disagreement and dissension within the community. But it also implies a community within which there must be agreement and consensus. There is no small political problem here. If society is to be at all a rational process, some set of principles must motivate the general participation of all religious groups, despite their dissensions, in the oneness of the community. On the other hand, these common principles must not hinder the maintenance by each group of its own different identity.[41]

Murray sees the engagement of difference in a pluralistic society as modeled, not on the structure of warfare, but on the structure of dialogue. Vigorous engagement, even argument, around the "common table" is vital to a democratic society. It is vital also to the health of religious faith so that we appropriate our faith not by habit or heritage alone, but by making it our own within the context of dialogue with people of other

faiths. Such dialogue is aimed not at achieving agreement, but at achieving relationship. Whether in the public school, the city council, or the
interfaith council, commitments are not left at the door. The "common
table" of American civic life has grown, and its shape has been refigured
with each new group of participants, each new seat added. Indeed, the
"naked public square" so repudiated by the conservative Christian
thinker Richard Neuhaus is now likely to become the multireligious public square in which many new religious voices are heard.

Finally, the process of pluralism is never complete but is the ongoing
work of each generation. In America, we might go further to say that part
of the engagement of pluralism is participating in the "idea of America."
After all, America is a nation formed not by a race or a single people, but
by the ideals articulated in the succession of founding documents, beginning with the Declaration of Independence. To say "We hold these truths
to be self-evident" is not to hold these truths in the safe deposit box of the
past, but to keep them alive through argument and dialogue in the present.
As Murray puts it, "The American consensus needs to be constantly
argued."[42] This was also the view of state of California's Board of
Education when, in 1991, it issued a new set of guidelines for teaching history and social science. It took the motto of the American republic as its
title: *E Pluribus Unum,* "Out of Many, One." The California educators made
clear that this motto does not define an already-finished ideal but one that
is dynamic and must be claimed anew in the context of new civic and social
challenges. They wrote, "The framework embodies the understanding
that the national identity, the national heritage, and the national creed are
pluralistic and that our national history is the complex story of many peoples
and one nation, of *e pluribus unum,* and of an unfinished struggle to realize
the ideals of the Declaration of Independence and the Constitution."[43]

In 1988, to commemorate the bicentennial of the Constitution, the
Williamsburg Charter Foundation drafted "The Williamsburg Charter,"
a reaffirmation of the principles of religious liberty found in the Bill of
Rights, signed by representatives from government and law, education,
and business, as well as by representatives of Christian, Jewish, Muslim,
and Buddhist communities. The preamble ends with words that envision
this charter as a basis for civic pluralism:

> The Charter sets forth a renewed national compact, in the sense
> of a solemn mutual agreement between parties, on how we view
> the place of religion in American life and how we should contend

with each other's deepest differences in the public sphere. It is a call to a vision of public life that will allow conflict to lead to consensus, religious commitment to reinforce political civility. In this way, diversity is not a point of weakness but a source of strength.[44]

The Williamsburg Charter affirms that America's distinctive experiment in religious liberty is not simply a landmark of the past but an ongoing challenge to be met in each generation. The arguing and reaffirmation of a freely chosen consensus, as embodied in the Williamsburg Charter, is what some have called "chartered pluralism." Today, as the religious landscape of America becomes multireligious, the foundational legacy of Jefferson and Madison is being appropriated anew by Muslim, Buddhist, and Hindu Americans. In the process of reconfiguring a new and more complex pattern of pluralism, might we begin to listen to what they have to say about being Americans?

Let us begin with a Buddhist, C. T. Shen, one of the foremost teachers of the Chinese Buddhist community in America, who speaks of a spirit of sympathy between the Buddhist and the American vision. In his well-known "Mayflower" speech, given at the Cathedral of the Pines in New Hampshire on July 4, 1976, he links the imaginative power of the Mayflower crossing the Atlantic to the Buddhist image of crossing the waters of danger and turbulence to the "far shore" of freedom. His use of the word *we,* linking himself to the ancestry of his new "imagined community," is revealing.

> May we Americans, in this Bicentennial year, reaffirm the dedication of our ancestors and raise our Mayflower flag to sail across the vast ocean of hatred, discrimination, selfishness, and arrive on the other shore of loving-kindness, compassion, joy, and equanimity.
>
> May we Americans, in this Bicentennial year, reaffirm our determination to extend our love of brotherhood to all people on earth, and may we be guided by the collective wisdom of all world religions to save ourselves from self-destruction. Today our greatest fear is not of nature. Our greatest fear is of ourselves.[45]

A Hindu physician in Nashville, Dr. Somayaji, one of the founders of the Ganesha Temple in the western suburbs of the city, put it this way: "We Hindus say *Ekam sat vipraha bahudha vadanti.* 'Truth is one, people speak of it in many ways.' What does this mean for us here in America? It means that we Hindus can show, in America, an example of tolerance. We do not talk of superiority. We do not talk of conversion. But we have an important role: to add tolerance to the mix in America." Having lived for over twenty years in Nashville and having encountered a dominant and exclusivist Christian ethos more than once, Dr. Somayaji has become an active member of the National Conference for Community and Justice, an interfaith group dedicated to promoting cultural, racial, and religious harmony. He and members of the Nashville temple have endeavored over the years to articulate a Hindu voice in the civic life of Nashville.

A Hindu professor of English at Southern Utah University, Dr. S. S. Moorty, lives in Cedar City, Utah, where there is no Hindu temple or community. He articulates in different terms the way in which his religious tradition enables him to participate in American society. In an article called "My Small American Town," he writes, "My coat closet in my home is my temple." He maintains his traditions of daily worship, sings devotional *bhajans* with his family, and observes the rituals of the calendar year in his home shrine, the former coat closet. It is the Hindu spirit of respect for other religious traditions that has enabled him to flourish in America, even as a Hindu in Cedar City. A few years ago, Dr. Moorty wrote to me,

> During all my seventeen years of geographical isolation, I have never felt that I have lost touch with my religion. In fact, without disowning me, my faith allows me to attend the local Catholic Church Christmas Mass or socially relate to the activities of the Church of the Latter-Day Saints. Yet I am neither a Catholic nor a Mormon. Every inch I am a Hindu.

We might also listen to the editor of a Sikh newsletter in Washington, D.C., who reflected on his participation in a bill-signing ceremony at the White House in 1994. He wrote,

> This was almost a hundred years after the first Sikh migrants came to North America. Today over 300,000 Sikhs have adopted United States as their home. As we grow as a community, future generations of Sikhs will carry on the universal and eternal message of Guru Nanak here in the United States. Our Guru's vision continues to hold true today in America as it was in India five hundred years ago—of a society where people are constantly aware of the Infinite within, where they live by honest labor and share with others.[46]

The public voice of American Sikhs has become stronger with each year, and in late September 2000 Dr. Rajwant Singh, president of Sikh

Council on Religion and Education, spoke at a Washington rally supporting the anti–hate crimes legislation pending before Congress. He said,

> I stand before you today as an advocate of anti–hate crimes legis-
> lation. Hate crimes are a challenge to all religious believers. While
> religion preaches that we are all God's children, hate crimes are
> evidence of a pernicious belief that those who are different, be it
> in race, creed, ethnicity, or sexual orientation not only cannot
> claim God's grace, but may actually be subjected to physical harm.
> This is a belief that no religion can accept, and it is particularly
> anathema to Sikhs, with their traditions of tolerance and mutual
> understanding. . . . America is a nation of diversity, and it is strong
> to the extent that we respect each other's beliefs, customs, and
> achievements. Passage of anti–hate crime legislation will put the
> practitioners of hate on notice that they cannot do violence to
> those whom they may not like and expect to get away with it.[47]

In Los Angeles a group of Muslim leaders speak to us of their vision
for America as Muslim immigrants to America. Hassan Hathout, Fathi
Osman, and Maher Hathout, all leaders of the Islamic Center of Southern
California in downtown Los Angeles, have written extensively about a
Muslim vision for America in a small book called *In Fraternity.* "There is an
opportunity for Islam in America, and there is an opportunity for America
in Islam," they begin. "There exists a mutual suitability between America
and Islam and Muslims." Because of Islam's insistence on the universal
equality and dignity of all human beings and because of the very diversity
and plurality of the Muslim community, they see Muslims as "qualified and
ready to take their place in the American mainstream and to be an active,
positive component of American pluralism."[48]

Islam, they write, is a "universal call," not an Arab or Middle Eastern
religion. Now, they say, "America is our mother country. Our children and
grandchildren after us will live in this country." They conclude that the
main strategic goal of Muslim institutions is "to be an effective, viable,
radiant part of American pluralism." This does not mean becoming a
majority. "All that is needed is an organized movement, a movement
which embodies the teachings of Islam in individuals and organizations,
capable of interacting with the American reality to affect its values and to
contribute positively in the decision making process. The movement has
to share Islam horizontally with all elements of the American society, and
vertically to the upcoming Muslim generations.[49]

During the 1990s the symbolic public response to America's new religious reality has been visible as never before. Sikh festival days, like the annual observance of Guru Nanak's birthday, have been noted at local, state, and federal levels with official greetings to the Sikh community. The Sikh Day parade each November in Yuba City, California, attracts as many as forty thousand participants. In 2000 the Hindus received a presidential greeting on the occasion of the fall festival of Diwali for the first time in American history. The month of Ramadan has become the occasion for public notice, newspaper articles, and official greetings during the 1990s, and in the year 2000 the U.S. Postal Service unveiled a new postage stamp for Eid, the feast day at the end of Ramadan. On February 20, 1996, at the end of the month of Ramadan, First Lady Hillary Rodham Clinton welcomed Muslims to the White House for the first Eid al-Fitr observance ever to take place there. Mrs. Clinton said,

> This celebration is an American event. We are a nation of immigrants who have long drawn on our diverse religious traditions and faiths for the strength and courage that make America great. For two centuries, we have prided ourselves on being a nation of pluralistic beliefs, united by a common faith in democracy.[50]

One of the Muslims who spoke on this occasion was an eleven-year-old, Marwa al-Kairo, from Herndon, Virginia, who in many ways represents both the challenges and changes of an increasingly plural America. She is a Girl Scout and came to the podium in her Girl Scout uniform, a reminder to those who may have followed the controversy that in 1993 the national Girl Scouts organization opened its pledge to the breadth of religious language, allowing scouts like Marwa to pledge, "On my honor I will try to serve Allah and my country. . . ." Standing at the lectern in her green felt hat, Marwa said, "Only in America people from different parts of the world can come together and become one community. I am proud to be an American Muslim."

The Girl Scouts have seen clearly and perceptively the new world in which we live. They are way ahead of most of the rest of us, and they have come up with a statement of pluralism we might all learn from. "Pluralism means being inclusive and respectful of people or groups with different backgrounds, experiences, and cultures. In a pluralistic organization, like the Girl Scouts, we value development of common traditions, respect for diversity and individual differences, preservation of everyone's cultural heritage and individual rights." They go on to make a distinction we have tried to make here as well:

> Diversity and pluralism are not the same, and although you can have diversity without pluralism, you cannot have pluralism without valuing diversity. Diversity can simply mean counting the variety of people. Pluralism means that we value people for the variety they bring to the group.[51]

Today, the United States is in the process of understanding and negotiating the meaning of its pluralism anew. Sociological, political, and philosophical contributions to this discussion are coming from a wide range of voices. However, in this new struggle to understand who "we" are in the new millennium, it is clearly critical to hear the voices of America's many religions, new and old, in shaping a distinctively and boldly multireligious society. It is critical to hear and value the many new ways in which the variety of American peoples bring life and vibrancy to the whole of our society. Today we have the unparalleled opportunity to build, intentionally and actively, a culture of pluralism among the people of many cultures and faiths in America. We may not succeed. We may find ourselves fragmented and divided, with too much *pluribus* and not enough *unum*. But if we can succeed, this is the greatest form of lasting leadership we can offer the world.

NOTES

1. *American Muslim Council Report* (Summer 1991).

2. Frank James, *Old Colony Memorial* (November 25, 1998), A17.

3. Peter J. Gomes, "The Hard Work of Reconciliation," *Boston Globe,* November 26, 1998.

4. Roger Williams, citation from his trial in First Liberty Institute, *Living With Our Deepest Differences* (Nashville, Tennessee: Freedom Forum First Amendment Center, n.d.), 32.

5. *Publications of the Narragansett Club,* ser. 1, vol. 3 (1867): 3–4.

6. *Flushing Remonstrance,* brochure distributed at Bowne House, Flushing, New York; original manuscript in the New York State Library, Albany, New York.

7. Henry Steele Commanger, *Documents of American History,* 8th ed. (New York: Appleton-Century-Crofts, 1968), 124–25.

8. James Madison, "Memorial and Remonstrance," *Letters and Other Writings of James Madison* (Philadelphia, 1867), 1: 162ff.

9. Thomas Jefferson, "An Act for Establishing Religious Liberty," in *The Life of Thomas Jefferson in Three Volumes,* ed. Henry S. Randall (New York: Derby and Jackson, 1858), 1: 219–20.

10. John Winthrop, "A Modell of Christian Charity," Winthrop Papers, Collections of the Massachusetts Historical Society, ser. 3, vol. 7 (Boston: Massachusetts Historical Society, 1838), 31–48.

11. Alexis de Tocqueville, *Democracy in America* (New York: Vintage Books, 1990), 1: 308, 303–4.

12. Robert Handy, *A Christian America* (New York: Oxford University Press, 1971), 100.

13. Isaac Kramnick and R. Laurence Moore, *The Godless Constitution* (New York: W. W. Norton, 1997), 146.

14. Kramnick and Moore, *The Godless Constitution,* 148.

15. Richard Hughes Seager, ed., *The Dawn of Religious Pluralism: Voices from the World's Parliament of Religions, 1893* (LaSalle, IL: Open Court, 1993), 25.

16. Quoted in Robert Handy, *A Christian America,* 167

17. Julie Canniff, "The Story of Watt Samaki," Pluralism Project Research, 1993.

18. Josiah Strong, *Our Country* (Cambridge: Harvard University Press, 1963), 73–74.

19. Leonard Dinnerstein, *Antisemitism in America* (New York: Oxford University Press, 1994), 35, 94–95. He refers, in the first instance, to an article by immigration activist Gino Speranza, and in the second to a series of 1920–21 articles in the *Saturday Evening Post* by writer Kenneth Roberts.

20. *Congressional Record* (February 28, 1882).

21. Robert R. Swartout Jr., "From Kwangtung to the Big Sky: The Chinese Experience in Frontier Montana," in *Montana Heritage: An Anthology of Historical Essays,* ed. Robert R. Swartout Jr. and Harry W. Fritz (Helena: Montana Historical Society, 1992), 78.

22. *Proceedings of the Asiatic Exclusion League* (San Francisco, July 16, 1911), 134–37.

23. *Proceedings of the Asiatic Exclusion League* (San Francisco, April 12, 1908), 22–23.

24. "National Quotas for Immigration to End," Congressional Quarterly Almanac, v. 21, 1965, 476–77.

25. Billy Redwing Tayac, Pluralism Project interview, 1996.

26. Alma Abdul Malik, Pluralism Project interview, 1996.

27. John Quincy Adams, *Niles' Weekly Register,* vol. 18, April 29, 1820, 157–58. This was a letter Adams wrote to Baron von Fürstenwaerther in 1818 when he was Secretary of State.

28. Israel Zangwill, *The Melting Pot* (New York: Macmillan & Co., 1919), 36–37.

29. Philip Gleason, "Melting Pot, Symbol of Fusion or Confusion," *American Quarterly* (Spring 1964).

30. Frederick Douglass, "Composite Nation," in *Racism, Dissent, and Asian Americans from 1850 to the Present: A Documentary History*, ed. Philip S. Foner and Daniel Rosenberg (Westport, CT: Greenwood, 1993), 215–30.

31. Horace Kallen, "Democracy Versus the Melting Pot," *The Nation* 100, no. 2590 (February 18–25, 1915): 190–94, 217–20.

32. *U.S. v. Bhagat Singh Thind, The Supreme Court Reporter*, October 1923, 338–42.

33. Dinnerstein, *Antisemitism in America*, 151ff.

34. Will Herberg, *Protestant, Catholic, Jew* (Chicago: University of Chicago Press, 1983), 23.

35. Herberg, *Protestant, Catholic, Jew*, 40.

36. Herberg, *Protestant, Catholic, Jew*, 85.

37. Vivek Maru, Pluralism Project interview, 1996.

38. Tom Morgenthau, "American: Still a Melting Pot?" *Newsweek*, August 9, 1993, 16–23.

39. Peter Brimelow, *Alien Nation: Common Sense About America's Immigration Disaster* (New York: Random House, 1995), 258

40. Arthur M. Schlesinger Jr. *The Disuniting of America: Reflections on a Multicultural Society* (New York: W.W. Norton & Company, 1991).

41. John Courtney Murray, *We Hold These Truths* (New York: Sheed & Ward, 1960), x.

42. Murray, *We Hold These Truths*, 11.

43. "Moral and Civic Education and Teaching About Religion," (Sacramento: California Department of Education, 1991).

44. The Williamsburg Charter (Williamsburg, Virginia: The Williamsburg Charter Foundation, 1988).

45. C. T. Shen, *Mayflower II: On the Buddhist Voyage to Liberation* (Taipei: Torch of Wisdom Publishing House, 1983), iii.

46. Editorial, Guru Gobind Singh Foundation Newsletter, Spring 1994.

47. "Episcopal Bishop in Roanoke Urges Congress to Move Hate Crimes Bill," *U.S. Newswire*, Washington, D.C., September 28, 2000.

48. Hassan Hathout, Fathi Osman, and Maher Hathout, *In Fraternity: A Message to Muslims in America* (Los Angeles: The Minaret Publishing House, 3–4, 1989), 11–12.

49. Hathout et al., *In Fraternity*, 16–17.

50. Remarks of Hillary Rodham Clinton. Old Executive Office Building, February 20, 1996.

51. Girl Scouts of America Statement on Diversity and Pluralism, www.girlscouts.org/adults/plural.html.

CHAPTER THREE

AMERICAN HINDUS: THE GANGES AND THE MISSISSIPPI

★

E *pluribus unum,* "From Many, One," could easily come from the ancient Rig Veda, with its affirmation: "Truth is One. People call it by many names." To be honest, the Vedas take the *unum* a giant step further. This affirmation of oneness is not sociological or political but theological; it is an affirmation about the very nature of ultimate reality. God or Truth or Ultimate Reality is one, though people speak of that One in many ways and try to realize it in their lives through many paths. On the face of it, Hindu immigrants would seem natural participants in the American project. Unity in diversity is a keynote of Hindu civilization: so many paths, so many gods, so many sects, and yet the deeply held affirmation of one common humanity animated by the one reality called Brahman, roughly translated as Truth, Ultimate Reality, or even God

Throughout our history, the United States has been dominated by the influence of Christianity—strongly monotheistic, with many Christian voices articulating an exclusivist view of "the way, the truth, and the life." At the same time, our Constitution has enabled a plurality of ways to flourish because of its strong stand for freedom of conscience. Thus, the positive civic view of pluralism implicit in the freedom of religion clauses of the Constitution clashes directly with the negative religious views of pluralism held by some conservative Christians. Hindus bring something unique to America—a theology of religious pluralism. Not only do they participate in the civic pluralism, which guarantees their right to freedom of religion, they also offer a worldview based on religious pluralism. It is a worldview in which the manyness of religious ways, paths, and understandings of God are not conflicting but consonant. They sound out the cosmic mysteries together, like the symphony of civilization imagined by pluralist sociologist Horace Kallen. Perhaps more appropriately, they glide like the intricate movements of an Indian raga, disciplined by scale and rhythm but created ever anew at each performance by the inspired innovation of each artist.

This consonance also has its dissonance. Hindu understandings of the Divine may seem distant to Americans of Jewish, Christian, Muslim, or even secular backgrounds, as they did to me when I first went to India as a young student. I am acutely aware of this as I meet people here in the U.S. who are encountering the panoply of Hindu gods for the first time and trying to comprehend it.

Understanding the manyness of the Divine is a good place to begin in our discussion of the Hindu tradition in America. In the fall of 1997 I received a call from a former student who was the pastor of a church in the town of Woburn, north of Boston. She was an enthusiastic member of the Woburn Clergy Association, and when a Hindu community bought the old Unitarian Church and she began to see worshipers in saris going in and out, she inquired whether this new community might be invited to join the Woburn Clergy Association. The association sponsors cooperative work like the Domestic Violence Task Force and community events like the interfaith Martin Luther King Day observance and the annual Thanksgiving service. Most members of the association were delighted, but one pastor was vehemently opposed. He wrote a lengthy letter to the association:

> I believe that the inclusion of the Hindu Community into the Clergy Association is making either an explicit or implicit statement to the community at large that other religions are valid and that Jesus is not unique but one of many! Is that what the association wants to purport to the community? And what exactly are we going to teach and preach with the Hindu Center in the Association? Will there be any room for a message about Jesus Christ crucified or will that view be "excluded" and Jesus now relegated to only one of 66,000 Hindu Gods?

Most of us who have had some contact with Christianity in America recognize the concern of this pastor. How do Christians reconcile claims to the uniqueness of Jesus as "the way, the truth, and the life" with appreciation of other ways of faith, especially a Hindu faith that expressly

underlines the multiplicity of ways? The Woburn pastor vastly underestimated the problem, however. Hindus usually say there are 330 million
gods, not 66,000. But the Hindu claim is not really about numbers anyway; 330 million is obviously not a numerical god count but a gesture in
the direction of infinity. There are as many manifestations of divine presence as we have eyes to see. Even so, the particular gods and the divine
images through which they are worshiped confront many Americans with
religious ways we simply do not understand. One nation under many
gods sticks in the throat—for both Hindus and Christians. We need to
come closer, ask questions, and listen carefully.

If you were to come with me to visit two typical American Hindu
temples, as I did on a Saturday in late February of 1999, we could observe
clearly and vividly the manyness of Hindu visions of the divine that
underlies this one-and-many worldview. Those of you not familiar with
Hindu worlds of image and ritual would probably experience both the
dissonance and the consonance.

In Sunnyvale, California, the Hindu Temple and Cultural Society
occupies a former warehouse on Persian Road, which runs parallel to the
freeway. I stop first at the Indian market in the mini-mall next door,
stocked with bags of basmati rice, spices, and condiments and thousands
of CDs and audiotapes organized by language—Hindi, Tamil, Telugu,
Marathi, Gujarati. I am looking for a tape of the "Hymn to the Goddess,"
the Sanskrit Devi Mahatmya—and there are many to choose from, along
with devotional songs, *bhajans,* from every region of India and dedicated to
every god. Next door is the temple, which repeats this eclecticism in a
sacred key. The building itself is a graceless single-story building with no
architectural distinction whatsoever. From the small palm-lined parking
lot, swinging glass doors lead into a huge carpeted hall with flat fluorescent
ceiling lights. I take off my shoes at the door and walk across the room
toward the altars, which host one of the most dazzling arrays of metal and
stone images and polychrome posters I have seen anywhere. I press my
palms together in front of my chest, a *namaste,* a gesture of greeting and
respect. I catch the eye of the *pujari* who attends the deities on the altar and
assists worshipers in their *puja* and *namaste* to him as well. Standing right
here in Sunnyvale is a good place to introduce ourselves to the Hindu gods.

At the center is a foot-high metal image of Ganesha, the rotund
elephant-headed Lord of Beginnings and Remover of Obstacles, worshiped at the outset of every ritual. He is wreathed with a dozen flower
garlands. In front of him is a Shiva *linga,* the cylindrical shaft that repre-

sents in abstract form the supreme presence of Shiva, who is beyond all faces and forms. According to Shaiva theology, this *linga* is a tiny representation of the shaft of sheer light that rose from the depths of the sea and pierced the highest heavens as the gods were arguing about which of them was supreme. Just to the right, in a small shrine with interior mirrors, is the Baby Krishna, a small brass image dressed in bright blue clothing and reflected in all directions into infinity. In the second row of altar images, Krishna also appears as the saucer-eyed Jagannatha special to the state of Orissa and as the black-faced and wide-eyed Shrinath-ji from Rajasthan. To the left of Ganesha stands Vishnu, here under the name of Shri Venkateswara Balaji, whose hilltop temple in South India is one of the most popular pilgrimage places in India. Behind this whole array are polychrome poster pictures: prominent teachers like Guru Nanak and Satya Sai Baba; the image of Lord Rama, bow in hand, with his brother Lakshmana and his wife Sita, the devoted monkey Hanuman kneeling before them. Behind them all is a huge Hanuman somehow overseeing the whole altar display. A second altar just to the right bears the various forms of the divine Goddess. Vaishno Devi, a hilltop goddess from Jammu in Kashmir who attracts pilgrims from all over North India, is in the center, riding her tiger and bearing weapons in her many arms. Around her are more benign images, like the gracious Sarasvati, and fearsome images, like the black dancing Kali garlanded with a necklace of skulls. If you weren't a Hindu, and perhaps even if you were, you would want a guide through the welter of deities. On these crowded and colorful altars appears some image large or small for every Hindu from every region and sectarian movement.

This multitude of deities is the conservative Woburn minister's worst nightmare. I think about him and the distinctive nature of America's encounter with Hinduism on my forty-minute drive west to the Shiva-Vishnu temple in Livermore. How does one explain all this to people encountering it for the first time? Why so many gods? Why the images? These certainly are the questions of anyone reared in the monotheistic traditions of the West. Not only the many gods, but the prolific imaging of the divine is a problem. The taboo against the "graven image" runs deep in our consciousness, and most people don't take the time to study Hinduism and ask just what it all means. My own metaphor has always been the kaleidoscope, with its multitude of tiny parts and pieces, colors and forms, the whole glittering altar at Sunnyvale. And yet, with a twist of the wrist, all these pieces fall into a different pattern; there are many centers and many intricate displays of the periphery. As if this weren't enough, each of the great gods repeats its own version of the One and the many. Each has many names; each has many forms; and each form may have many arms, even many heads and many faces. The well-known image of the dancing Shiva has at least four arms: one hand holding the drum of creation, another bearing the fire of destruction, another raised in a gesture meaning "fear not," and another pointing toward his gracefully raised foot, inviting the devotee to take refuge in his mercy.

Nearing Livermore, I pull off Interstate 580 onto North Vasco Road, I am in the midst of a brand new suburban development, its large houses and condominiums all variations on a white, beige, gray, sand, buff theme. It does not seem a likely place for a South Indian Hindu temple. I am convinced I must be in the wrong neighborhood, until I actually reach the wrought iron gates. I am surprised to see it there, a fine brick temple set back from the road, with an ornately decorated white tower over the central doorway and two elegant spires to either side. The whole building is trimmed with decorative cement castings. A well-kept long green lawn stretches toward the temple, with plenty of parking on either side. The lot is full on a Saturday afternoon with perhaps sixty or seventy cars.

Though I have been visiting American Hindu temples for nearly ten years now, I am still amazed at the very existence of a splendid temple like this one right in the midst of a markedly Walmart-suburban neighborhood. I remove my shoes at an outdoor shoe rack, overflowing this sunny Saturday afternoon with Reeboks and sandals. It is California, and I walk barefoot toward the door. Entering the spacious temple room, I find that a twist of the kaleidoscope has brought me to a very different space than that of the temple I left an hour ago in Sunnyvale. Here, as in so many of the new American temples, the various deities are accommodated not on a single altar, but each in its own chamber—on the right the shrines of Vishnu and his entourage and on the left those of Shiva. Each shrine is also labeled, which makes navigation easier, perhaps deceptively so: "Ganesha, Remover of Obstacles, Son of Shiva," "Shiva, Destroyer of Evils, Lord of Music and Dance," "Vishnu, The Supreme Protector," and "Sreedevi (Lakshmi), Goddess of Wealth, Wife of Lord Vishnu." The temple has made an effort to be user-friendly—for visitors who may know nothing of the Hindu tradition, for children who are growing up in the tradition, and even for their parents.

In India, a temple called "Shiva-Vishnu" would be unusual, to say the least. Every temple has an array of images but usually centered on a single central deity. Many American Hindu temples have chosen that pattern too, like the grand temple in the Penn Hills of Pittsburgh, dedicated to Vishnu under the name Sri Venkateswara. The other deities are there, but Vishnu occupies the central sanctuary. In Flint, Michigan, Shiva has his place at the center in the Kashi Vishvanatha Temple, named for Shiva as he appears in the sacred city of Banaras in India. In Houston, it is the Goddess Meenakshi who is honored at the center. But here in the Bay Area, the growing and diverse Hindu community has improvised creatively on the notes and rhythms of Hinduism and has chosen a dual center: worshiping both Shiva and Vishnu equally under one roof and dedicating the temple to both. Each of these great and complex deities, Shiva and Vishnu, is understood to be supreme, each a visible form of the Ultimate Reality whose names are many. The eclecticism here is also architectural. The shrine of Shiva and the spire that rises above it are designed in the beehive Kalinga style of the great Bhubanesvar Temple in Orissa in eastern India, while the shrine of Vishnu and its spire duplicate the Chola style of the Tirupati Temple in southern India.

As I think about the *pluribus* of gods here, I am also struck by the multiplicity of the temple's ritual life. This afternoon a range of religious rituals are being held concurrently, for Hindu temple life is not usually congregational in form. Families come and go. A small group of worshipers gathers near the door of the Ganesha shrine watching reverently as the priest lifts a six-wick oil lamp holder to illumine the face of the deity. He turns and comes out of the inner sanctum, offering the lamp to all of us. I too pass my fingertips through it, touching them to my forehead and eyes, appropriating the blessing of the Lord's light. A loudspeaker announcement informs us that a *puja* for Lord Vishnu is about to begin across the temple hall, and some of the worshipers reassemble there. The priest begins to sing the "Thousand Names of Vishnu" as he begins the *puja*. However, my attention is diverted by a family seated on the floor in front of Krishna's shrine a few feet away. The young parents are having their newborn baby named and blessed. Seeing my interest, they beckon me, a complete stranger, to sit down with them. They introduce themselves as Venkat and Radhika, and their baby is named Vikas. They have come from their home in Castro Valley, a few miles to the west, for the formal naming ceremony. Under the guidance of one of the staff priests, Venkat traces his own name, the name of his father, and the name of his little son in a large round stainless steel plate of rice grains. The couple both prostrate toward Lord Krishna, and then they guide the little baby in his first full prostration. All of us gathered round are given a few grains of rice to shower on little Vikas, adding our own blessings to the occasion. Finally, as I leave the temple, a shiny black Toyota Corolla is parked at the front door for what I discover is a new-car blessing, a *vahana puja.* Young men in snappy khakis stand in casual reverence while the temple priest sprinkles the vehicle with water sanctified by contact with the deity.

Hindus come by their pluralism naturally. The very environment of worship reinforces it—whether in the plain surroundings of Sunnyvale or the finely made new temple of Livermore. Whatever one's conception of God, whatever one's sect or perspective, one worships in the context of many others. Worship does not begin at an appointed hour, move through a program of liturgies and song, and then conclude. Rather, worship is multiform and simultaneous. One never forgets that there are divergent ways of worship, divergent understandings of the divine presence. This is a worldview that seems ready-made for America: one understanding of God, one ritual form or path, does not preclude the flourishing of others right next door. The Puritans of the old Massachusetts Bay Colony would not have liked it, but I suspect that Roger Williams with his vision of "soul liberty" might have managed an appreciative response, at least with a little coaching.

The language of the One Reality and the many paths is comfortably abstract for most Americans, but when their new Hindu neighbors introduce them to Shiva, Vishnu, or Ganesha, they might well find these gods strange, off-putting, even frightening. I suspect that many of the neighbors in this new suburban development find the forms of worship here at the Shiva-Vishnu temple alien. The words *polytheism* and *idol worship* might come to mind as they try to grasp the meaning of these divine images of granite and bell metal, clothed now in bright swatches of saris and dhotis, honored with incense, flowers, bells, sweets, bananas, and camphorscented water. Any temple trustee, any priest, any worshiper, indeed the young couple from Castro Valley, could eagerly explain to them the oneness of the Divine and the vivid variety of what they call "names and forms" in which the Divine is manifest. If the people next door spent some time here with these new Hindu neighbors, they would surely begin to glimpse the meanings of these ways of worship, perhaps even appreciate them, perhaps even gain deeper insight into their own understandings of the One they call God. It would be time well spent.

The past thirty years in America have seen the rise of temple-based Hinduism in the United States. This is new for America. Makeshift temples like the one in Sunnyvale abound. A cavernous former warehouse in

Woodside, Queens, is the Divya Dham temple, a veritable universe of Hindu gods and shrines. A former church at the corner of Polk and Pine in Minneapolis houses the Hindu community of the Twin Cities. Beyond these kinds of adaptive use, Hindus have initiated the building of brand-new temples, like the one in Livermore, as they have put down roots in the American landscape. The temple Hinduism of the new immigration has brought the Hindu gods permanently to America, beginning with the first full-scale Hindu temples dedicated in 1978. That year, on a hilltop outside Pittsburgh, the Sri Venkateswara temple for Lord Vishnu was consecrated; and in Flushing, Queens, a landmark temple to Lord Ganesha, the elephant-headed remover of obstacles, was opened. So it began, and year after year since that time, Hindus have consecrated new temples all over the United States. As I often tell my students, there is no better place than America for studying Hindu rites of consecration, for in India most of the temples are old and were consecrated centuries ago, while in America all of the temples are new.

For Hindus, consecrating and installing images of the gods in these temples is no small matter. It requires a long-term commitment and a vision for the future. When these rites establish divine breath in a granite image and ritually open the eyes of the Divine, they provide more than green cards for the gods; they, in effect, make the them permanent residents of American cities. And so it is that Lord Rama resides in Chicago, Vishnu in Pittsburgh, the Goddess Meenakshi in Houston, and the Goddess Lakshmi in Boston. Since the arrival of these Hindu gods deeply challenges the assumptions of many Americans, concerned about polytheism and idolatry, we should have a closer look at how a Hindu community creates its temples and brings its gods to life.

BRINGING LAKSHMI TO LIFE IN NEW ENGLAND

I saw my first American-built Hindu temple in the suburbs of Boston, just off Route 135 where the Boston Marathon begins each April. Over the years, I had logged thousands of hours in temples all over India from the high Himalayas to the ocean shores of Tamil Nadu, but not until I pulled off Route 135 in suburban Ashland into the construction site of the Sri Lakshmi Temple in early 1990 did I actually see a temple being built from the ground up. I had already missed the ritual groundbreaking, which had included the rites of *bhumi puja,* the "worship of the earth." Then the huge machinery of a Wellesley engineering firm had moved in and begun digging and shoving tons of earth around. By May of 1990, a boxy cinderblock building formed the basic structure of the temple. It was capped with four white spires intricately ornamented with the images of the gods and their supernatural attendants.

The story of the Sri Lakshmi Temple is typical of many American Hindu communities. In the 1970s new Indian immigrants to Boston, most of them professionals who had come during their student years, took jobs and settled in New England. They all intended to return to India, eventually. Then they began to have children, and before long their children were in grade school. By now, these young families were putting down deeper roots in America and beginning to look toward a future here. They realized that their children would have no cultural or religious identity as Hindus at all unless they themselves began to do something about it. So in 1978 a group of Tamil families from South India, who had been meeting for holidays in one another's homes, incorporated as the New England Hindu Temple and began planning to build a temple. Each couple donated an auspicious $101, and the project began to roll. For the next few years they worshiped in makeshift quarters—a Knights of Columbus Hall in Melrose and the Village Club in Needham. They brought glossy colored prints and small metal images of the deities. Ranjini Ramaswamy described the life of the nascent community. "We used to go there once a month on a Sunday morning, clean up the whole place, rearrange the chairs, arrange the deities on a table, and worship from about ten to two. Then we would eat together, clean up the place, and go." By 1981 the growing group had collected $30,000 in donations—enough to buy a parcel of land set back from the road in suburban Ashland.

As the prospects for a temple became a reality, they first had to decide which deity to place in the sanctuary. Here they took a noncontroversial and practical approach. They selected the Goddess Lakshmi. She would be especially appropriate for New England's first temple because, they said, she is the Goddess of Fortune who has blessed them in America. Of all the forms of Shakti—the powerful energy of the Great Goddess—Lakshmi is a wholly auspicious form. She has nothing of the dark ambiguity of Kali or the fierce-weaponed Durga. Lakshmi is an aspect of the Goddess beloved of all Hindus. To her sides would be representatives of two families of Hindu devotion: Vishnu, in the popular form of Sri Venkateswara, and Ganesha, son of Shiva.

These Hindus were engineers and doctors, metallurgists and biochemists, not temple builders. In fact, many of them had not been actively religious at all in India. Had they returned to Madras or Banga-lore, they would never have become involved in the building or admin-istration of a temple. But here in America their education as Hindus took on a new and practical form. They brought a traditional temple architect from India to survey the building site, to orient the temple, to draw its design according to ritual canons, and to sketch the sanctuaries and the divine images that would occupy them. Plans in hand, the com-munity was faced with the challenge of explaining the proposed temple and its activity to the zoning board in the town of Framingham. "They knew nothing of Hinduism, nothing of what a Hindu temple in the neighborhood would be like or what it would mean. We had to explain it as best we could," said T. A. Venkataraman, the Boston Edison engi-neer who spearheaded the project. "Finally, I took some of them in my car and drove down to the Ganesha temple in New York, so they could see with their own eyes what we were up to." In the end, there was no resistance. The design of the ritual architects was translated into work-ing drawings by the engineering firm, which excavated the founda-tion and constructed the large shell of concrete block. The artisans called *shilpis* came from India to live in the temple. Theirs was the task of pouring, casting, and installing all the ornamentation that would cover the temple spires and the several sancta of the temple within. On my second trip to the temple, I climbed up onto the roof with Venkataraman, known as Venky, who had volunteered hundreds of hours after work and on weekends to supervise the site. There I could see the *shilpis* at work on the spires, cementing the ornamental castings in place.

In May, the week of the consecration arrived. A great yellow-and-white-striped tent was pitched next to the temple to provide the ritual space for the consecration rites that would take place over the span of six days. Hundreds of Hindus gathered, morning and evening, as priests from India and a dozen American temples invoked the spiritual power of the Divine at each of seven fire-altars. Each sat cross-legged before one of the brick fire-altars, kindled the fires, chanted invocations, and invited the Divine presence. They poured oblations of clarified butter, grains, incense, honey, and spices into the flames, all to the ceaseless chanting of hymns from the Vedas, the very oldest hymnic record of India, preserved in memory alone for three thousand years. Before there were any temples at all in India, indeed before there were any images of the gods at all, these altars were the place of worship and praise.

Every day that week, I drove the twenty-five minutes from Cambridge to Ashland to see the unfolding sequence of rituals I had not witnessed in years of fieldwork in India. In this elaborate consecration process, the priests not only invoked the power of the Divine into the fires but also transferred it, through a stream of hymnic recitations, into hundreds of clay and metal water pots arrayed around fire-altars. These pots, each sponsored by a member of the temple community, contained the waters of the Ganges River in India, mingled with the waters of the Mississippi, the Missouri, and the Colorado Rivers of America. At the end of the week, these waters would be poured lavishly on the temple towers and on the images of the gods within.

As the weekend approached, the activity at the temple reached a fever pitch. Volunteers were sweeping and cleaning the shrines inside the temple. They prepared the central shrine for the image of Lakshmi, the auspicious goddess of wealth and blessings. The shrine on the right would house the image of Vishnu and the left, Ganesha. The dark granite images of the gods, sculpted by sacred artists south of Madras, had been shipped to Boston in crates. For weeks they had stood in the construction site, unconsecrated but carefully and respectfully treated. Now, during this week of ceremonies, they were prepared and bathed. All of us, Hindus and visitors alike, were amused at the distinctive and ingenious arrangements for the ritual bathing: large, brand-new, plastic splashing pools, covered with Big Bird, the Cookie Monster, and other characters from *Sesame Street*. Lying in their pools, they were submerged sequentially in flower petals, in grains, in milk, and in water. Through it all, they were bathed in a constant stream of Sanskrit hymns and chants.

On Friday, a sparkling May morning, the eyes of the gods were opened. I stood in the sunshine outside the temple with a group of thirty or forty Hindus who had taken the morning off from work for this landmark event. Inside, in a corner of the temple sequestered behind office dividers, priests and ritual artisans were carving pupils on the eyes of the granite images, and the eyes of the Divine were ritually opened. The term *darshan* is central to Hindu worship. It means, literally, "seeing," more specifically, the exchange of gaze between the human and Divine. We humans both see the Divine through the lens of this image and receive, in return, the blessed gaze of God. It is said that the first burst of sight released from the image is too powerful for any mortal to bear, so a mirror is placed before the image and the first gaze falls upon the mirror, reflecting back upon God. This morning, we were told that the mirrors had been set up and that when we finally entered the temple, we should look at the Divine image first in the mirror.

As we chatted in the sunshine, waiting for the rituals inside to be completed, a large transport truck pulled up bearing the name of a dairy farm down the road. The farmer opened the rear, pulled down the ramp, and out came a golden brown cow whose name, we were told, was Darling. One of the priests and Ranjini, a member of the temple board, greeted Darling, garlanding her with a necklace of pink rosebuds. Darling would be the first living being to be seen by the gods. The dairy farmer, wearing overalls and a baseball cap, visibly intrigued by his role in these events, led Darling into the sanctuary, past the powerful gaze of the gods. When they emerged, the small crowd gathered at the temple door moved quickly toward Darling, touching her, circling her, garlanding her, pressing the auspicious red marks of kumkum on her forehead—all ways of honoring the cow, now blessed with the holy gaze of the gods, and appropriating those blessings for themselves. These Hindus would insist that cows are not worshiped in India, as some of their American neighbors might imagine, but they are indeed loved and honored as auspicious bearers of blessings. That morning everyone was delighted with Darling, including the astonished farmer who had never before seen her so bedecked.

The young girls of the temple were next after Darling in the pecking order of auspiciousness. About fifteen of them, dressed in their best outfits, had taken the morning off from school. They entered the sanctuary and after five minutes emerged again, excited and pleased, each bearing the *prasad,* the blessed gifts given them by the priest: a piece of silk that had wrapped one of the deities, some sweets and a banana that had been offered to the deities, and a Susan B. Anthony silver dollar. Priti, a twelve-year-old, told me that she was going to write about the event for her fifth-grade class in Lexington. As they posed for photographs, it was clear that all of these girls would long remember this day and their roles in opening this temple. Finally, the rest of us were permitted to go in. We filed past the images of the gods, taking care, as we had been told, to look first into the mirrors before looking directly at the deities. I had been in countless Hindu temples for *darshan;* I had even written a book about this form of worship in India and the importance of the exchange of gaze that takes place between the Divine and the worshiper. It is not just that we humans reach out with our eyes to touch the divine presence, but the Divine sees us as well. Here in the soft greenery of a New England May, the Divine beheld New England Hindus. It began to dawn on me what a great threshold had been crossed. A lifelong Methodist, I found myself touching the feet of each of these images in reverence.

The Divine is fully present in these images but obviously is not limited to them. And just in case any one of us might be tempted to take the images too literally or narrowly, that same night eight grandmothers of the temple were also honored as embodiments of the Goddess Lakshmi. I arrived at the temple about eight in the evening to find the whole community gathered there for this special rite, Suvasini Puja. Eight of the most senior women of the temple were consecrated for this one night as Lakshmi. They were all women who had been active in the life of the temple and had the two qualifications of auspiciousness: they were mothers of children and wives of living husbands. They sat in a row, while the younger women of the temple community honored them by performing a *puja*. At some point in the long ritual, the whole battalion of Brahmin priests from all over the world entered the crowded hall and prostrated fully on the floor before these grandmothers, honoring the Goddess in these living women. My mind was filled with the strains of the great hymn to the Goddess:

> *That Goddess who is present among all creatures as women,*
> *Praise to her, praise to her, praise to her again and again.*

The next night was Saturday, the night before the final consecration. The men of the temple joined in the task of moving the granite images of the gods into the three inner shrines of the temple and securing them in place. It was no small task. It required wedges, ramps, hoists, ropes, and a lot of muscle power. Early the next morning, the priests kindled their fires once again in the great tent next door and invoked the divine presence, now with the intention of imbuing these granite images with the symbolic breath of life. My hosts explained that the divine power was ritually transmitted from the fire-altars through silver threads, which ran from the tent into the temple and around the stone images. In this amazing week of rituals, the stone images from India had become, for the Hindu community, the bearers of the very life of the Divine. Bringing images to life in this way is no small commitment. From this moment on, the community must be sure there are priests in attendance so that worship can be offered every day of the week—morning, noon, and evening—whether other worshipers are there or not. On this Sunday morning, Lakshmi, Vishnu, and Ganesha became the permanent divine residents of suburban Boston.

The whole temple was also consecrated that Sunday morning. Perhaps three thousand New England Hindus attended as the ceremonies came to a climax. They carried hundreds of round water pots out of the tent-sanctuary and around the new temple, circumambulating the sacred precincts of the gods. Priests, now hoarse with the chanting of thousands upon thousands of *mantras* and *stotras,* led the procession, bearing the largest and heaviest pots on their heads. They rode a hydraulic hoist up to the temple rooftop to pour the consecrated river waters of India and America over the ornate towers. All the rest of us stood below, cheering and stretching our hands heavenward to catch the blessings of the water sprinkled from above.

It is clear that for these Hindus of New England building a temple meant building a community too. As the process came to fruition that May, everyone participated—preparing lemon rice for thousands of visitors, stringing flower garlands, putting up twinkling lights, managing parking and shuttle buses, directing traffic, distributing lunch, sweeping and cleaning at the end of each day. By the time of the tower sprinkling at Sunday noon, the whole Hindu community had come together at New England's first temple. Building and consecrating a temple had created a new community. At the close of the day, my friend Venky surveyed the multitude of volunteers and said to me, "This is what I want to see. What is gratifying is to have the participation of all these people. What is wonderful is, now, to be able to stand aside while others do the work. This is real success."

A woman from Framingham summed up what must have been the emotions of many that day: "We have been living here for twenty years now and have been longing for a temple. This is a day of sheer happiness for us," she said. "As I drove home last night and in a few minutes came to downtown Framingham, I could scarcely believe that this had finally happened. I felt as if I had covered the distance between India and America in such a short time."

In the 1980s and 1990s, these rites, called *kumbhabhishekha,* literally, sprinkling (*abhishekha*) with the waters of the water pots (*kumbha*), have been repeated in dozens of new Hindu temples all over America. They have become the first great public rites of American Hindus as they claim a visible place in the American landscape—in Atlanta and Memphis, in Cleveland and St. Louis. In Boston, these rites reached out to the community. Members of the town council came to the consecration, as did the mayor, who was garlanded with a necklace of flowers and introduced to the Goddess Lakshmi. The local Framingham newspaper told the tale in its headline: "Goddess of Beauty and Abundance Radiates Shakti in Yankee New England."

During the next few years, the bare cinderblock of the temple would be ornamented and painted, an entry pavilion with skylights would be constructed, and a huge ornamented tower called the *rajgopuram,* the "royal gateway," would be built over the entryway. The whole temple, painted a gleaming white, would become one of the architectural gems of the Boston area.

THE "EASTING" OF OLD NEW ENGLAND

Less than ten miles from the Sri Lakshmi temple is the town of Concord, famous for the "rude bridge that arched the flood" where the first volley of the American Revolution was fired. Ralph Waldo Emerson's home is a long stone's throw from the bridge today, and it is here in the quiet of his study in the old house among the elms that we might look for some first roots of America's fascination with Hinduism. Emerson met the Hindu tradition and its philosophies the same way I did as a college student—in Hindu texts. He was an undergraduate at Harvard when he was introduced to Hindu literature through his aunt, Mary Moody Emerson. As early as the 1820s, Emerson began to write about India in his journals. His early entries expressed his astonished disapproval of the "goddery" and the "ostentatious ritual of India."[1] He probably would have had a hard time with Sri Lakshmi and the many other deities at the Ashland temple. Of course, in those days he had no neighbors in Concord who were Hindus, as he surely would today, and he had no opportunity to visit a Hindu temple or hear how the Hindu faithful understand their many gods.

By the 1830s Emerson had a copy of the Bhagavad Gita, the "Song of God," which revealed to him a more exalted view of Hinduism. He wrote, "I owed—my friend and I owed—a magnificent day to the Bhagavad Geeta. It was the first of books; it was as if an empire spake to us, nothing small or unworthy, but large, serene, consistent, the voice of an old intelligence which in another age and climate had pondered and thus disposed of the same questions which exercise us."[2] In the Gita, Emerson glimpsed something of the breadth of the Hindu tradition. He learned, for example, that religious life can be lived in different ways according to our temperament. For the activist, there is the path of ethical works, or *karma.* For the contemplative and meditative soul, there is the path of wisdom, or *jnana.* And for those yearning to direct their love and emotion toward God, there is the path of *bhakti,* devotion. For Emerson, *bhakti,* even in the muted form found in the Song of God, might well have seemed too close to the Christian evangelicalism rampant in the second Great Awakening of his day. He was more drawn to the path of ethical action, but he was attracted most of all to the path of philosophical insight, or *jnana*. Emerson referred to it as "gnosis," knowing, and indeed that Greek term is related as a distant cognate cousin to the Sanskrit *jnana*. It was the deeply speculative wisdom literature of the Upanishads and Vedanta philosophy that caught and carried the imagination of Emerson toward the "unity of spirit" that seemed to pervade the Hindu view of the world. The Transcendent, which Emerson referred to as the "unbounded, unboundable empire" is the one light "which beams out of a thousand stars" and at the same time the "one soul which animates all men." He perceived that the "highest object of their religion" is to restore the bond linking the soul, called *atman,* to the Eternal, called *paramatman,* which Emerson referred to as the "Over-Soul."[3] While he speaks of it as "their religion," in one sense experiencing the unity of this Over-Soul became his own. In Emerson himself the perspectives of the ancient Indian Upanishads and the nineteenth-century Transcendentalists came together, directing our human vision toward the oneness of spirit underlying the whole universe.

Emerson's vision led to the publication of what he called the "Ethnical Scriptures." In his view, scripture now needed to be seen in the plural. The "Bibles" of the world, like the Bhagavad Gita, are many, and the spiritual paths of humankind are many as well. Emerson's vision had a certain Hindu hue and tenor to it—a wideness of spirit, a recognition of the many revelations of truth, and a sense that America was the place where the transcendent unity of religions might indeed be realized. His work, woven seamlessly and sometimes without attribution with citations from his reading of Hindu and Buddhist scriptures, is a kind of literary testimony to the incipient meeting of East and West.

Emerson's younger friend Henry David Thoreau also participated in the "Easting" spirit of the mid–nineteenth century. Thoreau developed some familiarity with the texts to which he had access—a copy of William Jones's translation of the *Laws of Manu,* loaned by Emerson, who had borrowed it from the library of Boston's Athenaeum, copies of H. H. Wilson's translation of the *Vishnu Purana,* and a copy of Rammohan Roy's translation of the Upanishads. When he built his cabin at Walden Pond in the outskirts of Concord, Thoreau clearly had the Bhagavad Gita with him. He wrote from his retreat in 1845, "In the morning, I bathe my intellect in the stupendous and cosmogonal philosophy of the Bhagvat-Geeta . . . in comparison with which our modern world and its literature seem puny and trivial."[4] He marveled at both the physical and mystical connections between his beloved Walden and the holy Ganges, as big blocks of ice from the pond he called "God's Drop" were cut and hauled up to the train tracks that skirted Walden, sent by rail into Boston, and by ship to India.

Some say Thoreau's interest in yoga practice and his self-image as a kind of yogi on the shores of Walden was simply a literary self-presentation, a faddish device. But a few scholars, more familiar with the Indian litera-ture Thoreau knew, see Thoreau as finding in yoga—which he under-stands generally as contemplative practice—a confirmation of his own ecstatic, mystical experience. Thoreau was not a Hindu. In fact, he insisted, "I do not prefer one religion or philosophy to another. . . . I pray to be delivered from narrowness, partiality, exaggeration—bigotry." Even so, he found illumination in the India he came to know in his imagination and states of consciousness. "Farthest India is nearer to me than Concord & Lexington," he wrote, referring to the India he had found echoed within his own soul.[5]

VIVEKANANDA: AMERICA'S FIRST HINDU

If we imagine ourselves in New England in the 1890s, where Hindu thought had been shifting the mental and spiritual furniture of Boston's intellectuals for more than fifty years, we may be astonished to realize that few New Englanders had ever met a Hindu face-to-face. What came to be called Hinduism was a religious perspective borne on the trade winds from the East. As such, it was susceptible to both the condemna-tion and romanticism that characterized the "orientalist" perspective. Western observers measured the exoticized "other" against their own norms and needs. Some saw India as pagan, polytheistic, and idolatrous in the light of their own Christian assumptions; others reached for India as the homeland of the most universal and sublime religious aspirations, somehow filling an empty space in their own religious lives. So in the late summer of 1893, when a handsome thirty-year-old Hindu reformer, Swami Vivekananda, arrived in Boston for a month's stay before the opening of the World's Parliament of Religions in Chicago, it is no won-der that he attracted a great deal of attention. For most New Englanders, his was the very first Hindu voice they had ever heard.

Vivekananda was a disciple of the Hindu saint of Calcutta, Sri Ramakrishna. He had come by ship from Calcutta to Vancouver and then traveled by train to Chicago, arriving more than a month early for the parliament, which was to be held in September of 1893 in conjunction with the Chicago World's Fair. He quickly ran out of money. Fortunately, on the train from the West Coast he had met a Boston woman, Kate Sanborn, who graciously invited him to her house in the country outside Boston—not far from where the Sri Lakshmi Temple stands today. Sanborn had been a professor of literature at Smith College. At her estate, she introduced Swami Vivekananda to a number of Bostonians, including Harvard classics professor J. H. Wright. At Professor Wright's invitation, Vivekananda delivered his first public lecture in the U.S. at the Unitarian Universalist Church on the North Shore. In the next few weeks, he caused a stir wherever he appeared in the area clad in his silk tunic and turban. Here was an articulate, well-educated Hindu who spoke English eloquently, could explain the religious ideals of far India, and could respond to all their questions—from the mysteries of yoga to the mistreatment of women.

At the parliament in Chicago, Vivekananda was received with enthusiasm. Perhaps America's own burgeoning universalist spirit was eager to hear that spirit echoed by a young Hindu reformer from the other side of the world. As the parliament opened, Vivekananda had uttered only five words, "Brothers and Sisters of America . . ." when the audience burst into applause. In his speech he called for a universal religion "which would have no place for persecution or intolerance in its polity, and would recognize a divinity in every man or woman, and whose whole scope, whose whole force would be centered in aiding humanity to realize its Divine nature."[6] To underline the unity of the adherents of all religious traditions assembled, he proclaimed,

> It is the same light coming through different colors. . . . But in the heart of everything the same truth reigns; the Lord has declared to the Hindu in his incarnation as Krishna, "I am in every religion as the thread through a string of pearls. And wherever thou seest extraordinary holiness and extraordinary power raising and purifying humanity, know yet that I am there."[7]

Through the writings of Emerson and Thoreau and the various stripes of Unitarians and Transcendentalists, the audience had some familiarity with Hindu ideas—the eternal soul, universal and common to all people, and its oneness with the Divine. But here was a man who spoke this message with passion from the heart and, as he put it, on behalf of the three hundred million Hindus of India. One journalist wrote of him, "Vivekananda's address before the parliament was broad as the heavens above us, embracing the best in all religions, as the ultimate universal religion—charity to all mankind, good works for the love of God, not for fear of punishment or hope of reward."[8]

After the close of the parliament in September of 1893, Vivekananda stayed on in the U.S. for two years, lecturing and teaching, hoping to raise money for the humanitarian work of the Ramakrishna Mission in India. He not only visited the large East and West Coast cities but also spoke to eager audiences in Des Moines, Memphis, Detroit, and Minneapolis. He returned to Boston many times, speaking at the Methodist church in Lynn, at the Procopeia Club on St. Botolph Street, at Radcliffe College, and at Harvard. During the summer of 1894 Vivekananda settled at a farm called Green Acre in Eliot, Maine, where he taught Vedanta to a summer encampment of Transcendentalists and seekers. The local paper reported, "Each morning he meets a company of men and women under a large pine tree in the woods, and sitting cross-legged, discourses to them of the things of the soul."[9]

During this time, Swami Vivekananda sowed and tended the seeds of what would become America's first Hindu organization, the Vedanta Society. Vivekananda not only was fluent in English, he also became fluent in the distinctive American idiom necessary to translate Vedanta for the West. If we had gone to hear him on January 12, 1896, at Hardman Hall in New York, for example, we would have heard a discourse on "The Ideal of a Universal Religion." Following along with his lecture gives us a glimpse of the kinds of Hindu ideas that might have appealed to late-nineteenth-century Americans and continue to have appeal even today.

He began with a sober look at the record of religion, which resonates all too well a hundred years later: "No other human interest has deluged the world in so much in blood as religion; at the same time nothing has built so many hospitals and asylums for the poor . . . as religion. Nothing makes us so cruel as religion, nothing makes us so tender as religion."[10] All religions seem to be susceptible to what he called the "disease of fanaticism." He looks at the clear evidence. "Each religion brings out its own doctrines, and insists upon them as being the only real ones." In the area of mythology, each invests its own with reality and dismisses the other.

> The Christian believes that God took the shape of a dove, and came down, and they think this is history, and not mythology. But the Hindu believes that God is manifested in the cow. Christians

say that is mythology, and not history: superstition. The Jews think that if an image be made in the form of a box, or a chest, with an angel on either side, then it is to be placed in the Holy of Holies; it is sacred to Jehovah; but if the image be made in the form of a beautiful man or woman, they say "This horrible idol; break it down."

As for rituals, Christians look at the Hindu worship of the *linga* and see it as phallic worship, while Hindus look at the Christian sacrament of communion and are repulsed by its symbolic cannibalism.

Religion is not the place to look for what is universal, he said. Religion, after all, is a human expression, and religions are as different as our cultures. For our universal kinship we must look not to religion, but to God and to our deepest humanity, which is the soul, struggling godward. Vivekananda quotes the apostle Paul in the appeal he made to the Athenians on the Areopagus, where he speaks of the many gods of the Greeks and the "unknown god," the one "in whom we live and move and have our being." It is this God who is the unity running through all these religions, like a thread through a string of pearls. To illustrate, he presented his New York audience with an age-old Hindu analogy:

Suppose we each one of us go with a particular pot in our hand to fetch water from a lake. . . . He who has brought the cup has water in the form of a cup, he who brought the jar, his water is in the shape of a jar, and so forth. . . . So, in the case of religion, our minds are like these little pots, and each one of us is seeing God. God is like that water filling the form of the vessel. Yet He is One. He is God in every case.

Vivekananda brought more than ideas; he brought a path of realization. Spiritual growth comes from inside out, he explained, like the growth of a plant. A teacher can help remove the obstructions, but spiritual growth is the flowering of one's innate oneness with God. Vivekananda considered the burden of original sin, which the Christian tradition placed so heavily upon the soul, a "standing libel" on human nature, which is inherently divine. The paths toward realizing that divine one within are many. They are called yogas, religious disciplines, and different paths suit our different natures. As we have seen, the path of action is *karma yoga,* the path of devotion, *bhakti yoga,* and the path of wisdom, *jnana yoga.*

The particular path Vivekananda taught he called Raja Yoga, the "royal path," which he described as both mystical and psychological. It is a form of spiritual discipline based on the cultivation of concentration. That night in New York he described it this way:

> In the present state of our body we are so much distracted, the mind is frittering away its energies upon a hundred sorts of things. As soon as I try to calm my thoughts and concentrate my mind upon one object of knowledge, thousands of thoughts rush into the brain. How to check that, bring it under control, this is the whole subject of Raja Yoga.

Concentration is the key to this "psychological way to union." The chemist, the astronomer, the professor, the working person—all are able to excel in what they do only by concentration, bringing the mind to one-pointedness. So it must be with the spiritual life, the disciplines of body and mind that will lead to clarity and concentration in the realization of God. In short, in this and many of his American lectures, Vivekananda set forth a form of Hindu thought and practice that would be, he thought, both appealing and useful in the American context.

When Vivekananda's little book called *Raja Yoga* was published in 1900, it provided, in summary form, the basics of yoga practice: the postures of the body (*asanas*), the control of the breath (*pranayama*), and the stages along the path of realization. It has been in print for nearly a century and is still widely read. The yoga described here is both psychological and experimental. Vivekananda repeatedly uses the term *scientific* to convey the way in which the path of yoga and the markers along the way have been verified by generations of practitioners, right to the present day.[11] As we shall see, the notion that Hinduism is the religion for the age of psychology, secularism, and science is one that will be sounded repeatedly in the decades that follow.

Not only did Vivekananda launch the Vedanta Society in America to bring Hindu spirituality to the West, he also launched the Ramakrishna Mission in India, complete with an order of monks dedicated to religious service. When Wendell Thomas surveyed the history of Vedanta and other early Hindu movements in the U.S. in 1930, in a book with the alarming title *Hinduism Invades America,* he made the provocative observation that "While India is getting more of the Christian side of Vivekananda's dual religion of renunciation and service, America is getting only the strictly Hindu side." Indeed, the Ramakrishna Mission in

India was establishing hospitals and schools, engaging in the kind of service ministry that some associated with Christian missions. In America, however, Vivekananda had seen a kind of spiritual bankruptcy and placed a heavy emphasis on the cultivation of the inner life. In pondering what the Hindu conservatism of the American Vedanta Society meant, when contrasted with the Hindu liberalism of the Ramakrishna Mission in India, Thomas wrote, "It means that of all the countries of the world including India itself, the United States offers the most fertile soil for the growth of conservative Hindu ideals."[12] He insightfully conjectured that America is a land of both pioneers and religious seeking, and Americans tend to participate aggressively, single-mindedly, and whole-heartedly in whatever they do. By the 1930s the Vedanta Society appealed particularly to nominal, liberal Christians, who came to see Christianity anew in the context of the Hindu claim to the equality of all religious traditions. It also appealed to secular seekers with no previous stake in any religious tradition who were attracted by its "scientific" language and yoga practice.

THE VEDANTA SOCIETY TODAY

One blustery March morning, I found the brownstone on New York's Upper West Side where the Vedanta Society of New York makes its home. It is the oldest of America's some two dozen Vedanta Societies, tracing its history to 1894 and Swami Vivekananda's stay in New York following the parliament. I rang the bell and was greeted by a soft-spoken young woman. "The swami is on his way down," she said, as she invited me into the front hall and settled me in the sitting room. I looked into the adjacent chapel while I waited.

The chapel looked much like others I had seen in Vedanta Societies across the country. It is a peaceful, carpeted room, softly lit, with about a hundred chairs arranged in rows facing the altar. The woman who received me explained that the chapel is filled to capacity on Sunday mornings. On Tuesday and Friday evenings when Swami Tathagatananda lectures on the Gita, there is a smaller group. In the past ten or fifteen years, however, the number of Indian American immigrants has steadily increased and now constitutes nearly half the congregation. From my observation, this shift in the composition of the old, fairly white, Vedanta Society is happening all across America. In this Vedanta Society, new Hindu immigrants find an already-assimilated form of Hindu religious life that emphasizes universal ideals. The multitude of glittering gods we saw in Sunnyvale have no overt presence here.

At the center of the altar is a black-and-white photograph of Vivekananda's teacher, Sri Ramakrishna, the Bengali mystic who spoke of experiencing the Divine One in all the panoply of names and forms— tasting the Divine as Krishna, Shiva, and the Goddess, as the Buddha and the Christ. A visitor first encountering a photograph of the stubbly-bearded, crooked-smiling face of Ramakrishna might well be puzzled to see him there on the altar, flanked by two vases of fresh flowers. This ecstatic saint of Calcutta might seem out of place on the urbane Upper West Side. But Ramakrishna was a powerful engine of spiritual energy, and anyone born in India would recognize this face immediately.

To either side of Ramakrishna on the altar stand images of Jesus and the Buddha, expressing the spiritually eclectic message of Vedanta. On the right wall is a portrait of Sharada Devi, Ramakrishna's wife, who became his celibate companion whom he honored as a goddess, and on the left wall is a portrait of the young Vivekananda. The altar confirms the plurality of the Hindu universe but in a different key than the altars of Sunnyvale and Livermore. Here oneness of the many extends beyond the gods and spiritual ways of India to the religious ways of the wider world.

After a few minutes, Swami Tathagatananda appeared, wearing a faintly orange velour sweatshirt—a dim signal of the orange robes of the *sannyasi,* "renouncer," of India—along with slacks and running shoes. The swami has been in New York for decades, and his summary of the teachings of Vedanta has been honed to a few bare points for an American audience. He touched on them skillfully as we talked:

- God is one; people worship him in different forms.
- Humanity, in its essential nature, is divine.
- The goal of humanity is to realize this divinity.
- The ways to realize this divinity are innumerable. They are called the yogas. As Sri Ramakrishna declared, "As many faiths, so many paths."

As we spoke, it was clear that the swami, like Vivekananda before him, cares little for the outward structures of what we call religion. He would understand, but not be eager to participate in, the life of the Sri Lakshmi temple in Ashland or the Sunnyvale temple in the Silicon Valley. His favorite American is Abraham Lincoln, whom he admires for his truthfulness, humility, and inner strength as well as for his disregard for institutionalized religion. The Vedanta Society does not proselytize, advertise, or press its message on the public. It is here for those who seek. "This is the temple that counts," he said, pointing to his heart. "They say people in America are very religious, meaning they frequent churches or synagogues or temples. They have an altar at home with a cross or a picture of Kali. That is that. But nothing changes in their lives. But I tell you, it is not what you do or know in your head that matters. Finally, it is whether your heart is transformed, whether your life is transformed. That is the only thing that matters."

The distrust of institutions and the transformation of the heart sounded familiar to me as a Protestant, for this was the very stuff of the Reformation and the religion of the heart the very drumbeat of my own Methodist tradition. But I also thought of the too-often exclusivist narrowness of born-again faith. I asked, "And what of the Christian fundamentalists who have a strong heartfelt experience of transformation and are born again but insist theirs is the only way?"

"To think you own the Almighty cannot but be counterfeit," he replied. "No real experience of the infinite presence of God can leave you condemning your neighbor. When Christ suffered on the cross, he did not condemn either the thieves next to him or the executioners. God within us is 'the way, the truth, the life.'"

You won't hear the Vedanta swamis of today confronting or debating the chauvinism of new fundamentalist Christianity, or new fundamentalist Hinduism, for that matter. Their style is almost wholly oriented toward teaching, and modest newspaper notices will tell you where and when you might hear them at one of America's some twenty Vedanta Societies.

When Vivekananda returned to India in 1896, after three years in America, he sent Swami Abhedananda to take up the reins of the small New York community, the predecessor of the community I visited that morning. Swami Abhedananda was a vigorous organizer and a fine lecturer. He delivered hundreds of lectures on Vedanta in Manhattan in the late 1890s. Vivekananda returned to the U.S. for a second stay in 1899 and started the second Vedanta Society, in San Francisco, putting Swami Turiyananda in charge. There in 1906 the first real Hindu temple in North America was erected: a whimsical Victorian architectural delight with cupolas, steeples, domes, and spires all testifying to the *pluribus* within. Somehow it survived the earthquake that same year, and you can still see it today. It is a Victorian architectural expression of the universal embrace of Vedanta.

Unfortunately, Swami Vivekananda did not live to see his splendid San Francisco headquarters. He left America for the last time in 1900. Debilitated by diabetes, he died in 1902—on the Fourth of July. He was only thirty-nine years old. By then the institutions he had begun were strong enough to continue without him, though it can only be imagined what growth would have taken place had his immense, cyclonic energy continued to infuse the movement for another thirty years. The flow of monks to the U.S. continued as dozens of swamis from the Ramakrishna Mission in India came in succession to the United States to take the lead in the growing number of Vedanta Society centers—in Los Angeles, Pittsburgh, Providence, Boston, Portland.

Despite its long history in America, the Vedanta Society has never gained wide attention, primarily because its form of organization did not become truly American. There was no unified national Vedanta Society structure. Instead, each center retained and still retains a direct relation with the headquarters in Calcutta, and each received its religious leadership from headquarters, even though there have been Euro-American *sannyasis* involved for one hundred years now. As early as 1895, Vivekananda had invited a small group of American followers to an intensive training retreat on one of the islands of the St. Lawrence River. There he initiated two Western followers as *sannyasis*. A small order of Euro-Americans who speak of themselves as monks and nuns continues today. They are associated with both the urban temples and rural retreat centers. The Vedanta Society of Southern California, for example, has a convent at Montecito near Santa Barbara and a monastery in Trabuco Canyon near Los Angeles. The Vedanta Society of Chicago has a monastery and retreat center in a town in Michigan, appropriately named Ganges, Michigan. All this time, however, the leadership of the Vedanta Society centers has remained firmly in the control of Indian monks of the Ramakrishna order, sent from the headquarters in Calcutta.

The Vedanta Society became very American in one sense, with chapels and chairs, Sunday morning services and weekday evening study classes. Some swamis took American citizenship, leaving behind the monastic orange robes for suits and ties, even orange velour sweatshirts and Reeboks. Yet still the culture of the leadership always came from Calcutta. Not until the new post-1965 immigration did the Vedanta Society experience a burst of growth, this time from new Indian immigrants who discovered the legacy of Vivekananda in their new homeland.

YOGANANDA AND THE "SCIENCE OF RELIGION"

For forty years—from the 1930s to the 1970s—the most popular Hindu movement in America was the Self-Realization Fellowship. Yogananda, its founder, was another Hindu teacher who, like Vivekananda, came to America for a conference and stayed to launch a religious movement. He came from Bengal to a meeting of the International Congress of Religious Liberals held in Boston in 1920 and sponsored by the Unitarian Church, and he stayed for over thirty years.

Yogananda's theme song was one that struck a popular chord in America: the uniting of science and religion. Many Americans tended to see science and religion as opposites, so as one moved into the world of science and rationality, one would have to move away from religion. Yogananda insisted that the Hindu yoga tradition was itself a science—the "science of religion." Like Vivekananda before him, he pointed out that religion cannot be a secondhand matter learned from authorities in churches or temples, acquired by reading scriptures or by learning doctrines. Religious life must be firsthand: based in and confirmed by experience. In this, religion is like science, a worldview tested through experiment and experience. As Yogananda put it in that very first lecture in Boston, "Yoga is a system of scientific methods for reuniting the soul with the Spirit."[13] In 1925 in Los Angeles he founded the Yogoda Satsang, which eventually became known as the Self-Realization Fellowship, with the aim "to unite science and religion through realization of the unity of their underlying principles" and "to disseminate among the nations a knowledge of definite scientific techniques for attaining direct personal experience of God."

Yogananda looked every bit the exotic swami, but he spoke of the principles of the inner and spiritual world as very much like those that govern the physical world. They can be observed and confirmed repeatedly. "The principles that operate in the outer universe, discoverable by scientists, are called natural laws. But there are subtler laws that rule the hidden spiritual places and the inner realm of consciousness; these principles are knowable through the science of yoga." India's yogis have experimented for hundreds of years in the inner realm. They have refined their knowledge of inner terrain. Far from being abstract and mystical, this path is very practical and embodied. This body of flesh and bones is not at odds with some other entity called the spirit but is the very vehicle of spiritual practice. As the body learns stillness, the mind learns stillness.

Though today we might associate yoga primarily with the postures that have become popular for health and fitness, the broader basis of yoga taught by Yogananda was the discipline of the mind, the practice of inner one-pointedness. In this practice, there are markers along the path of inner development toward "self-realization." One needs a teacher both to get started, and to check one's progress along the path. For thousands of Americans, Yogananda was that teacher. He developed a mail-order self-study course covering 180 lessons, enabling distant learners in Minneapolis or Schenectady to cover one lesson a week, practice at home, and periodically attend a Self-Realization Fellowship convention for personal guidance along the path.

This remarkable swami had a great inclination toward and gift for organization. By 1930, in addition to the Los Angeles center, there were twelve centers in major U.S. cities, claiming some twenty-five thousand members. For him, yoga was not a specifically Hindu practice but a practice that could benefit everyone. Yogananda's students and supporters included scientists like Luther Burbank, an architect from Cleveland, and a New York textile manufacturer. He emphasized that one could be a Catholic yogi or a Methodist yogi. Indeed, Yogananda spoke of what he called the "original Christianity," which teaches the realization of "Christ-consciousness" within. Like some Christian teachers, he encouraged yoga practitioners to offer testimonials to the value of yoga practice in their own lives, and the issues of the publication *East-West* are filled with the stories of yoga practitioners testifying to the transformation the practice brought to their lives.

Yogananda put yoga on the map in America. He liked America. It became his home, and he developed distinctively American organizational strategies and public relations. He posed for photos with President Calvin Coolidge and prescribed a vegetarian diet for the president's health. He observed the Fourth of July and Lincoln's Birthday with public greetings. At his ashram headquarters in Los Angeles he gathered the Self-Realization Fellowship to celebrate Christmas, Easter, and Thanksgiving. There were greeting cards, Christmas cards, SRF pins and insignia items, and sheet music for the "Song of Brahma" and "Om Song." All this led Wendell Thomas to conclude, "Swami Yogananda is even more American in method than in message." The popularity of Yogananda was further enhanced in 1946 with a book tie-in—the publication of his famous *Autobiography of a Yogi*, which has been continuously in print and basic reading for those on the path of yoga for more than fifty years.

The great yogi died on March 7, 1952. On that day, he is said to have entered into a deep state of meditation and passed away, according to all medical measurements. However, his body remained incorruptible for twenty days before interment. So remarkable was this fact to the mortuary director, Mr. Harry T. Rowe, that he had an affidavit drawn up and notarized:

> The absence of any visual signs of decay in the dead body of Paramahansa Yogananda offers the most extraordinary case in our experience. . . . No physical disintegration was visible in his body even twenty days after death. . . . This state of perfect preservation of a body is, so far as we know from mortuary annals, an unparalleled one. . . . He looked on March 27th as fresh and unravaged by decay as he had on the night of his death.[14]

Today the Lake Shrine Center that Yogananda established in 1950 is a sanctuary of the spirit in Los Angeles, where Sunset Boulevard meets the sea. Of the ten other SRF ashrams and centers in the U.S., eight are in California, and SRF meetings are held in virtually every state. But the Lake Shrine Center is the jewel in the crown. It is a leafy spiritual oasis, with its facilities circling a small lake, a world away from the world. Visiting the center in the mid-1990s, I picked up a copy of one of Yogananda's most popular writings, the little book called *Scientific Healing Affirmations,* and, looking through its pages, was struck by the contemporary sound of the mind-body language he uses.

In this little booklet Yogananda writes about the power of words and thoughts to shape consciousness and therefore to influence our health. "The mind, being the brain, feeling, and perception of all living cells, can keep the human body alert or depressed," he writes. "Just as we concern ourselves with the nutritive value of our daily food menus, so should we consider the nutritive potency of the psychological menus that we daily serve the mind." An issue of the SRF journal from the Lake Shrine bookstore confirmed my hunch: the movement does indeed see Yogananda as the forerunner of today's mind-body medical movement, anticipating many of these developments by at least four decades.[15] It cites parallels with Dr. Carl Simonton, who pioneered the use of mental visualization in cancer treatment. It cites Norman Cousins, who wrote, "What we put into our minds can be as important as what we put into our bodies. . . . Negative emotions, persisting over a long period of time, can impair the immune system, thus lowering the body's defenses against disease." And, of course, it mentions Yogananda's kinship with the medical pioneer of the mind-body movement, Dr. Herbert Benson of Harvard Medical School, who subjected meditators to scientific testing and found,

> Through meditation . . . you can set the stage for important mind- and habit-altering brain change. . . . Scientific research has shown that electrical activity between the left and rights sides of the brain becomes coordinated during certain kinds of meditation and prayer. . . . The implications are exciting and even staggering.

By the 1980s doctors in white coats were teaching a simple version of some of the kinds of meditation exercises that Indian swamis in orange robes had been teaching for hundreds of years.

Until 1965 the Self-Realization Fellowship was the most extensive Hindu organization in the U.S. Thinking back on both Vivekananda and Yogananda from today's standpoint, we can see that both introduced to America a body of thought and practice that had attracted considerable attention even before the great turning East of the 1960s and 1970s, even before the new immigration, even before the great wave of gurus who came with the new immigration. They began the process of slipping a holistic worldview under the crumbling foundations of American secularism. By the 1980s it would be called New Age, and by the 1990s it would gain the currency of a prevailing way of looking at things. Even the Harvard University Health Services would have a Mind-Body Clinic. In this view, science and religion, body and mind, matter and spirit are seen not as contending opposites but as inextricably interrelated. Health is a spiritual matter, just as spirituality is a form of fitness. Call it yoga, call it New Age, call it Hindu—this has become a holistic way of thinking that is prevalent in the U.S. today as never before.

TRANSCENDENTAL MEDITATION AND THE MIND-BODY CONNECTION

After Yogananda, the next great teacher in the record book of Hindu America is the Maharishi Mahesh Yogi, who became known simply by his title, the Maharishi. The form of simple meditation practice he taught has become virtually a household word in America—TM, short for Transcendental Meditation. The Maharishi was trained in the monastery of the Shankaracharya of Jyotimath high in the Indian Himalayas. In the late 1950s he launched what he modestly called a mission for the "spiritual regeneration" of the whole world, settings his sights on Europe and the U.S. His first trip to the U.S. was in 1959, and he gave his first lecture on this form and philosophy of meditation in San Francisco, traveling next to Los Angeles, New York, London, and Germany. Those in my generation in the 1960s remember the Maharishi as the guru of the Beatles. The campus-based movement he launched in the U.S. became known as the Students International Meditation Society (SIMS), and by the 1970s there were SIMS centers at over a thousand American colleges and universities. By the early 1980s, the society estimated that more than 1.5 million Americans had received a mantra and begun practicing TM under a teacher's instruction. Today the TM movement has meditation centers, a university—Maharishi International University in Fairfield, Iowa—and a political party, the Natural Law party.

TM literature describes the practice as a "simple, natural, effortless, easily learned mental technique practiced for 15 to 20 minutes twice daily, sitting comfortably with the eyes closed." The movement insists this is not Hinduism, indeed not religion at all, but a technique of concentration. Focusing on a mantra, a powerful sound or word imparted by the teacher at the time of initiation, the meditator is able to realize the natural and blissful state of completely relaxed, yet wakeful, consciousness. No uncomfortable lotus postures are necessary, no exotic clothing, prayer shawls, beads, or cushions. Just sit in a chair, in comfortable clothing, at home. Anyone can learn TM, no matter what one's religion or culture, age or educational background.

The Maharishi was a spiritual entrepreneur in the best sense. TM introductory sessions were frequent and free. However, the course of training that led to receiving a mantra for meditation cost enough money to take it seriously. The Maharishi must have perceived, and rightly so, that Americans are very practical people, like to do things for themselves, and are more apt to commit themselves to those things they pay for. New practitioners who had just invested in their initiation were likely to put in their twenty minutes of practice twice a day—at least for long enough to begin to realize the fruits of practice. And there was no question the practice would bear fruit. Fifteen or twenty minutes of simple meditation, twice a day, would be good for just about anyone. It did not need to be called Hindu, for in the fast-paced and stress-filled life of mid-twentieth-century America it was just a common-sense dose of sanity.

The success of TM is attributable, in part, to its playing down any distinctively Hindu context of meditation and emphasizing instead its scientifically demonstrable value as a technique for concentrating and stilling the mind, enlarging and focusing awareness, relaxing the body, and lowering metabolism. While scholars can see the continuities with India's forms of meditation, many practitioners would find these links inconsequential for themselves and do not identify as Hindu in any way. In their view, this is not a religion, not a philosophy, but a technique—like turning on a light switch or using a lever to move a big rock. It can be practiced, so they say, by Christian ministers, Jewish rabbis, and people who have no religious affiliation at all.

Today TM is practiced by corporate executives and lawyers, school-teachers and professors, even by military personnel and blue-collar workers. "TM Can Improve Job Performance" was the headline of the Kankakee, Illinois, *Daily Journal* (February 23, 1997). The reporter, Tracy Ahrens, began,

> Business people, locally and around the world, are jumping at the opportunity to offer transcendental meditation (TM) to their employees in order to increase job performance and decrease the number of work absences due to illness. TM is a simple technique that is performed for 20 minutes, twice a day in a fairly quiet location. Today, over four million people around the world practice this form of meditation.

The TM movement appeals to Americans who are practical about their spirituality. In this way it stands clearly in the traditions that had been cultivated in the U.S. by both Vivekananda and Yogananda. Like his predecessors, the Maharishi used the language of science to explain spiritual exercises to a scientifically minded American audience. He courted the verification of scientists as part of the presentation of TM in the American context. The earliest research on TM meditators was pioneered by UCLA physiologist Robert Keith Wallace for his Ph.D. thesis in the late 1960s, entitled "The Physiological Effects of Transcendental Meditation: A Proposed Fourth Major State of Consciousness." In the early 1970s TM meditators approached Dr. Herbert Benson, a Boston Harvard-affiliated physician, and volunteered to be hooked up to instruments that would measure the physiological changes that took place as they entered into states of deep meditation. In 1975 Benson's popular book *The Relaxation Response* put into plain English the results of his research: that meditation can produce the decreased metabolism that researchers referred to as a hypometabolic state, a deep rest that can reduce blood pressure and begin to diffuse stress. Benson's research is part of what, by now, seems a virtual explosion of mind-body clinics and meditation workshops for people with chronic pain, heart disease, cancer, and stress.

A 1991 pamphlet on TM says on its cover, "A Scientifically Validated Program." TM is described as developing "the simplest form of human awareness, where consciousness is open to itself." The meditation practice is described as "the technology of the unified field," which develops the physiology of deep rest, with decreased respiratory rate, lower plasma lactate levels, and increased basal resistance. Research published in the *American Journal of Physiology, Scientific American,* and the *International Journal of Neuroscience* is cited, and it is noted that over the past twenty-five years there have been more than 500 scientific research experiments on TM at 210 research institutes and universities in 33 countries. Here the specifically Hindu language of the yogis has been completed replaced by the language of science. One of the primary TM Web sites today describes the Maharishi as "the foremost scientist in the field of consciousness."

For a time in the 1980s and early 1990s, the Maharishi linked his dedication to mind-body medicine with that of Deepak Chopra, a Boston medical doctor of Indian origin. Chopra's book *Quantum Healing,* a work written during a period of close collaboration with the Maharishi, describes the "quantum mechanical human body," where astonishingly, on a day-to-day basis, the drama of the mind-body connection is enacted. Thought—the thought of fear, for example—is transformed into neuropeptide, a form of matter. Health is not the absence of invasion by disease but the presence of homeostatic harmony of body, mind, and spirit. Chopra sees the foundation of mind-body medicine as the link between our states of mind and the physiology and biochemistry of our bodies. By the dawn of the new millennium, it is a medical doctor of Indian origin, not a swami, who speaks of the "science of awareness," the process that enables one to move through the sheaths or vestures of the soul described by Vedanta, from the material body to the breath to the mind to pure consciousness, and, finally, to pure bliss.

The term *holistic* has become the common coin of what is sometimes called the New Age, a way of thinking and living that tries to break free of the dualistic opposition of science and spirit, outer and inner, body and mind. This turn of mind has gradually saturated the whole of American culture with essentially Hindu, more broadly Asian, ideas without speaking of them as such. Swami Yogananda, who had spoken of the science of religion and had an avid interest in the relation of spirituality to health decades before all this flowered, would surely have looked on the emergence of this "new age" with satisfaction.

GURUS AND THE NEW RELIGIOUS AMERICA

When the 1965 immigration act opened the door to immigration from Asia, among the beneficiaries of the new policy were not only the engineers, computer scientists, physicians, and nurses who came to the U.S. in great numbers, but also religious teachers or gurus, like the Maharishi. The term *guru* entered into the American vocabulary with the steady stream of teachers who brought their philosophies, meditation practices, spiritual leadership, and eccentricities to America. In the Hindu tradition, becoming a teacher has traditionally meant receiving the blessing and authority to teach from one's own teacher. It is not a matter of academic degrees but of recognizing that the student has learned deeply the wisdom of the tradition and can teach it with authenticity. Hindus in India know, however, that there are all kinds of gurus, some more fully in possession of the insights of the tradition than others. And in India it is taken for granted that some alleged gurus are downright bogus. In America, however, who was to say? All had a chance to attract a following. In the past thirty-five years, gurus have come and stayed, and come and gone.

Of the many Hindu gurus who came, exploded like the fireworks on the Fourth of July, and eventually disappeared, I will mention only two of the most memorable. In 1971 we saw the meteoric rise of the young boy-guru of the Divine Light Mission called Guru Maharaj Ji. By 1973 he was said to have initiated fifty thousand people who had "received knowledge" through him. He rented the Houston Astrodome for what was billed "the most significant event in human history." It was unclear what was supposed to have happened, but the event was not well attended, leaving his organization in debt half a million dollars and on the road back to India. Bhagwan Shree Rajneesh also had a brief life in America. In the 1970s his ashram in Pune, India, had attracted young Americans and Europeans to a cathartic form of Hindu tantric meditation practice. In 1981 he established an ashram community in the small town of Antelope, Oregon, and the movement became widely known in the U.S., partially because of the controversies that ensued. Suddenly the small town had more than three thousand residents and a legendary fleet of

Rolls Royces for the guru. The city council refused the group new building permits, but soon the Rajneesh followers elected themselves to the
council and changed the name Antelope to Rajneeshpuram, the "City of
Rajneesh." In 1985 the ashram disintegrated amidst a flurry of legal controversies and internal dissent. Eventually, Rajneesh returned to India.

Of the long-lasting new gurus of America, the senior statesman is
Swami Satchidananda. He came in time for Woodstock in 1969, where he
spoke a word of spirituality and attracted some of the assembled hippies of
the day to the practice of yoga, and he stayed right on through the seventies and eighties. In 1993 he was at the Parliament of the World's Religions
in Chicago, and in September of 2000 he was there with orange robes and
long, now white, hair at the Millennium World Peace Summit at the
United Nations. Swami Satchidananda's 750-acre Integral Yoga Institute
in the green hills of rural Virginia continues to attract yoga practitioners
even today. Here you will find what is perhaps the most astonishing piece
of spiritual architecture in the whole country: the Light of Truth Universal
Shrine, or LOTUS. It is a domed, lotus-shaped temple of pink glass sitting
like a huge glass flower in the green countryside. Entering this temple, you
will find at the center an open shaft of light, reaching upward toward the
infinity of the sky. Around it on the lotus petals of the periphery are twelve
chapels, each dedicated to the Divine as seen in one of the world's religious
traditions. Hindu eclecticism has found a home here, with these lotus
altars embracing all the religious traditions of America.

At the Siddha Yoga Dham Ashram in South Fallsburg, New York,
this eclecticism takes a slightly different form, as the followers of the styl-
ish Gurumayi observe *pujas* not only for the Hindu festivals of Diwali and
Shiva Ratri, but also for Christmas, Passover, and Easter. Here in the
Catskills, once famous as the spa country of America's urban Jewish culture, Gurumayi's own teacher, Swami Muktananda, established a retreat
center in the late 1970s. A disciple of a long line of revered Hindu gurus,
Muktananda taught a path of inner awakening called *siddha yoga,* aimed at
awakening the transformative spiritual power that is deep within each of
us. The touch of the guru's *shakti,* or energy, can enable us to experience
the divine consciousness within and to recognize that divine consciousness in others. When Muktananda died in 1982, there was a brief period
of instability, intrigue, and turmoil while the two young gurus he had
appointed his successors found their spiritual feet. Eventually, the young
woman he had named Swami Chidvilasananda took over the movement. Known to her followers as Gurumayi, she has created a vibrant,

somewhat upscale, following. She teaches and bestows *shakti pat* in her primary ashrams at South Fallsburg in New York and Ganeshpuri in India and also conveys instruction through a network of smaller ashrams in places like Oakland, California, and Atlanta, Georgia. The Web site iconography of Siddha Yoga leaves behind distinctively Hindu motifs for a more universal iconography of autumn leaves, nautilus shells, and abstract images from the world of nature. For the time being, it seems that Gurumayi has made a critical transition in creating an American context for teachings and meditation practices that had traveled for centuries in Indian spiritual lineages.

The guru Ammachi creates a very different scene in the United States, with a soaring popularity that is astonishing for a woman from Kerala in India who communicates primarily in Malayalam, the language of Kerala. But her real language of communication is unconditional love, dispensed liberally to thousands who wait in line for hours to receive her blessing in the form of a hug. Her full name is Mata Amritanandamayi. She was born in a fisherman's family on the coast of Kerala and even as a child is said to have displayed an uncommon devotion to the Divine, first as Krishna and then as the Goddess. Her inborn nature, she says, was always to pour forth an unbroken stream of love toward all beings. Her ashram communities in India make clear that social service goes hand in hand with devotion. She runs two hospitals, an orphanage for about four hundred children, and a school committed to serving the poor through education. Ammachi first came to the United States in 1987 and since then has made regular tours through major American cities each summer, attracting both Indian immigrants and Euro-American seekers. For those who follow her or come to see her, this unselfconscious woman seems to become the "universal embodiment of Mother Love," and apparently there is a yearning and thirsting for this maternal love. Whether in the outskirts of Boston or midtown Manhattan, whenever her gatherings are announced many hundreds of seekers line up, sitting for hours on end, anticipating the moment she will embrace each one on her shoulder with the hug that is her special blessing.

America seems to have begun to learn the ropes of the gurus. It has kept some, let others go. There are frequent debunkings. But the power and importance of the guru—the presence, the word, the touch, and the image of the guru—were not concocted by the wild imaginings of the anticult movement of the 1970s, which saw untold dangers in such spiritual authority. The spiritual authority of the guru is central to the Hindu tradition, in which religious knowledge is transmitted personally to the disciple from one who knows, not merely intellectually, but experientially. As Swami Muktananda put it in an article entitled "What Is a True Guru?"

> The Guru is not a human being. The Guru is the grace-bestowing power of God. He transmits the power, the Shakti of God into you and awakens your own inner power.[16]

It would be fitting to round out our brief view of the new gurus of America with one who would have to be called an antiguru, so averse was he to precisely the guru described by Muktananda. That was J. Krishnamurti, who first visited the United States in 1911 and whose final years were lived out in the Ojai Valley of California until his death in 1986. As a young man, Krishnamurti had been hailed by the Theosophical Society's Order of the Star of the East as the long-expected world teacher for our age. In 1929, however, he called his followers together and dissolved the order, maintaining that the very impulse to follow a teacher and cling to his teachings is what keeps us from realizing our own true nature. "I maintain that truth is a pathless land, and you cannot approach it by any path whatsoever, by any religion, by any sect."[17] While Krishnamurti taught for decades, moving back and forth from India to Europe to America, and while he filled lecture halls in California and London, in Banaras and New York, he did not wish the label or the following of a guru, much less a Hindu guru.

When I first heard Krishnamurti in Banaras in 1965, I found that his teaching style relentlessly challenged our habitual propensity to label, compare, judge, and classify everything we hear, everything we experience. "Choiceless awareness" was the quality of mind that he tried to elicit in those he encountered: experiencing for ourselves the ground of our consciousness, before we build upon it the superstructures of our interpretations and the organized systems of our religions. Meditation can help cultivate this choiceless awareness, but even meditation can become too rigid. As he put it, "I am concerning myself with only one essential thing: to set man free. I desire to free him from all cages, from all fears, and not to found religions, new sects, nor to establish new theories and new philosophies."[18] It was, of course, one of the ironies of Krishnamurti's life that people followed him, listened to his lectures, and recorded his teachings as if to map that trackless land. After Krishnamurti died, the ranch home he kept in Ojai, California, has continued to flourish as a teaching center, and the Krishnamurti Foundation of America there promotes the teachings of this antiguru of the age through an extensive library and a school aimed at cultivating in young people the freedom of mind that was his.

LORD KRISHNA COMES TO AMERICA

Another of the great gurus to come to America once we opened the door to Asia was A. C. Bhaktivedanta, a sixty-nine-year-old teacher who arrived in New York in 1965. His story has all the elements of a great American immigration epic. The former manager of a chemical firm in Calcutta, Bhaktivedanta had been instructed by his own spiritual teacher to carry devotion to Krishna from India to the West. He arrived nearly penniless in New York City and began his mission to America, chanting "Hare Krishna, Hare Rama" in Tompkins Square Park. He attracted a few followers in his joyful, even ecstatic, chanting, and within a few months he opened the first Krishna temple in America—a Second Avenue storefront on the lower east side. Within five years, his eager following had temples in thirty American cities. Such was the origin of the International Society for Krishna Consciousness, ISKCON. This was not drugs, not heady philosophy, and above all not easy for young Americans of the sixties; it was hard-core devotional Hinduism of a sort America had never before seen.

One of his first followers was a young English instructor from Ohio State, who recalls the early life of the movement with the teacher they came to call Prabhupad, a title of reverence.

> Prabhupad had prodigious energy. He was up every morning before any of us. He pounded the drum, exhausted everyone at kirtan, chanted hymns, danced, delivered lectures, translated books, cooked and supervised all affairs. And he was triple the age of any one of us.[19]

This distinctively devotional style of Hinduism did not seem a likely magnet for young Americans in the turmoil of the sixties. It was not a transcendental or universalist approach, it did not have the countercultural cachet of meditation or yoga. It was a very particular, distinctive form of Hindu devotionalism, called *bhakti*. Unlike TM, it was ritually complex. Unlike TM, it was unabashedly Hindu, and it drew Krishna's new devotees into a world of Hindu worship, chanting, and devotional singing. Astonishingly enough, it attracted a dedicated group of young people.

I first encountered the Hare Krishnas in September of 1969 when I came to Harvard as a graduate student. I was a serious young scholar with furrowed brow, taking first-year Sanskrit and launching into the study of Hinduism. There they were in Harvard Square—Caucasian Hindus in saris and dhotis, dancing in a snake line to the rhythm of their hand cymbals and bells, chanting, "Hare Krishna, Hare Krishna! Krishna, Krishna! Hare Hare!" They pressed magazines, books, and free sweets on anyone who would listen. Cambridge did not seem to me a likely spot for such energetic devotion or for any possible conversions. I wanted to cross the street when I saw them, but I also wanted to know who they were. So I finally took them up on their invitation to visit the temple, an old house in a working-class district across the Charles River from Cambridge.

I found that the fervent devotional piety could be traced to Chaitanya, an ecstatic saint who lived in Bengal in the late fifteenth and early sixteenth centuries. He popularized the form of worship called *kirtan,* the chanting and singing of the holy name of God. The teachings of Vedanta philosophy and the practice of yoga did not touch the heart, he said, not like the singing of God's name. And the rituals of the Brahmins were too expensive, too long, too caste bound with rules of purity and pollution. But the singing of God's name required only love and broke down the barriers that divided people one from another. The followers of Chaitanya were not only caste Hindus but untouchables, even Muslims. It was a religious path defined by the love of God, not the rules of men. Chaitanya came to be seen by those who knew him as the living presence of Lord Krishna. Indeed, he came to be seen as an incarnation of Krishna and his beloved Radha in one body, demonstrating that the relation of the soul and God is as close as that of lover and beloved.

The Hare Krishna movement has been the most visible, though certainly not the largest, of the new Hindu movements in the United States. The path of *bhakti,* loving devotion, continues in ISKCON temples even today. Devotees are up at dawn, chanting the name of Krishna and participating in a traditional form of Hindu temple worship. They present offerings of food, flowers, water, and sweets to the divine presence of Krishna and Radha and receive, in turn, the divine grace, called *prasad.* They offer water to Krishna, pouring it over his feet through a conch shell, and then receive the sprinkled water as a blessing. They offer food and fruit and then eat together what had been consecrated by the Lord. They offer incense and then breathe its fragrance. They circle oil lamps before the face of Krishna and then pass their fingers through the flames and touch their foreheads with reverence. While all this is the common ritual fare of a Hindu temple, it was a more richly sensual form of worship than young Americans of the sixties had ever known. It involved sight and sound, touch and fragrance, color and movement, chanting and dancing.

Introducing Swami Bhaktivedanta to an audience at Ohio State University in the spring of 1968, Allen Ginsberg said, "It's strange that so far out and ritualized an Indian form should take root in the United States a little more naturally than the more protestant Vedanta Society."[20] But from the standpoint of American religious history, perhaps it was not so strange. The fervent devotion of the Hare Krishnas and their sidewalk evangelism seems a natural cousin to the heartfelt evangelical streams of American Protestantism—from the Great Awakening of the seventeenth century to the born-again Christianity of the twentieth century. Though ascetic and renunciatory at the core, Krishna Consciousness also brought religion back to the senses—with movement and music, incense and ecstasy. It is also a mission movement, with the specific aim of enabling all to hear the sound of God's name, "Hare Krishna, Hare Rama," providing a much-needed opportunity for turning, if only for a moment, to God-consciousness. Of course, Krishna devotees annoyed merchants and passersby in Boston and St. Louis just as they had in north Indian market towns four hundred years ago.

The Hare Krishnas experienced the full impact of the anticult movement of the 1970s and 1980s. They were accused of brainwashing and mind control, much like the accusations that Protestant nativists had flung at Catholic monastic movements in America a century before. At the instigation of concerned parents, devotees were kidnapped by deprogrammers who tried to rescue them from the "cult" of Krishna. There were suits and court cases, accusations by disgruntled former members. There were testimonials by loyal devotees about the ways in which the community, the discipline, and the devotion of ISKCON had saved them from drugs and aimlessness. Like all religious movements, ISKCON has included a wide range of devotees, and it certainly cannot be painted with a single brush, even today.

Because of its demanding lifestyle, the Hare Krishna movement never gained a wide membership in America, but it has nonetheless persisted for more than thirty years. In the 1970s, when Hindu immigrants began to settle down in America in significant numbers, the Hare Krishna temples were the only temples they found. On Sunday afternoons they could show up for the worship of Krishna, complete with devotional chanting and a lecture on the Gita, usually delivered by an eager and well-trained Caucasian devotee wearing the faded orange robes of a Hindu monk. They could enjoy a Sunday vegetarian meal and observe the great festival days that made them most nostalgic for their homes in India—the birthday of Krishna, the Diwali festival of lights, or the vigil of Shivaratri. In some cities, the ISKCON temple was a transitional space where they could settle and feel at home before organizing, or even building, a new temple. But in many American cities, the Hare Krishna temple has continued to create a community that serves both its Euro-American devotees and the new Hindu immigrants. The ISKCON temples in Dallas, Chicago, Denver, and Los Angeles, for example, have continued to involve both Euro-American and Indian American members. A young Indian man in Denver, when asked how he felt about attending the Krishna temple, put it this way: "Why should I feel funny there? They practice Hinduism. They're Hindus. What's the difference?" His wife remarked, "In a lot of ways, I feel we should be grateful to them. I mean here they are, Americans, working to bring our culture here."

Every summer in Denver and Boston and in many other American cities, Krishna devotees celebrate their annual Chariot Festival, or Ratha Yatra. They bring the saucer-eyed images of Lord Krishna, his brother Balarama, and his sister Subhadra out of the temple and place them on a large chariot, or *ratha,* which they pull through the streets of the city on a pilgrimage among the people, a *yatra.* These public processions of the gods are common throughout India. They bear some resemblance to the festival processions of St. Anthony, the Virgin Mary, or Jesus through the streets in Italian or Portuguese Catholic cultures. For Hindus, this is a time when the movement of people to temple is reversed, and the deity leaves the temple to greet them in the streets. Among India's most famous festivals of this sort is the Ratha Yatra of Lord Krishna at the seaside temple of Jagannatha in Puri in the eastern state of Orissa. There the image of Krishna is seated on a chariot with wheels some ten feet high. As devotees lean into the ropes, the wheels begin to roll with the inexorable momentum that gives us the word *juggernaut.* It is this festive procession, albeit with a smaller and more easily controlled chariot, that is repeated in America's Festival of the Chariots. In Boston they pull the tall brightly decorated chariot up Beacon Hill, past the State House, and around Boston Common; in New York they pull Krishna's chariot down Fifth Avenue; and in Los Angeles they treat Krishna to a trip along Venice

Beach. In the Hindu view, not only do the passersby have the opportunity to view Lord Krishna, but the Lord has the opportunity to behold the people and the urban landscape of the United States.

In the 1970s and early 1980s many Americans would have equated the Hare Krishnas with Hinduism in America. Most of us did not notice the gradual religious changes that were percolating with the new immigration. By the late 1980s, however, those who had worried about whether a few youngsters would don orange robes and worship Krishna suddenly found that their surgeon or anesthesiologist was now a Hindu, settled in the suburbs, and perhaps a worshiper of Krishna himself. Those who had worried about the brainwashing of devotees who chanted the name of Krishna now had to contend with psychiatrists of Indian origin who had known this devotional chanting from childhood and could not be enlisted in the anticult hysteria. For these new immigrants, chanting Hare Krishna was as familiar as the strains of Ravi Shankar's sitar.

GANESHA AT THE GATES

At the time of the 1970 census, six thousand Indian immigrants had settled in New York City. By 1990 the number had grown to ninety-four thousand and the 2000 census will expand this number considerably.[21] In Flushing, Queens, stands the first temple Hindus built in the U.S. from the ground up, the great Hindu temple formally called the Sri Maha Vallabha Ganapati Devasthanam. The temple is dedicated to Lord Ganesha, also known as Ganapati, the portly, elephant-headed god who sits above the doorway of homes and temples as the remover of obstacles and the lord of new beginnings. As the temple brochure puts it, "Everything in Hinduism begins with the worship of Ganesha." So it is fitting that this temple is dedicated to him.

It would be safe to say that all Hindus love Ganesha. They make a place for him in their home shrines and at the doorways of their temples, where he guards the threshold into sacred space. They worship Ganesha at the beginning of every ritual, at the outset of every wedding, at the launching of a business deal, at the outset of a journey, or on the first day of the school year. Why does he have an elephant head? According to one version of the story in Hindu mythology, Ganesha was created by the goddess Parvati from her own body and set to guard her doorway as she bathed. When Lord Shiva, her divine husband, came home and demanded entry, Ganesha obediently and bravely refused. A terrific battled ensued, and Ganesha lost his head. When Parvati saw what had happened, she was distraught, and Shiva, chagrined. He set off to replace the boy's head with another. The first candidate he found for this emergency surgery was an elephant, and so it is that Ganesha has the head of an elephant.

Like every temple in India, the Queens temple has a founding story. One of the men responsible for the project, Dr. Alagappa Alagappan, reports that he had a vision. The astral form of an ancient Indian sage named Agastya told Alagappan that Lord Ganesha would take up residence in the city of New York. The temple of Ganesha would become a bridge between India and America, bringing scholars, priests, artists, and musicians to the U.S. and initiating a movement of temple building on the American continent. There was one final, intriguing point to the vision: Agastya told him that one day in the distant future, when the waters rise up to Ganesha's waist, Ganesha would save New York City from a great disaster. This, of course, remains to be seen.

With this commission, Dr. Alagappan organized and formally established the Hindu Temple Society of North America on January 26, 1970, India's Republic Day. More than seven years of hard work later, America's first Ganesha Temple was dedicated on July 4, 1977, America's Independence Day. A bridge in time was created between the two great independent democracies, and every year the Ganesha temple community celebrates its founding day on the Fourth of July. It is fitting that the image of Ganesha was one of the first to be duly consecrated in the U.S. and to be placed at the eastern gateway of America in New York City.

The Ganesha Temple has now become an important hub for the Hindu communities of the Northeast. The annual Ganesha Chaturthi—the celebration of Ganesha's birthday in late August or early September—is now a tradition in Flushing. During the nine-day festival more than ten thousand people come to the temple. Their rituals eloquently express their love for Ganesha. They donate 108 conch shells, they recite 100,000 mantras of Ganesha, and they decorate the great granite image of Ganesha in the central sanctum of the temple with flowers, sandal paste, and pearls. For the children, there is a children's *puja* in which the temple's youngsters sit in the sanctuary with plates of offerings before them. They learn how to proffer the flowers, lights, water, and incense to Lord Ganesha.

The highlight of the festival is the Ratha Yatra, when the processional image of Ganesha, a portable duplicate of the great granite image in the temple, is taken out of the temple for a chariot pilgrimage through the streets. The people place Ganesha on the chariot, decorated to be a portable temple, and pull the chariot through the streets of Flushing. Musicians take the lead, playing the reedy instrument called the *nada-swaram*. Devotees by the hundreds lend a hand to pull the Lord's chariot by its long ropes. There is dancing and chanting, the singing of devotional *bhajans,* all along the parade route. "It's difficult to believe we're not in India!" exclaim participants. Yet for the children who skip along with the procession in excitement, this festival has no association with India but is squarely a part of the America they know.

On this same festival day across the continent on San Francisco Bay is another famous Ganesha procession. Many new American Hindus who have come from Gujarat and Maharashtra in western India used to celebrate Ganesha Chaturthi back home by honoring temporary, finely made clay images of Ganesha in their homes and neighborhoods. At the end of this time, the clay images are returned to a body of water—the sea or a river—which is the proper way to dispose of an image that has once been the temporary focus of worship. Back home in India at the conclusion of Ganesha Chaturthi, there are great processions in which worshipers bring hundreds of images of Ganesha from neighborhood and temple shrines to the seacoast for the rite of immersion, called *visarjana.* In 1991 Hindus from all over the San Francisco Bay area launched this tradition in America. Gathering at the Baker Beach parking lot, they formed a parade with their painted clay images of Ganesha, carrying them to an artillery site in the old Presidio that they had converted into a temple for the occasion. They broke coconuts at the feet of Ganesha and then immersed the images—all biodegradable—in San Francisco Bay. For the first time in history, the mayor of San Francisco issued a proclamation declaring the date, September 22, 1991, Golden Gate Ganesha Visarjana Day. The reporter from *India Abroad* wrote, "It is believed to be the first time that a mayor of a city in the United States has honored the Hindu deity."[22]

Ganesha is found in almost every American Hindu temple, and in some temples he is the central deity. When the diverse Hindu community of Nashville set out to build a temple in the western suburbs of the city, it took a vote as to which deity should occupy the central sanctum. It was a truly American solution to the inevitably difficult problem of negotiating so many Hindu differences in the creation of a single house of worship. Ganesha won by a landslide, and today he presides in the elegant marble sanctuary of the temple, balancing a row of Shaiva shrines on one side of the hall and Vaishnava shrines on the other. When I first visited the temple in 1995, a warm and articulate woman from the temple community accompanied me and explained to me what she no doubt says to the temple's countless visitors, from schoolchildren to elder-hostel tourists: "Ganesha is the aspect of the Supreme Being responsible for the removal of obstacles, both in a practical sense and in a spiritual sense. On the spiritual path, our obstacles might be our weaknesses or our ego. When we pray to Ganesha, we ask him to help remove those obstacles within the self." She told the story of Shiva and Parvati and the elephant's head but then went on, "But for me, I think that when Hindus long ago imagined the divine form who would remove obstacles from the path, it is natural that they saw the mighty elephant as such a form." She has clearly developed a symbolic, spiritualized explanation of the gods and myths of India, which makes an effort to bridge the gap of culture and tradition separating the temple life of Hindu immigrants from the suburban life of their American neighbors.

The immense interpretive task that falls to Hindus in America cannot be underestimated. The introduction of Hindu temple culture in late-twentieth-century America is comparable in importance to the introduction of Hindu ideas by Swami Vivekananda in the late nineteenth century—but very different. A century ago the seeds of Vedanta and Yoga, which have always claimed a universal applicability, were transplanted and grew to have a wide appeal in the American context. But today we are seeing the transplanting of a more particular idiom of Hindu worship, liturgy, art, and symbol, hitherto rooted primarily in the cultural soil of India and the places of the Hindu diaspora—in East Africa, Trinidad, Malaysia, and Fiji. The first fruits of this transplanting are America's new Hindu temples—with their finely proportioned architecture, their intricate ornamentation, their exquisitely rendered images of the gods, and the elaborate ritual culture of Hinduism. Americans now encounter, not just the ideas of Hindu philosophy, but the many gods of the Hindu kaleidoscope and the prolific ritual and artistic expression of Hindu life.

LORD OF THE MEETING RIVERS: PILGRIMAGE TO PITTSBURGH

India is a land of pilgrimage, where every village and hilltop has its story and every story its location somewhere in the sacred geography of the land. Visiting these sacred places, called *tirthas,* literally, "crossing places," is one of the most dynamic forms of religious life in Hindu India. These *tirthas* are spiritual crossings where the river of this earthly life may be safely forded to the far shore of immortality. If we were to imagine *tirthas* in America, most of us would probably not think first of Pittsburgh, but in the late twentieth century it became one of America's premier places of Hindu pilgrimage.

Pilgrims to America from the very beginning have brought the places of their homeland with them. Plymouth and Boston, Cambridge and Salem, New York and New Orleans—all were place-names of the old world transcribed in the new. And, of course, for the Native peoples of America, the landscape has always been linked to their spiritual lives, from the Black Hills of South Dakota, sacred to the Lakota Sioux as the Paha Sapa, to the Medicine Wheel sites of the Plains Indians in the Bighorn Mountains of Montana, to the Kootenai Falls, sacred to the Kootenai Indians in western Montana. Like European immigrants, Hindus have brought the places of home to their new homes in America. But Hindu immigrants to America also share something of the strong Native American sensitivity to the inherent sacredness of the natural world. The places of India are charged with religious significance, and Hindus have brought that sense of sacred geography to America.

For instance, in Pittsburgh, the Allegheny, Ohio, and Monongahela Rivers join together, the confluence of rivers Hindus call a *sangam*. The most famous *sangam* in India is the juncture of the Ganga, Yamuna, and Sarasvati Rivers at the ancient pilgrimage place known as Prayag, the modern Allahabad, where pilgrims come from all over India to bathe. Pittsburgh's *sangam* is not so holy, and there are no bathing rites in these waters, but the symbolism is important. An Indian American who had lived in Pittsburgh for over twenty years put it this way in our conversation: "We have come to love Pittsburgh because of these rivers. In India all of our holy places were built on the banks of rivers or at the place where rivers join." Then he laughed a bit and added, "Of course we don't bathe here in the rivers here in Pittsburgh, but the meeting rivers are still a reminder that this is an auspicious place."

The Sri Ventakteswara Temple in Pittsburgh duplicates an important pilgrimage shrine in India—the hilltop temple of Tirupati in southern India where Lord Vishnu dwells as Sri Ventakeswara, known lovingly as Balaji. In Pittsburgh, Hindus also chose a hilltop for their temple. They started to build in the Penn Hills about the same time as the temple builders in New York City. "The environment was supposed to be very carefully selected," said Mrs. Rajshri Gopal, one of the leaders of the Pittsburgh temple, as we sat in her Pittsburgh home. She was eager to talk about how the site was selected. "Most of the ancient temples are on river-banks or seashores or peaks of mountains. A beautiful environment was supposed to have a very beneficial effect on the mind. So we did select a mountain, here in Pennsylvania. When we did the testing for mines, we could not build on the summit, but we built as close to the peak as possible. We built on the slope, and this actually proved later to be an added attraction because the backdrop of the green trees behind the white temple makes it like a gem studded in the emerald hills of Pennsylvania."

When the Sri Ventakeswara Temple first opened in 1977, just a month before the New York temple, it immediately attracted Hindu visitors. For most of the 1980s, more than twenty thousand visitors a year were recorded, coming from all over the country. Today, Hindu pilgrimage traffic in America is more diffuse. The Pittsburgh temple retains a kind of preeminence, but temples dedicated to Sri Venkateswara have also been built in DuPage County, west of Chicago; in the Malibu hills north of Los Angeles; and in Milwaukee.

Vasudha Narayana, a scholar of Hinduism at the University of Florida who is originally from South India, has studied the creation of new ritual forms and new devotional songs (*bhajans*) in the communities of Hindu America. In Pittsburgh, for example, she discovered a temple cassette of *bhajans* that includes one with the refrain, "Victory to Govinda, who lives in America, Govinda who with Radha resides in Penn Hills!"[23] Govinda is one of the names of Krishna, also a name of Sri Venkateswara. Radha, of course, is his beloved. The two are praised here as residents of the Penn Hills.

Indians often transpose and duplicate sacred spaces to make them more available to people far away from the original sites. For example, the city I first studied in India, the sacred city of Varanasi, also called Banaras and known to Hindus as Kashi, is duplicated north, south, east, and west in India. The Kashi of the North is in the Himalayas, and the Kashi of the South in Tamil Nadu. Thus, the fruits of a pilgrimage to a city far off can be claimed in a place much closer at hand. Today, the Kashi I knew so well on the Ganges in India can be found spiritually duplicated in Flint, Michigan, where Lord Shiva is worshiped in the Paschimakasi temple—the "Kashi of the West." And Kashi can also be found in Sebastian, Florida, where the American guru Ma Jaya and her followers have created Kashi Ashram, a community dedicated to service on the banks of their own Ganges River.

Now in America, Hindus are fast developing a whole set of temples and sites that bring to these shores some of the most beloved sacred places of India. The temple of Sri Meenakshi in Houston specifically transports the goddess of the holy city of Madurai in Tamil Nadu to Texas. The Divya Dham temple in Woodside, Queens, has created a replica of a powerful goddess shrine of northwest India, Vaishno Devi, located in a cave on a hilltop near Jammu and attracting hundreds of thousands of pilgrims yearly from across North India. In one corner of the Divya Dham, worshipers climb a set of stairs on an artificial hillock to enter into a cave chamber for the *darshan* of Vaishno Devi.

In rural Pennsylvania, a hand-painted sign points the way to Vraj, a name Hindus readily recognize as the homeland of Lord Krishna south of Delhi. Here, in the countryside near Schyukill Haven, a Krishna devotional movement has created its own Vraj. The stream that runs through the temple property has been named Yamuna, after the holy river that runs through the land of Vraj in India. Another part of Krishna's sacred homeland is duplicated near Austin, Texas, where Hindus have established a large temple complex called Barsana Dham, named for Barsana, the hometown of Radha, Krishna's beloved. As one of the Texas devotees wrote,

> It is not possible for everyone to visit Vraj in India. For many people family and business commitments or economic considerations make travel to India difficult. With the Grace of Shree Swamiji, Barsana Dham has been established in Texas, U.S.A., where the same Divine-love vibrations of Vraj may be experienced by the devotees.[24]

To my mind, the most eclectic pilgrimage temple in the United States is the Shiva-Vishnu temple located in the suburbs of Washington, D.C., in Lanham, Maryland. I have traveled all over South India, visiting the many great temples associated with both the Vaishnava and Shaiva traditions, and the many interior shrines of the Shiva-Vishnu temple in Lanham duplicate them all, reproducing virtually the entire sacred geography of South India from Tirupati to Trivandrum. Shortly before my visit, the pilgrimage to the hilltop called Shabarimalai in Kerala, the home of Lord Ayyappa, had been added to the site. In India, pilgrims visit this temple by undertaking the ascetic discipline of a long foot journey through the forest, chanting, "Swamiye Ayyappa!" as they ascend the steep hill. At the very end of the journey, they climb a set of eighteen sacred steps to the temple. Here in suburban Maryland, the eighteen steps are also replicated, bringing pilgrims to the shrine of America's Ayyappa, chanting, "Swamiye Ayyappa!"

As a native of Montana, I have often marveled on my visits to

Yellowstone Park how we in America have tended to set aside parks, build boardwalks around the geysers, and create lookouts for a vista of a beautiful mountain range or waterfall, whereas Hindus would have constructed wayside shrines or built temples. Our *darshan* is in the form of snapshots, and we come to gaze, or perhaps we come for general spiritual refreshment, but we usually do not come to worship. In Hindu India, on the other hand, the natural beauty of nature is one of many reasons a place may gain spiritual luster. In Hawaii, a temple is being built on a site near the Wailua River on the island of Kauai, where Swami Sivaya Subramuniyaswami had a vision of Shiva. Kauai is a place of spectacular natural beauty that Native Hawaiians called Pihanakalani, "Where Heaven Touches Earth." A natural six-sided crystal, weighing seven hundred pounds, discovered in Arkansas, has been brought to be installed in the San Marga Iraivan Temple there as a rare and healing manifestation of the Shiva *linga*. Tons of granite stones destined for the temple are being carved near Bangalore in a village of some seventy-five craftsmen and their families. In the next few years they will be transported to Kauai, and the temple will be erected at this new site of pilgrimage in Hawaii.

Consecrating temples and divine images with the waters of American rivers has also added to the luster of the land of America. The waters of the Ganges are said to be a liquid form of divine energy, and they purify the waters of the Mississippi or the Hudson with which they are mixed in sacred rites. But these rivers too are beginning to be invoked in ritual prayers, their names recited in the Sanskrit prayers called *sankalpa,* prayers that locate the worshiper in the geographical context where he or she stands.

THE MICHIGAN MARRIAGE OF LORD RAMA

I was in Detroit for Rama Navami, the Hindu holiday celebrating Lord Rama. My Hindu host, Dr. T. K. Venkateswaran, gave me careful directions to the Bharatiya Temple in Troy, a leafy northern suburb of the city. For two days I had been plying the streets of Detroit visiting mosques and Islamic centers. But as I drove into Troy for the Hindu festival, I was in another world, the one created in the aftermath of the terrible Detroit riots of 1968 as urbanites fled to the suburbs. It almost seemed rural, with winding roads lined with trees, long driveways leading to private homes, and only an occasional stoplight. I found the temple and turned off the road toward a wooded hillside.

The Bharatiya Temple is intentionally pan-Hindu. It is not built in either North or South Indian style but is rather a temple of modern design, with only the scalloped arches at the entryway gesturing toward Indian architectural elements. Mr. Venkateswaran greeted me and showed me around. The first thing I noticed was the "mud room." This was the first American temple I had seen, and by now I had seen dozens, where the removal of shoes and coats had been incorporated in the architectural design. The ritual architects from India simply didn't think of it, and temples like the Sri Lakshmi temple in Boston struggled for years with piles of shoes, boots, and coats and nowhere to put them. Here, in a muddy mid-March, I was happy to find a superb cloakroom, with benches to sit on and remove shoes, cubbyholes in which to place them, and hooks for the hanging of coats.

The community was gathering in the temple sanctuary, a large carpeted room with four soaring wooden trusses supporting the roof. Ample windows and skylights brought the natural light of the late afternoon into the sanctuary. A broad raised platform at one end of the room served as the altar area. There was no fixed *sanctum sanctorum* for any of the deities; rather, they could be placed on a central altar table as the occasion required. That day Lord Rama was center stage on the altar, for this was celebrated as the day the Lord Vishnu became manifest on earth in the human incarnation of Rama. While it was a birthday, it was also celebrated as the wedding day of Rama and his bride, Sita, so she too was on the altar next to Rama.

The story of Rama's life is well known in Hindu communities like this one: his miraculous birth as the prince of the kingdom of Ayodhya, his heroic youthful years, his marriage to the princess Sita, their tragic exile from Ayodhya, and their sojourn in the forest. Hindus know by heart how Sita was suddenly kidnapped by the demon Ravana and how the divine monkey Hanuman came to Rama's aid to try to find her. Hanuman, son of Lord Shiva and son of the Wind, became the invaluable accomplice, servant, and devotee of Rama. All this was told in the Sanskrit Ramayana more than two thousand years ago and retold many times in the vernacular languages of India.

As the celebration began, I joined more than three hundred people seated on the carpeted floor in the sanctuary for the Wedding of Rama and Sita, a ritual enactment particularly popular in South India. The priests sat cross-legged next to the small granite images of Rama, who was dressed in a yellow silk dhoti, and of Sita, dressed in a red silk sari and pearls. The two families who were the sponsors of the rite were also seated at the altar. They were, I learned, representing the families of Rama and Sita at their wedding. One of the most auspicious moments of the wedding is called the "Gift of the Daughter" (*kanyadana*), when the bride's father makes the greatest gift of all: his own daughter to the groom's family. Nothing on earth is harder to give away than one's own child, and nothing gives more blessings than this gift. In every Hindu wedding, this is, for me, a moment of dissonance with my own feminist consciousness and a moment of poignant awareness that in Hindu traditions daughters are said to be born for someone else's family. In this Michigan wedding, the priest did something unusual. He asked the whole congregation to join in repeating the words, "I make the gift of my daughter in marriage, *kanyadanam aham karishye.*" Then a member of the groom's family, acting in Rama's behalf, placed a necklace called a *mangala sutra* over the head of Sita. It is a symbolic marker of marriage, like the wedding ring. In many Hindu weddings, the giving of the *mangala sutra* is said to recall this very moment in the wedding of the ideal divine couple, Rama and Sita.

As the wedding concluded, the priest again asked the whole congregation to join in prayer. "Please pray if your daughter or son is of the age to get married," he began. A deep and prayerful silence fell across the hall. "Pray that they will get a good match and will enjoy the blessings of a good marriage." This brief prayer was clearly heartfelt, for these Indian immigrant parents who have chosen to settle in Detroit are uncertain what it will mean for their children and grandchildren. For most, a "good marriage" means to a Hindu young man or woman hailing from their own strata and part of India, but here in the United States, most will be grateful for a good marriage to any young Hindu man or woman. The intermarriage rate among Indian Americans is high. As I sat at Rama and Sita's wedding in Detroit, I could not help thinking of my friends in Pittsburgh and in Louisville, both active in founding temples and both graciously accepting the reality that their own daughters married non-Hindu Americans.

When the wedding was over, the whole congregation adjourned to the adjacent community hall, a large auditorium with a full-fledged stage. We settled into our seats, and the program began—greetings, dance and musical numbers, and an impromptu talk I was asked to give on my research on Hindu temples. The final act was unforgettable. The junior high group of the Hindu Heritage class had written and rehearsed a play called *Hanuman Meets Superman,* which was the hit of the evening's cultural program.

As the play opened, young Arun Mehta came onstage dressed in a fine Hanuman costume, his long monkey tail flowing behind him. Then entered Mohan Kapur as Superman, with the S logo on his chest. A hip teenage gang gathered at the microphone, looking at the two heroes. "What is really the difference between Hanuman and Superman?" one of the boys asked. A girl volunteered, "Hanuman can move with the speed of wind. After all, he is the Son of the Wind. He leapt to the island of Lanka to find Sita. He flew to the Himalayas in the heat of battle to get a mountain of healing herbs for Rama's dying army."

"But Superman can move with speed through the air, too," countered another. "'Faster than a speeding bullet,' you know what they say."

"Well, Hanuman has amazing strength. After all, when he couldn't figure out which healing herbs to pick for Rama, he just picked up the whole mountain of herbs and brought it to Lord Rama."

"But, Superman is awesome too. He leaps tall buildings in a single bound."

Back and forth they went, comparing the heroes. Finally, the youngest in the group, stretched on his tiptoes, barely able to reach the microphone, cried, "Wait! I know one thing Hanuman has that Superman doesn't have! He has Lord Rama in his heart!" And sure enough, Hanuman knelt and tore open his chest to reveal the presence of Rama and Sita in his heart. More than his strength, more than his speed, more than his heroism, it is this—his love for the Lord—that has made Hanuman who he is.

The celebration of Rama Navami came to a close. The divine marriage was completed. The talent show concluded in the auditorium, and the whole community gathered for a supper of rice and curry dishes, mango chutneys and lemon pickles, with water tumblers on every table bearing the insignia of the Detroit Tigers. On this day I had seen a new phase of assimilation. This temple did not maintain the cultural distance that is distinctive of many of America's big South Indian temples, where the Sanskrit liturgies are extensive and the young people too often flee to the parking lots with their Frisbees. Here a new space had been created where Hindu immigrants could experiment with the work of building a new culture. Hindus of all ages were involved, and imaginative, creative bridge building had taken place to link the ritual and mythic world of Hindu India and the suburban world of Detroit, Michigan.

FIRST HOLI IN NEW JERSEY

On Washington Road in Sayreville, New Jersey, just past the Dupont Laboratories and Our Lady of Victory Knights of Columbus Hall, is a temple dedicated to Lord Krishna as the divine child. It is an important stop on our journey, for it gives us a real sense of the intensity of devotion and love that Hindus sum up with the term *bhakti,* which means the love of God. The temple began in anything but an atmosphere of love, however. It was opened in 1994 in a former YMCA building after years of community resistance and a court case. The temple-to-be had been defaced with the words, "Get Out Hindoos! KKK!" But the days of ugliness and contention seemed to be over when I first visited the temple. It was the springtime of 1995, and the old Y had been freshly painted a pale pink. The name Dwarakadish Temple appeared boldly on the signboard. I left my shoes in the rack outside the door and entered a large room with a carpeted floor.

At one end the curtain was drawn before the shrine, and presumably young Krishna was within. Temples in this Hindu community have *darshan,* the viewings of Krishna, six times a day. Devotees will say, "We take *darshan,* and Krishna gives *darshan.*" For them, beholding Krishna is, indeed, a gift, and I recalled the great anticipation of *darshan* in the temples of this community in India and the palpable delight people expressed as the curtain was drawn back for Krishna to be revealed. At the other end of the room sat a cluster of women, chatting in a mixture of Gujarati and English and participating in what they called the *seva,* or "service," of Krishna. One was making a fresh flower garland that Krishna would wear at the next *darshan.* Two other women were sewing, making the tiny clothes that Krishna would wear during *darshan,* especially at the *shringara darshan* in the midmorning, when Krishna is dressed for the day.

Here Krishna is worshiped especially as a child. One of the many tastes of human love Hindus use to describe, by analogy, our love of God is the unconditional love parents have for their children. At Krishna Janmashtami, the festival of Krishna's birth in the late summer, they tell the story of how Krishna was born in the city of Mathura in North India. He was born in prison to his mother, Devaki, and father, Vasudeva, locked up by the wicked King Kamsa when he learned that their child would grow up to conquer Kamsa's kingdom. But when the baby was born, Vasudeva was miraculously able to steal out of prison. The door was unlocked, the guards were asleep, and Vasudeva took baby Krishna through the flooding waters of the Yamuna River to a village on the other side. There he placed him in the foster care of two simple villagers, Nanda and Yashoda, who raised Krishna as their own. The stories of

Krishna found in the Bhagavata Purana tell of his childhood as a mischievous and lovable baby, his boyhood as a hero and companion to his village friends, and his life as the sweetest, most playful, and most passionate lover of the *gopis,* or milkmaids, of Vraj.

Here in Sayreville at the Dwarakadish Temple it is his childhood with Nanda and Yashoda that is especially remembered.[25] "This is Nanda Baba's house," explained one of the women as she stitched away. "When we come to the temple, we say in our hearts that it is going to Nanda Baba's house, where Krishna lived as a child." The bell rang for the 5:15 evening *darshan.* The temple room had begun to fill with people stopping by after work. By the time of the next *darshan* from 6:30 to 7:30, just before Krishna retires to bed, the room would be completely full. The women stood at the altar rail, hands pressed together in a gesture of greeting, honor, and prayer as the curtain was pulled back. "Jai Shri Krishna!" they exclaimed as they received his *darshan.*

The black image has four arms and bears the traditional emblems of Krishna—the club, the conch, the discus.[26] This image of Krishna, now elaborately decked with clothing, garlands, and necklaces, is the permanent, consecrated one. At his feet, however, is a smaller metal image of Krishna as the child, endearingly called Lalji. It is this fully consecrated image that is moved from place to place during the day, duplicating the presence of Krishna in the larger image. In this form Krishna is taken from the altar into the back chamber of the temple at bedtime, is awakened in the morning, is brought once again to the altar for *darshan,* and is moved at special times into the swing next to the altar to enjoy the pleasures of swinging.

The religious feeling, called *bhava,* that is nurtured here is that of the spontaneous, tender love that parents have for their child. For the priests this a full-time job. They wake Krishna and put him to bed, they cook for Krishna, dress him, change his clothes 365 days a year. The priest explained, "The *bhava* I feel is of being both mother and father at once. I often think of myself, in this service, as Krishna's mother, Yashoda." Here in this temple, men and women take the raw materials of human emotion—the instinctual caretaking and loving of parents—and direct them toward God. The women who sit making garlands and sewing tiny clothes would laugh at the suggestion that the Supreme Lord actually needs these offerings, but we human beings need to refine and practice the arts of loving—even with the gods. Krishna's presence in this temple enables his devotees to do just that. "I moved to the U.S. in 1972," said one of the women. "There was no temple then, not really any community. I was so lonely. I used to cry every day. And now all this." She gestured with delight toward the altar and the fine image of Krishna. "Now we have a temple right here. I come every day for at least one *darshan.*"

The springtime festival of Holi is popular in North India where it is celebrated with a Holika bonfire and the revelry of greeting one another with the red powder called *gulal.* For a few days, all social rules seem to be suspended while celebrants greet one another, streaking a smear of red *gulal* across each other's faces. The Holi festival in America is evolving. A few years ago *India Abroad* announced that a Maryland group held its Holi celebration in an Indian café in the mall, the Bihar Cultural Association of Chicago celebrated Holi at a hall in Skokie, and the Hindu Temple of Metropolitan Washington observed a Holi celebration in a local high school. There was even a gala Holi at the Trump Palace in Atlantic City. For the Hindus of Sayreville, New Jersey, however, the first real Holi was in 1995 at the newly completed Dwarakadish Temple. Having been through several jubilant Holi celebrations in India and emerged a multi-colored crimson-haired spectacle, I accepted the invitation to Holi with some trepidation.

A forty-five-minute drive out to Sayreville from Manhattan brought me to an already crowded temple, with the evening *darshan* of Lord Krishna about to begin. Some fifty women were singing the songs of Holi as a drummer kept the beat. A few of them began dancing to the lively rhythm. Suddenly the bright red *gulal* powder appeared. Someone must have pulled a small plastic packet surreptitiously from her pocket. At once a dozen people seemed to have their own supply. One woman seized a fellow dancer by surprise and grazed her face with a streak of bright red. Before long pink puffs of powder hung in the temple air as the worshipers bestowed dots and streaks of *gulal* upon one another. "Jai Shri Krishna! Hail to Lord Krishna!" they cheered. Soon I too was emblazoned with a streak of red. Providentially, the carpets of the large sanctuary had been covered with bright blue plastic tarps. At 6:30 P.M., the bells announced the evening *darshan.* The doors to Krishna's inner sanctum were opened to show Lord Krishna, dressed for the holiday. The Holi play continued, with Krishna as a participant. The priests flung pinches of blue, green, red, and yellow powder on the image of Krishna. Then, in turn, and on

Krishna's behalf, they pitched handfuls of powder into the congregation, where all received it as a blessing.

Behind the temple in the parking lot, the teenagers of the Hindu community, delighted with the celebration and covered with color, had kindled a huge bonfire, called the Holika fire. It is said to burn the symbolic demoness, Holika, who had tried unsuccessfully to destroy young Krishna. The young people careened around the fire, bestowing "Happy Holi!" greetings of red. A swelling crowd of red-faced revelers streamed from the rites inside the temple and joined them, circling the fire in dance and song. For many of these revelers, this was not only the first Holi here in the Dwarakadish Temple, but their first real Holi in America, bonfire and all. The rented halls and temporary dwellings of the community had never been the right place for such a celebration. The fire of Holi also marked a kind of new year, consuming things of the past and starting afresh. That night the bonfire crackled with the popping of grains thrown into it as auguries of a new season of life. Clearly a new season was beginning for the Hindu devotees of Krishna in New Jersey.

I left the celebrations late that night, and as I peeked at myself in the rearview mirror, I realized just what a wild sight I was. My entire face was red, with a few dots of green and blue, and my long hair was a brilliant lion's mane, given body by red powder and the smoke of the fire. I made my way to the New Jersey turnpike and assured the startled keeper of the first toll booth that I was fine. The parking lot attendant in Manhattan where I was staying was completely blasé. I passed dozens of people as I walked toward the place I was staying and greeted the doorman, who seemed unconcerned about my appearance. This was New York, I concluded, and people could clearly take Holi in their stride.

GROWING UP HINDU IN AMERICA

The first time I visited the beautiful temple of Sri Venkateswara, just over the hills from Malibu Beach, I was in the company of several members of my extended family. They were evangelical Christians, and I was not sure how they would respond to a Hindu temple, with its multitude of gods. The temple itself was breathtakingly beautiful, sitting on a hillside in Casabalsas, its white decorated towers rising amid a forest of green, woven with brilliant bougainvillea. We parked and approached the main gate of the temple, and as luck would have it, we arrived in the main sanctuary just as another family was arriving: a Hindu couple with a tiny baby.

The young couple and their small group of family members approached the priest who was officiating at the sanctum of Vishnu, here present as Sri Venkateswara. They presented two plastic bags, bulging with fruit to be offered in the service of worship. As we waited before the sanctum for the *puja* to begin, the young man explained to me that this was the three-week-old baby's first outing. Here, as in India, it is often the custom that the mother and child do not go out or visit in people's homes for a certain period of time after the baby is born. The first real outing of mother and newborn baby is traditionally to the temple, and so they had come that day. Even fifteen years ago, this ritual first journey to the temple would not have been easy, perhaps not even possible, in most American cities.

We stood a few steps behind this family as the *puja* began. As each offering was made—the water, the flowers, the fruit, the oil lamp—it was returned as God's grace to bless the couple and their baby and the rest of us as well. No ritual could have created a more readily accessible bridge to Hindu life for my family members. They beamed with delight at the blessing of this newborn and felt honored to be witnesses of this event. When the fruits were returned, blessed by Vishnu, they did not hesitate to receive the bananas and apples, which now seemed to link our family and theirs. There were many things they found perplexing and alien as we continued our tour of the temple, but this ritual blessing had established a common ground of humanity that set everything else in perspective.

Rites of passage in the Hindu tradition are called *samskaras,* those rites that shape and perfect human life. They begin with prenatal rites, then rites of birth and childhood, such as the name giving we saw in Livermore. There are rites that accompany the first outing, as we saw in the Malibu hills, rites that accompany the child's first solid food and the first learning of the alphabet, and so on. Among the most important, for boys, is the *upanayana,* in which a young boy in his early teens is brought to a guru or teacher to begin his religious education. He receives the sacred thread worn by men of the three upper castes in traditional India and receives the mantras and instruction that will guide him in a life of sacred learning.

I attended the *upanayana* of two young cousins, Tejas and Shridhar, one Sunday morning in Bridgewater, New Jersey. It took place not in the temple sanctuary but in the large adjoining auditorium. There more than two hundred family and friends gathered to witness this rite of passage, as they might gather at a nearby synagogue for a bar or bat mitzvah. The event began with a meal, which the boys shared with their mothers, in former times marking the last such meal they would share with the women of the household. In the long series of rites that followed, the boys signified their readiness for what lay ahead by standing on a stone slab, symbolic of the firmness of resolve that must accompany a life of learning. Each received the sacred thread, a white three-stranded cord that was tied by the father and the guru around the boy's chest, over the right shoulder, and under the left arm. They will wear this sacred thread for the rest of their lives. Toward the end of the ceremony, the whole assembled family was called to attention for the Brahmopadesha, the receiving of the sacred teachings. The teaching took place under the cover of a white silk cloth, a kind of womb of rebirth, where the guru, the father, and the mother gave the initiate the mantra that marks his spiritual adulthood. This is the Gayatri mantra, said to symbolize the wisdom of the whole tradition.

I found the ritual symmetry of the rite moving. The initiates began the morning as boys, fed by their mothers, and ended the morning as new students of sacred wisdom, symbolically setting off from home. As such, they had to learn to beg for alms. Holding their alms dishes, the boys practiced by trying it out for the first time on the most likely donors—their own mothers, who responded generously with rice and sweets. At the conclusion, everyone in the assembly blessed the boys by throwing upon them handfuls of yellow flower petals and rice grains.

In America today, the temple is the locus of many life-cycle rites, even those that might normally be performed at home in the Indian context. And today American temples are inventively creating the kind of temple life that will enable young people, like Tejas and Shridhar, to grow up in a temple, with the attendant forms of education and rites of passage. In India, with its multitude of temples and its more assimilative environment for learning Hindu practice and traditions, there is little precedent for the deliberate forms of temple life that have begun to take root in the U.S. Hindu temples here are evolving dozens of new forms to meet the challenges of a new society. Traditional rites of passage may be supplemented with new ritual forms, such as Graduation Puja for high school seniors or Mother's Day Puja for children to honor their mothers on Mother's Day.

New forms of Hindu instruction are also coming into being in the U.S., and with them new and more systematic formulations of Hinduism. At the Hindu Temple Society of Greater Chicago in Lemont, Illinois, the youth program called "In the Wings" brings young people together for weekend classes and summer camps to enjoy one another's company and learn about their tradition. In Boston, the Shishu Bharati School brings

Hindu children and their families together at an elementary school each Sunday for classes. Hindu Heritage classes abound in temples all over the country, some with makeshift curricula and others using materials that are being explicitly produced to teach Hinduism in the West. For example, Swami Dayananda and his staff at the Arsha Vidya Gurukula retreat center in Pennsylvania have developed a Vedic Heritage curriculum—with both student workbooks and teacher's guides. The Saiva Siddhanta curriculum of the Himalayan Institute, based in Hawaii and California, has modeled its study around the family home-study programs of the Mormons, complete with discussion questions and multiple-choice test questions. What is fascinating about these developments is the attempt to systematize and codify a tradition that for over three thousand years has proliferated into so many forms as to defy simplification. What is being worked out, in the American context, is not so much the reclaiming of ancient traditions but the creation of a new emergent form of Hinduism.

While the first generation of Hindu immigrants has learned to negotiate a new American identity through the process of community formation and temple building, the second generation faces new challenges, among them to identify what parts of the Hindu tradition they will claim for themselves and what parts they will let go. The American-born baby presented for blessings at the temple, surrounded by Indian-born parents and family members, will likely grow up in Los Angeles and attend grade school and high school there. Boys like Tejas and Sridhar will finish high school and go off to college. Their lives will be lived in the complex American contexts of race, religion, culture, and politics. At every step of the way, these youngsters will be weaving a new pattern of Hindu life that will include the traditionally Hindu, the overwhelmingly American, and their own wholly new creations.

A photo album of America's second-generation Hindus will include snapshots of traditional rites, like the hundreds of photos taken at the *upanayana* of Tejas and Sridhar. It will also include new images that may puzzle those back home in India. The high school youth group at the Hindu Temple in Minneapolis poses in the snow on their ski trip. A few months later they stand in the temple in cap and gown for their Graduation Puja. In Boston, the youth group strides along a parkway, participating in the Walk for Hunger. In Michigan, a chapter of the Hindu Students Council stands with garbage bags beside the section of the public highway they have signed up to maintain. The photo album also includes many images of summer camps. At the Pittsburgh temple camp at Slippery Rock Community College, the junior high group strikes a pose from the play of the Ramayana they are producing. At the Chinmaya Mission camp in North Andover, Massachusetts, campers paint T-shirts with images of Ganesha. At a Hindu Students Council camp in New Jersey, college students sing *bhajans* around a campfire. And there will be photos of marriages. A young man from a Vermont Protestant background rides a white horse up the hill to the Pittsburgh temple, where he will marry a Hindu woman at the sacred fire-altar. The next week, a young Hindu woman from Pittsburgh poses with her groom at a white Protestant church in Vermont. These photos will find their way into family albums in both India and America. Some will be displayed on Web sites and printed in temple newsletters. What they present to us is a complex picture of the multitude of ways in which new moments of cultural creation have taken place.

ONE HUNDRED YEARS LATER . . .

Pulling off Highway 101, which winds through the Poconos into Saylorsburg, Pennsylvania, I found a Sunday flea market set up in a large field. Booths had been set up selling blue bottles, canoe paddles, lamps, quilts, used books, and Confederate flags. But across the road, in a grove of tall pines, was the place I was looking for, Arsha Vidya Gurukulam, "Wisdom of the Sages School," roughly translated, where a week-long Hindu family camp was getting under way. The flea-market folks were going about their business unaware of what was happening on the margins of their Sunday encampment, just as most Americans are unaware of the new life on the margins of a familiar culture. What was happening across the road is typical of the new life that is changing America forever.

Just a hundred feet from the road under the pines was a cluster of summer cabins and an open meadow where American-born Hindu teenagers were throwing a football. A beautiful new Hindu temple was secluded in the pines, with attached kitchen and dining hall to accommodate campers. Here the negotiation of old and new, Indian and American, first- and second-generation, was in full swing.

I arrived just in time for the opening session. A Hindu swami in traditional orange robes was speaking to a group of summer campers on the subject of *viveka*, "discrimination," in Hindu philosophy. The temple room where we were all seated was a peaceful space, the high arched ceiling supported with wooden trusses, with floor-to-ceiling windows along the walls. The whole room was covered with soft blue carpeting and spread with floor cushions and backrests for the small congregation of forty or so who had gathered. They were middle-aged men and women, with pullover sweaters and reading glasses. For many of the professionals among them, this week of Vedanta in the Poconos *was* their summer vacation. They opened their loose-leaf texts, containing the text of the *Tattva Viveka* in Sanskrit and English. They begin with a prayer for under-standing:

> Om. May He indeed protect both of us. May He nourish both of us. May we together acquire the capacity to study and to under-stand. May our study be brilliant. May we not disagree with each other. Om, peace, peace, peace.

I found that Arsha Vidya holds frequent family camps—at Thanks-giving, at Christmas, and over the Fourth of July weekend, creating a Hindu context for the great days of the American calendar. Youth camps for high school and college students take place in summer, and for adults there are Vedanta camps to study a particular text and stress-management camps for busy professionals. This camp is but one knot in a web of new sites where American Hindu life is now being created all across the coun-try, and perhaps it is a good place to conclude our own journey.

More than one hundred years after Swami Vivekananda planted the seeds of Vedanta in American cities, the Hindu tradition has truly taken root in America—and in ways Vivekananda could not have imagined. Were he to return to the U.S. today, Vivekananda would be pleased to find these Indian professionals studying Vedanta under the pines in Pennsylvania, and he would recognize the forms of their study and prac-tice. But traveling across America today, he would be astonished at the array of Hindu life he would find here. He would find Bengalis from his own part of India gathering for summer picnics in Boston and Telugu speakers from the South gathering for summer conventions. He would find practitioners of Indian Ayurvedic medicine in Seattle and yoga classes in hundreds of health clubs. He would find a temple youth choir learning Sanskrit chants and Hindi devotional songs in suburban Maryland and a group of zealous devotees singing the Hindi Ramayana straight through in Chicago. He would see the procession of Lord Ganesha through the streets of New York and the celebration of Krishna's birthday in a huge convention center in Houston. Were he to return to Harvard, where he lectured in the 1890s, he would find students crowding into a gaily decorated dorm room for the celebration of the Diwali Festival of Lights, he would hear the chanting of the Rig Veda at the baccalaureate of the senior class, and he would wonder, as we do, how these young people, destined for American life in public service, medicine, and science, will carry their tradition with them in the years ahead. A new and somehow American Hinduism is coming into being.

NOTES

1. Cited in Arthur Versluis, *American Transcendentalism and Asian Religions* (New York: Oxford University Press, 1993), 52.

2. Edward Waldo Emerson and Waldo Emerson Forbes, eds., *Journals of Ralph Waldo Emerson* (Boston: Houghton Mifflin, 1909–14), 7:11.

3. Cited in Versluis, *American Transcendentalism,* 57, 66.

4. J. W. Krutch, ed., *Thoreau: Walden and Other Writings* (New York: Bantam, 1962), 324–25.

5. Alan Hodder, "Ex Oriente Lux: Thoreau's Ecstasies and the Hindu Texts," *Harvard Theological Review* 86:4 (Spring 1994), 437.

6. Richard Hughes Seager, ed., *The Dawn of Religious Pluralism: Voices from the World's Parliament of Religions, 1893* (LaSalle, IL: Open Court, 1993), 431.

7. Seager, ed., *Religious Pluralism,* 430–31.

8. Mary Louise Burke, *Swami Vivekananda in America: New Discoveries* (Calcutta: Advaita Ashram, 1966), 67.

9. *Portsmouth Daily Chronicle,* July 31, 1894, quoted in Elva Nelson, *A Bird's Eye View: Vivekananda and His Swamis in Boston and Vicinity* (Boston: Ramakrishna Vedanta Society, 1992), 49.

10. Swami Vivekananda, *Address on Vedanta Philosophy by Swami Vivekananda: The Ideal of a Universal Religion* (New York: Vedanta Society, 1896).

11. As Swami Prabhavananda put it in introducing yoga in Los Angeles many years later, "Religion is, in fact, a severely practical and empirical kind of research. You take nothing on trust. You accept nothing but your own experience." Carl Jackson, *Vedanta for the West* (Bloomington: Indiana University Press, 1994), 75.

12. Wendell Thomas, *Hinduism Invades America* (New York: Beacon Press, 1930), 106–7.

13. Yogananda, "Yoga: The Science of Religion," *Self-Realization* 64, no. 2 (Spring 1993), 9.

14. Yogananda, *Scientific Healing Affirmations* (Los Angeles: Self-Realization Fellowship, 1985), 81–82.

15. *Self-Realization,* vol. 64, No. 1, Winter 1992, 44–49.

16. Swami Muktananda, "What Is a True Guru?" *Meditate* 1, no. 4 (Spring 1979).

17. Krishnamurti's speech, "Truth Is a Pathless Land," can most easily be found on the Web site of the Krishnamurti Foundation of America: www.kfa.org/truth.html.

18. Krishnamurti, "Truth."

19. Hayagriva, *Back to Godhead,* no. 26 (1969), 28.

20. Allen Ginsberg, *Back to Godhead,* no. 28 (1970), 4.

21. *New York Times,* June 11, 1991.

22. *India Abroad,* September 6, 1991.

23. Vasudha Narayanan, "Victory to Govinda Who Lives in America!" (unpublished paper, University of Florida, n.d.).

24. Sushree Meera Devi, Barsana Dham, 1994.

25. The Dwarakadish Temple is named for the particular form of Krishna who is honored as the divine child in the hills of Rajasthan at the Pushti Marga temple in Kankroli.

26. These, of course, are also seen as the emblems of Vishnu or of any form of Vishnu. For the Pushti Margis, however, Krishna is the Supreme Lord.

CHAPTER FOUR

AMERICAN BUDDHISTS: ENLIGHTENMENT AND ENCOUNTER

★

The Buddha's Birthday is celebrated for weeks on end in Los Angeles. More than three hundred Buddhist temples sit in this great city facing the Pacific, and every weekend for most of the month of May the Buddha's Birthday is observed somewhere, by some group—the Vietnamese at a community college in Orange County, the Japanese at their temples in central Los Angeles, the pan-Buddhist Sangha Council at a Korean temple in downtown L.A. My introduction to the Buddha's Birthday observance was at Hsi Lai Temple in Hacienda Heights, just east of Los Angeles. It is said to be the largest Buddhist temple in the Western hemisphere, built by Chinese Buddhists hailing originally from Taiwan and advocating a progressive Humanistic Buddhism dedicated to the positive transformation of the world. In an upscale Los Angeles suburb with its malls, doughnut shops, and gas stations, I was about to pull over and ask for directions when the road curved up a hill, and suddenly there it was— an opulent red and gold cluster of sloping tile rooftops like a radiant vision from another world, completely dominating the vista. The ornamental gateway read "International Buddhist Progress Society," the name under which the temple is incorporated, and I gazed up in amazement. This was in 1991, and I had never seen anything like it in America.

The entrance took me first into the Bodhisattva Hall of gilded images and rich lacquerwork, where five of the great bodhisattvas of the Mahayana Buddhist tradition receive the prayers of the faithful. The bodhisattvas are the enlightened and compassionate beings who come to the threshold of nirvana or enlightenment and yet choose to remain in the world of birth and death to help others along the path. Among them I recognized the popular Kuan Yin, carrying a branch of willow and a vessel, often approached for the blessings of health and beneficence. I moved with the stream of Chinese families into the huge open-air field-stone courtyard that is the center of the temple and monastery complex. It was brilliantly alive with hundreds of people dressed in their festive best. Across the courtyard was the broad staircase leading up to the main Buddha Hall. For the occasion of the Buddha's Birthday and the afternoon garden party that was to accompany the celebration, a dozen American flags were posted on either side of the staircase, snapping in the blue May morning. I climbed the stairs, turning every few steps to view the scene. Ten minutes ago I had been driving down Main Street, U.S.A., and now my vision of America was in radical transformation.

In the Buddha Hall, more than four hundred people were on their knees on red cushioned kneelers. The room was resonant with chanting. In the front rows were the many black-robed nuns who are the backbone of Hsi Lai and behind them the multicolored multitude of Chinese families. The whole hall was standing, bowing, kneeling. Gongs resounded, bells tinkled. I took a seat along a side bench and began to absorb the magnificence of this great Buddha Hall.[1]

On the high altar were three large, seated, golden Buddhas. In the center was Shakyamuni, the historical Buddha, whose birthday was being observed today. He was born a prince, Siddhartha Gautama, in the foothills of the Himalayas. Despite the comfort of his palace life, he was disturbed by the suffering of sickness, old age, and death and set out from the palace to find the cause of suffering and the path to freedom from suffering. To one side sat Amitabha or Amida, the Buddha of Infinite Light, who attained enlightenment and vowed to create a Pure Land where people may be reborn and attain peace. On the other side sat the Medicine Buddha, whose vows on behalf of humanity included the healing of body and mind. The walls of the great hall were covered with thousands of small Buddhas, each lit by a tiny light and bearing the name of a donor. In the Mahayana tradition of East Asia it becomes clear that the awakened mind of enlightenment cannot be limited to one historical Buddha but is potentially infinite.

In front of me, a four-year-old girl with a ponytail knelt beside her mother, watching her carefully, peeking up to her side to see if she had done it right. Bowing, her mother turned her palms upward as if to receive blessings from above. Now, the child was turning her tiny palms upward too, learning the forms of prayer that come with centuries of tradition. To me, and perhaps to this child, the whole universe seemed filled with the rolling rhythm of chanting and the movement of hundreds of people at prayer. Here, as in so much of the Buddhist tradition, it is not silence but chanting that brings the heart and mind to stillness.

As the chanting subsided, I heard a woman's voice on the loudspeaker announcing the significance of this occasion. "Two thousand five hundred thirty-five years ago the Buddha was born in the Lumbini Garden in present-day Nepal. The Buddha is like a lamp in this world of suffering, shining the way for us. Today we have a special ceremony in which we symbolically bathe the image of the Baby Buddha. In bathing the Baby Buddha, we also purify defilements such as greed and anger that are within ourselves." As she spoke, people began to rise and line up for this simple ceremony. I fell in line with the mother and her ponytailed daughter. They were from a nearby suburb that is now more than half Chinese. It was her first Buddha's Birthday, in fact her first time at the temple. The announcer continued, "The pure nature of the Buddha is innate in us all. It is covered up with these defilements. We need to clean off the dirt so that we can shine. When the sun is covered by clouds, we are unable to see the sun shining. So when we bathe the Buddha, keep in mind that what we want to purify is our own defilements, so that our pure nature can shine." She concluded, "If you would like to transfer the merits of this act to others, you are invited to do so." This is the Buddhist practice of engaging in an act of faith or charity, all the while asking that the credit for the action be put on someone else's account.

Near the door of the Buddha Hall, a small standing image of Baby Buddha with his right hand lifted heavenward was set in a basin inside a beautiful flower-decked pagoda. According to the accounts of miracles that attended the Buddha's birth, the child was born standing up, and at his birth the heavens burst forth with a shower of flowers. Each person approached the Baby Buddha, bowed, and took one of the long-handled bamboo ladles to scoop up the liquid from the basin and pour it over the infant's shoulders. The woman next to me told me it was sweetened tea, and indeed I could see that the same liquid was being handed out in cups for all to sip. I helped lift her four-year-old high enough to grasp the bamboo ladle for herself and pour her sweet offering over the Baby Buddha. As I held her up, my mind was a rush of thoughts. I wondered what the Buddha would mean to the girl as she becomes part of the energetic, homogenizing, diversifying combustion of American culture. I wondered if this place and the tradition it embodies would become important parts of her life, if she would come here for classes or meditation, if she would become involved as a young adult and seek the advice of the nuns, or if she would come to the temple only to observe the death of an uncle, a grandfather, or her mother. Or she might espouse secular values and never return at all. As I took the bamboo ladle myself, I quietly prayed to transfer whatever merit I might gain from this offering to her.

Hsi Lai means "Coming to the West," meaning the journey of Buddhism to America. Of course, from the standpoint of Asia, Buddhism has moved steadily eastward from India through Central Asia, to China, Japan, and Korea, and now across the Pacific to America. But in the global scope of things, America is still seen as the "West." This temple was built by and is linked to a mountaintop temple-monastic complex in Taiwan called Fo Kuang Shan, the center of the Humanistic Buddhist movement guided by its founder, Master Hsing Yün. The temple here sits on fourteen acres, the building complex alone being over one hundred thousand square feet and costing some thirty million dollars. It has a membership of more than twenty thousand, drawn largely from the Chinese immigrant community from Taiwan, making it on a scale with the largest of America's new megachurches. Surveying the whole from the top of the grand staircase, I looked down on the courtyard surrounded by a large compound of monastic residences housing nearly one hundred monastics, mostly nuns. Across the court were a conference center with an auditorium and facilities for simultaneous translation; a museum of Buddhist ritual and visual arts; and a library of some fifty thousand volumes. At the periphery of the building was an impressive bookstore of Buddhist books in English and Chinese, cassettes, prayer beads, incense, and images; and beneath us was a large cafeteria specializing in vegetarian food.

The very existence of this temple is a tremendous achievement. While my new ponytailed friend will take for granted a landscape that includes Hsi Lai and other spectacular Chinese Buddhist temples, this was not part of the religious landscape of California even twenty years ago. It took some five years to gain the zoning clearances to build here. Townspeople were stunned by the news that a large Chinese temple would be built on the hillside, and they turned up in droves at zoning meetings determined to thwart the project. Dozens of meetings took place, both public and private, with promises and compromises on all sides. Finally, the cornerstone was laid in 1986, and by the end of 1989 the building was dedicated—on Thanksgiving Day. Still, it took time to win a place as citizens in Hacienda Heights. The next year a float created by the temple for the Fourth of July parade was met with boos and heckling along the parade route. After that, the temple began a series of initiatives to build bridges with these new neighbors—food baskets for the needy on Thanksgiving and Christmas, invitations to the whole community to come to dinner at the temple in the days preceding big events like the Buddha's Birthday or Chinese New Year. The temple also invited outside groups to use its conference room facilities, and community groups took them up on it. The outreach seems to have been a success. By 1991 five hundred people from the community accepted the invitation to the Chinese New Year community banquet.[2]

The Buddha's Birthday was a day for the family. Multicolored helium balloons floated aloft bearing the temple's insignia; at food stalls around the courtyard tickets could be exchanged for spring rolls, fried rice, shrimp, and delicacies. In the reception room, individuals and families consulted with nuns regarding questions from their daily lives. I spent the day eating and talking. From Venerable I-Han I got a glimpse of the strength and grit of the nuns who had been virtually at the helm of this multimillion dollar construction project. From Venerable Yun-Kai I heard about the outreach programs of the temple—teaching meditation at a hospital drug dependency center, visiting inmates at the Terminal Island Penitentiary, conducting weekend classes for children, arranging meditation retreats for non-Chinese seekers.

The Venerable Man-Ya explained to me the vision of Master Hsing Yün's Humanistic Buddhism. "It revolves around the needs of people," she said. "He speaks of building the Pure Land on earth, not simply looking beyond this life to Amitabha's heavenly Pure Land." She explained that many Chinese people expect Buddhism will be important to them only at the time of someone's death, when they will call monks or nuns to chant and when they will come to the temple for special rites. But Master Hsing Yün insists that the Buddha's teachings are concerned with the living, not just the dead. The ebullience of this temple seems a confirmation of that vision. Man-Ya sat at a table just outside the Buddha Hall, and as we talked she signed people up for the Three Refuges ceremony. Participants would affirm their faith in the three great "treasures," by taking refuge in the Buddha, the Dharma, and the Sangha—the teacher, the teachings, and the community of Buddhists. Taking refuge in these three treasures is the formal act of affirming one's participation in the Buddhist tradition, and the list for the afternoon ceremony was many pages long.

By the end of the day, I had begun to realize that the serious social vision of Buddhist Humanism was combined here at Hsi Lai with the sheer happiness of having created a landmark center for the Chinese Buddhist community in America. The community was justly proud of this place, but learning the ropes of participation in American life would pose some difficulties.

Five years later, Hsi Lai became the focal point of a presidential campaign finance controversy when Vice President Al Gore visited the temple in the 1996 election campaign. Was it a civic luncheon that he attended or a fund-raiser? In October of 1996 the story began to break. As a *Washington Post* writer put it, "With its pagoda-style ochre roofs and red-pillared Hall of the Buddha and robed monks wandering piously through Oriental gardens, the Hsi Lai Temple seems more like an island of spiritual tranquility in this bustling Los Angeles suburb than the focal point of a growing controversy over questionable big-money contributions to a presidential reelection campaign."[3] But controversy there was, and the temple that had reached out to become involved in civic life was now at the center of a public dispute. It was alleged that the event was a fund-raiser, in which case it was illegal for a tax-exempt religious institution. Distressed members of the lay temple community responded to the controversy with a statement expressing their "sadness" at the allegations. "For years, Hsi Lai Temple has been our second home and we have an intimate understanding of the temple's operations." They characterized the event as a "civic luncheon" and recalled how the vice president spoke movingly about learning from one another, respecting one another's traditions, and cooperating "to offer the best resources of our minds and hearts to the United States."[4] The vice president's speech there had praised the practice of placing one's palms together as a gesture of greeting. He said, "The placing of palms together is very much in the American spirit. To bring together one, two, three, four, so many, is simply wonderful. It is an act of cooperation, union, mutual respect, and harmony."[5]

This group of temple members explained what even a brief visit to Hsi Lai makes clear: that this is a Chinese temple community trying very hard to undertake the most American of activities, that is, participation in civic life. They wrote,

> Trying to westernize Buddhism and do more to benefit the American people, Hsi Lai Temple monastics have chosen to be actively engaged in American society. For example, they have

helped the American Heart Association with the annual Heart Run; they have given lectures on Buddhist teachings in response to invitations by colleges and universities; they have invited local religious groups to participate in New Year's Peace Services; they have held a wide variety of charity events and recycling drives; they have joined Fourth of July parades and celebrations; they have shared joy with the community through our Chinese New Year community outreach event. The invitation to the Vice President was also done out of the same understanding, as a way for cultural integration and exchange of friendship.[6]

Far from coming to know the Hsi Lai temple through its impressive achievements, most Americans first learned of it through this oft-revisited controversy. For this Buddhist community, the learning curve on America's strict view of the separation of church and state was steep, and yet some felt that their temple had been unfairly criticized because they were Chinese. Clearly, in its first decade, Hsi Lai Temple has experienced the full range of "coming to the West," from zoning hearings to gala celebrations to hot political controversy.

MANY BUDDHISMS

As impressive as it is, Hsi Lai Temple is only a small part of the American Buddhist story. In the past thirty years Buddhism has come to America to stay, with Buddhists from all over Asia—Koreans and Chinese, Vietnamese and Cambodians, Thais, Tibetans, and Sri Lankans. Nowhere can we see the whole panorama of Buddhism as clearly as in Los Angeles.

I had the usual East Coast stereotypes of Los Angeles as a sprawling, smoggy city with no center and no periphery, but when I went to L.A. to do research on Buddhism in America, I discovered a city I came to love. Of course, all I really know of L.A. is its Asian religious life, which is every bit as ebullient and astonishing as its world of entertainment. L.A. is unquestionably the most complex Buddhist city in the world, with its vast variety of Buddhist temples and meditation centers representing the whole spectrum of Asian, and now American, Buddhism. Wat Thai in North Hollywood anchors two generations of Thai immigrants, and Kwan Um Sah on Western Avenue gathers Korean Buddhists in a former Masonic hall, its plush red-carpeted chamber now the shrine room for gilded images of the Buddha. In Long Beach there are Cambodian temples, the largest in a former union hall, and in Orange County dozens of sub-urban homes have become the temple centers of a large Vietnamese community. The elegant Jodo Shinshu Temple in South Central L.A. is one of several temples that serve third- and fourth-generation Japanese Americans. In Los Angeles, Buddhists who would never have met one another in Asia find themselves neighbors, often with very different cultural experiences of Buddhism. Like so many other religious traditions, seemingly coherent wholes from the outside, the Buddhist tradition becomes more variegated and complex the more closely one looks.

The Asian forms of Buddhism are only half the story, for there has also been a turn toward Buddhism on the part of native-born Euro-Americans and even African and Hispanic Americans. The Zen Center of Los Angeles, occupying half a city block, answers its busy phone lines with an array of automated options: sittings, retreats, study groups, evening Dharma talks, directions to the center. And there are a dozen other Zen centers in the area. The Tibetan Dharmadhatu Center, the Vipassana sitting groups, and the International Buddhism Meditation Center provide homes for various forms of Buddhist practice that have attracted native-born Americans. The Soka Gakkai International, a group with strong roots in Japan and an active mission outreach, has its American headquarters in Santa Monica.

In the 1950s one might have mistaken the Beat Zen of the counterculture for a fad that would fade, but with each succeeding decade Buddhism has become more vibrant. Today Buddhism has given its own distinctive hues to the tapestry of American religious life. Its traditions of meditation appeal to frank, practical Americans. As teachers in American Dharma centers often say, Buddhism is not a set of beliefs to be taken on faith but a set of observations about life, the sources of suffering, and the end of suffering to be tested in our own experience. Even more, it is a set of practices that enable people to cultivate the equanimity, mental clarity, and self-awareness needed to observe clearly, in their own experience, whether or not these postulates are true. "Come and see," is the invitation. For the past three decades, Americans in unprecedented numbers have accepted the invitation. They have tried it out, and whether they have ended up calling themselves Buddhists or not, many have stuck with it. By 1997 more than a thousand Buddhist meditation and practice centers were listed in the new edition of *The Complete Guide to Buddhist America.* Los Angeles has its fair share, to be sure, but there are also centers in Elk Rapids, Michigan, and Omaha, Nebraska. No part of the United States today is untouched by the presence of this form of Buddhism based in meditation practice.

The past three decades have not only brought Buddhist immigrants from all over Asia in unprecedented numbers, they have also seen ancient lineages of Buddhist teaching, passed from teacher to disciple in Asia for over twenty-five hundred years, cross the Pacific to America. The torch of teaching has been handed to a new generation of non-Asian teachers, many of whom are women, almost all of whom are laity. Few monastics are among them, so they are more likely to be dressed in slacks and T-shirts than saffron or gray robes. They teach in living rooms and conference centers, hospitals and prisons, elegant urban centers and mountain retreat centers. In their style and language, in their social and environmental activism, they are slowly but surely developing something we can call American Buddhism.

Here in America, Buddhists from all over the world are discovering their own diversity, their many Buddhisms. Not surprisingly, a gulf of experience and understanding separates the old Chinese and Japanese immigrant communities, some of whom have been in the U.S. for nearly one hundred years, and the new Thai, Vietnamese, Cambodian, and Chinese immigrant communities just getting started. Another separates the first-generation immigrants and their American-born children, who straddle the culture of Buddhist temple enclaves and the culture of their American high schools and colleges. Wide differences also separate Asian Buddhists who light incense and shake fortune sticks before the Buddha altar and American-born meditation practitioners who may consider such rituals extraneous to the teachings of the Buddha. Buddhism in America today is experiencing its own internal struggles with pluralism as cultures and generations express their different understandings of what it means to be Buddhist.

Buddhists are also developing their own forms of unity in urban and regional ecumenical councils. Yes, Buddhism is diverse, just as American Protestantism, Catholicism, and Judaism are internally diverse. In a sense, its very diversity signals its coming of age in the American context of competitive, voluntary religious associations. The story of the emerging Buddhist landscape of America over the past hundred and fifty years is nothing short of amazing, and it has attracted the attention of fine scholars and writers in the past decade.[7] As we look more closely, we will follow a few of the many strands that make up the multicolored fabric of Buddhism in America.

For all their diversity, Buddhists seem to hold one thing in common—a reverence for what they call the three treasures of the tradition: the Buddha; the Dharma, or teachings; and the Sangha, or community. Taking refuge in the three treasures is, as we saw at Hsi Lai, the closest thing there is to a Buddhist affirmation of faith. For American newcomers to Buddhism, Cambodians of the Theravada tradition, or Chinese of the Mahayana Pure Land tradition, being Buddhist means taking these as central for one's life. In ancient Pali or in a dozen other languages, Buddhists chant three times over, "I take refuge in the Buddha, I take refuge in the Dharma, I take refuge in the Sangha." As we shall see, however, just what Buddhists mean by these three treasures has varied widely.

TAKING REFUGE IN THE BUDDHA

Buddhism challenges many Americans at the very core of their thinking about religion—at least those of us for whom religion has something to do with one we call God. Two thousand five hundred years ago, a prince of a small kingdom in the Himalayan foothills of India renounced his kingdom to seek spiritual truth. Amid the philosophies and ascetic practices of his day, the prince ultimately found his own path to deep insight, clear vision, and inner awakening. He became known as the Buddha, the one who is "awake." After this awakening, or enlightenment, the Buddha taught for over fifty years in the cities and towns of north India. His teachings, collectively referred to as the Dharma, have nourished human beings over the centuries and around the whole world. But they have nothing to do with the kind of supreme being we refer to as God, although there is a very deep understanding of what is called the unconditioned, or sometimes the far shore.

This startling fact—a religion without God—was noted with some alarm in a news item in the *San Francisco Chronicle* when the very first Japanese Buddhist teachers, Dr. Shuje Sonoda and the Reverend Kahuryo Nishijima, arrived in the U.S. in 1899 to minister to the Japanese immigrant community. The reporter, having interviewed and photographed the two teachers, wrote, "They will teach that God is not the creator, but the created; not a real existence, but a figment of the human imagination, and that pure Buddhism is a better moral guide than Christianity." This was, no doubt, interpreted with less nuance than it might have been, but it put forward in journalistic fashion a theological matter that has been a stumbling block for many Western theists in their approach to Buddhism. The very idea of a religion with no God makes for a rocky start in the nation that now prints "In God We Trust" on its coins and pledges "One nation, under God, indivisible . . ." Nearly one hundred years later, the Japanese Buddhist descendants of those first teachers in San Francisco weighed in on the school prayer issue with a resolution that even now alarms those who understand religion in presumed Christian categories. It says, in part: "Prayer, the key religious component, is not applicable in Jodo Shin Buddhism which does not prescribe to a Supreme Being or God (as defined in the Judeo-Christian tradition) to petition or solicit; and allowing any form of prayer in schools and public institutions would create a state sanction of a type of religion which believes in prayer and 'The Supreme Being,' would have the effect of establishing a national religion and, therefore, would be an assault on the religious freedom of Buddhists."[8]

Those of us who are not Buddhists are likely to view the image of the Buddha, found in every Buddhist temple and meditation center, as something close to the idea of God. From the high altar of Wat Thai in North Hollywood to the much more modest altar of the Cambridge Insight Meditation Center just a few blocks from my home, the seated meditating Buddha reigns in a peaceful pose. When Larry Rosenberg, the resident teacher here in Cambridge, enters the meditation room to take his seat at the front of the hall, he presses his palms together in a gesture of reverence and bows deeply three times to the image of the Buddha. If we were to drive into the northern industrial suburb of Lynn, to the Khmer Buddhist Center of Massachusetts situated in a former church building, we would find Cambodian refugees gathered in the sanctuary, lighting incense and bowing in reverence before the image of the Buddha and teaching their children to do so. As the focus of such reverence, the Buddha has the look and feel of a divine being or at least a saint. Clearly, Buddhists have many understandings of the figure we so readily identify as *the* Buddha, and we have some work to do if we are to grasp the significance of this central figure.

At the World's Parliament of Religions in 1893, Buddhist delegates tried to explain to their Christian hosts that theirs was a tradition in which the language of God as creator of the universe was not relevant; the Buddha did not create the universe, with its intricate interdependence and its laws of cause and effect, but he discovered the true nature of the universe through the insight of his enlightenment. The Buddha was, in the view of some, the pioneer, the human being who became truly enlightened and found a path to freedom. The promise of his enlightenment is that it is possible for us all. One hundred years later at the centennial of the parliament held in Chicago in 1993, the Buddhist delegates again found they had not been understood. After nearly a week of speeches in which there were all too many universalizing platitudes about the many faiths and the one God, they got together and wrote a letter expressing their astonishment that "leaders of different religious traditions define all religions as religions of God and unwittingly rank Buddha with God." They went on,

> We found this lack of knowledge and insensitivity all the more surprising because we, the religious leaders of the world, are invited to this Parliament in order to promote mutual understanding and respect, and we are supposed to be celebrating one hundred years of interfaith dialogue and understanding! We would like to make it known to all that the Shakyamuni Buddha . . . was not God or a god. He was a human being who attained full Enlightenment through meditation and showed us the path of spiritual awakening and freedom. Therefore, Buddhism is not a religion of God. Buddhism is a religion of wisdom, enlightenment, and compassion.

The Buddha had said as much himself, according to an early tradition. When two wayfarers met the newly enlightened one, they asked, "Are you a heavenly being? a God? an angel?" And he responded, "No, I am awake." Indeed, the word *Buddha* was not the name of Prince Siddhartha but an honorific title expressing his awakening. Of course, the subtext is that most of us, most of the time, are not fully awake. Awakening was not, however, the unique quality of the historical Buddha. Because he woke up to the true nature of reality, there must be other Buddhas in other times and realms. The Pure Land tradition speaks of Amida Buddha, for example, as reigning in paradise. There are also multitudes of bodhisattvas, the enlightened ones who vow to serve in this world until all beings realize their true nature. Some speak of this as our "Buddha nature," meaning the capacity for enlightenment and deep knowledge that is within all sentient beings, which includes not only humans but all living things. As Buddhists read so many meanings in the serene image of the Buddha, it is not surprising that the word *God* would come to our minds, but if we were to mean by that a transcendent creator, immanent and yet beyond the creation, we would be misled. The historical Buddha spoke often of the useless abstract questions "that lead not to edification," and they include such questions as the origin of the universe, whether the soul is or is not eternal, whether it is or is not divine. To insist that we human beings know the answer to these questions is spiritually pointless. What we can know is fathomless, including the unfolding insight into ourselves, our own spiritual condition, the experience of suffering, the sources of our suffering, and the ways in which we might let it go.

Lama Surya Das, an American-born Tibetan Buddhist meditation teacher, put it this way as he spoke to the first Conference on Buddhism in America, held in Boston in 1997: "We are all Buddhas by nature. And not Buddhists." The form of meditation he teaches is called Dzogchen, and he explains,

> Let's just call it cutting through, or seeing through, as in seeing through the veil of illusions, seeing what is right there. As my own teacher Kalu Rinpoche said, "You are what you are seeking. You are the Buddha. You are it." Then why don't we know it? What would it take to know it? To awaken, to recognize who and what we are.[9]

Getting from where we think we are to where we really are is the key. It takes many forms, but the Buddha is both a guide to this process of realization and its goal.

Interviewing the Zen poet Gary Snyder in the early 1990s, my friend Michael Camerini, a filmmaker, asked him, "Who is the Buddha?" He responded with a story from his own Zen teacher. The roshi asked his three fourteen-year-old students, "How old is the Buddha?" The first responded, "The Buddha was born 2500 years ago in India." The second responded, "The Buddha is eternal." And the third responded, "The Buddha is fourteen." All, in a sense, were right. But the one who said "The Buddha is fourteen" hit the mark straight on.

TAKING REFUGE IN THE DHARMA

The second of the treasures is the Dharma, the teachings. The teachings are many, for the historical Buddha is said to have lived a long time, gathered many followers, taught in many ways. He explained the experience of his realization to the full-time renouncers, the monks who left their homes to seek spiritual freedom. He also taught townspeople whom he met along the way who had no inclination to leave the affairs of the world behind. And he taught urbanites in the growing cities of North India, including the kings and queens who created retreat centers at the edge of the city for him and his companions to settle for the three months of the rainy season each year. The Buddha's view of teaching was what he called "skill in means," teaching skillfully to each situation, to communicate with farmer and king, monk and philosopher. The first set of teachings, called "Turning the Wheel of the Dharma," comprised what came to be known as the Four Noble Truths. They were the observations he had made, the insights he had, as the turbulence of his mind settled in deep meditation and he saw directly into the heart of things. These truths, he taught, were the very essence of the religious journey of discovery.

America's Declaration of Independence sets forth what it calls self-evident truths—"that all men are created equal; that they are endowed by their Creator with inherent and unalienable rights; and that among these are Life, Liberty, and the Pursuit of happiness." American Buddhists are likely to point out that the teachings of the Buddha, called the Dharma, also begin with evident truths: that life is suffering, sorrowful, out of joint; that suffering has a cause, which is our tendency to desire, to grasp, to want to hold on to a process that is constantly changing and imperma-nent; that there is freedom from suffering; and that there is a path of ethics and practice that leads to freedom from suffering. These Noble Truths are not held as a Buddhist dogma or a Buddhist creed but as a set of observations about life that one is invited to see for oneself. They are not seen as peculiarly Buddhist truths but as universal truths about human life.

Lama Surya Das, who speaks of himself in the American colloquial as a "Dharma-farmer," summarizes the Buddha's approach to these teachings:

> As the Buddha said, "Don't believe in it just because the Buddha said it. Don't believe it just because the scriptures say it. Don't believe it just because the elders say it or just because everybody else says it or because it is written down." Check it out for your-selves. Find out if it is true, if it is conducive to the good, the wholesome, and the rest, then adopt it. Otherwise leave it and go. I think that is a good touchstone for us all.[10]

Starting with the painful truth of suffering is not necessarily the most attractive advertisement for Buddhism in America, where wealth, enter-tainment, sports, and consumerism seem to promise happiness. The desire to be happy, as the Dalai Lama so often reminds us, is also univer-sal, so it is important to understand the gnawing unsatisfactoriness, the suffering, that makes up human experience. Teachers struggle for the right translation of the Sanskrit term *dukkha*. It means suffering, sorrow, pain. It is the opposite of *sukha*, which is happiness. *Dukkha* is a particular pain—like the pain of a bone out of joint, the creaking of a wheel that is off its axis; it is the pain of disharmony. It is not only the overt suffering of old age, sickness, and death, which are the standard human inheritance, but the suffering that comes from losing what we love or having to stick with things we don't like. It is intrinsic to the human condition, whether we are rich or poor. When Chogyam Trungpa Rinpoche began teaching in America, he used the term *anxiety* as a translation for *dukkha*, the complex psychological sense that, for a variety of reasons, things are not all right. Why should this Buddhist worldview that begins with suffering and anxiety become so popular in the United States, as indeed it has?

Sylvia Boorstein, a Jewish-Buddhist meditation teacher, recalls her own first encounter with the Dharma: "What a relief it was to me to go to my first meditation retreat and hear people speak the truth so clearly— the First Noble Truth that life is difficult and painful, just by its very nature, not because we're doing it wrong. . . . I thought to myself, 'Here are people who are just like me, who have lives just like mine, who know the truth and are willing to name it and are all right with it.'" Such expressions of the appeal of this tradition in the American colloquial set us on the track to an answer. Sylvia Boorstein was born Jewish and had a lively practice as a psychotherapist before she came to Buddhism. Today she is a grandmother and one of the guiding teachers at the Vipassana meditation center called Spirit Rock in Marin County north of San Francisco. She attests that her journey into Buddhist practice has also made her a more observant Jew. In speaking about the Four Noble Truths, Boorstein makes what she sees as an important distinction. "In the First Noble Truth," she writes, "the Buddha explains that in life 'pain is inevitable, but suffering is optional.' The Buddha didn't say it in those exact words; he spoke in his vernacular. My rendition in a more current idiom carries the sense of what the Buddha meant to convey. . . ." She goes on to explain that the difficulties of sickness, old age, death, grief, and loss are just part of the human condition. No one escapes them in life, but how we encounter them is up to us. Do we imagine that we have been singled out for suffering? Do we name it, cling to it, and rehearse it to ourselves and to others? But suffering is only the beginning. The second truth is that there is a cause for suffering—our ceaseless desire and grasping, trying to hold on to things as if they were permanent in a world of constant change. Sylvia Boorstein puts it this way:

The Second Noble Truth explains that suffering is what happens when we struggle with whatever our life experience is rather than accepting and opening to our experience with wise and compassionate response. From this point of view, there's a big difference between pain and suffering. Pain is inevitable; lives come with pain. Suffering is not inevitable. If suffering is what happens when we struggle with our experience because of our inability to accept it, then suffering is an optional extra.[11]

Thich Nhat Hanh, the widely popular Vietnamese meditation master, sums up the importance of working with suffering this way: "The Buddha called suffering a Holy Truth, because our suffering has the capacity of showing us the path to liberation. Embrace your suffering, and let it reveal to you the way to peace."[12]

The third truth is that there is a way out of suffering. Here we might listen in to the explanation of Robert Thurman, who was among the very first Euro-Americans to study the Tibetan tradition seriously in the 1960s. He was ordained to monastic training by the Dalai Lama himself. In speaking about the Dharma, he articulates the third Noble Truth, that there is a way out of suffering:

> The Buddha said: "Come, monks, go to the four directions. Proclaim to everyone the door to nirvana is open. Everyone can go and become free of suffering. I see that this is possible. I became so free. It is possible for people to do it." He didn't say, "Go and proclaim everything is suffering."[13]

The possibility of letting go of the constant grasping that is at the root of suffering is truly good news, for it means that there is the hope of freedom from suffering.

The fourth Noble Truth is the path to freedom from suffering, called the Eightfold Noble Path. It begins with basic ethical behavior—right speech, right action, right livelihood—and moves on to the disciplines of body, breath, and mind that create the conditions of freedom. Here again, Thich Nhat Hanh might gives us a sense of the modern colloquial as we think about the path today.

> There is a story in Zen circles about a man and a horse. The horse is galloping quickly, and it appears that the man on the horse is going somewhere important. Another man, standing alongside the road, shouts, "Where are you going?" and the first man replies, "I don't know! Ask the horse!" This is also our story. We

are riding a horse, we don't know where we are going, and we can't stop. The horse is our habit energy pulling us along, and we are powerless. We are always running, and it has become a habit. We struggle all the time, even during our sleep. We are at war within our selves, and we can easily start a war with others.

We have to learn the art of stopping—stopping our thinking, our habit energies, our forgetfulness, the strong emotions that rule us. When an emotion rushes through us like a storm, we have no peace. We turn on the TV and then we turn it off. We pick up a book, and then we put it down. How can we stop this state of agitation? How can we stop our fear, despair, anger, and craving? We can stop by practicing mindful breathing, mindful walking, mindful smiling, and deep looking in order to understand. When we are mindful, touching deeply the present moment, the fruits are always understanding, acceptance, love, and the desire to relieve suffering and bring joy.[14]

The Dharma includes, in addition to the Four Noble Truths, many kinds of teachings, some distinctive to the monastic traditions of the Theravada, the "way of the elders" of South Asia, others cherished by Mahayana Buddhists of East Asia, and still others central to the Vajrayana traditions of Tibet. A year after my first visit to Hsi Lai Temple, I returned to hear Master Hsing Yün of the Mahayana tradition teach in his own style, very different from the down-home style of Sylvia Boorstein. He sat on the high altar, wearing his robes and a crown, and expounded the Vimalakirti Sutra, especially popular in China because the seeker is not a monastic but a businessman. When Buddhism first came to China with visiting monks in the third century C.E., the message of world-renouncing monasticism encountered deep resistance in Confucian culture, with its ethos of filial piety, family, and respect for parents and elders. The Vimalakirti Sutra was a teaching directly relevant to early Chinese Buddhism, for here the Buddha teaches a layperson, a businessman named Vimalakirti, how to live a good Buddhist life as a layperson.

That evening at Hsi Lai the grand Buddha Hall was full again, this time with an audience of eager Chinese immigrants, ready to receive the teachings of Master Hsing Yün, who was to lecture in the tradition of a grand master of the Dharma. It was not a lecture like any I had ever seen as a college professor, but a formal Dharma teaching. As the gongs sounded, a delegation of eight lay devotees left the Buddha Hall to approach the master, bow to him, and formally request that he give instruction. When Master Hsing Yün entered the Buddha Hall, the leader of the lay delegation led us all in bows and chanting and offered incense to the ten directions. He concluded with the words, "Now listen to the teaching of the Buddha!" The whole community prostrated three times—to the Buddha, the Dharma, and the Sangha—and the master ascended a high podium in front of the altar, where he sat cross-legged directly in front of the central image of the Buddha and began his teaching. For those of us who did not understand Chinese, there was simultaneous translation. Here in California, few of the sons and daughters of the new immigrants are likely to become monks and nuns, so understanding this teaching is especially important. Leading a good Buddhist life as a businessman is extremely important and fits right in with the Humanistic Buddhism at the core of the Hsi Lai vision.

TAKING REFUGE IN THE SANGHA

In Asia, the Sangha usually refers to the community of monastics, primarily monks. A Buddhist takes refuge in the Sangha because this community is charged with preserving the way of life and teachings of the Buddha. The Sangha is important, even to a community of laity. While there were nuns in the early Theravada tradition of South Asia, the lineage of nuns did not continue, and only in recent times have monastic orders for women been reintroduced. The Mahayana traditions of China and Japan, however, included an ongoing lineage of nuns, so in Taiwan both monks and nuns are part of the Sangha. Indeed, the majority of the Hsi Lai monastics are women, like the friends I met at the temple who ran everything from the construction project to the daily ordering of temple life. When I attended a full monastic ordination at Hsi Lai, called the Triple Platform Ordination, many of those ordained were women, including women who came from other streams of the Buddhist tradition and were seeking full ordination through this lineage.

In some traditions of Buddhism, however, the Sangha has a wider meaning. For example, when the Japanese teacher Shinran launched the Jodo Shinshu devotional Buddhist tradition in the twelfth century, he made a break with monasticism altogether, insisting that no special acts of renunciation would merit the favor of Amida Buddha and rebirth in the Pure Land. The gracious beneficence of Amida was available to all who called upon his name. So he introduced a radical lay orientation in this tradition, somewhat akin to the priesthood of all believers in

Protestant traditions. Ministers in the Jodo Shinshu tradition, including women ministers, see to the instruction of the congregation, but the term *Sangha* refers to the whole community.

The Nichiren tradition of Japan also made ample room for the laity. Dating from the thirteenth-century reformer Nichiren, this movement was revitalized in postwar Japan as the Nichiren Shoshu and its lay movement, Soka Gakkai, the Value-Creation Society. As Soka Gakkai developed into a political movement in Japan and as Soka Gakkai International developed into a global movement with adherents around the world, it split away from the old Nichiren Shoshu, which continued to be dominated by a high priesthood based at Taisekiji. The controversy over this parting of the ways had much to do with the role of hierarchical leadership, and the new Sangha of the Soka Gakkai International, under the leadership of Daisaku Ikeda, is truly a multiracial and multiethnic lay community. The form in which one encounters this movement in the United States today is as SGI-USA, and its core chanting practice is done in an essentially domestic setting, before the home altar of one of its members. Its strong inclusive community makes it America's most multiracial Buddhist group, with many African-American and Latino members as well as Asians of Vietnamese or Chinese origin. Its firm conviction that chanting the name of the Lotus Sutra, *Namu-myoho-renge-kyo,* will transform one's life for the better fits in well with the practical, evangelical stream of American religiousness.

The lay emphasis is also evident among the Zen and Vipassana meditation communities in America. Here the Sangha most often means simply the community of practitioners. America has no homegrown traditions of monasticism, and America's populist spirit leans toward a nonhierarchical structure. The individualism of the Buddhist path also appeals to many Americans. The traditional last words of the Buddha to his disciples are said to have been, "Be lamps unto yourselves. Work out your own salvation with diligence." In other words, awakening is not anything others can do for you. You have to put your foot on the path, one step at a time. Yet this individualism is tempered with a strong sense of the strengthening experience of community practice. Bernard Tetsugen Glassman, one of today's most prominent Zen teachers, described it this way when we interviewed him for the Pluralism Project: "It's a little bit like joining an orchestra. It's much easier for you to get in tune when you're part of that group than if you're just by yourself."[15] Other teachers describe the mutual strengthening of practice with different images.

When I visited Jakusho Kwong at the Sonoma Zen Center north of San Francisco, he told me with a broad smile about his discovery of the meaning of Sangha at a monastery in Japan. He had been asked to clean a bucketful of small, somewhat hairy, potatolike vegetables. He started scrubbing them one by one, until a senior monk came in, laughing as he saw Jack's efforts, and showed him how to clean them by putting some water in the bucket and shaking them together until they made one another clean. "This is what the Sangha is for us," he said. "With our efforts together, we help one another."

At least so far, even traditional Theravada communities of Cambodian and Thai immigrants, for whom the Sangha means the monks, find that few of the second generation choose monasticism as a vocation. Monastic leadership has to be imported from elsewhere. Only time will tell how this cycling of traditional leaders into a changing American community will work. Walpola Piyananda, abbot of a Sri Lankan community in central Los Angeles, has reflected a great deal on being a monk in America and has taken steps toward change. When he spoke at the Chicago Parliament of the World's Religions in 1993, he described his early days as a monk in America, giving us a vivid sense of the complexities of translating an Asian monastic tradition into a new context. "My ignorance of U.S. culture and geography led me to arrive in Chicago on Christmas Day wearing only my traditional robe and sandals," he said. He had no sweater, no coat, not even a pair of closed shoes. Even so, he observed, the Sri Lankan community did not want to see monks wearing boots and parkas or driving cars and shaking hands with women.

> I constantly faced the challenge of meeting the social customs of the U.S. head on, dealing with things which did not seem to coincide with the letter of the Vinaya, our Buddhist monastic code of discipline. I needed to drive, as Los Angeles is virtually uninhabitable if you can't get around, and it certainly makes a monk useless if he cannot reach his community. In addition, I studied at several universities and was myself often invited to give talks to groups which were not necessarily Buddhist. This often meant shaking hands with all in the audience, regardless of sex. I had to take a rational attitude towards the application of my discipline to the social realities of life here.[16]

Now, Walpola Piyananda not only wears shoes, socks, and sweaters but also drives around Los Angeles and is experimenting with new forms of Buddhist training closer to those of Western clergy. The first level of training prepares one to teach Dharma school, give talks on the Dharma, and conduct meditation classes; the second requires four years of college, three years of training with a qualified senior monk, and prepares the initiate to be a lay Buddhist minister. This would be a step short of fully ordained monasticism but would enable one to conduct religious services such as weddings and funerals and to be a chaplain in a university or hospital. In a 1995 article, Walpola Piyananda writes, "The question of genuine Buddhist 'tradition' is a huge one and one which every one of us Sangha members must confront for ourselves, but it is also important in the future development of Buddhist institutions in the West. We must feel safe enough to come to an agreement about what is common to Buddhism and what is strictly cultural, otherwise Buddhism will never become engrained in western countries like the U.S. except as a kind of 'countercultural' manifestation."[17]

There is no more spectacular evidence of the sheer diversity of the Sangha than at a gathering of the Sangha Council of Southern California. A few days after my inaugural Buddha's Birthday visit to Hsi Lai, I was invited to the annual ecumenical Buddha's Birthday observance by this council, one of a growing number of pan-Buddhist organizations trying to find "what is common to Buddhism." It was held that year at the Dharmaseal Temple in Rosemead, another eastern suburb of L.A. The congregation gathered in the former church, now Buddha Hall, the altar soaring with gladiolas, the Baby Buddha standing in his flower-decked basin before the altar. I joined the official members of the Sangha Council outside in the parking lot, where they were beginning to line up for the opening procession by the rear door, which still bore the sign "Sunday School."

When the procession of Buddhist leaders finally began, it was a dazzling display of Buddhist regalia, all following the color guard bearing the American flag and the six-colored Buddhist flag. Walpola Piyananda and the abbot of Wat Thai wore the bright saffron robes of South Asia, the Venerable Thich Man Giac of L.A.'s oldest Vietnamese temple was in his light gold robes, the Venerable Do An Kim of the downtown Korean temple wore gray with a brown shoulder sash, Geshe Gyeltsin from the Tibetan tradition had robes in deep maroon with a gold shoulder sash, Maezumi Roshi and the representatives of the Zen Center were in black, the Reverend Ito of the Japanese Buddhist Church wore a business suit, as did Julius Goldwater, the much-revered American Buddhist who had helped the Japanese community during its World War II internment.

The nuns of Hsi Lai wore their black robes, and the Venerable Karuna Dharma wore the golden robes she had received at the time of her monastic initiation by a Vietnamese master. The procession gave visual evidence of an emerging and much wider sense of Sangha than any of these participants could possibly have experienced firsthand in his or her own Buddhist community and culture.

"The Sangha members gathered here represent thousands of people. But if the whole Sangha were to come there would not be enough space to gather all the people, so we represent them by our presence here." The speaker and master of ceremonies was Dr. Havanpola Ratanasara, the Sri Lankan monk who had been instrumental in launching the Sangha Council in 1979. This sense of a community reaching across the differences of language, culture, and lineage and including both monks and lay leaders is relatively new in Buddhism. Like every religious tradition, Buddhism is not a neat box of doctrines and practices but a vibrant river of faith with many tributaries and branches, all flowing today in America. Nowhere is the real challenge of Buddhist diversity presented so clearly as in metropolitan America.

The next year I was back in L.A. for the Sangha Council's Buddha's Birthday. This time it was hosted by Kwan Um Sah, a Korean temple in downtown L.A. Driving to the temple was not easy that year. Streets were blocked, and those that were open took me through parts of Koreatown that had been burned to the ground. It was May 10, 1992, just after the rioting that had torn and scarred the city of Los Angeles. The verdict of innocence in the controversial case in which policemen had been charged with brutally beating an African-American man, Rodney King, had exploded long-simmering tensions between blacks and Koreans. Korean small businesses had succeeded where black businesses had failed, often right in the midst of black neighborhoods. Koreatown was thriving with glitzy glass mini-malls, and once again new immigrants seemed to claim the economic success denied to blacks.

At Kwan Um Sah, the atmosphere was somber as the many monks, lay leaders, and members of the ecumenical community came forward, one by one, to honor the Baby Buddha. But as leaders spoke, it became clear that crisis had helped them remember and affirm what they had in common as Buddhists here in America—a commitment to creating peace in the midst of urban strife. The American flag was posted next to the tall golden image of the Buddha in the stately chamber, which had been converted from its former use as a Masonic Hall. The miniature flower-decked image of the Baby Buddha, his forefinger pointing upward, seemed to point to the banner stretched across the hall directly above: "Pray for the Los Angeles Disaster of April 29." As I sat in the multiethnic congregation, all Buddhists, including a few African Americans, I was struck by this symbolic juxtaposition of religious and national symbols, the Buddha and the Stars and Stripes. The words of Rodney King, who had gone on television to deplore the violence, hung in the air, posing the question of our times for everyone, "Why can't we all just get along?" It seemed the whole world had converged in Los Angeles, with both its problems and its promise.

"We have to take the plant of Buddhism out of its Asian pot and plant it in the soil of Arizona," I recalled the words of that Vietnamese monk in Phoenix, interviewed by one of our Pluralism Project researchers. Taking root in American soil takes time. The Buddha, the Dharma, and the Sangha—Buddhism's three treasures—will all be expressed in new ways as the various forms of Buddhism begin to grow. So far, the plant is still young. As we wait to see how it will grow, we can look back upon America's Buddhist history. After all, Buddhism has been here for over 150 years, and each of its lineages beckons us to look more closely.

GOLD MOUNTAIN: THE CHINESE IN AMERICA

America's encounter with Chinese religion, including Buddhism, began in the 1850s when Chinese workers arrived on the West Coast, eager to have a part in the Gold Rush in the land of opportunity they called Gold Mountain. Some of these newcomers became miners. Like the forty-niners who swarmed into California, some were lucky and many more were not. Most of the Chinese who sought their fortune here eventually became cooks and fishermen, farmhands and loggers. Chinese work crews were "workin' on the railroad," with pickaxes, shovels, and dynamite, forging a rail link through the Rocky Mountains and across the heart of America.

Chinese workers brought to America a complex worldview that included Buddhist, Taoist, and Confucian traditions. Some surely brought small images of the Buddha and of the Bodhisattva of Compassion, Kuan Yin, along with Taoist deities like T'ien Hou. Among the first Chinese temples in the U.S. were those in San Francisco's Chinatown, eight of them by 1875. One of them was the T'ien Hou Temple on Waverly Place, dedicated primarily to the Taoist goddess of the sea, who saw them safely over the vast Pacific. It is still there today, in a second-floor sanctuary up a steep staircase from the streets of Chinatown. As Chinese immigrants settled throughout the West they created many makeshift temples, like the log temple in Weaverville, California, now a state historical landmark. By the end of the century, hundreds of Chinese temples and shrines could be found along the West Coast and in the Rocky Mountains.

In my home state of Montana, temples were built in Helena, Butte, and Virginia City. In 1870 one-tenth of the non-Native population of the Montana territory was Chinese. Few of the Chinese there were miners. Most were laborers, small businessmen, farmers, and even doctors practicing Chinese medicine, like Dr. Chen in Butte whose portrait standing next to his storefront office is in the archives of the Montana Historical Society. A few years ago, I spent many hours in the historical society library in Helena during a January blizzard, reading the fat sheaf of newspaper clippings chronicling the early history of the Chinese communities. In the sheaf was a striking 1890s photograph of a Chinese woman standing in traditional dress next to the temple in the frontier mining town of Virginia City, along with an anonymous account by a pioneer who recalled the temple.

> It was a two story log building: upstairs was where they went to pray to the Buddha. As I remember, there was one [Buddha] in the center of the room and two on the north wall and a kneeling pad before each one, and a platform or stage for their orchestra which always played for their New Year's services. This was always in February and lasted for a two week period. During this Chinese New Year there were Chinamen who came from all over the state and it is estimated that there were as many as six hundred Chinamen in Virginia City at this time.[18]

The more I read, the more makeshift temples I found in frontier Montana. Before the end of the day, the librarian had taken me into the basement of the historical society museum to see an elaborate Chinese altar kept in storage there.

The booming mining town of Butte seemed to have an active Chinese religious life. In the folder of articles was one from *Butte Weekly Inter Mountain* dated November 23, 1882, recalling the arrival in Butte of the sacred image of the Buddha, referred to as the Joss.

> The great Chinese Joss arrived last night by express from California, and is being feasted today with all the delicacies of the

season. . . . The room in which he has taken up his quarters is gaily decorated with flags, roast hogs, chickens, drums, and a thousand and one articles which defy description. [The Chinese] will wind up with a grand free lunch to-night, at which at least three hundred will be present.

We know that the Chinese of Butte did not have an easy time of it. Discrimination was part of the experience of this community, though many lived here for decades. We well remember the dictum from the Butte editorial, "The Chinaman's life is not our life, his religion is not our religion. . . . He belongs not in Butte."[19]

In the folder of articles, many had to do with funerals and death anniversaries. Death often provides an idiom of connection across language and culture; people of every religion and none are sympathetic toward the rituals that accompany this great transition. For instance, the *Helena Weekly Herald* of April 8, 1869, announced: "Today is the (Chinese) annual Josh Day, on which occasion their custom is to visit the burial places—as our China men and women have done, closing their ceremonies about 2 p.m.— burn incense and innumerable small wax candles about the head stones or boards of the graves, deposit a liberal lunch of choice eatables and drink- ables, designed for the spirits of the departed; recite propitiatory prayers to their savior (Josh), and otherwise show themselves sacredly minded of the welfare of their dead."[20] China Row in Helena's town cemetery became the final resting place of dozens of Chinese pioneers. A concern of many immi- grants has been providing for death rites and respectful care for those who died far from home and family, and Chinese family associations provided this service to those who lived in America. According to the Helena records, at least one San Francisco–based Chinese family association came to retrieve the bones of the dead who were association members. They placed them in small wooden boxes and sent them home to China, according to arrangements previously made. The practice of sending bones home for burial proved to many critics that the Chinese were unassimilable and clan- nish, therefore unfit to participate in the demands of citizenship.

Looking back to the 1850s when the Chinese first came to the U.S., we certainly find evidence that the spirit of reception began on an upbeat note. For example, at a celebration of California statehood in 1850, Justice Nathaniel Bennett declared,

Born and reared under different governments and speaking dif- ferent tongues, we nevertheless meet here today as brothers. . . .

You stand among us in all respects as equals. . . . Henceforth we have one country, one hope, one destiny.[21]

The Chinese were often referred to as the "Celestials," and the hope expressed in the pages of the *Daily Alta California* in 1852 was optimistic: "Quite a large number of the Celestials have arrived among us of late, enticed thither by the golden romance that has filled the world." The paper predicted that "the China boys will yet vote at the same polls, study at the same schools, and bow at the same altar as our own countrymen."[22]

Taking a longer view of history, perhaps this optimism was justified. Today, Chinese Americans of early and recent immigration do indeed stand as equals in America, voting at the same polls and studying at the same schools. They also play in the same symphony orchestras, work in the same law firms, and shop in the same malls. All do not worship at the same altar, however, and there is still evidence of discrimination and prejudice. The road from the 1850s to the present has been difficult. As we have seen, the idea that Chinese immigrants would stand on equal footing was not to be a reality for more than a century. The anti-Chinese movement began almost as soon as Chinese workers arrived, culminating in a series of Chinese exclusion acts that made new immigration from China difficult and began to set a tone for widespread discrimination. Throughout the West anti-Chinese demonstrations led to laws prohibiting Chinese from owning property and prohibiting marriage between Chinese and white Americans. In Montana when the city of Great Falls made its bid to be the state capitol it offered the slogan "Great Falls for the Capitol. No Chinese." In 1903 an article in the *Great Falls Tribune* boasted of the city's "unwritten law" barring Chinese. It reminded the public that a decade earlier an unwelcome Chinese newcomer was pitched over the Great Falls of the Missouri where he fell to his death.[23] As Montana historian Robert Swarthout put it, prejudice against the Chinese was "so pervasive that recognition of the Chinese role in the development of modern Montana would come only after most of the Chinese pioneers and their descendants had left the state."[24]

Today, after decades of renewed immigration from Taiwan, Hong Kong, and mainland China, the sentiments of the raw prejudice that surfaced so publicly a century ago seem distant. Discrimination still takes place, however, as do hate crimes, such as the murder of Vincent Chin, a Chinese-American draftsman who was chased down by two disgruntled Detroit auto workers and beaten to death on a June night in 1982.

Despite the brutality of the murder, the sentence handed down by the judge was a fine and three years' probation. The ensuing appeals and court processes never produced a prison term for either assailant, but the tragedy did yield a heightened vigilance among Asian-American advocacy groups. Despite cases like that of Vincent Chin, nothing today quite matches the publicly tolerated anti-Chinese movement of a century ago. There are still urban Chinatowns in San Francisco, New York, and Boston, but there are also Chinese-dominated suburbs like Monterey Park, California, more than half Chinese. While the nineteenth-century Chinese were largely laborers, those who come to America today are looking for a different Gold Mountain, that of higher education and professional employment, especially in science and technology. Today's Chinese have established themselves in America in larger numbers than ever before, and the new immigration has charted new territory. Some identify themselves primarily by their Chinese ethnicity as Chinese Americans; for others, Buddhist or Christian identity is also important; and for others the accent is on being American and Chinese identity becomes a little-used cultural marker.

Hsi Lai, where we began this journey, is a striking architectural symbol of Buddhism having finally arrived, and spectacularly at that, not in the narrow back streets of nineteenth-century Chinatowns, but on the hilltops of suburbia. Its new branch temple in Austin, Texas, signals the robust expansion of this Humanistic Buddhism, as does its high-rent storefront not far from Harvard Square. But Hsi Lai is far from alone. When our researcher Stuart Chandler surveyed the complex landscape of Chinese Buddhism in the U.S. in the mid-1990s, he found over 125 Chinese Buddhist temples or organizations. Many of the temple complexes are as impressive as Hsi Lai, though perhaps not as large, and all of them are growing. Let me mention just three of the most splendid in order to extend our sense of the Chinese Buddhist landscape of America.

First is the City of Ten Thousand Buddhas, located on more than four hundred acres of land in Talmadge, California. It is the most extensive of some twenty institutions affiliated with the Dharma Realm Buddhist Association.[25] Its founding teacher, Master Hsuan Hua, immigrated to the United States in the 1950s. In 1970 he established the Gold Mountain Monastery on Sacramento Street in San Francisco's Chinatown and within a few years began creating the spacious study center in a former junior college facility in Talmadge, about three hours north of San Francisco. It includes a research library, a university, and two full-time schools. The monks and nuns, a few of them Euro-Americans, have devoted themselves to translating Chinese Buddhist texts. Others are full-time schoolteachers. In their religious lives, they combine the disciplines of meditation associated with Ch'an or Zen Buddhism and the chanting more widely associated with Pure Land Buddhism.

I met one of the American-born monks, Heng Sure, in the early 1990s when he came through Cambridge. I will never forget our conversation because of the photographs he showed me of his unusual trip up the West Coast of California, perhaps the slowest trip ever on record. He did full prostrations, marking with his outstretched arms the distance in front of him and then moving forward to place his feet there and prostrate again. Prostrations are part of the monk's training, and Heng Sure made his repeated bows while covering the length of the state of California. In 1997, although he was a Western monk, he was invited to take part in the ordination of nearly six hundred monks and nuns at a monastery near Shanghai. He saw it as completing the circle of Buddhism coming to America and returning again to China. Reflecting on this at a conference on Buddhism in America, he said,

> I guess this would be a kind of testimony to how far Buddhism has come into this country and put down roots—that the Chinese Sangha when they wanted to ordain monks and nuns, came to America looking for masters and certifiers. . . . We went back to China in a religious role: Westerners trained in America and Taiwanese monks who came to America for their training, went back to stand in front of six hundred ordainees from China, men and women who had decided to follow the Buddhist path of renunciation into the Sangha.[26]

Our second stop is the Jade Buddha Temple in Houston, located along a highway of sprawling strip malls. It's formal name is the Texas Buddhist Association, and its Web site is available in both Chinese and English.[27] At the entryway stands the Bodhisattva of Compassion, Kuan Yin, surrounded by blooming lotuses in an artificial pond of water. The temple complex includes two large Buddha halls, a library, a kitchen, and a community center. It offers Sunday morning meditation sessions in English, followed by Dharma talks. The meditation group uses an eclectic range of books, including *Mindfulness in Plain English* by the Theravada Thai monk Gunaratna or *Being Peace* by the Vietnamese monk Thich Nhat Hanh. The Jade Buddha Temple also has an extensive program of service and youth work, and it boasts a one-hundred-voice Bodhi Choir that sings Buddhist hymns in performance, with a mission "to preach Buddhist Dharma with music." This temple stands in striking continuity with both the great temples of Hong Kong and the giant Baptist megachurches of Houston. Like Hsi Lai, the Jade Buddhist temple is part of a larger network. Indeed, the Thousand Buddha Temple in Boston is linked to this network of temples by virtue of the involvement and teaching of the Venerable Wing Sing, a Hong Kong–based monk.

The third stop on our tour of spectacular Chinese temples is the Chuang Yen Monastery in Kent, New York, in the rural fringe of Westchester County north of New York City. Its setting could not be more different from that of the Jade Buddhist Temple. Here the road winds into the temple property past a large lake, with an image of the Bodhisattva Kuan Yin welcoming visitors from a midlake island. The Kuan Yin Hall set in a clearing of maples and oaks is impressive enough, but next to it is an even more spectacular temple, a large Buddha Hall with a thirty-five-foot-tall image of the Buddha, the largest in North America. The Buddha is seated under the huge vaulting wooden beams that hold the roof, leaving the view of the Buddha completely unobstructed throughout the hall. The monastery also includes a research library, just across the lake, and a hillside shrine for the interment of the ashes of the deceased. The whole complex is part of the Buddhist Association of the United States, founded by the Chinese teacher C. T. Shen.[28] Among his first centers is a modest Ch'an meditation center in Elmhurst, Queens, Ch'an being the Chinese predecessor of Zen Buddhism in Japan. The Chuang Yen Monastery is the capstone of C. T. Shen's efforts. This landmark temple combines the elegance of contemporary architecture with traditional Chinese architectural forms.

Although the Chinese have been in America longer than other Asian groups, most of their Chinese Buddhist institutions have been built during the past thirty years in the context of the new immigration. Those who have studied Chinese Buddhist communities also report that as many as half of those involved became actively Buddhist only once they arrived in America. Buddhism is a way of sustaining a link to their traditional roots in Taiwan, Hong Kong, or China, yet as Stuart Chandler notes, "First-generation Chinese Americans who become Buddhist are not maintaining a directly inherited identity so much as reconstructing one."[29] One might well expect in Chinese communities a new face of Buddhism that is quite open to change and innovation.

JAPANESE BUDDHISTS IN AMERICA

Though the Japanese immigrants came decades after the Chinese, they put down religious roots more quickly, in part because the men were able, eventually, to bring their wives to the U.S. They could not return to Japan to marry, but many unmarried young men who had established themselves in the U.S. brought "picture brides" from Japan, women to whom they were betrothed by their families back home, without ever having met them. When the young women arrived in San Francisco, their prospective husbands identified them by the photographs sent from Japan. For all its inadequacies, this system of marriage enabled the Japanese community to have families and put down more permanent roots in America. Their temple communities go back to the very first years of the twentieth century, and their level of institutionalization and assimilation was fairly high by the end of the 1930s. All this was painfully shattered with the bombing of Pearl Harbor and the mass detention of America's first two generations of Japanese Buddhists. The story of this strand of Buddhism is an important one for the history of American Buddhism and the history of America.

For more than half a century, Japanese-American Buddhists have gathered for worship at Senshin Temple in South Central Los Angeles. It is a Jodo Shinshu temple, part of what is now called the Buddhist Churches of America. This form of devotional, lay-oriented Buddhism has claimed the largest number of Japanese-American followers for more than a century. The Senshin congregation renovated a building for its first temple in the late 1930s. During the years from 1943 to 1946 when the minister and members of the congregation were interned in detention camps, Julius Goldwater, one of the early Euro-American members of the community, took an active role in protecting the temple and the property of the community that was stored within. After the war, when the community slowly began to grow again, the group laid plans for a new temple, which was built in the 1960s. It is an architectural gem, its simplicity of line partaking of Japanese architecture and its gracefully bowed entry arch reminiscent of the Japanese torii.

I first visited the Senshin Temple in the early 1990s, escorted by its minister, the Reverend Masao Kodani. When we entered, I was surprised to find, not a large meditation hall, but a space that resembled, at first glance, a modern Protestant church. We passed through a foyer, and inside the sanctuary we encountered rows of pews and a carpeted central aisle leading to the altar. But at the altar the Protestant resemblance came to a halt. Suddenly my eyes were busy taking in a rich gold-hued complexity that reminded me more of the icon screen of an Orthodox Christian church. It was an elaborate threefold altar, suffused with the warm light of lanterns, bearing the image of Amida Buddha in the center, flanked by subsidiary chapels on either side with the images of the twelfth-century Japanese founders, Shinran and Rennyo, who pioneered this form of lay-oriented, devotional Buddhism. Reverend Kodani explained that before Shinran's revolutionary approach to Buddhism, the altar area in a temple was very big and could be entered only by the monks who conducted rituals while the laypeople were simply observers. "Shinran considered all people to be 'fellow travelers' on the path," he said. "In his view, ordinary laypeople were to be participants in the ceremonies and rituals of Buddhist life, not observers. All of us are in this together." I was reminded of the story of the arrival of the first Jesuit missionaries in Japan. When they discovered Jodo Shinshu Buddhism with its emphasis on the laity and on salvation by the gracious vow of Amida Buddha, they wrote home that the "Protestant heresy" seemed to have already reached the shores of Japan.

Shenshin Temple's Buddhism emphasizes the grace and compassion of Amida Buddha, teaching that this "Buddha of Infinite Light," called Amitabha in Sanskrit, moves with grace toward human beings. As Kodani put it, "Amida is the mythical or cosmic Buddha, a representation of the wisdom and compassion that are the content of the Buddha's enlightenment."[30] We cannot pull our selves up by our bootstraps, so to speak. It is only by faith in the wisdom and compassion represented by Amida Buddha that we develop the wise, compassionate mind in ourselves. He speaks of "other-power" as opposed to the "self-power" of, say, Zen meditation, to describe this form of Buddhism.

That morning as people assembled for Sunday worship at Senshin Temple, each person walked to the front of the sanctuary to the incense burner set on a stand in front of the main altar. With a deep bow, each grandmother, each teenager, each small child lit a stick of incense and placed it on the bed of glowing ashes in the burner. I took my place in the pew and noticed the familiar hymnbook in a pew rack in front of me. The organ began playing, and the Sunday service was under way. At every phase of the service, I found myself struck by the extraordinary juxtaposition of what was familiar to me as a Protestant and what was quite different. The ritual idiom reminded me of my hometown Methodist

Church in Bozeman, Montana. We stood for a hymn, sat for a scripture reading, stood for a responsive reading, just as I had all my life. And yet the content was Buddhist, and the overall feeling I had as a worshiper was of a Methodist-Buddhist blend, the Methodism being supplied from my own religious background. The hymn we sang together seemed to be a direct adaptation of Protestant hymnody. We sang:

Sweet hour of meditation, The quiet hour of peace,
When from life's care and turmoil I find a blest release.
In silent contemplation, New faith and hope I win.
More light and deeper knowledge, New strength to conquer sin.

The reader took his place at the front of the congregation to read from scripture, the Avatamsaka Sutra: "Do not seek to know Buddha by his form and attributes; for neither the form nor attributes are the real Buddha. The true Buddha is enlightenment itself." At one point in the service we all stood for what I would call an affirmation of faith. Opening to a page in the worship book, we recited a version of "The Threefold Refuge." Reverend Kodani led off, saying:

Difficult it is to receive life in human form, now we are living it.

Difficult it is to hear the Dharma of the Buddha, now we hear it.

If we do not cross over to the Truth in the present life, in what life shall we cross over? Let us with sincerity and true reverence take refuge in the Three Treasures of the Truth.

The congregation responded, "I take refuge in the Buddha. I take refuge in the Dharma. I take refuge in the Sangha."

Reverend Kodani preached a sermon, kneeling at a low lectern at the front of the Buddha Hall. His subject was the upcoming observance of the birthday of the Buddha. He reminded us of the story of the Buddha's birth and how all of nature resounded with the great event. Trees blossomed out of season, and earthquakes shook the hills. "The story sticks in your head because it is so real," he said. "When a child is born, when you go to first grade, when you go to your first day of high school, there is all the beauty of springtime newness. But there are also earthquakes. Beauty and newness come with earthquakes too. Nothing stays springtime forever. This is the teaching of *dukkha.* It is the pain of being off-center like a wheel. When you are in the midst of enjoyment, you begin to hold on to it, and you lose it. When you are in pain, the minute you look at the pain, it is already beginning to dissipate." There was nothing sentimental about this very Buddhist sermon, and yet this sunny, even jocular preacher, connected the evanescence of springtime with the pain of life without a trace of cynicism or negativity.

Announcements concluded the service, including that of a lively junior high schooler who said she would be going to Japan for the summer. Reverend Kodani chuckled and said, "Wait till you get to Japan. Within twenty minutes of getting off the plane, you know you are in a foreign country, even though everybody looks just like you!" Everyone laughed. Finally, the temple celebrated all members with birthdays that month, and right there in the sanctuary a longtime member gave out cupcakes with lighted candles.

After the service, people lingered to socialize in the foyer and in the outside courtyard. Some hurried off to "Sunday school" Dharma classes. I visited two children's classes. In one, second and third graders were coloring Dharma School workbook pages entitled "My Obutsudan." One of the children explained that an *obutsudan* is a Buddha altar. It is found in every Jodo Shinshu temple and home, and there was one in the classroom too. At the center of the page was the standing image of Amida Buddha, surrounded by an incense burner, a bouquet of flowers, a candle, and a small dish of rice. The children colored and cut out the Buddha altar, putting Amida Buddha and the various offerings in the proper places. Placing their palms together in the gesture of reverence called *gassho,* they recited a prayer that emphasizes one of the cardinal virtues of the tradition—gratitude.

> Amida Buddha,
> I offer rice to say "thank you."
> I burn incense to say "thank you."
> I offer beautiful flowers and say "thank you."
> I light the candle and say "thank you."
> Namu Amida Butsu

"'Praise to Amida Buddha,'" the teacher said, "is the Buddhist way to say 'thank you.'"

In another classroom, I sat with a group of six- and seven-year-olds. Their lesson emphasized another of the deepest teachings of the tradition: the interdependence of all things. We are linked in a vast, intricate web of relationships that ultimately extends to the whole of life, what the Vietnamese monk Thich Nhat Hanh calls "interbeing." The students were cutting strips of yellow construction paper, which they circled and taped into a paper chain. They explained to me that they were creating Buddha's "golden chain." They all knew by heart the recitation that goes with this chain making, for they say it week after week in Dharma School and often in the Sunday services when they go with their parents. It is the childhood creed for these young Shin Buddhists:

I am a link in Amida Buddha's golden chain of love that stretches around the world. I must keep my link bright and strong. . . .

May every link in Amida Buddha's golden chain of love become bright and strong, and may we all attain perfect peace.

The Jodo Shinshu Buddhist tradition has considerable experience in teaching Buddhism to the younger generation, for these Buddhists are now in their fourth and even fifth generations in the U.S. They have led the way in developing a Dharma School curriculum for use with children on Sundays. The education department of their national headquarters in San Francisco produces Buddhist educational materials that are supplied to temples throughout the country. It is a distinctively American curriculum, modeled on the kinds of exercises that will enable children to appropriate their faith for themselves.

When I first met him, the Reverend Kodani told me that America's Japanese community has a name for every generation, and there have been many. The Issei were the first to come in the late nineteenth and early twentieth centuries. Their children are the Nissei, the first to be born in America. Reverend Kodani is Sansei, the third American generation. I thought to myself that I would most likely be part of that generation—a Sansei Swede. The Yonsei are the fourth generation, like the college-age Dharma-School teachers I had met. And there are beginning to be Gosei, the newborns. A few weeks later, a dozen of the very youngest generation were brought to Senshin temple with their parents to be presented to the Buddha and the Sangha for the first time, a rite called Hatsu Mairi.[31] It combined elements of a Christian infant baptism and a Hindu first outing to the temple, only here many couples presented their babies at once. Calling the parents forward, the Reverend Kodani spoke each child's name and touched the child on both sides of the head and on the top of the head with a rolled paper scroll containing the teachings of the Buddha, a form of initiation. A finishing touch was a tiny gift: a baby-sized Senshin Temple T-shirt.

This Shin Buddhist community dates its heritage in mainland America to the 1880s when the first Japanese immigrants began to arrive.

Japanese immigration was far more controlled than that from China. Those eager to come to America were screened by the Japanese government and often received support and training from the government lest they elicit the same animosity that was being directed against the Chinese. By the early 1890s, there was already an organized Buddhist community in Hawaii. In 1898 a Young Men's Buddhist Association, modeled on the YMCA, was chartered in San Francisco with some thirty members. As that group grew, it petitioned Shin Buddhist headquarters in Japan to send a Buddhist teacher, because without a teacher, as they put it, "there is no possibility of basking in the Compassionate Life of the Buddha."[32]

Two teachers responded to the call, and Dr. Shuye Sonoda and the Reverend Kakuryo Nishijima arrived in San Francisco. The *San Francisco Chronicle* of September 13, 1899, carried the photographs of these newly arrived "representatives of the ancient creed" and the story we noted earlier about their beliefs, which dispensed with the notion of a creator God. In the next few years, communities of Jodo Shinshu Buddhists were organized. The first was in San Francisco, where the reconstituted Young Men's Buddhist Association adopted the name Buddhist Church of San Francisco. Then came the Buddhist Church of Sacramento and the Fresno Buddhist Church. The community in Seattle began in 1901. Portland followed in 1903 and Salt Lake City in 1912, by which time there were some twenty Shin Buddhist "churches," most of them headed by ordained ministers sent from Japan.

Group photographs show these immigrants standing in front of their "churches" in suits and ties, wearing long dresses and carrying parasols, looking very much like Swedish, German, or English grandparents. But their seeming assimilation did not succeed in halting the rising tide of anti-Asian public rhetoric. Japanese immigrants did not have equal rights by any stretch of the imagination. In many states they could not own land, and above all they could not become citizens. Their children were citizens by birth, but in 1906 the state of California launched a policy of separate education for Japanese children. By 1924 new immigration from Japan was cut off entirely. The rising tide of blatant discrimination against the Japanese in the first two decades of the twentieth century might have served to bolster the Buddhist communities. In a climate of discrimination and adversity, some Japanese who may have hesitated to be openly Buddhist sought out Buddhist communities for support. By the late 1930s dozens of Buddhist churches and ministers, most of them on the West Coast, stretched from San Diego to Seattle.

The Japanese bombing of Pearl Harbor on December 7, 1941, turned the world upside down for Japanese Americans. No other immigrant community in U.S. history has ever been singled out for such intense scrutiny or subject to such discriminatory sanctions as those of Japanese origin after Pearl Harbor. In their temple histories, they recall the rising sense of isolation and fear.

> While news flashes were constantly printed onto the screens of the movie theaters and continued interruptions made through-out the radio broadcasts announcing the bombing of Pearl Harbor, tension and insecurity were rising in the Japanese American public. It was not something they had expected, yet whether in a theater, restaurant or other public places, the eerie feeling of being eyed as an enemy Japanese was the paramount feeling on this particular day, December 7, 1941. The newsboys shouting out, "Extra! Extra! Pearl Harbor bombed by the Japs!" rang out throughout the main streets of American cities.
>
> What were once the gay and lively "Japanese Towns" of the Pacific Coast area soon turned into ghost towns, seemingly overnight. Store owners closed shop early for fear of reprisal. Doubt, suspicion and anger cast their shadows upon the Japanese community; moreover, without any warning, the leaders of these communities were incarcerated into jails, immigration stations, Federal prisons and military camps. The Japanese Buddhist leaders were not an exception.[33]

Buddhist ministers and community leaders were immediately rounded up by the FBI because they were thought to be particularly prone to disloyalty. The truth is, they were members of a little-understood minority religion. Their wives and children saw them wrenched from their homes and taken off to detention camps. The official Jodo Shinshu history records,

> A large number of the ministers were removed from their temples and homes. And, with the ministers and the many Buddhist lay leaders incarcerated, leaving only the wives and young children stranded, massive chaos in the religious institutions was the order of the day. The membership was apprehensive about approaching their temple for fear of being apprehended.[34]

During this time of fear, Buddhists were especially vulnerable. The history continues, "Those who had little confidence in their own religious beliefs believed that any association with a Buddhist organization would be to their disadvantage. Possession of Japanese writings became suspect and a source of concern; thus, the fearful ones removed their Buddhist altar, destroyed their sutra books and burned their family albums containing photos of relatives or friends in uniform."

In February of 1942, President Roosevelt issued his famous Executive Order #9066 authorizing the establishment of internment camps and the forcible relocation of people of Japanese ancestry. Evacuation orders were posted in cities and towns up and down the West Coast. This was unprecedented in American history. There was a rush to pack personal belongings, to make arrangements for homes and temples, to move valuables to a safe place, often in the temple itself. This was the story of 110,000 people, more than 60 percent of them Buddhist, who were essentially taken prisoner. Japanese men, women, and children were held in these camps for the duration of the war, and the detention experience became a major marker in the story of every Japanese-American Buddhist community and family. While Protestant and Catholic Japanese had some networks of support from their coreligionists, the Buddhists had none.

The names of these relocation camps have resounded in the history of America's first Buddhists. Manzanar and Tule Lake in California, Poston in Arizona, Heart Mountain in Wyoming. In each of these camps, Buddhist ministers and leaders constructed a religious life as best they could. At Heart Mountain camp, one of the members recalled the first observance of the Buddha's Birthday in the camp when there was no figure of the standing Baby Buddha. A young man who later became a Buddhist minister carved a Buddha figure from a carrot that he took from the mess hall kitchen.

In the detention camps the Japanese were subjected not only to the hardship of barracks life, but also to loyalty oaths and questionnaires. The second generation were American citizens and were asked if they would volunteer to fight in the U.S. military. Japanese civil rights activists in the camps were among the first to point out that they should not be expected to serve in the military unless their basic civil rights were restored. Nonetheless, the U.S. instituted a draft in the internment camps, and it was met with both draft resisters and volunteers. Both should be recognized as patriots in their own ways, but those who received the most public recognition were the second-generation Nisei Japanese who formed the 442nd Regimental Combat team, one of the most decorated units in World War II. Recalling this history, Congressman Phillip Burton of

California read a statement into the Congressional Record in 1974 at the time of the seventy-fifth anniversary of the Japanese Buddhism community in America: "In the century old history of the Japanese in America, the most courageous act of total commitment was demonstrated by the young men who volunteered from behind these barb-wire fenced concentration camps into which their own country had forced them, to fight—and die as many of them did—in the defense of their homeland." Burton recalled examples of their heroism, such as Sadao Munemori of Long Beach, California, who threw himself on a live grenade to save his comrades, and Frank Hachiya of Hood River, Oregon, who died capturing Japanese defense maps through which thousands of others were saved. "Both were Buddhists," said Congressman Burton, "even though they—as American soldiers—were denied their Buddhist classification on their identification dog-tags and could not have their Buddhist insignia mark their graves should they be killed in action against the common foe."[35]

Buddhist leaders came together for a landmark meeting at Topaz, Utah, in 1944. At this meeting the name of the Japanese Shin Buddhist community was changed from Buddhist Mission of North America to the Buddhist Churches of America, emphasizing the word *America* and making clear a turn toward further assimilation. After the war, as the Japanese-American community began to regain its footing and reopen and rebuild temples, the look and feel of the congregations of the newly formed Buddhist Churches of America became distinctly Protestant, as I had seen at Senshin. Dozens of new BCA "churches" were built, each as elegant as the new Senshin Temple in Los Angeles.

On the rooftop of the Buddhist Church of America headquarters in San Francisco sits a treasure few non-Buddhists know about—a shrine for a part of the relics of the Buddha. It was presented to Bishop Masuyama by the crown prince of Thailand in the 1930s. A few years ago, my host at the Buddhist Church of San Francisco unlocked the door at the top of a flight of stairs and escorted me across a wooden walkway on the rooftop to the door of the small domed shrine called a *stupa*. Inside was a small altar, with space for two or three to sit or kneel in meditation. We stood in silence, our hands pressed together in reverence. Here, looking out on the skyline of San Francisco, a city scarcely two hundred years old, we stood in the presence of a tiny relic connected by tradition to the Buddha half a world away and twenty-five hundred years ago.

The assimilation of these Buddhists, now in their fourth and fifth generations, is considerable, and by all accounts the intermarriage rate is high. In absolute numbers, the community is shrinking. Even so, the deep tradition here gives Japanese Americans a sense of strong Buddhist identity, and their ability to change with the times gives them a strong American identity as well, as could be observed in the one hundredth anniversary of the coming of the first Japanese Buddhist teachers to the U.S., celebrated in August 1999. The Southern District of the BCA in California and Arizona gathered a thousand participants at a hotel to chant the devotional sutra written by Shinran Shonin in the twelfth century. The evening's entertainment included line dancing by the Buddhist Women's Association and a traditional folk dance led by BCA ministers wearing their black robes and sunglasses, dancing to the music of the movie *Men in Black.* From one end of the ballroom to the other, these long-time American Buddhists did the wave![36]

REACHING FOR THE EAST: THE PIONEERS

The Chinese and Japanese were America's first Buddhist immigrants, but America has another Buddhist history that began, not with immigration, but with ideas and books. In the mid–nineteenth century when largely illiterate Chinese laborers and small businessmen were struggling to make a living and gain a toehold in the American West, college-educated New Englanders a continent away were beginning to discover Buddhism. And, ironically, in the same years of the 1880s in which an increasingly comprehensive policy of Asian exclusion began to set the tone of America's immigration policy, the American Oriental Society was founded to study Asia, including the sympathetic study of its religions.

One place to begin the tale of America's fascination with Buddhism is certainly with Emerson and Thoreau, the Concord transcendentalists of the mid–nineteenth century who played such a major role in making Hindu thought known in the Unitarian circles of New England. They also received Buddhist texts newly translated into English. We often forget that knowledge of Buddhist thought and practice became available to English speakers relatively recently. The term *Buddhism* did not appear in English-language dictionaries until 1812. In the 1840s Henry David Thoreau got his hands on a French translation of the Lotus Sutra, an early Mahayana text two thousand years old, and rendered part of it into English. He wrote movingly of his newfound attraction to the figure of the Buddha, whom he called "my Buddha," in his essay, "A Week on the Concord and Merrimac." "I know that some will have hard thoughts of me, when they hear their Christ named beside my Buddha," he wrote, "yet I am sure that I am willing they should love their Christ more than my Buddha, for the love is the main thing. . . ."[37] Thoreau died in 1862, but had he lived another two decades he would have found himself in an intellectual ambience buzzing with interest in the Buddha.

In 1879 Edwin Arnold's book *The Light of Asia* was published in London and then in the United States. It became an international best-seller, bringing Arnold's poetic rendering of the life of Buddha to a wide audience in the West for the first time. The book sold well over half a million copies—enough to make even today's publishers envious, with their large market for the books of the Dalai Lama and Thich Nhat Hanh and the popular books of Buddhist writers like Robert Thurman (*Inner Revolution: Life, Liberty, and the Pursuit of Real Happiness*), Steven Batchelor (*Buddhism Without Beliefs*), or Dan Goleman (*The Art of Meditation*).

The most famous and controversial of America's first Buddhist sympathizers were Helena Petrova Blavatsky (1831–1891), a flamboyant Russian émigré Bohemian who immersed herself in an eclectic sea of spiritual phenomena, and Colonel Henry Steele Olcott (1832–1907), a Manhattan urbanite and reformer attracted by the growing knowledge of world religions and universalist ideas. The two of them, with overlapping visions, founded the Theosophical Society in New York City in 1875 to make known the esoteric knowledge of the spiritual masters of the Near East, meaning the ancient world of Egypt and Mesopotamia. In these teachings, they believed, lay a universal truth that would unite the spirituality of the East and the science of the West. Gradually, these first two Theosophists began to incorporate Hindu and Buddhist ideas into their spiritualist vision. By 1879 Blavatsky and Olcott were on the boat to India, and in 1880 they knelt at Wijananda Monastery in Sri Lanka and took refuge in the Buddha, the Dharma, and the Sangha. As far as we know, they were first Americans to do so.

The reformer Olcott became committed to creating a unified Buddhism throughout Asia, based on what he saw as the simple early teachings of the Buddha. Beginning in Sri Lanka, he started Buddhist educational programs like Sunday schools and a Young Men's Buddhist Association with echoes of the YMCA. It may well have been his distant influence that led to the creation of America's first YMBA among Japanese workers in San Francisco. In 1882 Olcott published a sort of Buddhist catechism, putting into question-and-answer form what he considered to be the essentials of Buddhist faith. These "essentials" had never before been cast as a set of beliefs, but Olcott set them forth as a creed, importing into his version of Buddhism a notion of belief that came straight from Western Protestantism.

Q: What is Buddhism?

A: It is a body of teachings given out by a great personage known as the Buddha.

Q: Was the Buddha God?

A: No. Buddha Dharma teaches no "divine" incarnation.

Stephen Prothero, whose book *The White Buddhist* is the most thorough scholarly treatment of Olcott, concludes that the structure of Olcott's thought remained distinctively liberal, reformist Protestantism.[38] This creolization of two traditions helps us understand many of the Western transformations of Buddhism. Olcott's creedal, "Protestant" Buddhism had significant influence. Two of the Asian Buddhists who traveled to the World's Parliament of Religions in Chicago in 1893—Anagarika Dharmapala from Sri Lanka and Soyen Shaku from Japan—had become students or at least younger associates of Olcott, and when they spoke in Chicago of Buddhism as the religion for the modern age of science, it was as if they echoed Olcott's own voice back to his native America.

When Colonel Olcott died in 1907 at the Theosophical Society headquarters at Adyar near Madras, his body was laid out in the main hall of the society, a room containing the scriptures of all the traditions he considered his own—Christian, Buddhist, Hindu, Muslim, Sikh, Jain, and Zoroastrian. As Prothero writes, "In the center of this theosophical space lay Olcott's body, encircled by a ring of flowers and draped with twin symbols of his personal allegiances: the Buddhist flag and America's 'Old Glory.'"[39] He was carried by Hindus and Buddhists to the cremation ground; half his ashes were scattered on the Indian Ocean and half taken to the sacred river Ganges at Banaras in north India.

William Sturgis Bigelow (1850–1926) was a "Boston Brahmin" who had been born to wealth and position, had attended Harvard College and Harvard Medical School, and had became Boston's first Buddhist. Bigelow was nearly twenty years younger than Olcott, but in the 1880s both were in different parts of Asia finding their way into Buddhist life. Instead of becoming a doctor, as his father expected, Bigelow had become fascinated by the culture of Japan, in part from a series of lectures in

Boston given by Professor Edward Morse, who had been teaching zoology at the Imperial University of Tokyo. By this time Morse had already recruited another Bostonian to the Imperial University, a poet and art historian named Ernest Fenollosa (1851–1903), who had studied philosophy at Harvard and attended Harvard Divinity School.

In 1882, the very year the U.S. Congress was debating the Chinese Exclusion Act, William Sturgis Bigelow went to Japan and joined Ernest Fenollosa in what would become for both of them a deepening interest in both Buddhism and Japanese art. Fenollosa was the tireless aesthete and art collector, Bigelow the cultured financier. In 1885, both Fenollosa and Bigelow received the Buddhist precepts and were initiated into Buddhist practice.

No one spoke in those days of Buddhist-Christian dialogue, but it was clearly going on—within Bigelow himself. After a visit from Boston's charismatic Episcopal bishop Phillip Brooks in 1889, Bigelow wrote to him:

> Living off here, one is always grateful for the importation of a strong charge of home magnetism, to set one's compass by. I was especially glad to get a talk with you about Buddhism, &c, as you are I think the only man whose preaching ever made a sensible difference in my life. I shall stick it out here a little longer, till I find the bottom of the thing or make sure there isn't any, and then come home.

He was interested not only in "getting to the bottom" of Buddhism, but understanding the relation of Buddhism with psychology. "What I want to get at is the point where the two meet," he wrote. "Unless all the collateral evidence is misleading, there is something big at that point of contact."[40] Bigelow was instinctively right. He would be fascinated by the range of today's mind-body clinics and programs, including those sponsored by his own alma mater, the Harvard Medical School. In exploring the mind-body link, Buddhist meditation practice has becomes the starting point for psychological and physiological healing.

In the early 1890s when both Bigelow and Fenollosa returned to Boston, they contributed in different ways to the intellectual and spiritual encounter of the West with the Buddhist tradition. Much of the Japanese art they had collected became the core of the Museum of Fine Arts Far Eastern art collection, and Fenollosa became its first curator. In 1892, he composed a poem called "East and West" for the Phi Beta Kappa literary exercises at Harvard. He imagined the harmonious blending of eastern spirituality and western science. He clearly saw himself as an interpreter between East and West, for he had received the imprimatur of the government of Japan from the Meiji emperor, who honored him with a citation: "You have taught my people to know their own art. Going back to your country, I charge you to teach them also."[41]

As for Bigelow, he returned to his life among Back Bay Boston Episcopalians, only a few of whom knew much about his Buddhist meditation practice. From Bigelow's letters and papers, gathered in archives at Harvard, it is clear that Bigelow felt increasingly spiritually isolated. These were days when one's sense of continuity with a spiritual life rooted on the other side of the world must have been hard to maintain.

Even though he returned several times to Japan and corresponded with his mentors there, he finally had to go it alone. When he died, he was laid out in his Buddhist robes in his elegant townhouse on Beacon Street, looking out on the Boston Common. His funeral was at Trinity Church, where he was a member. Half his ashes were buried in Mt. Auburn cemetery in Cambridge and the other half sent for interment in Japan.

Sitting in Trinity Church, I often think of Bigelow and wish he could return to Boston today. What companionship he would find in his dedication to Buddhist practice. More than a dozen Buddhist centers offer training, like the Cambridge Buddhist Association where D. T. Suzuki and, more recently, Maureen Stuart Roshi led practice; the Cambridge Insight Meditation Center with its intensive Vipassana training; the Cambridge Zen Center with its Korean Zen tradition; and the Boston Dharmadhatu for Tibetan practice. He would find that some of the thousands of Bostonians who repair to these centers on a weekly or daily basis are Episcopalians, as he was, somehow balancing and merging two traditions of faith.

EAST COMES WEST:
BUDDHISTS IN THEIR OWN VOICE

The 1893 World's Parliament of Religions in Chicago opened a new chapter in America's history of Buddhism, just as it did for Hinduism. After decades of travelers' reports, Americans for the first time could hear Buddhist teachers in their own voices. Dharmapala came to the Parliament from Sri Lanka. In his lecture on "The World's Debt to Buddha" he challenged the presumptive universalism of Christianity. In seeking "universal" values, most parliament liberals really meant that

Christianity was the emerging universal religion, able to stretch its canopy over the whole world, including Buddhism. Dharmapala showed how the universal teachings of the Buddha had come many centuries before the advent of Christ.

Soyen Shaku from Japan was the first Zen master to come to America, and he explained the law of cause and effect, challenging the Christian notion that religion has to have something to do with a creator God. He set Buddhism's more scientific spirit over against the Christian idea of God as the creator and prime mover. The Buddhist view, he said, was more compatible with the emerging inquiries of science and the spirit of rationalism.

Many of Soyen Shaku's followers knew the atmosphere of discrimination against Asians that existed here and urged him not to come to a country as backward and uncivilized as America. They argued it was simply not befitting the station of a Zen master. But Soyen Shaku came anyway. His countryman Hirai Ryuge Kinzo addressed most directly the discrimination that Japanese were experiencing. He offered pointed examples: the barring of a Japanese student from a university on the basis of his race; the exclusion of Japanese children from the San Francisco public schools; the processions of American citizens bearing placards saying "Japs Must Go!" He concluded, "If such be the Christian ethics, well, we are perfectly satisfied to be heathen."[42]

In a speech so overtly and justly critical, Hirai Kinzo also had warm words for the American people, expressing his belief that discrimination does not represent the best of Christian morality and justice. He offered his own view of America's vision:

> Especially as to the American nation, I know their sympathy . . . by their emancipation of the colored people from slavery. I know their integrity by the patriotic spirit which established the independence of the United States of America. . . . I cannot restrain my thrilling emotion and sympathetic tears whenever I read in the Declaration of Independence the passages: "We hold these truths to be self-evident, that all men are created equal; that they are endowed by their Creator with certain inalienable rights; that among these are life, liberty, and the pursuit of happiness. . . ." We, the forty million souls of Japan, standing firmly and persistently upon the basis of international justice, await still further manifestations as to the morality of Christianity.[43]

In the days following the parliament, these Buddhist voices entered into more extended conversations. Dharmapala lectured on Buddhism in Chicago at the start of what would be a long lecture circuit around the United States. It began on a striking and auspicious note, for at the conclusion of this first lecture, a New Yorker of Jewish background, Charles T. Strauss, came forward to take refuge in the Buddha, the Dharma, and the Sangha and became the first American to become a Buddhist in this fashion on American soil.

Soyen Shaku's voice continued in conversation through his association with Paul Carus, a freethinker who pioneered in making the intellectual connections of religion and science, which he published in a journal called *The Open Court.* Through Soyen Shaku, Carus made his most important contact with the Buddhist world—the young D. T. Suzuki (1870–1966), who had translated Soyen Shaku's parliament address into English.

In the late 1890s, at the urging of Carus, D. T. Suzuki agreed to come to America and work with Carus at the headquarters of *The Open Court* in LaSalle, Illinois. Suzuki was not yet thirty. He spent more than a decade in Illinois, working on a translation of the Tao Te Ching and translations of Mahayana Buddhist texts. "My decision to write in English originated as a result of my many conversations with Dr. Paul Carus," he reflected later in life. "My conviction gradually emerged that Westerners did not understand Buddhism."[44] In the course of this long apprenticeship, Suzuki also became the first real cultural translator of the Zen tradition. D. T. Suzuki's name is so familiar now that it is easy to forget just how groundbreaking his achievement as a Buddhist pioneer in America really was. He was the first to put Zen Buddhism into the idioms and ideas of the West, producing more than twenty books in all. He was not a meditation master, but he was steeped in the traditions, arts, and culture of Japanese Zen and is sometimes called "the first patriarch of American Zen."

Eventually Suzuki married an American woman, a Radcliffe graduate, Beatrice Erskine Lane, who worked at his side in both the U.S. and Japan until her death in 1939. Suzuki's longest sustained period in America was in the 1950s when, throughout his eighties, he lectured at the Claremont Colleges in California and then at Columbia University. He had many Western students, like Alan Watts, who wrote that he "had to get out from under the monstrously oppressive God the Father," and Philip Kapleau, who eventually went to Japan to undertake meditation practice and wrote the classic *Three Pillars of Zen.* Psychologists such as Erich Fromm and Karen Horney attended his lectures, leading to the first major conference on Zen and psychoanalysis in Cuernavaca, Mexico, in 1957. In that same year, Suzuki also came to Cambridge, Massachusetts, for an extended visit with the Zen philosopher Shinichi Hisamatsu, who taught for a short time at Harvard Divinity School. This visit marked the beginning of the first Buddhist center in Boston, the Cambridge Buddhist Association. All the while, Suzuki was writing books that people bought and read—*Essays in Zen Buddhism, Zen and Japanese Culture, An Introduction to Zen*—and articles about him were published in such popular magazines as *Vogue* and *The New Yorker*. All this contributed to a growing "Zen boom" in intellectual circles. In the last few years of his life Suzuki lived in Japan, where he died in 1966.

Suzuki was the interpreter, the scholar, even the embodiment of Zen, but he was not a teacher of Zen practice. It was another of Soyen Shaku's students, Ngoyen Senzaki, who would become one of the first Zen meditation teachers in the U.S. He came to the U.S. to join his teacher in San Francisco in 1905, when the elder Zen master was living as a guest of Mr. and Mrs. Alexander Russell, a couple who had a strong interest in Buddhism. Mrs. Russell received instruction in koan practice from Soyen Shaku, making her perhaps the first formal student of Zen meditation in America.[45] There Nyogen Senzaki worked for a time as a houseboy and an attendant monk before his teacher sent him off on his own. When the two parted for the last time on the streets of San Francisco, Soyen Shaku is said to have told Senzaki not to teach for twenty years. He told him, "Just face the great city and see whether it conquers you or you conquer it."[46]

Senzaki began his long years of study, working at humble jobs while keeping his silence, reading books on Buddhism, and readying himself to teach. Eventually, in 1922, with twenty dollars, he rented a hall, and for an evening it became a zendo—the first in America. He would continue to teach whenever he saved enough money for a public hall or whenever he was invited to a private home. His students called it the "floating zendo." Senzaki moved to Los Angeles in 1931, and the floating zendo tradition continued until the Japanese attack on Pearl Harbor, when Senzaki, like the many other Japanese religious and community leaders, was ordered to report to a relocation camp. During these years, the floating zendo found a mooring at the Heart Mountain detention camp in Wyoming. After the war, when he was released, Sensaki was again homeless, with a suitcase, as were so many Japanese Americans whose homes, businesses, and temples simply did not survive the years of exile. In 1945 he wrote a poem commemorating the death day of his teacher, Soyen Shaku:

For forty years I have not seen
My teacher, So-yen Shaku, in person.
I have carried his Zen in my empty fist,
Wandering ever since in this strange land.
Being a mere returnee from the evacuation
I could establish no Zendo
Where his followers should commemorate
The twenty-sixth anniversary of his death.
The cold rain purified everything on the earth
In the great city of Los Angeles, today.
I open my fist and spread the fingers
At the street corner in the evening rush hour.
(*October 29, 1945*)

After coming to the U.S. at the beginning of the century, Senzaki made only one return trip to Japan, in 1955. He died in 1958 and was buried in the Japanese cemetery in Los Angeles. By that time he had opened his fist into the traffic of L.A. and let loose the practice of Zen into the rush hour of America.

TRAFFIC EAST AND WEST

The last half of the twentieth century was energized by increasing spiritual traffic across the Pacific, creating a web of relationships, teachers and disciples, seekers and immigrants, that launched a new phase in the Buddhist tradition. It began with the counterculture of the fifties and early sixties and moved within a few decades into the mainstream of American culture with bankers, doctors, and teachers who have become serious Buddhists. It began with Jack Kerouac and the *Dharma Bums* and moved into the world of Dharma Executives, Dharmanet, and Dharma on line. It began with the dropouts and the hangers-on and moved into a spectacular array of Buddhist institutions—monastic centers, temples, rural and urban retreats, service programs, and clinics. In some places it lost the name "Buddhism" altogether. All this happened in the past fifty years of American Buddhism.

The story began in the 1940s when the slow-motion ebb and flow across the Pacific began to quicken. Senzaki and Sokei-an and a few other Zen pioneers were teaching in the United States, and Americans were crossing the Pacific to study in Asia. More than sixty years after Bigelow and Fenollosa, Robert Aitken found himself in Japan in quite different circumstances—in a World War II detention camp near Kobe. His own interest in Zen was stimulated by the fact that one of his fellow prisoners was Robert Blyth, an Englishman who had written on Zen and whose works Aitken had admired. After the war, Aitken became a student of Senzaki in Los Angeles. He returned to Japan for further instruction and eventually became, in his own right, one of the first American-born Zen teachers and the founder of the Diamond Sangha in Hawaii. Ruth Fuller Sasaki was another pioneer who went to Japan to study Zen. She was introduced to Zen in Japan in 1932 by D. T. Suzuki, and after a few months she returned to New York to become part of a small circle of students around Sokei-an, the master of what became the First Zen Institute of New York. Sokei-an, like Senzaki, was imprisoned in a detention camp during World War II. When he was released in 1945, he and Ruth Fuller married, although his health was so weakened by life in the detention camp that he died later that year. After his death, Ruth dedicated herself to her own practice and to finding the right teacher to replace him at the newly formed First Zen Institute of America in New York. She returned to Japan and became accomplished in Rinzai koan practice at Daitokuji in Kyoto. Another passenger across the Pacific was the poet Gary Snyder who had studied Buddhism while a student at Reed College in Oregon and learned how to sit in meditation by studying the images of the Buddhas in the Seattle museum. Living in Berkeley in the 1950s, Snyder met and became part of the circle of Beat poets, including Allan Ginsberg and Jack Kerouac, and then set out for Japan in 1956. Jack Kerouac based *The Dharma Bums* on a figure much like Snyder. Allan Ginsberg first discovered Zen in the New York Public Library and then through the First Zen Institute of America. Kerouac's first encounter was reading Thoreau, then discovering Ashvaghosa's *The Life of Buddha* and a book called *The Buddhist Bible* published in 1950 by Dwight Goddard, who wanted to make Buddhist scriptures readily available to Americans.

In 1957 Alan Watts, an Episcopal priest turned Zen practitioner, published *The Way of Zen*, a book that became, for many, as it was for me, a first introduction to Zen. Watts had come into the circle of Sokei-an in New York, where he met and eventually married the daughter of Ruth Fuller Sasaki. He was convinced that the new Western interest in Zen was not a passing fashion. He wrote, "The deeper reason for this interest is that the viewpoint of Zen lies so close to the 'growing edge' of Western thought."[47] He meant that we in the West were beginning to reach the limits of our fascination with the objects of the material world; we were beginning an inward turn. In 1958 Watts edited a special issue of the *Chicago Review* in which his famous article, "Beat Zen, Square Zen, and Zen," appeared. Here he set forth distinctions that would become well known—the Beat Zen of countercultural poets and rebels; the Square Zen of serious practitioners, including the likes of Kerouac and Snyder; and just plain Zen, as it was practiced in Japan.

Philip Kapleau would surely have been in the Square Zen group. He was an American court reporter who had become interested in Zen when he had heard D. T. Suzuki lecture at Columbia. Wanting to move from appealing ideas to real practice, he packed up and went to Japan where he worked with Zen masters for thirteen years, eventually studying with the famous Rinzai master, Yasutani Roshi. Out of these years of firsthand experience, Kapleau wrote one of the most enduring books on the foundational Zen practices of sitting, breathing, and concentration. *The Three Pillars of Zen* was published in 1965, and when Kapleau returned to the U.S. he became the founding and guiding teacher of the Zen Meditation Center of Rochester, New York. It was in his itinerant work as a teacher that I had my own first taste of Zen practice. He did not lecture on the university circuit but rather led day-long practice sessions where students like me could come with our cushions, notebooks, and misconceptions and practice "just sitting" all day long, counting our breaths, returning our attention to the breath when the mind wandered, trying our best to ignore our aching knees and our sleepiness.

THE FLOWERING OF ZEN IN AMERICA

Zen was America's first form of Buddhist practice, including both the Soto practice of "just sitting" and the Rinzai practice of wrestling with a question called a koan, like the famous "What is the sound of one hand clapping?" Among the first and most widely influential teachers to establish Zen community practice was another Suzuki—Shunryu Suzuki, who set off from Japan for America in 1959. He did not intend to teach Zen to American seekers but rather came to serve Sokoji, the Japanese American Soto congregation in San Francisco. There he began attracting American students wanting instruction in meditation, many of them more eager and serious about meditation than the Japanese community. He invited them to join his meditation at 5:30 in the morning, probably not expecting many takers. Amazingly, they showed up, and by 1970 Suzuki and his

American followers had started the Zen Center of San Francisco, one of America's first great urban residential Zen centers.

Zen postures—legs crossed in a lotus position, back straight, chin tucked in—were demanding and required training and discipline, but the American seekers were up for the challenge. Even so, they encountered a deeper challenge than the physical posture of sitting: the can-do American spirit, putting energy and heart into the achievement of something, always instrumental, always on the go. This too had to be transformed. As long as one was training to gain something, one would never get anywhere, for Zen practice was not about yet another kind of achievement in an achievement-oriented culture. As Suzuki Roshi would put it, "These forms are not the means of obtaining the right state of mind. To take this posture is itself to have the right state of mind." The way Japanese Zen masters had put it, "An inch of sitting is an inch of Buddha." Suzuki's collection of teachings, Zen Mind, Beginner's Mind, became the introduction to Zen for a whole generation of Americans. It brought the encouraging message that it is an advantage to come to the practice of meditation without a head full of preconceptions, ideas, expectations, and philosophy. The tabula rasa of beginner's mind is good soil for Zen practice.

The Zen Center of San Francisco became the flagship for the Americanization of Zen. Over the past thirty years, all the issues that have challenged a new American Zen Sangha have cropped up here. They developed regular sitting groups and week-long intensive practice periods, called sesshins. For serious Zen practice, they created a rural mountain retreat center, the rustic and elegant Tassajara. Responding to the AIDS crisis, Issan Roshi, one of Suzuki's students, created the Bay Area AIDS action project and the Hartford Street Zen Center. Those who took the environmental movement most seriously and engaged the fundamental issues of sustainable agriculture created Green Gulch Farm, a rural farming practice center in Marin County. At Green Gulch Farm, gardening, pruning, cooking, and brewing tea become part of spiritual practice. From SFZC and Green Gulch Farm grew the fashionable San Francisco vegetarian restaurant called Greens. All this was part of the flowering of a Zen center, continually dynamic and constantly finding new ways of practice. A recent schedule of SFZC events includes meditation instructions in both Spanish and English and Zen sitting retreats for the over-sixty crowd and for young people ten to thirteen years old. The center boasts some fifteen residential teachers.

The question of leadership has been one of the great challenges of Zen community building in America. In the early 1980s SFZC experienced the sting of scandal and betrayal as Shunryu Suzuki's successor, Richard Baker Roshi, was found to have misused his teacher's role by having intimate relations with a married student. Members of the center had to confront their expectations for spiritual and moral authority. These were painful years, but eventually SFZC took an entirely new and very American turn, deciding to designate its leaders by election. In the 1990s, abbot Norman Fischer and abbess Blanche Hartman were the elected spiritual leaders of the community, and by the year 2000 Fischer's term had come to a close and Jiko Linda Cutts was selected to share the leadership with Blanche Hartman.

While Shunryu Suzuki was launching a Zen community in San Francisco, Maezumi Roshi was pioneering Zen life in Los Angeles. He left Japan for California in the 1950s. Like Shunryu Suzuki, he went first to a Japanese Soto Zen community in L.A. but soon began to attract Western Zen students. Although he was a Soto teacher, he was intensely interested in Rinzai koan practice as well. Maezumi Roshi returned to Japan for intensive study of this form of practice. This combination of both sitting and koan practice, both Soto and Rinzai Zen, shaped Maezumi Roshi's teaching legacy at the Zen Center of Los Angeles.

For more than thirty years Maezumi Roshi taught at ZCLA, a complex of bungalow homes in a largely Latino neighborhood of central Los Angeles. There he lived with his own family—an American wife and two children—and with a community of serious students who undertook daily Zen practice, beginning and ending their days by sitting in the zendo at ZCLA. In the early 1980s Maezumi Roshi also was involved in scandals, alleging drinking and intimate liaisons with a student and Dharma heir. When I met Maezumi Roshi some ten years later, the community was smaller and he himself was clear eyed, steady, and genuinely humble. Among Maezumi Roshi's students are outstanding first-generation American-born Dharma heirs. Bernard Tetsugen Glassman was an aerospace engineer when he took up Zen practice and was eventually ordained. When he left Los Angeles he founded the Zen Community of New York and pioneered in the creation of American-style Zen work projects in Yonkers, one of the country's most depressed urban areas. This was, as he put it, "an experiment in applying Buddhist principles to community development." One of the Buddhist principles he brought to the inner city was "the simple notion of starting with the ingredients at hand rather than starting with one's expectations." First he opened a successful bakery, which made deliveries all over urban New York City. He explained, "We asked what are the skills that the people have? What are the skills they don't have? And we created a production line based around the skills they already had; we started where they were at."[48] Then he started a construction company to provide employment and housing in the inner city. Both enterprises enabled workers to practice arts of attention and interdependence in daily life. "Wherever you are, there is the zendo," he would say. He also took his students to the streets for their *sesshins,* setting forth into Manhattan without a penny in their pockets, learning the arts of compassion and the truths of interdependence from the life of the streets. We will discuss his work further when we look at the contributions of Buddhists to participatory life in American society in chapter 7.

Another of Maezumi Roshi's Dharma heirs is John Daido Loori, abbot of the Zen Mountain Monastery in Mt. Tremper, New York, a beautiful and active mountain retreat center with an energetic schedule of retreats, *sesshins,* work-practice, and publication. He holds retreats for families with children, for artists, and for environmentalists and conducts rigorous canoe trips for Zen practice in the woods of the Catskill Mountains. A very different Dharma heir is Jan Chozen Bays, the leader of the Portland, Oregon, Zen center. She is a pediatrician with a busy practice in Portland. Out of both necessity and creativity, her forms of teaching and practice are grounded fully in American soil, in the life of a full-time professional.[49]

When Maezumi Roshi died in 1994, the circle of those who had worked with him gathered. It was an extraordinary witness to the first-generation of Zen teachers, sown in the soil of America and growing toward maturity. For more than thirty years, ZCLA had been in the hands of Maezumi Roshi, and for 750 years Soto Zen teaching had been in the hands of Japanese teachers. Together, these American-born teachers trained by Maezumi Roshi formed the White Plum Sangha. The writer Peter Matthiessen, who had also been among Maezumi Roshi's students, reflected at a 1997 conference on American Buddhism held in Boston, "In American Zen, with Maezumi-roshi's death, in a sense the great era of Japanese Zen teachers began to draw to a close. There are still some here, but that was, to me, a benchmark, an indication that the Dharma is being left in our hands now." Indeed, of the ninety-nine Soto teachers in America in the late 1990s, eighty-three were American born.[50]

In June of 1999 Wendy Egyoku Nakao was installed as the new abbot of ZCLA. She had been a longtime resident of the Zen center. Following

Bernard Glassman's initiative, she had undertaken "street retreats," living for three days with her students among the homeless on the street. As the new abbot of one of the nation's preeminent Zen centers, Wendy Nakao is now striking out on a distinctive path, adding a feminist perspective to the discipline of Zen practice, adding the names of women teachers, long neglected in the Soto hierarchies, to the liturgical recitations. Her style is also egalitarian rather than hierarchical. Reporting on her installation, the *Los Angeles Times* said, "True to Nakao's East-West style, she offered well-wishers both formal bows and warm kisses, chanted ancient sutras and tossed out on-the-spot quips. The ceremony was rich with both Japanese tradition—she offered incense and poems at different altars— and such American touches as a specially crafted celebratory song with guitar accompaniment."[51] In the White Plum Sangha, new plum blossoms are growing on the old branch.

MINDFULNESS: THE VIPASSANA MOVEMENT

The Insight Meditation Society sits on country acreage outside the small Massachusetts town of Barre. The large Georgian brick house with its rambling accumulation of wings, additions, and dormitories, formerly a Catholic retreat center, was bought in 1976 by a group of American meditators trained in Southeast Asia. It is the largest center in the country for serious meditation practice, and the acquisition of a neighboring farm down the road for a study center has created a Buddhist subculture on this country road. Plans are well under way for a long-term practice center for experienced meditators. Driving the two miles from Barre, one sees meditators along the roadside, walking alone, slowly, practicing the mindfulness of walking.

The resident guiding teachers of IMS are Joseph Goldstein and Sharon Salzberg, both of whom took up meditation practice in the 1960s. Joseph, a graduate of Columbia University, went to Thailand in the Peace Corps in 1962 and stayed after his stint to study Vipassana meditation in Bodh Gaya, India, with Anagarika Munidra, a student of the Burmese master Mahasi Sayadaw. He describes his first five minutes of meditation:

> I did not know anything about meditation at the time, and I became very excited by it. I gathered all the paraphernalia together, sat myself down on a cushion, and set my alarm clock for five minutes. But something very important happened even in

those first five minutes. I realized that I could do it. That realization is a turning point in everyone's spiritual life. We read books and hear people speak about it, but then we reach a certain point in our lives when something connects and we realize, "Yes, I can do this." This does not mean that in those first five minutes I reached any great state of awakening; I did not. But I saw very clearly that there is a way to look inward. There is a path. There is a way to explore the nature of the mind, the nature of our lives.[52]

The 1960s and 1970s found many young Americans in India and Thailand undertaking the serious practice of Buddhist meditation with some of the leading meditation masters of the Theravada tradition. Jack Kornfield studied with the forest monk Achaan Chaa in Thailand. Jack and Joseph met during the first year of the Naropa Institute's summer school in 1974 in Boulder, Colorado, and began teaching together. In 1976, as we have seen, the first major Theravada retreat center in America opened in Barre, Massachusetts. In 1985 Jack Kornfield and others on the West Coast started Insight Meditation West and began the creation of the Spirit Rock Center in Marin County. Today there are dozens of Vipassana meditation centers, large and small, and the group of prominent guiding teachers has expanded to include women like Sylvia Boorstein, whose teachings combine meditation practice with the deep wisdom of an experienced psychotherapist, and Sharon Salzberg, whose teachings enable people to cultivate the practice of compassion, beginning with compassion in everyday life.

Insight Meditation is a basic, no-frills teaching. Neither the students nor the teachers wear robes for their sitting practice, as you might find in a Zen or Tibetan center. The sitting room is an unadorned hall, large enough for two hundred people, who sit row upon row, each place marked with a jumble of cushions, shawls, and blankets. On the altar at one end of the hall is an image of the Buddha, seated in meditation, the very exemplar of the plain practice that goes on here, hour after hour: a breath-centered practice called *shamatha,* calming or concentrating the mind. Merely attending to the in-breath and the out-breath begins to quiet the restless mind and create the stillness necessary for clear insight. This concentration practice is joined to the practice of *vipassana,* sometimes translated as "mindfulness," sometimes as "insight meditation." Vipassana is the practice of observation, focusing on the comings and goings of thoughts, emotions, and sensations. These are simple forms of practice, but they are not easy. Even a taste of breath-centered practice reveals to a beginner just how wild the mind can be, how little we are able to focus on the in-breath and the out-breath without being drawn into fantasies, into trains of thought, into the turbulence of emotion. It is little wonder that the process of meditation is a lesson in self-discovery that people of every religious tradition and none have found illumining. An IMS publication summarizes the basic practice in plain English, with not even a hint of Buddhist jargon:

> The core of insight meditation is the practice of mindfulness, a quality of awareness which sees without judgment. Mindfulness is developed and strengthened through sitting and walking meditation. Meditation practice may begin by simply paying careful attention to the breath, in and out, and returning over and over to the breath when the mind wanders. The deepening stability and calmness of mind developed through this practice slowly renders the mind fit to see more clearly into itself. Such clear seeing gradually sets us free, dissolving barriers to the full development of wisdom and compassion.

Today the Insight Meditation Society has a year-long series of short-term retreats, and the Barre Center for Buddhist Studies offers classes that bridge the gap between academic Buddhist studies and the traditions of practice on which Buddhist philosophical texts are based. Each fall, IMS offers a three-month retreat, a completely silent retreat in which the daily routine consists of sessions of sitting meditation, walking meditation, work-practice in the kitchen or dining room, silent meals, and a daily evening Dharma talk. The only speech during the entire three-month period is during the periodic instruction interviews each participant has with one of the resident teachers. Even reading and keeping a journal are discouraged, as these tend to provide a diversion from the primary focus on moment-to-moment awareness. These three months are a time-out, constructed in such a way as to intervene in the rush of activity, thinking, planning, grasping, self-aggrandizement, and self-recrimination that dominates most of our lives. Despite the rigor of this program of meditation practice, reservations for the three-month retreat must be made nearly a year in advance, and even then there is often a lottery for places.

Insight Meditation groups span America, from San Diego to New Hampshire, meeting in homes and practice centers. Because this tradition of meditation practice is also part of the life of South and Southeast

Asian immigrant Buddhist communities, many temples have become meditation centers for Buddhists of all races. I think especially of communities like Wat Dhammaram in Chicago, a Thai temple that gathers the Thai immigrant community together for festivals and worship and also gathers a mixed Thai-American community for regularly scheduled insight meditation retreats. The Bhavana Society in the forests of West Virginia was established by a Sri Lankan monk, the Venerable H. Gunaratana, who is also its guiding teacher. Here again, old monastic traditions of Asia have begun to grow in America, providing a place of both refuge and practice for American laypeople who have no intention of becoming monks but are yearning for a way to clear a space for Buddhist practice in the thicket of their lives.

TIBETAN VAJRAYANA TRADITIONS

The most familiar Buddhist in the world today is the Dalai Lama, the spiritual head of the Tibetan Buddhist Gelugpa tradition and the exiled leader of the Buddhist kingdom of Tibet. Maroon robed, stooping ever so slightly forward in a gesture of humility, smiling broadly, combining deep spirituality with infectious laughter, the Dalai Lama has become the closest thing there has ever been to a worldwide Buddhist leader. He is respected by Buddhists across cultures and around the world. This is not a respect inherited, but one conferred by Buddhists in virtually every stream of the tradition. While he is the leader of a refugee Tibetan community now scattered across the globe, he directs his political and moral force not to the issue of Tibet alone, but to the support of a wide range of humanitarian and environmental causes.

My first glimpse of the Dalai Lama was at Harvard in the mid-1970s, when he delivered a series of lectures on Buddhist philosophy and then made one public appearance in a huge campus theater packed with three thousand students. After he was introduced, the Dalai Lama sat in a single chair on the stage and spoke straightforwardly, winningly, about the sense of "I," the problems of egotism, and the difficulty most of us have grasping the truth that "I" is only a mental construct. The next day, the *Harvard Crimson* story reported on the sense of "eye" and the difficulties of understanding "eye" as a mental construct! It must have been written either by a freshman innocent or an interloper from the *Harvard Lampoon*. In the next few years, I met the Dalai Lama several times in quite different settings: at a Harvard Medical School mind-body conference at MIT, at the

Parliament of the World's Religions in Chicago in 1993, and most important, at a special Christian-Buddhist intermonastic dialogue at Gethsemani Abbey in Kentucky in 1996. For me and for many Americans, the Dalai Lama speaks with a voice of global acuity and authority, matched only in the Christian world by someone like Archbishop Desmond Tutu or Pope John Paul II. In some ways, his role as the leader-in-diaspora of a politically oppressed religious community enhances his stature, for unlike the pope, he does not have the power and authority of a worldwide hierarchical structure at his command. It made perfect sense for him to receive a delegation of American Jews in 1991 to discuss their common questions of exile and survival, the story of which is told in the delightful book *The Jew in the Lotus* by Rodger Kamenetz.

Although most of us identify Tibetan Buddhism with the Dalai Lama, the Vajrayana tradition of Buddhism is a really complex skein of traditions, with at least four main lineages—Kagyu, Gelugpa, Nyingma, Sakya—all of them present in the United States. Among the first teachers to come was Chogyam Trungpa Rinpoche of the Karma Kagyu lineage, who arrived in the early 1970s and began teaching Buddhist philosophy and practice in the distinctively American vernacular of psychology. He established the first Tibetan centers, which he called Dharmadhatu Centers, in rural Barnet, Vermont, and in Boulder, Colorado. By now, however, his network of centers, united by the Vajradhatu organization and Shambhala International, includes dozens of centers in every part of the country, making this America's most extensive Tibetan Buddhist infrastructure.

Trungpa Rinpoche, who dressed as often in a business suit as in maroon Tibetan robes, steered into the heart of nondualist Vajrayana teachings with a personal style that scorned the expectations of holiness and, too often for some, included heavy drinking and sexual liaisons. But his teachings, first published as *Cutting Through Spiritual Materialism,* emphasized the ways in which spirituality itself can become an ego trap, a form of grasping identity that is every bit as deceiving as materialism. At Karme Choling in Boulder, practice included the use of mantras, mandalas, and visualizations, all harnessing sense, sound, and sight to spiritual realization. His cremation on a green hillside in rural Vermont, circled by hundreds of maroon-robed Tibetan monks and American followers in jeans and in business suits, was the first of its kind in the United States. The story made the New York Times and gave many Americans a first glimpse of the Tibetan high liturgical tradition.

Tarthang Tulku of the Nyingma lineage arrived in the U.S. just a little earlier than Trungpa Rinpoche. He began the Nyingma Institute in Berkeley in the 1970s with the support of students he had met in India. The institute, adjacent to the campus of the University of California, gradually grew, launching dozens of meditation programs, educational programs, and a publishing enterprise. By the mid-1990s, Tarthang Tulku had opened a spectacular center for the preservation, study, and practice of Buddhist traditions in the hills of northern California. Named Odiyan, this complex includes a grand copper-domed temple with an eighty-four-thousand-text library and an eleven-story golden stupa streaming with multicolored prayer flags—all set amid meadows and giant Douglas firs.

By 1998 I had visited the Nyingma Institute in Berkeley with its huge walk-around prayer wheel in the backyard, I had spent a few days at the epicenter of the Dharmadhatu at the Boulder Karme Dzong temple, and I had made deep bows to the Dalai Lama, but my first introduction to the distinctive forms of Tibetan meditation was with a teacher named Tsoknyi Rinpoche, recognized as a reincarnation of Lama Drubwang Tsoknyi, in the Kagyu and Nyingma traditions. The practice he taught was called Dzogchen, and the method was to move beyond the stillness of *shamatha* practice, which still maintains a kind of subject-object dualism, to the soft-focus, nondualistic sky-mind of clear seeing. I thought of it as sky gazing. That summer, Tsoknyi Rinpoche was teaching at Wisdom House in Litchfield, Connecticut, a retreat center run by a group of Catholic sisters who practice the arts of hospitality by opening the place to people of other spiritual paths. The large carpeted chapel room had been emptied of chairs and was filled with row upon row of the multicolored zafus and zabutons brought along by a very diverse group of meditators. Rome notwithstanding, Sophia, Our Lady of Wisdom, reigned at the front of the chapel, looking sufficiently androgynous that one could readily mistake her for either Christ or Kuan Yin. In front of her was the elegantly decorated throne, covered with rich yellow, blue, and red brocades, where the young rinpoche would sit to teach. Except for his heady teachings on the nature of the mind, it would be a week of silence. One could call it summer camp, in a way. The daily regime was clear—sitting, teaching, sitting, interviews, discussion, meals, sitting. But there was no interaction among the campers. Meals were taken in silence, and in the breaks we sat on the long porches and green lawns gazing silently toward the sky.

Rinpoche began by reminding us that we have spent our entire lives cultivating a particular habit of mind, that is, directing our minds outward to one thing after another, past, present, and future, apprehending and investigating objects, people, places, experiences, investigating every-thing except the mind itself, never coming home, never resting in itself, never glimpsing its own nature—pristine clarity and unbounded space. So the main activity of this camp was to recognize the "mind essence," called *rigpa* in Tibetan, which Rinpoche described as "empty in essence, cognizant in nature, unconfined in capacity."

For an hour we would sit with our eyes open, dropping all concep-tion. This was not easy. The fan churned the hot summer air, the colors swirled in soft focus. Like everyone else, presumably, I would drift off, wondering from my cushion at the very back of the hall who these two hundred people were, balding and graying men, slim and fit-looking middle-aged women, who seemed to have chosen a week of sitting in silence over a week in the Berkshires or the Hamptons. As the mind reached for this or that, we were instructed to drop it and to rest in awareness in the space, the "gap," as he called it, between thoughts; grad-ually the space expanded. There was nothing to do but to drop it and look directly into the gaps, again and again.

The other side of this bare-bones practice were quite elaborate liturgies that I warmed to immediately. They took place in the evenings, in the last session of the day, bringing an imaginative luminosity to the last hours of the day. Tsoknyi Rinpoche sat on his teaching throne, and we all sat in silence for a short while. Then he began speaking, slowly and clearly above the low sawing of the crickets outside. "Imagine a white, eight-petaled lotus. On it sits the Buddha, golden, his right hand touching the earth in front of him, his left hand in his lap. A brilliant light issues from his forehead, and it touches your forehead, eliminating all defilements of body. Brilliant light issues from his throat, and touches yours, eliminating all defilements of speech, that we may speak only words of compassion. Light from his heart touches your heart, eliminating all defilements of mind. The Buddha dis-solves in pure light. That light suffuses your whole body. . . ."

There was a concluding prayer:

May the light of the Buddha shine, spreading its rays like the ris-ing sun. May the Nectar of Dharma satisfy all beings. May all beings attain success and happiness. May the rains come. May the crops grow and reach maturity.

It seemed to be a perfect prayer for the growth of Buddhism in America. The dawn had clearly passed, and the light of the Buddha seemed to be spreading like the rays of the sun.

THE RIPENING OF BUDDHIST AMERICA

The many tonalities of Buddhism in America signal its maturity here. This diversity is in keeping with the whole of the tradition, for the languages, cultures, and forms of the Buddhist tradition have been many—the Theravada traditions of South Asia, the Mahayana traditions of China, Japan, and Korea, and the Vajrayana traditions of Tibet. The continuities that are called "Buddhism" have taken on the colors and forms of the cultures into which they have moved. Buddhism has always maintained a certain continuity of thought while adapting its language and syntax to each new culture. Each form of Buddhist teaching and practice has a utilitarian purpose—to enable us to cross the flood of birth and death, suffering and desire, getting and keeping, to what is called the "far shore." But when you have reached the far shore, they say, there is no point in remaining attached to the boat. Don't haul it along with you on your back.

The past one hundred fifty years, and especially the past thirty years, have seen the crossing of these boats of Buddhism to the new world of America and the development of distinctive ways of speaking that are American, or at least Western. We have also seen the development of Buddhist institutional life, with meditation centers that number now in the thousands and form the institutional infrastructure of the Buddhist tradition in America. Central to all three of these streams of Buddhism is the emphasis on Buddhist practice. While Buddhism had been understood and received sympathetically by readers of D. T. Suzuki and other popular writers, it was not until the 1970s that Euro-American Buddhism focused intently on the discipline of meditation practice and began to build the communities and centers to sustain such practice. In 1988 when the first edition of Don Morreale's *Buddhist America: Centers, Retreats, Practices* was published it included descriptions of 163 Mahayana centers offering instruction in some form of Zen practice; 72 Theravada centers with Vipassana meditation practice; and 180 Tibetan or Vajrayana centers. When the next edition was published ten years later, the numbers had grown to 423 Mahayana centers, 152 Theravada centers, 352 Vajrayana centers, and another 152 centers that referred to themselves as generically Buddhist. On the whole, this accounting did not even begin to include the whole scope of new Asian immigrant temples. Even so, Don Morreale begins with a good summary of what he thinks has happened in this critical decade. "Everything has changed in Buddhist America," he writes.

The wildness of the early days is over and meditation is no longer the province of a handful of visionaries and poets. Buddhism has gone mainstream. At retreats one is likely to find oneself sitting next to a stock-broker or a therapist or a retired social worker who may or may not claim to be a Buddhist. It is an older crowd as well, with fewer and fewer people in their twenties and more and more in their forties, fifties, and sixties.[53]

This demographic indicator tells us something significant about the appeal of Buddhist practice, not so much to college-age people and twenty-somethings, but to people more mature and with plenty of experience in the turbulence of life and growth. Don Morreale's catalog of Buddhist centers also reveals that these are not limited to the big cosmopolitan coastal cities. We learn of the Zen Center of Las Vegas, the Nebraska Zen Center, and the Nashville Zen Group, and we find a Pentagon Meditation Center profiled, with the motto, "Love is the ultimate first-strike capability."[54]

Not surprisingly, by the end of the 1980s, in each of these traditions—Theravada, Mahayana, and Vajrayana—a number of American-born and American-trained students of Buddhist teachers had emerged who had received Dharma transmission and could be said to be second-generation teachers. These teachers represent the first step in truly indigenizing and Americanizing Buddhism. In the last two decades of the twentieth century, age-old Asian lineages crossed the Pacific, and for the first time in history they were passed to American-born Buddhists. This is one of the great new facts of the Buddhist tradition as we enter the twenty-first century. It is no longer the case that we are speaking of a neo-Buddhism that falls short of the real thing; it is no longer the case that we are speaking merely of America's interest in Buddhism; now American-born teachers—the grandchildren of Polish Jews or Norwegian Lutherans—are recognized teachers in ancient Buddhist lineages.

One day in the fall of 1992, I drove to the Providence Zen Center in Cumberland, Rhode Island, for just such a historic event: the Dharma transmission of one of the great Korean Zen teachers, Zen Master Seung Sahn. For the first time on American soil, he was publicly entrusting the authority to teach to three American-born disciples. A huge festival tent had been set up on the lawns of the Providence Zen Center, and on the rows of chairs inside sat a range of Buddhists whose very presence seemed to bridge the gulf that often separates Euro-American Buddhists from new Asian immigrants. The front row of chairs was reserved for the dozens of teachers who had come to witness the transmission: monks from Zen Master Seung Sahn's order in Korea, Jakusho Kwong Roshi from the Sonoma Mountain Zen Center and Shunryu Suzuki's Soto Zen lineage, and Mahaghosananda, the patriarch of the Cambodian Buddhist community.

Twenty years earlier, Zen Master Seung Sahn had made the Pacific crossing himself. He arrived in Providence in the early 1970s, speaking little English and earning his living by repairing washing machines. He offered meditation instruction to a few dedicated students who eventually became the core of the Providence Zen Center. He comes from a Zen tradition, called Chogye in Korea, and part of his teaching practice is the kong-an or koan, testing the student's insight by responding to a question posed by the master. Now there are more than sixty branches of the Kwan Um School of Zen worldwide. That fall day, in his first major Western Zen center, Zen Master Seung Sahn publicly tested his three heirs—a Euro-American man, an Asian-American man, and a Euro-American woman. He would pose seemingly impossible questions: "This stick and your mind—are they the same or different?" In the midst of this kind of "dharma combat," these new teachers were able to respond in ways that demonstrated—at least to the teacher, if not to the appreciative but puzzled audience—their razor-sharp presence of mind.

While the East-West-East movement of spiritual teachers and seekers across the Pacific was going on, powerful currents of migration were also bringing hundreds of thousands of new Asian Buddhists to America. From Sri Lanka, Thailand, Taiwan, and Korea they came as immigrants, and from Southeast Asia they came as refugees from the aftermath of America's war in Vietnam. By the time the United States pulled out of Vietnam in 1975, hundreds of thousands of Vietnamese were ready to emigrate to the U.S., and within a few years hundreds of thousands of Cambodians were ready to be transported from refugee camps in Thailand. A new wave of Buddhist immigration to America had begun.

VIETNAMESE BUDDHISTS IN AMERICA

In 1965 the world's attention was arrested by the vivid front-page story of a monk, seated in the serenity of meditation, aflame with fire. His name was Thich Quang Duc, a monastic leader who opposed both the Communist regime of North Vietnam and the alliance of the U.S. with the

Diem regime in South Vietnam. He had walked calmly to the center of the main intersection of Hue, poured gasoline over his body, and set himself ablaze. I was like millions of others around the world for whom the story and the photo were a vivid awakening. Despite the burgeoning protest movements on American city streets, never did we imagine this form of protest. What did it mean? Where did this kind of self-sacrificing serenity come from? His soft-spoken monastic colleague, Thich Nhat Hanh, came to the United States to tell us, bringing to us the voice of Buddhist resistance to the war in Vietnam. His book *Lotus in a Sea of Fire* explained the role of Buddhism in protesting the war. It is a short and powerful book, and in 1965 it was the first book on Buddhism that I ever read.

Like many Americans, I encountered Buddhism during these years of the war in Vietnam, years that spanned my studies in college and graduate school. Few of us in college, even those of us who considered ourselves religious, understood anything at all about Vietnamese religion, especially its Buddhist traditions, which brought together influence from both the Mahayana traditions of China and the Theravada traditions of Southeast Asia. Links existed to our world through Dr. Martin Luther King Jr. and through the Trappist monk Thomas Merton. Both men knew of Thich Nhat Hanh and had an inkling of the issues that Buddhist resistance placed before the world: the fruitlessness of armed struggle and the high toll such a war takes on the ordinary people who are its victims. Thich Nhat Hanh's first trip to the United States was sponsored by the Fellowship of Reconciliation, and it was the beginning of four decades of Thich Nhat Hanh's teaching in America. The monk's outspoken critique of the war in Vietnam meant that he was unable to return to Vietnam.

From his retreat center called Plum Village in the south of France, Thich Nhat Hanh has continued to teach and speak for peace and has become one of the primary teachers of what is called "engaged Buddhism." He emphasizes the Buddhist teaching of the interdependence, what he calls the "interbeing," of all things. Nothing exists unto itself alone, but we "inter-are," our lives are entwined with those of others and with the natural environment that sustains us. This foundational teaching becomes the basis for a form of peacemaking and social transformation that begins within. We need to practice not just making peace but "being peace," by cultivating an awareness of our very way of being in the world. If we can see deeply into our own suffering, anger, and frustration, we can let the springs of compassion water and nurture peace within. Only then can we be effective peace builders in the world. When Thich

Nhat Hanh first toured in the United States in 1966, there were no Vietnamese temples here. The tragedies that brought a flood of refugees, many of them the boat people who escaped from the advancing Vietcong in a flotilla of crowded boats, were still a decade away. But that human displacement that came from the war has now created a new Vietnamese subculture in America. It is a legacy of the conflict against which Thich Nhat Hanh spoke so relentlessly.

The first Vietnamese Buddhist monk to settle in the U.S. was Thich Thien-an, who came to Los Angeles in the late 1960s, taught at UCLA, and became involved in creating both the International Buddhist Meditation Center in 1970 and the first Vietnamese temple in America, Chua Vietnam, in central Los Angeles, in 1976. The fall of Saigon to the Vietcong in 1975 triggered the movement of refugees from Vietnam, Laos, and Cambodia to settle the U.S., so in April of 1975 alone some 86,000 Vietnamese were airlifted from Saigon and transported to the U.S. By the end of 1975, 130,000 had come, including many who could not escape by the airlift and became boat people, who set to sea in inadequate craft to escape from the takeover of Saigon. By 1985 the total Vietnamese population of the U.S. was estimated to be 643,000. This number includes both Roman Catholics and Buddhists, but all share the experience of profound dislocation. By 1990 the number was well over a million.

In Vietnam the temples were the residence of monks, so not surprisingly the small homes monks were able to rent and, eventually, to buy, became the first Vietnamese Buddhist temples in America. I first learned the term *home temple* through the work of one of my students and researchers, Chloe Breyer, who spent a summer in Los Angeles exploring the Buddhist communities of L. A. and Orange County. Among them was the Lien Hoa temple on Bixby Street in Garden Grove, a one-story suburban home in a residential neighborhood. Shoes were piled at the front door, and the living room was the Buddha Hall, containing an altar for the Buddha and a small family memorial altar bearing the photos of the dead. The Confucian ethos of China that both remembers and venerates ancestors is very important here, and of course in this community there are many dead, both those who died in the war and those who died in flight as refugees. Just behind the temple, out the backdoor, was the patio, which functioned as the community hall, with picnic tables for dinners and blackboards for meetings and classes.

Lien Hoa was like dozens of home temples in Orange County, where the greatest density of Vietnamese settled in an area that has come to be called Little Siagon. On an average day perhaps two dozen regulars would stop at the temple for prayers, chanting, tea, and conversation, but on special holidays such as the Buddha's Birthday and at important occasions such as a funeral, there might well be three or four hundred people in the course of a day. Traffic would be dense, and cars might be parked all over the neighborhood. As we shall see in chapter 6 when we investigate the interrelations of new religious neighbors in the U.S., the conflicts of these Vietnamese communities with local zoning ordinances have stretched over more than a decade. Our Pluralism Project researchers found small temples of this kind throughout the U.S.—in Denver, Houston, New Orleans, Oklahoma City, and Chicago. A small booklet published in Westminster, California, in 1992 listed over one hundred forty Vietnamese temples, most of which are located in what were once suburban homes.

In late August of 1992 I visited another temple called Lien Hoa, this one in Olympia, Washington, the state capitol. I was on my way to a Labor Day gathering of my own family on Hood Canal and had been invited to stop in Olympia for an occasion that the temple president described as "Vietnamese Mother's Day." I found the temple without much difficulty in a verdant suburban neighborhood. From half a block away temple teenagers were busy directing traffic into the lot next to the temple. Chua Lien Hoa was formerly a Korean Christian Church, so the congregation had avoided any zoning battles. It was much too small for the community on this festival day, however. They had stretched out multicolored parachutes over every available outside space to serve as canopies for cooking and serving an elaborate community meal. And they had clearly planned for the surfeit of traffic and checked with the neighbors.

I made a round of the busy life outside the temple, getting a sense of the intense activity. The ceremonies inside were about to begin, so I found my host, one of the temple lay leaders, and he introduced me to his wife, who stood at the doorway with a huge bouquet of roses. Greeting me, she asked if my mother was living or deceased. I was very happy to say she was still alive and was given a red rose; those whose mothers were no longer living received white roses. The sanctuary, with its original pews supplemented by extra folding chairs, was crowded with young families, grandmothers, young singles, and several pews of guests from the surrounding neighborhood. In front of me sat a Caucasian family with four children, all clutching their red roses: three little boys and a very excited eight-year-old girl, the eldest, all decked out in her party dress with a straw hat and black ribbons flowing from her hatband. I learned that they lived right across the street, but this was their first visit to the temple.

On the altar at the front of the sanctuary was the Buddha, seated amid many porcelain vases of flowers and plates of fruit. Behind him was a painted scene of what appeared to be Washington's own Hood Canal with the Olympic Mountains in the background. About ten monks made their entry. Most were Vietnamese, but they were joined by a Thai monk and a Tibetan monk from Seattle, a Euro-American leader of one of the meditation centers, and my friend from Los Angeles, Dr. Ratanasara, who had come to encourage the formation of pan-Buddhist fellowship in the Pacific Northwest.

It was a long Mother's Day program. Monks spoke, both in English and Vietnamese. A woman vocalist sang a traditional Vietnamese song. The Buddhist youth group put on a skit. The whole congregation joined in chanting. Finally, the little girl in the straw hat began to squirm, and her brother fell sound asleep. In the course of the hour or so, I learned that Vu-Lan, or Vietnamese Mother's Day, comes at the end of the annual period of monastic retreat called the "rainy season retreat" in South Asia, where it does, in fact, coincide with the end of the rainy season. It is called Ullambana in much of the Buddhist world. Here in the Pacific Northwest, it was noted, it is always the rainy season. Already full participants in the regional humor, everyone laughed. Vu-Lan is a time for laity to honor the monks and for monks to dedicate the merit of their retreat season to the benefit of their parents, especially those who have died. The laity also join in dedicating offerings to their parents.

While I can understand my many reformist Buddhist friends, including the nuns of Hsi Lai, who want to emphasize the life-oriented teachings of Buddhism and deemphasize the death rites, I was deeply touched in Olympia by this communal memorial. Perhaps it was because my visit took place during a week of reunions for my family that I was intensely aware how much the dead are missed and how few rituals we Protestants have for collectively remembering them. Family gatherings often include toasts and shared memories but nothing very reliable for honoring those who have passed over to the far shore. I was happy to have been here for Vu-Lan, and I stayed for the sumptuous meal after the service, served in generous Styrofoam plates with separate compartments for each dish, before making my way back onto the road to Hood Canal.

The future of Vietnamese Buddhism in America in the next generation is uncertain. Few of the monks who have come from Vietnam are
able to communicate effectively with the rapidly assimilating American-
born young people. Cuong Nguyen and A. W. Barber, who have written
about the subject, note that American-born Vietnamese are unlikely to
become monks, and their parents are far more concerned with their
material and educational success than with their education and commitment as Buddhists. But in my view there are real signs of positive adaptation and change. For example, when I returned to Olympia in the summer of 1999 a new monk was in charge—a Sri Lankan, who was very
effective as a Buddhist teacher. The Vietnamese Buddhist Youth Association seemed to be flourishing, and its Web site listed a host of activities: a retreat with youth from the Portland temple, a friendship camp
with Canadian youth in Vancouver, and a Lion Dance performing arts
group. These second-generation youngsters, born or at least raised in
America, are the future for temples like Lien Hoa.

Thich Nhat Hanh has also had a significant role as a bridge between
the first generation of refugees and their very American children. He has
not yet been able to return to his native Vietnam, but he comes regularly
to America, where both Vietnamese and non-Vietnamese Americans
flock to hear him and to undertake week-long or day-long retreats with
him as he teaches sitting and walking meditation. Especially for the second generation, Thich Nhat Hanh provides an important bridge to a Vietnamese tradition that is inaccessible to them in the traditional temples of
their parents, where the monks rarely speak English. In one of the
Vietnamese temples in Boston, for example, the temple leaders, Dr. and
Mrs. Nguyen, are typical of the increasingly professional middle class who
find Thich Nhat Hanh's teachings spiritually deepening. While the temple
community holds traditional services, with chanting and sutra recitation,
services also include the silent mindfulness meditation that Thich Nhat
Hanh has popularized in the West. During the potluck meal following
the service, there is a brief period of mindfulness practice as people begin
eating. Every few months, the temple hosts its own Mindfulness Day in
the style of Thich Nhat Hanh: taking a full day at the temple to attend
mindfully and gratefully to every breath and each action. His style of
teaching addresses the particular woundedness of the Vietnamese experience in America. By attending mindfully to this very moment, he says,
one can both heal the past and plant the seeds of the future.

FROM CAMBODIA TO AMERICA

In his suburban home in Long Beach, California, a Cambodian teenager, You Korn, showed me a framed photograph of his family that has become one of the most enduring images imprinted in my mind from the Cambodian experience. It was an eight-by-ten color photo of the whole family taken just a year earlier. Inside the glass, along the right edge of the photograph, was a strip of black-and-white mug shots that had been taken of each member of the family—his parents, his brother, his three sisters, and himself—as they were processed into the refugee camp in Thailand after fleeing the Killing Fields of Cambodia. They lived as refugees in Thailand for six years from 1979 to 1985, when they gained entry into the United States. The juxtaposition of the color print and the mug shots was startling, and the care taken to create this montage of two worlds and to display them together in this Long Beach living room was moving.

Along with the Vietnamese, Laotians, and Hmong, Cambodian refugees have also come to the U.S. in the wake of the war in Southeast Asia. It was not even their war, at least to begin with, but by 1969 the United States began bombing in Cambodia in an attempt to destroy Vietcong bases and supply routes, and in 1970 a U.S.-backed coup put General Lon Nol in charge of the government. U.S. ground forces then invaded Cambodia as part of a strategy to destroy the countryside bases of the Vietcong. It is little wonder that disaffection and the seeds of revolution were strong enough to nurture sympathy for Cambodia's own Communist movement, the Khmer Rouge. Even after the U.S. had left Vietnam, the civil war in Cambodia continued. When the Khmer Rouge marched into Phnom Penh and deposed Lon Nol in April of 1975, many hoped for a new start.

But the new start the radical Khmer Rouge initiated was disastrous. They proclaimed 1975 "year zero" and tried to reconstruct Cambodia as a classless, agrarian, anti-Western society, by erasing its history, its social and family structures, its religious life, and its intellectuals. This reconstruction was done by force—marching people from the cities and enforcing manual labor in the countryside. Between 1975 and 1979 during the full power of Pol Pot and the Khmer Rouge, Cambodia was virtually sealed off from the outside world. We later found out that two to three million Cambodians had been killed. Most of Cambodia's 3,600 temples were destroyed, and only about 3,000 of Cambodia's 50,000 monks survived the genocide. Millions fled the villages and fields of

Cambodia, which became known as the Killing Fields, pouring across the border into refugee camps in Thailand. Between 1979 and 1985 more than 150,000 Cambodians came to the U.S. They were, on the whole, a traumatized population, most of whom had come, like You Korn's family, from the refugee camps in Thailand.

Among those who met the refugees at the Thai border was a monk who brought to his countrymen—who had witnessed unspeakable horrors, who had seen parents and children killed before their eyes—the most difficult message of all: the message of nonviolence and forgiveness. The monk's name was Mahaghosananda, and his message came straight from the first verses of the Dhammapada, the classic source of Buddhist ethics:

> In those who harbor thoughts of blame and vengeance toward others, hatred will never cease. In those who do not harbor blame and vengeance, hatred will surely cease. For hatred is never appeased by hatred. Hatred is appeased by love. This is an eternal law.

Mahaghosananda had grown up in the Mekong delta and had attended the Buddhist university in Phnom Penh and Battambang. He went on to study in Nalanda in India and spent several years training with the forest monks of Thailand in the discipline of mindfulness meditation. He was there in Thailand during the Khmer Rouge reign of terror. When the survivors of the Pol Pot regime and the Killing Fields poured across the Thai border, he was the first active and openly robed monk they had seen in years.

Mahaghosananda has worked relentlessly with his people, bringing to those who meet him the spirit of nonviolence, compassion, and forgiveness, even for the oppressor. He established temples in the refugee camps and then came to the U.S. with the Cambodian migration. He has been instrumental in establishing some thirty temples in the U.S. and Canada. Since 1988 he has been called the Supreme Patriarch of Cambodian Buddhism. His very countenance bespeaks the peace he hopes to bring, step by step, on his many peace marches.

The last time I saw Mahaghosananda was in July of 2000. During the past few years, he has been living the life of a monk in a Cambodian temple built on a forested hillside outside Leverett, Massachusetts. The Cambodian community of the Amherst area built the temple and takes pride in Mahaghosananda's presence among them. "If we don't build temples," said the aging monk, "our culture won't survive in this country." It was a sunny day, and we were sitting outside under the trees,

Mahaghosananda in his cotton saffron robes, his shoulders bare. It seemed possible to imagine something of Cambodian religious culture surviving here. I asked about winter in New England, imagining this hillside temple on a snowy February afternoon. Mahaghosananda simply laughed, his eyes dancing. "When it is hot, it is hot," he said. "And when it is cold, it is cold." Completely unvexed by the polarities and dualities of the world, Mahaghosananda's spiritual equanimity is the secret to creating an infectious kindness, even in the heart of the world's worst cruelty.

The largest concentration of Cambodians in America—some fifty thousand in all—live in the Long Beach area of California, where there are several small temples and one large temple, Khemara Buddhikarama, housed in a former union hall of ninety-one thousand square feet. It is a hub of daily activity for the Cambodian community, housing several monks and a least half a dozen elderly men and women. The abbot of the temple is the Venerable Kong Chhean, and he was my host on the several visits I made to Khemara Buddhikarama. We had been students at Banaras Hindu University in India at about the same time, so we fell into talk of familiar places and people before our conversation turned to Cambodia and Long Beach.

Dr. Kong Chhean came to the United states in 1979 along with thousands of traumatized refugees. The temple he leads has provided an important anchor for this uprooted Cambodian community. Acutely aware of the educational, counseling, and social needs of his community, Dr. Kong Chhean, fluent in English and already holding a doctoral degree, returned to school to get a master's degree in counseling psychology and a Ph. D. in clinical psychology.

Today Dr. Kong Chhean leads a complex life, straddling and linking two worlds. After his morning rituals at the temple, he drives to his office in the Long Beach Asian Pacific Mental Health Department, where he is a Mental Health Services Coordinator. At his lunch break, he returns to the temple for the noontime meal, the last meal he eats during the day, according to his monastic vows. There, one day, he invited me to partake of the platters of rice, shrimp, and noodles brought by lay families as offerings to the monks and served to the small community gathered at the temple at noon.

After lunch Dr. Chhean returns to his office, and that day I accompanied him. At the county office building this saffron-robed monk introduced me to the police guard and nodded a greeting to several co-workers as we walked down the hall to the Asian Pacific Mental Health Department. A small American flag was posted on his desk, which was piled high with fold-ers. On the wall behind him were handsome color photographs of the six living American presidents, the U.S. Capitol, the White House, and the Lincoln Memorial building. He described his most important role in Long Beach as that of helping his own Cambodian people adjust to life in American society. Most of the refugees were farmers in Cambodia and were not literate even in Khmer. The generation of parents knew little English, but their children picked it up quickly, and soon the parents were depen-dent upon their children for basic information and mobility. Both parents and teenagers have difficult intergenerational issues over everything from homework to dating, all the usual problems compounded by deep cultural issues. Dr. Kong Chhean has started counseling programs, alcohol educa-tion programs, parenting programs, and support programs for the elderly.

I gained a sense of the ways in which he has begun to stretch the tra-ditional roles of both monk and mental health worker. The temple fami-lies who bring their food offerings to Wat Buddhikarama have little sense of what Dr. Kong Chhean does at the county office building. On the other side, the police officer at the county office building no doubt has little idea of what goes on during Dr. Kong Chhean's lunch hour at the temple, which he probably has never entered. Dr. Kong Chhean seems to straddle the two worlds with ease, but in both he is a pioneer.

For most Cambodians, preserving the Buddhist tradition in the U.S. has been of critical importance. As one young man put it, "When you leave Buddhism, eventually you will lose your Cambodian identity because Buddhism is the foundation of Cambodian culture."[55] So it is that today a latticework of Cambodian temples has been built all across the United States. Near Boston there are temples in Lynn, Lowell, and Revere. In the rural area south of Minneapolis, a new Cambodian temple has been built in the farmlands. And in Silver Spring, Maryland, outside Washington, D.C., is a beautiful Cambodian temple and monastery, with ochre-tiled sloping roof lines, the whole complex set on a grassy, spacious lot. Today, even as the changing political landscape of Cambodia offers some promise of return, the Cambodian American Buddhist community has put down some deep, if fragile, roots in the United States.

You Korn, the teenager I met in Long Beach, was a senior in high school, about to become a monk for the summer following his gradua-tion. This form of temporary monasticism is common in Southeast Asia. It combines a rite of passage into adulthood with a way of returning thanks to one's parents, whose stock of spiritual merit will swell as their son becomes a monk. When I visited You Korn, I also met his elderly grandmother, who had a portable oxygen pack. I asked her what she thought of her grandson's ordination, and she beamed a smile. I asked if she would be able to go to the ordination. Nodding and smiling vigorously, she got up from the couch, removed the oxygen tube from her nostrils, and demonstrated just what she would do—how she would get down on her knees and bow at her grandson's feet. Reversing the roles of respect ordinarily shown to elders, this grandmother will bow in respect to a new monk. A few weeks later, You Korn was ordained, his hair and eyebrows shaven in tonsure.[56] You Korn and his generation will determine the future of their Khmer Buddhist tradition in the U.S.

THAI BUDDHIST COMMUNITIES

My first visit to an American Thai temple was Wat Thai, the flagship temple of the American Thai community, located in North Hollywood. Its steeply pitched, orange tiled roof, mounted with golden finials, soars into the blue sky. On the Saturday I first visited, the temple grounds were bustling with students gathered for a weekend school. Most wore uniforms of blue trousers or skirts and white shirts, bearing the Thai school emblem. They stood at the flagpole in front of the temple and sang the national anthems of Thailand and the U.S., raising both flags as well as the six-colored Buddhist flag. Then the classes began, in Thai language and culture as well as Buddhism. Around the temple grounds merchants had set up food stalls and were grilling succulent skewers of chicken and offering egg rolls and soups for sale. Sweetened Thai iced coffee was being ladled from enormous plastic vats. We met some of the monks who lived in a residence on the temple grounds, and we spent some quiet moments in the temple, where monks were receiving baskets of offerings from the laity—everything from rice to robes and toiletries. The atmosphere at the temple was palpably welcoming.

The Thai community purchased this site in North Hollywood in 1972, and the temple hall was opened at a ceremony in 1979, presided over by the supreme patriarch of Thailand. A year later the Buddha image, which had been made in Thailand, was installed in the main hall, and by 1983 five monks were in residence. Like the wats of Thailand, this was a full-fledged temple-monastic complex. Here in Los Angeles it served as the center of a far-flung Thai community with educational, social, and religious programs. Thai immigrants to the U.S. came under the provisions of the 1965

Immigration and Naturalization Act, which gave preferences to professionals and skilled workers; some came as the families of U.S. military personnel who had married Thais during the war in Southeast Asia. Their cultural and financial security is certainly far greater than that of Thais whose route to the U.S. was as refugees. Very few Thais, either in Thailand or the U.S., are Christian, and it is often said, "To be Thai is to be Buddhist."

I returned to Wat Thai many times. At a celebration of the king's birthday, the portrait of the king was set in honor in the teaching hall of the temple, banked with an elaborate floral display of pink and white orchids. The girls of the temple honored the community with traditional Thai dancing. In the spring I attended the festival of Songkran, the "water festival," which had all the elements of a celebration of springtime. The temple was decked with multicolored streamers and balloons, and the courtyard was filled with thousands of people and dozens of festive food stalls. Under a large tent canopy, a rummage sale was in full swing, and a new Chrysler was being raffled off as a teen band with synthesizers and electric guitars boomed out Thai and American soft-rock music. A Buddha image had been moved outside and placed under a flower-decked, four-postered canopy. People lined up with small vials of perfumed water, incense, and flowers, as well as paper-thin gold leaf, to make offerings to the Buddha. One by one, each came before the Buddha, lit the incense, and then stood for a moment, hands folded in prayer, before stepping up on the platform to pour water on the Buddha and apply a paper of gold leaf. Inside the temple women from the temple sat at special tables to receive donations for the baskets of food and supplies, including new, folded saffron robes, that would be presented to the monks sitting on the raised platform along the side of the temple hall. On festival occasions like this, a piece of Thailand is truly recreated in America.

My most recent count yielded some ninety-four Thai temples in the United States, including those in Bolivia, North Carolina; Converse, Texas; Fort Smith, Arkansas; and Florissant, Missouri. Let me take you to three of the temples I have visited during my research. In Chicago, I was the guest of the Venerable Chuang Pham at Wat Dhammaram, a Thai community located in a huge utilitarian building that was formerly a neighborhood school. Once inside, however, I had the feeling of entering a world set apart. The school gymnasium had been transformed into a large Buddha Hall, and the high ceilings made possible a high multilayered altar at one end of the room bearing the images of a dozen gilded Buddhas.

Another temple is Washington Buddhavanaram, located in a verdant area of Auburn, between Seattle and Tacoma.[57] Its adopted symbol is a wheel of Dharma placed upon the map of the state of Washington, with a candle above, illumining the whole land. When our Pluralism Project researcher Jenny Song had visited the budding community in the early 1990s, the Thai monks in charge lived in a big double trailer sixty-four feet long. It had been moved to the site purchased for an eventual temple, and for several years it served as both monastery and Buddha Hall. In the summer of 1999, when I visited, the temple was finished—a beautiful four-gabled Thai temple, with full surrounding porch, set amid Douglas firs, its driveway lined with gardens of gladiolas and dahlias. A few months earlier it had been dedicated and its sacred boundaries established during a week of festivities. The monk and one of the lay members showed me the Buddha Hall, a huge space with arching A-frame Weyerhauser wooden beams that create a cathedral-like interior, where the view of the high altar of Buddhas is unimpaired from any angle. The first Thai community gathered in Seattle to incorporate for the purposes of building a temple in 1981, and the fruits of nearly twenty years of labor were spectacular.

Finally, I'd like to tell you about a much smaller temple, Wat Buddhanusorn, on tree-lined Niles Boulevard in Fremont, California. When I first visited the temple in the mid-1990s, it was all two-by-fours, framed but still under construction. A large bungalow-style home on the property housed several monks and provided space for weekend cultural classes; the Buddha Hall was a small converted garage, too small for the community of Thai, Lao, and Cambodian immigrants who came here on a regular basis. On that first visit a saffron-robed monk climbed with grace and confidence over the planks and into the space that would become the Buddha Hall, describing what it would eventually look like. Two years later the temple was complete: a jewel of a temple, with its four gabled roofs sloping out in the four directions, crowned with the traditional finials. In the Buddha Hall behind the altar, a member of the community who is a traditional Thai painter had hand-painted a background scene of the realms of heaven and earth. In the highest part near the roofline were heavenly angels and musicians; slightly below unfolded the story of the earthly Buddha and his disciples. And below that, in the realm of this world, I spotted Wat Buddhanusorn, the place we now stood, and in the distance the Golden Gate Bridge and the city of San Francisco.

This image is a vivid expression of the religious reality of this immigrant Thai Buddhist community. Wat Buddhanusorn is now a visible part of the religious life of Fremont and the drive down Niles Boulevard will never be the same because of its presence here. But conversely, the Bay Area is now a visible part of the life of the Thai community, painted right on the altar mural. The Golden Gate Bridge has become temple iconography. Just as Wat Buddhanusorn will have a role in reshaping the life of America, so will American life gradually reshape this Buddhist community.

THE BUDDHIST TAPESTRY IN AMERICA

No simple paradigm can adequately categorize the many Buddhist communities of America. They come from all over Asia—Cambodia, Thailand, Japan. And they come from the three historical streams of the Buddhist tradition—the Theravada of southern Asia, the Mahayana of east Asia, and the Vajrayana of Tibet and central Asia. To simplify matters, one could say there is Asian Buddhism and Euro-American Buddhism or that there are old Buddhists from Asia and new Buddhists from the West. The Buddhist tradition in America is every bit as complex and varied as it is in Asia, and each part of the tradition itself has multiple lineages. The chemistry of America and the formal requirements of religious nonprofit institutions create yet another set of influences on each Buddhist community.

At this point in time, nearly forty years into this new complex period of American Buddhist life, the many Buddhist communities have different agendas and priorities. The Buddhist temples of the immigrant groups also serve as community centers, helping to preserve cultural identity and teach language. The Thai and Cambodian temples have dance classes for young girls. The Japanese temples may offer Taiko drumming. Festivals are celebrated with elaborate food fairs of traditional dishes.

On the other hand, new American Buddhists find in Buddhism a way of rejecting materialist, indulgent, and dogmatic aspects of the American mainstream, including the religious traditions of Christian and Jewish life from which they may have come. They may see Buddhism as a vehicle for social transformation, as do the "engaged Buddhist" movements devoted to peacemaking, environmental consciousness, ministries of healing, and hospice work with the dying. While these new American Buddhists are respectful of the cultural traditions of immigrant Buddhists, they are not particularly interested in duplicating Asian cultural traditions here in America. Traditional gender roles or temple-based ceremonies are seen as cultural trappings that do not need to be part of an emerging new

Buddhism in America, and traditional monastic life with its rules and hierarchies is seen as unsuited for contemporary America.

While new American Buddhists are going about what Robert Thurman calls "inner revolution," new Buddhist immigrants are not rejecting the American mainstream but finding ways to become part of it, to comply with its building codes and organizational forms, to preserve the valuable strengths of their own tradition while assimilating to a culture that has tremendous influence in their new lives and those of their children. The decision about what we keep and what we change is part of every religious tradition in the twentieth century, but in immigrant communities this dynamism is accentuated as old-world Asian traditions put down roots in what, to them, is the new world of the United States.

There are some points of contact between immigrant Buddhists and the new Buddhists of America, however, as the many strands of American Buddhism are woven into a new, complex fabric. A number of these temples house parallel congregations of Asian immigrant Buddhists and American-born practitioners drawn to Buddhism's philosophy and meditation practice.[58] They may share festivals but have quite different forms of daily practice. A Thai temple like Wat Dhammaram in Chicago might have a group of Euro-American regulars who come on a daily basis for meditation classes and also participate in the festival life of the temple. The Chinese Humanistic Buddhism movement at Hsi Lai temple has started a Buddhist university at which most of the students and professors are non-Chinese. And there is another development: increasingly, American practitioners of one stream of meditation take on teachers from other strands, and their practice becomes a braided skein of Buddhist practice. A respected Vipassana meditation teacher may undertake long retreats with a Dzogchen Tibetan meditation master, for example. In America today, the Buddhist tapestry is shimmering with the liquid light of change.

Some teachers suggest that the deep quest for freedom unites the Buddhist and American visions. The image of crossing the waters of turbulence to the far shore of freedom is one both Buddhists and Boston's founding Puritans share. The Chinese teacher C. T. Shen has been active for decades in pioneering Chinese Buddhist institutions in the U.S., including the great Chuang Yen monastery in Kent, New York. He also took a lead in the Chinese Buddhist community's participation in America's bicentennial celebrations in 1976. As we have seen, on the Fourth of July that summer he gave us a Buddhist twist on the American story, linking the Buddhist image of crossing to the far shore, the goal of one's spiritual quest, with the American image of the Mayflower crossing: "May we Americans . . . reaffirm the dedication of our ancestors and raise our Mayflower flag to sail across the vast ocean of hatred, discrimination, selfishness, and arrive on the other shore of loving-kindness, compassion, joy, and equanimity. . . ."

Bishop Matsukage of the Japanese Jodo Shinshu tradition, who saw his besieged community through the crisis of the internment camps in World War II, nonetheless staked his future and that of his community on life in America. He wrote his own epitaph, engraved now on his grave-stone near San Francisco:

Bury my ashes
In the soil of America
And into Eternity
May the Dharma Prosper!

NOTES

1. This Buddha's Birthday ceremony at Hsi Lai is the opening episode of the WGBH-TV film *Becoming the Buddha in L.A.,* for which I was primary academic adviser. Directed by Michael Camerini and produced by Terry Rockefeller; available from WGBH in Boston.

2. Stuart Chandler, one of the first Pluralism Project researchers, wrote *An Introduction to Hsi Lai Temple for its Non-Buddhist Visitors* (1992), still available at the Pluralism Project, Van Serg 201, Harvard University, Cambridge, MA 02138.

3. William Claiborne, "Site of Tranquility in Cash Controversy," *Washington Post,* October 18, 1996.

4. Statement of the Hsi Lai Community, published on the Hsi Lai Web site (http://www.hsilai.org) for a short period during the controversy.

5. Stuart Chandler, "Placing Palms Together: Religious and Cultural Dimensions of the Hsi Lai Temple Political Donations Controversy," in *American Buddhism,* ed. Duncan Williams and Christopher Queen (Richmond, Surrey: Curzon Press, 1999), 36–56.

6. Statement of the His Lai Community.

7. Rick Fields, *How the Swans Came to the Lake,* 3rd rev. ed. (Boston: Shambhala, 1992); Richard Seager, *Buddhism in America* (New York: Columbia, 1999); Charles Prebish, *Luminous Passage: The Practice and Study of Buddhism in America* (Berkeley: University of California Press, 1999); Williams and Queen, eds., *American Buddhism.*

8. The Buddhist Churches of America National Council adopted a resolution opposing school prayer at its annual meeting, February 22–24, 1985.

9. Brian D. Hotchkiss, ed., *Buddhism in America* (Rutland, VT: Charles E. Tuttle, 1998), 104, 107.

10. Quoted in Hotchkiss, ed., *Buddhism in America,* 109.

11. Sylvia Boorstein, *It's Easier Than You Think: The Buddhist Way to Happiness* (San Francisco: HarperSanFrancisco, 1996), 17–18, 19.

12. Thich Nhat Hanh, *The Heart of the Buddha's Teaching* (New York: Broadway Books, 1999), 5.

13. Hotchkiss, ed., *Buddhism in America,* 233.

14. Nhat Hanh, *Heart,* 24–25.

15. Bernard Glassman, Pluralism Project interview, 1995.

16. Walpola Piyananda, "Buddhist Clergy in the West: Present and Future" (unpublished manuscript, n.p., 1995).

17. Piyananda, "Buddhist Clergy."

18. Manuscript, n.d., Montana Historical Society, Helena, Montana.

19. Cited by Robert R. Swarthout Jr., "From Kwangtung to the Big Sky: The Chinese Experience in Frontier Montana," in *Montana Heritage: An Anthology of Historical Essays,* ed. Robert R. Swarthout Jr. and Harry W. Fritz (Helena: Montana Historical Society, 1992), 78.

20. Swarthout, "Kwangtung," 75.

21. Ronald Takaki, *Strangers from a Different Shore: A History of Asian Americans* (New York: Penguin Books, 1989), 80.

22. Takaki, *Strangers,* 80.

23. Roger Clawson, "Immigrants Build Ribbon of Rail to West," *Billings Gazette,* December 25, 1988.

24. Swarthout, "Kwangtung," 79.

25. For more information on the Dharma Realm Buddhist Association, see their Web page at: www.drba.org/index.htm.

26. Quoted in Hotchkiss, ed., *Buddhism in America,* 5.

27. The Web site of the Texas Buddhist Association is: www.jadebuddha.org.

28. The Web site of the Buddhist Association of the United States is: www.baus.org/baus/index.html.

29. Stuart Chandler, "Chinese Buddhism in America," in *The Faces of Buddhism in America,* ed. Charles Prebish and Kenneth Tanaka (Berkeley: University of California Press, 1998), 24.

30. Masao Kodani, interview with author, Los Angeles, May 1992.

31. This Hatsu Mairi ceremony at Senshin Temple is included as an episode of the WGBH film *Becoming the Buddha in L.A.*

32. *Buddhist Churches of America: 75 Year History, 1899–1974* (Chicago: Nobart, 1974), 1:46.

33. *Buddhist Churches of America:* 1: 61–64.

34. *Buddhist Churches of America,* 1: 61–64.

35. The Honorable Phillip Burton, *Congressional Record,* 93rd Cong., 2nd sess., 1974, 1209, no. 180, pt. 2.

36. The account of the service is found at: www.vbtemple.org/sdnews.htm.

37. Henry David Thoreau, *A Week on the Concord and Merrimack Rivers* (Cambridge: The Riverside Press, 1893), 85.

38. Stephen Prothero, *The White Buddhist* (Bloomington: Indiana University Press, 1996), 7–9.

39. Prothero, *White Buddhist,* 171.

40. Bigelow to Brooks, August 19, 1889. William Sturgis Bigelow archives at Houghton Library, Harvard University.

41. Fields, *Swans,* 155.

42. The Rev. John Henry Barrows, ed., *The World's Parliament of Religions* (Chicago: Parliament Publishing, 1893), 1: 444–50.

43. Barrows, ed., *World's Parliament.*

44. D. T. Suzuki, "An Autobiographical Account" in MasaoAbe, ed., *A Zen Life: D.T. Suzuki Remembered* (New York: John Weatherhill, Inc. 1986), 24

45. Maureen Stuart Roshi says this of Mrs. Russell in her interview with Sandy Boucher, *Turning the Wheel* (Boston: Beacon Press, 1993), 200.

46. Fields, *Swans,* 172.

47. Alan Watts, *The Way of Zen* (New York: Pantheon Books, 1959), vii.

48. Bernard Glassman, Pluralism Project interview, 1996.

49. The Zen Mountain Monastery in Mt. Tremper, New York, can be found on the Web at: www.zen-mtn.org/zmm. The Portland, Oregon, Zen center is located at: www.zendust.org.

50. Matthiessen, quoted in Hotchkiss, ed., *Buddhism in America,* 397. On the numbers of American-born Soto teachers, see the Rev. Taiden Yokoyama of the Soto Zen Administrative Office, Los Angeles, quoted in Teresa Watanabe, "Zen Abbot Gives a U.S. Look to an Asian Faith," *Los Angeles Times,* June 19, 1999.

51. Watanabe, "Zen Abbot."

52. Joseph Goldstein, *Transforming the Mind, Healing the World* (New York: Paulist Press, 1994), 42.

53. Don Morreale, ed., *The Complete Guide to Buddhist America* (Boston: Shambhala Press, 1998), xv.

54. Morreale, *Buddhist America,* 351.

55. A young man interviewed in the remarkable film *Rebuilding the Temple. Temple: Cambodian in America,* produced by Claudia Levin and Lawrence Hott, 1991.

56. You Korn's ordination forms an episode of the WGBH film *Becoming the Buddha in L.A.*

57. This temple is the first of a sect of Thai Buddhism called the Dhammayuta. The history of this temple community was published in a celebratory booklet at the time of the consecration, June 19–27, 1999, translated by Justin McDaniel for the Pluralism Project.

58. Paul Numrich, *Old Wisdom in a New World* (Knoxville: University of Tennessee Press, 1996), has called attention to the development of parallel congregations, focusing his study on Dharmavijaya Buddha Vihara, a Sri Lankan community in L.A., and Wat Dhammaram, a Thai community in Chicago.

CHAPTER FIVE

AMERICAN MUSLIMS: COUSINS AND STRANGERS

★

When Siraj Wahaj, imam of Masjid al-Taqwa in Brooklyn, stood in the U.S. House of Representatives on June 25, 1991, and offered the first-ever Muslim invocation, he wove into his prayer one of the most oft-cited verses of the Qur'an: "Do you not know, O people, that I have made you into tribes and nations that you may know each other." The moment was historic, and the Islamic prayer for life in a pluralist society was arresting. Our religious and cultural differences should not be the occasion for division but, on the contrary, the occasion for the biggest challenge of all: that "we may know each other."

As Muslims become increasingly articulate about their place in the American pluralist experiment, they bring this particular Qur'anic teaching to bear on the question of difference. The problem of pluralism in America is from this perspective a God-given challenge. Difference is built into the scheme of things. How we respond to it is up to us. The Qur'an offers us all a good place to start: we should come to know each other. But knowing each other is not easy in the American context. Misinformation about Islam and, even more, sheer ignorance of Islam, are common. Even while American Muslims create mainstream mosques and Islamic centers, register to vote, and become active participants in the American democratic process, newspapers bring to American homes the images of Islamic Jihad and other terrorist organizations, their rifle-toting leaders and their hideouts, creating a view of Islam as dangerous, subversive, highly political, and anti-American. When a terrorist attack occurs elsewhere in the world, American Muslims may well be among the first to condemn the attack and to speak of terrorism as anti-Islamic, but their voices are usually not heard, let alone magnified by the popular press. American Muslims may also be among the first to feel the repercussions, as their mosques are pelted with stones.

In the media, Islam is too often painted with one brush, in bold and monochromatic tones. Ali Asani, one of my Muslim colleagues here at Harvard, is realistic about just how difficult the challenge to understanding is. "I think the levels of prejudice and the ignorance about Islam in this society are so deep that it's really going to be a long struggle to educate people in America about what Islam is, that Islam is not just this monolith, and that if Muslims do something it is not necessarily to be associated with their faith."[1] In reality, we know that every tradition has its extremists. Many Muslims would say in no uncertain terms that militant extremist Muslims are to Islam what the radical Christian identity movements, the Christian militias, and the Aryan Nation are to Christianity: one end of a wide spectrum, one thread in a complex pattern of faith and culture.

Getting to know each other may seem a modest goal, but in a world supercharged with mutual stereotypes—Muslims, Christians, and Jews provide enough examples—it is a good start. Many Muslims are convinced that America is the place to make that start. A decade ago, for example, one of the founders of the Muslim Public Affairs Council, Salam Al-Marayati, called for a "relationship of reconciliation" between Muslims and Jews to "begin in America where Jews and Muslims live together in a free society."[2] By the end of 1999 he had worked with other Muslims and with like-minded Jews in Los Angeles to sign a joint code of ethics that would support respectful, mutual relations between the two communities.

Coming to know each other is a good start, but Muslims often move on to cite further Qur'anic advice for the pluralist society: compete in righteousness and strive in virtue. Along with the foundation of freedom is the impulse to competition. "If God had so willed, He would have made you a single people," the verse reads. "But His plan is to test you in what He hath given you; so strive as in a race in all virtues. So the goal of you all is to God; It is He that will show you the truth of the matters in which ye dispute." (Surah 5.51, A. Yusuf Ali, trans.) According to Al-Marayati and many like-minded American Muslims, Islam and democracy go hand in hand, and the United States, in its respect for the dignity of each person and its commitment to freedom of worship and expression, rests on what he considers Islamic foundations. The challenge to know one another and to compete in goodness gives us a strong place to begin as we explore the landscape of American Islam today.

There is no phrase more commonly on the lips of Muslims than the greeting *salam alaikum,* "peace be with you." The response is *alaikum salam.* I know from experience what a pleasure it is to exchange this greeting of peace with Muslims, and what a difference it makes in establishing a tone for relationship. My own "hellos" and "how do you dos" feel pale by comparison with the baseline of an articulated, mutual wish for peace. Like anything, it may become merely habitual, but like all good habits, it instills an inner disposition.

THE NIGHT OF POWER

Toward the end of the month of Ramadan is the "Night of Power"— Laylat al-Qadr. It is the night God sent the angel Gabriel to the Prophet Muhammad and began revealing the Holy Qur'an. That night, that revelation, that Prophet would change the course of human history. As evening approaches on the Night of Power, I join hundreds of New England Muslims at the new Islamic Center in Sharon, Massachusetts, in the Boston suburbs. The holy night falls this year on a Sunday, and many of the young people have been at the Islamic Center all afternoon for classes in Islam and in Arabic, the language of the Qur'an. It is a chilly but sunny March afternoon, and the teenage boys are spending the last half hour before sunset in a quick game of basketball at the hoop in the parking lot of a full-time Islamic school, built in the meadow of what was once an eighty-acre horse farm. Up the hill from the school is the Muslim community center with a large prayer hall and a kitchen. My host points to the stand of maples on another hill where a mosque will eventually be built. Here at the intersection of past, present, and future, between the revelation of the Qur'an, the basketball game, and evening prayers is where I begin this story of Islam in America.

The unfolding of revelation we remember tonight in suburban Boston began on a mountain outside Makkah in the middle of the seventh century C.E. Now at the beginning of the twenty-first century, the Night of Power is observed all over the world—in Indonesia and India, the world's largest Muslim countries, in Egypt and Nigeria, in London and Los Angeles. For Muslims, the Qur'an is the clear and direct Word of God, not just for themselves but for all humankind. Building on the foundations of the prophets from Moses to Jesus, the revelation of the

Qur'an stands in a family tradition that links Judaism, Christianity, and Islam. Muslims are truly cousins in the so-called Judeo-Christian world of the United States, and yet to many they also remain strangers about whom most Jewish and Christian Americans know little beyond the rough-hewn stereotypes of mass culture.

As the sun sets in Sharon, some three hundred people gather in the community hall up the hill to break the Ramadan fast together. We sit around tables set with plates of dates, slices of melon, and glasses of juice and water. Next to me at the table are Mr. and Mrs. Husain, both originally from Pakistan. They have been in Boston for over thirty years now and are among the old-timers in the Islamic Center of New England. Offering the dates around the table, Mrs. Husain explains, "It's the tradition of the prophet. Even in places where we don't grow dates, we like to break our fast this way, because the prophet Muhammad did it like this." The imam takes the microphone and recites the traditional prayer for the breaking of the Ramadan fast, "O God, for you I have fasted and over your provisions, I have broken my fast. My thirst has gone. My veins have become wetted, and my reward will be sure, if it be your will."

I feel honored to be here. I have not been fasting today like my hosts, but as I take the dates I am quite conscious of the remarkable fact that all over the world, as evening falls today, Muslims are breaking their day-long fast in just this way. A fifth of the world's population got up this morning to have something to eat and drink before sunrise. They took nothing else all day, not even water. And as evening comes, they gather in homes and mosques in Jakarta and Delhi, Casablanca and, now, in Boston to share the breaking of the Ramadan fast. The minds and hearts of Muslims in this Boston community follow, no doubt, the lines of memory, family, and affection that link them to Muslims all over the world, joined in breaking the fast. These Muslims have come from India and Indonesia, Pakistan and Lebanon, Egypt and Somalia. They create not only a complex multicultural Muslim community here in New England but also a local community with a worldwide reach. Indeed, the creation of translocal and transnational communities is part of the world's new pattern of immigration. E-mails, faxes, and phone calls have linked those here today with homelands all over the world and communities all over the U.S.

As a guest of the community tonight, I note that my mind travels to the dozens of Muslim communities I have visited across the United States in the past few years. They too are coming together for the Night of Power in the huge old movie theater that is now the Muslim

Community Center in Chicago, in the Bosnian mosque in Northbrook, Illinois, in the suburban mosque in Pompano Beach, Florida, in the big downtown Islamic Center in Los Angeles, and in the huge prayer room of the Santa Clara Islamic Center in the Silicon Valley.

After breaking the fast with dates, we all move to the adjacent room, separated from the dining room by an accordion wall. The call to evening prayer is sounded. I take a seat against the wall toward the back as the congregation lines up in straight lines, men in front, women behind. They join together in the cycle of prayer postures that are familiar to all Muslims—bowing, kneeling, prostrating, kneeling again. This community prayer, shoulder to shoulder, powerfully attests to the oneness of the Muslim community, called the *ummah,* spanning the globe and linking Muslims of all races and nations.

Following the prayers, we return to the dining room for dinner. There will be a much longer period of prayer later, but now I find my tablemates, the Husains, my adoptive family for this festive, long-awaited meal. We pass plates of chicken and lamb with rosemary, Mediterranean salad with rice and olives, Indian bean curries and rice pilafs, Trinidadi bread. There is baklava for dessert. "The whole meal is a mixture of our cultures," says Mrs. Husain as she introduces me to the vice president of the Islamic Center, formerly a cook in Bangladesh, who has devoted his retirement to being the volunteer cook of the Islamic Center and the mainstay of these great community meals.

At the microphone, Imam Talal Eid calls people to attention and reads the names of the young people, mostly junior high schoolers, who have fasted for at least fifteen days during Ramadan, and the still younger group of grade schoolers who have fasted for one week. They stand as their names are read, and they receive applause and cheers of "Allahu Akbar," "God is Great!" "This is the future of Islam," says the imam, raising his arms toward the youngsters with pride and satisfaction.

After dinner most of the congregation assembles again in the prayer hall for the long rounds of prayer that are distinctive of this Night of Power. The men and women make their straight prayer rows—men in suits and socks, sweaters and slacks, women in pantsuits, long dresses, *selvar kamizes,* kaftans, *jalabiyas,* and long denim skirts. There are teens, boys and girls, in baggy jeans. One girl wears a sweatshirt from the Sharon High School soccer team. Here the dress, like the cuisine, spans the spectrum of the Islamic world, from New Delhi to New England.

"This whole month of Ramadan is the month of the birthday of the

Qur'an," begins Imam Talal Eid after the first cycle of prayer is finished. "On this Night of Power, we say the Qur'an was received in total by the Prophet, peace be upon him." I think of Christmas Eve, a single holy night in my own tradition that somehow receives the whole mystery of the divine revelation. The imam continues, "The Qur'an is the foundation of life for all humanity. Everything needed for our success is here. It is not a book, in the usual sense of the word. It is not a collection of inspired writing. It is God's direct word. It is a book meant for our teaching and guidance. It is really an address—to us."

Surely the Qur'an is the single most important fact of the Islamic tradition. It is not the inspiration of Muhammad but is understood by Muslims to be the revealed Word of God. In this sense its true counterpart in Christianity is not the Bible but Christ as the incarnate Word, revelation in the form of a person. Yes, the Qur'an is a book, indeed, *the* Book. But, more important, the Qur'an is an event, an outpouring of recitations, revealed in complete form over the course of twenty-three years. Muhammad's followers gathered these revelations together into one book of 114 surahs, or chapters. Under the third caliph, Uthman, an authoritative recension of the recitations was pronounced. They were roughly arranged from longest to shortest. The Qur'an begins, however, with a short opening surah, "Al Fatihah," which is the most common prayer of the Muslim tradition. That prayer is uttered tonight, and most of those present here repeat it every single day of their lives:

> In the Name of God, Most Gracious, Most Merciful.
> Praise be to God, the Cherisher and Sustainer of the Worlds;
> Most Gracious, Most Merciful;
> Master of the Day of Judgment.
> Thee do we worship and Thine aid we seek.
> Show us the straight way,
> The way of those on whom Thou hast bestowed Thy Grace,
> Those whose portion is not wrath,
> And who go not astray.
>
> —A. YUSUF ALI, trans.

Most of those who have come tonight will stay until midnight. There will be prayers and talks and time for reading the Qur'an. "This is the night when the angels draw near the earth," the imam continues. "It is a holy night, for we remember the gift of the Holy Qur'an. We do not understand exactly how the Spirit of God speaks in the Word of the Qur'an. But we say, this is the night of the descending of angels. They will come close to us."

Mrs. Husain brought her Qur'an and a wooden folding book stand, which opens to form a V-shaped cradle for the text. At dinner she said that she would stay until midnight. Many others will stay all night long, reading through the entire Qur'an if possible, as the angels draw near the earth.

ISLAM IN AMERICA: THE BEGINNING IN SHARON

The history of the Muslim community in Sharon, Massachusetts, is in some ways typical of a wide range of Muslim experience in America. This new facility is a branch, an expansion really, of the Islamic Center of New England in Quincy, located just south of downtown Boston and not far from the birthplace of America's sixth president, John Quincy Adams.

The community dates back to the early 1900s when immigrants came from Syria and Lebanon to work in the Quincy shipyards. There were more Christians than Muslims at first and more men than women. Before long, the Muslims came together for prayers and special observances. Seven families, in all, lived in the area of the shipyards. Mohammad Omar Awad volunteered as the imam, the leader of the prayers. In 1934 they formed a cultural, social, and charitable organization called the Arab American Banner Society. They met in a house on South Street in Quincy, organizing informal religious lessons for their children, gathering for Friday prayers, and celebrating the two big Muslims feast days, Eid al-Fitr at the end of the month of Ramadan and Eid al-Adha, the feast of sacrifice during the time of pilgrimage to Makkah. In 1962, after three decades of temporary housing, the leaders of this Muslim community decided to build a mosque on South Street. Almost as soon as the new building was dedicated in 1964, the community began to experience the impact of the new immigration. The small group of Muslims suddenly tripled in the decade between 1964 and 1974.

By the early 1980s the community took a giant step by hiring its first full-time imam, Talal Eid, who came from Lebanon and had been educated at the al-Azhar University in Cairo. He was jointly sponsored by the Quincy mosque community and the Muslim World League. Eid, along with his wife and two small daughters, arrived in New York with another Lebanese imam and his family. They had thought they would be neighbors in America, until they suddenly discovered that New England and New Orleans were more than a thousand miles apart.

Talal Eid has led the community now for over twenty years, somehow finding time for graduate work at Harvard Divinity School in the midst of an increasingly busy life. "Being an imam in America is totally different from being an imam in Lebanon," he said in an interview with the Pluralism Project. "There my role was limited to the mosque and dealing with the community, but here it is a combination: I lead the prayer, do the education, do the counseling, and deal with people of different backgrounds, cultures, nationalities, and languages. The Islamic Center of New England is a small replica of the United Nations, with more than twenty-five different nationalities." Today, Imam Eid has more than three hundred children enrolled in weekend education programs and two congregations in Quincy and Sharon.

Imam Eid's role has grown not only because of the expanding expectations of his own community, but also because of the expectations of clergy in America generally. This means taking on new roles such as hospital visitation and participation in interfaith clergy meetings and interfaith dialogue. "Its not only about educating the Muslims," he says, "but I also have to do my share in educating non-Muslims, because living in a pluralistic society you have to establish friendly relations with people who believe differently than you." As one of Boston's most prominent and visible Muslim leaders, Imam Eid participates in three or four interfaith Thanksgiving services and is called upon constantly to speak in churches, synagogues, civic organizations. He answers questions at Cambridge City Hall, rushes to the Quincy mosque for Friday prayers, then leads a session on Islam with nurses from the Children's Hospital. Imam Eid's daily rounds are as exhausting as those of the most harried of urban ministers.

Like many other Muslim communities in the U.S., the Muslim community of New England has experienced fear and pain along with growth. In March of 1990 a three-alarm fire swept through the Quincy mosque, causing an estimated $500,000 worth of damages. The fire was attributed to arson, but the investigation was inconclusive and no one was arrested. The experience was unsettling for the community. Imam Eid recalls, "In the past, whenever a sad incident involving Muslims would take place in the Middle East or in any part of the world, people would focus on us. We received harassing calls and threatening letters. Angry people came over to demonstrate in front of the Islamic Center. And then there was the arson. If it's cloudy anywhere in the world, it will rain on us here." For a year after the arson, Muslims pulled together and poured their resources and energies into rebuilding what had been destroyed—the dome, much of the prayer hall, and the education wing.

Even before the fire, however, the Quincy community was bulging at the seams in the South Street mosque and had been looking for a larger home. In 1991 the group found a large building for sale in Milton—an estate that had housed a Jesuit center with more than seven acres of surrounding land. It seemed perfect for a new Islamic center. Before long voices of resistance, apprehension, even suspicion were heard in Milton. Would there be too much traffic? Would there be enough parking? Would this be in keeping with the character of Milton? Dr. Mian Ashraf, a Boston surgeon and a prominent leader of the Muslim community, remembers the meeting with Milton neighbors. "They were worried we were going to destroy their neighborhood by bringing in a lot of people. A man from the newspaper asked me, 'Doctor, how many people are you expecting to come here to pray?' I said, 'Well, you know, on our great holy days, we will probably have thousands.' But of course there are only two such holy days a year. So the next day, the headline in the paper was 'Thousands of Muslims Coming for Prayers to Milton.' I was so upset."[3]

Negotiations to buy the property went forward, but while the Islamic community was finalizing its mortgage arrangements, a group of Milton buyers purchased the property out from under them for one and a quarter million dollars in cash. "That was a bitter pill to swallow," said Ashraf. "I questioned in my own mind, why did people do this to us? Is it true that they are discriminating against us? I didn't want to believe that because all my life nobody discriminated against me." Some in the Muslim community were determined to take the issue to court and fight for the right to be good neighbors. Others did not want to settle in a community that had already expressed such hostility. This is a difficult question, and it has been faced by one immigrant community after another in cities and towns across America as they negotiate to buy property and find themselves confronting the opposition of new neighbors. The community decided not to raise an uproar over the lost opportunity but to look toward the future and seek another property.

Happily, the opportunity soon came to purchase a former horse farm in Sharon, a small town of 15,500 that is more than half Jewish. "I got a telephone call," said Dr. Ashraf, "The man said, 'Doctor, I have just the place for your Islamic center. I've been reading in the newspaper what they've been trying to do to you. You want to build a house for worship, and I think I can help you.' He took me out to Sharon. He had fifty-five acres of peaceful land for sale. I fell in love with the place right away."

"Suppose the neighbors give us the same problem again?" asked Ashraf. "What will we do?" This time, the community came up with a plan to introduce themselves to the town of Sharon. To begin with, they gave an educational videotape on Islam to every neighbor on the road. "We told them, 'If you have any questions, come talk to us. We'll have a meeting. We'll sit down. We'll answer your questions.'" Their proactive energy seemed to work, and the town of Sharon began to open its doors to the new Muslims. The rabbi of Temple Israel, Barry Starr, told Ashraf, "I think you are going to enrich our town. You're going to bring new things here." Starr called a meeting of the Sharon Clergy Association, and all of them had the opportunity to meet representatives of the Muslim community. The clergy voted a unanimous welcome to the Islamic Center. They printed their endorsement in the local paper, under the headline "Sharon Welcomes Islamic Center."

I found my way to the property in Sharon for the first time on the day of the groundbreaking, a rainy spring day in 1993. Appropriately, it was an interfaith groundbreaking, with rabbis, bishops, pastors, and priests—all in hard hats—joining the members of the Muslim community. As they turned their shovels of earth that day, many commented that they were breaking new ground for all of their religious communities. The Muslims had erected a great striped tent for the occasion, and we all crowded inside to hear the greetings and words of congratulations. I remember especially a young Muslim woman, a teenager representing the Muslim youth group, who stood on a folding chair and said the words American Muslims have said thousands of times in explaining their religious tradition to their new neighbors. "Islam means peace," she said. "I hope there will be a day here in New England, which has always been the birthplace of new ideas and great movements, when religious beliefs will not be held against anyone but will be a tribute to that person's moral strength."

Two years later the new center was open for its first ever Eid al-Fitr, the feast day at the end of Ramadan. It was a few days after the Night of Power, a sparkling late-winter day after an ice and snow storm. The frozen field of the former horse farm was a vast parking lot for the thousands who had come to pray. Dr. Ashraf announced with a sense of pride, "Today Eid is a formal holiday in the Commonwealth of Massachusetts. Because of our efforts, Eid is a paid holiday for Muslim workers and a religious holiday for our schoolchildren too. We need to let people know that Eid is our holiday." He shared with pleasure a letter to the American Muslim community from President Clinton. "Greetings to all those who are observing the holy month of Ramadan. As dialogue replaces confrontation. . . . Hillary and I offer our greetings to Muslims everywhere."

After the Eid prayers, the crowd streamed down the hill, dressed in their holiday best—bright *selvar kamizes,* sequined and mirrored velvet jackets, bright pink parkas, brilliant African cottons—a festive and colorful congregation delighted and dazzled with the winter wonderland. "I have never seen an icy Eid like this!" grinned a young man from the Gambia in Africa. Juice, coffee, and doughnuts were served in the common room of the school at the base of the hill. "Eid Mubarak!" "Happy Eid!" greetings were exchanged in this growing congregation of Muslims, born in over thirty countries and forging now an American Muslim tradition.

The Islamic Center of New England is really a microcosm of Islam in America today, with its generations of history, its growing pains, its efforts to establish Islamic practice in a culturally diverse Islamic community, and its efforts to create Islamic institutions on American soil. Its saga of relations with non-Muslim neighbors is also a mirror of wider experience—from the threats and arson attack to the zoning battles and finally the successful effort to build new bridges of relations with other communities of faith.

THE MOST MISUNDERSTOOD:
COUSINS AND STRANGERS

Islam, like Judaism and Christianity, traces its heritage to the prophet Abraham, and Muslims consider Jews and Christians their cousins as "people of the Book." It is strongly monotheistic, looks to Moses and Jesus as communicators of God's message to humankind, and has an ethic of equality and justice for all. The faith is simple, as stated clearly in the *shahadah,* the closest thing to a creed in Islam: "There is no God but God, and Muhammad is God's messenger." Bearing witness to this once, with deep conviction, makes one a Muslim, and walking the path of Islam means aligning one's whole life with this conviction.

Despite this kinship, Islam is the religious tradition about which many Americans have the most negative stereotypes—extremist terrorism, saber-rattling *jihad,* and the oppression of women. In America the Muslim community feels misunderstood, maligned by the media, and subject to continuous low-level harassment. The resurgence of Islamic confidence and the rise of militant Islam throughout the world have shaped the public image of an Islam dominated by its most radical voices. It is no wonder that American Muslims place public education and information high on their list of priorities and that Muslim community leaders often spend countless hours interpreting Islam to non-Muslim neighbors.

Dr. Mian Ashraf of Boston's Islamic community reflected on this as he encouraged his congregation on the morning of Eid al-Fitr in 1995. "Muslims are going through an interesting period in America. Even though our numbers are increasing gradually, our position as Muslims in American society has not really improved," he said. "This is our fault. We have not taught people about Islam. We must educate our non-Muslim brothers and sisters about Islam. Children growing up as American know little of Islam. This center has taken the responsibility of educating non-Muslims about Islam. Consider yourselves the ambassadors of Islam in this country."

Islam is the most misunderstood of America's religious traditions. Ironically, Islam is also theologically and historically closer to Christianity and Judaism than the traditions of the East, which should make it easier to understand. After all, the world of Qur'an includes the figures of Abraham and Moses, Jesus and Mary, and the prophetic vision of justice that rings through the biblical texts also resounds in the Qur'an. But Muslims see the path of Islam to be one that corrects, completes, and fulfills the Jewish and Christian understandings of revelation. Thus, the very closeness of Islam to Christianity and Judaism can be a source of tension. There is a built-in supercessionism here: Muhammad is the last prophet and Islam the last religion.

Misunderstanding Islam is not new in the West. The growing Islamic world permeated and threatened the medieval lands of European Christendom from Spain and Italy to the Balkans. The direct and violent encounter of Christianity and Islam took place not only in the years of the Crusades and in the far-off Holy Land, but on the very soil of Europe. Europeans developed a centuries-long rhetoric of hostility and denigration toward the Islamic world. Not until the twelfth century was the Qur'an translated into Latin, and in the sixteenth century the first publication of the Arabic text of the Qur'an was ordered burned by the pope. In that same century, Luther spoke in favor of translating the Qur'an—but primarily so that people could see how full of lies it was. A seventeenth-century translation from French into English bore the subtitle *Newly Englished for the Satisfaction of all who desire to look into the Turkish vanities.* An 1884 book on Islam was called *Error's Chains.* And, from the

Muslim side, the legacy of hostility associated with Christianity is also considerable. From the Crusades to colonialism, Muslims of the Middle East have also spoken of Christianity in the language of power, exploitation, and the sword. There is plenty of misunderstanding on both sides.

This heritage of Islamophobia was certainly prevalent at the time of the World's Parliament of Religions held in Chicago in 1893. The caliph in Turkey did not send Muslim representatives to the parliament, and the sole Muslim speaker was an American, Mohammed Russell Alexander Webb, the son of newspaper publisher in upstate New York. Webb had attended private school and college and had worked as a journalist before being posted in 1887 as America's consul general to the Philippines. There he was exposed to Islam for the first time and converted to Islam. His background made him well aware of the mistrust most Americans had of his newly adopted faith. "I am an American of the Americans. I carried with me for years the same errors that thousands of Americans carry with them to-day," said Webb at the 1893 parliament, speaking of the stereotypes and ignorance of Islam.

> Those errors have grown into history, false history has influenced your opinion of Islam. It influenced my opinion of Islam and when I began, ten years ago, to study the Oriental religions, I threw Islam aside as altogether too corrupt for consideration. But when I came to go beneath the surface, to know what Islam really is, to know who and what the prophet of Arabia was, I changed my belief very materially, and I am proud to say I am now a Mussulman.[4]

Becoming a Muslim was a radical move for a nineteenth-century American. The image of Islam as the religion of the sword was prevalent, just as it is today: the horseman charging through the desert with upraised sword, Arab and Muslim identities conflated in a single image of violence. Webb addressed just this issue: "I have not returned to the United States to make you all Mussulmans in spite of yourselves. . . . I do not propose to take a sword in one hand and the Koran in the other and go through the world killing every man who does not say, *La illaha illala Mohammud resoul Allah*—'There is no God but one and Mohammed is the prophet of God.'"

Despite the stereotypes, Webb articulated a deep-seated confidence that true knowledge of Islam would prevail. He concluded with an important challenge: "I have faith in the American intellect, in the

American intelligence, and in the American love of fair play, and will defy any intelligent man to understand Islam and not like it." This is a challenge Muslims in America have continued to issue: have a look at Islam, not as you have received it secondhand through the media, but as it really is. Once you see it through the eyes of Muslims of faith, you will no longer be able to sustain the negative images.

The first generation of Syrian and Lebanese Muslims established in 1952 the Federation of Islamic Associations. The primary purpose of the association was to "band together to combat the false and degrading propaganda leveled at them and to present to the American public a true and unadulterated picture of the true Moslem."[5] If the founders of the FIA thought that educating non-Muslims was difficult in the 1950s, it is in some ways even more difficult today, as resurgent Islamist movements from the Middle East to Indonesia present images of a militant Islam easily magnified by the media. A new generation of American Islamic organizations developed in the 1990s, and each of these organizations tackles, in one way or another, the task of correcting misinformation about Islam.

Like Mohammed Webb in 1893, American Muslims today express the deep confidence that Islam is so clear and compelling that their main mission is simply to provide accurate information. The rest will follow. The Institute of Islamic Information and Education in Chicago, located next to the large Muslim Community Center, publishes dozens of brochures and booklets, distributing more than 3.5 million copies free. Its founders, Dr. Amir Ali and his wife, Euro-American convert Mary Ali, have dedicated themselves to correcting misinformation about Islam by providing readily accessible and accurate information. They operate an information line "Islam on the Phone," a computerized voice-mail service to answer questions about Islam. In Los Angeles, the Islamic Center of Southern California has its own line of brochures introducing Islam. Its introductory brochure *What Is Islam?* is also printed in Spanish, *¿Qué es el Islam?* for the increasing number of Hispanic seekers and converts. It explains the five pillars of Islam—profession of faith in One God and the Prophet Muhammad, five-times-a-day prayer, the obligation of almsgiving, the practice of fasting in Ramadan, and the pilgrimage to Makkah. It responds to the most commonly asked questions about Islam: How does Islam treat women? What is *jihad?* Who is Muhammad?

Perhaps the most focused effort to educate Americans about Islam is the nationwide Islam Awareness Week sponsored by the Muslim Students Association. More than one hundred campus affiliates of the MSA organize a week-long program to generate awareness and understanding of Islam among their classmates. "Cogito Ergo Islam: I think, therefore, Islam" was the motto of the 2000 Islam Awareness Week at Stanford University. The events of the week included dozens of speakers and Friday prayer outside on the Stanford oval. Here at Harvard, the Harvard Islamic Society set up loudspeakers on the steps of the library, and a freshman *muezzin* issued the call to prayer out over Harvard Yard.

My first experience of Islam Awareness Week was at Boston University in 1994. I arrived at the first evening event of the week and was immediately attracted to the display tables outside the hall, stacked with pamphlets and tapes aimed at helping non-Muslims understand aspects of Islam—*Introducing Islam, Is Jesus Really God?, Human Rights in Islam, Moral System of Islam,* and *How I Came to Islam* by Cat Stevens, whose conversion to Islam has made him a prominent voice in the Muslim world of the West. I was impressed with the tremendous energy for what we Methodists call outreach. I collected a few of the brochures and settled into a seat in the auditorium. The stage was hung with banners bearing brief Qur'anic quotations: "There Is No Compulsion in Religion," "Allah Commands Kindness and Justice," and "The best of you is one who is best to his wife."

A young law student introduced the event. "Unfortunately, most non-Muslim Americans don't understand Islam at all," he said. "All over the country this week, we are putting on programs for people to understand Islam from Muslim sources, not just from what they read in the papers." It interested me as I looked around that most of the people who had come out for the event seemed to be Muslims. Most of the women were sitting with one another on one side of the auditorium, and many were wearing *hijab,* the scarf or head covering that Muslim women wear in public. The whole center section was filled with Muslim men, mostly students. Few non-Muslims were present for what turned out to be an excellent evening. I was disappointed, mentally listing the people who should have been there—roommates, professors, deans, chaplains. But it also became clear that these programs serve a dual purpose. They not only educate outsiders, they also serve Muslims who live in a non-Muslim environment where they are constantly called upon to explain their faith. The sessions clearly doubled as a kind of training in Muslim mission, called *da'wah.* Muslims, like Christians, participate in a worldwide mission movement aimed at elucidating Islam and explaining its teachings to non-Muslims. Everyone in the audience that night has to respond, in some way, to the questions most people ask about Islam.

The speaker that evening was Jamal Badawi, a professor of management at Dalhousie University in Halifax, Nova Scotia. His own awareness of Islam had sharpened when he came to the U.S. as a student in the 1960s. "I was often asked by different groups to speak about Islam," he said, "so it was then incumbent on me to learn more about Islam." Now, decades later, Badawi is one of the most sought after speakers in North America. His dozens of tapes and books provide a clear approach to many facets of Islam—for Muslims and non-Muslims alike.

"Islam is not Mohammadanism," he began. "Islam is the only religion that has a name for itself—a name that is found right there in the Qur'an. It comes from the root which means peace, submission, and commitment. Islam is peace through submission to and commitment to God. It is aligning one's life with God. It is commitment to living under new management—God's management." As Badawi spoke, he raised questions, one after another—the most frequently asked questions about Islam.

What about God? "When I say God," he went on, "I mean Allah. God *is* Allah. *Allah* is the Arabic term for God. Sometimes people ask me if the God known by Christians and Jews is the same as Allah. That is like asking if the French who worship Dieu or the Germans who worship Gott are also worshiping God. Christians who worship in Arabic speak of God as Allah too. Allah is God's personal name, to me, but mind you it has no plural form, like gods, no feminine form, like goddess." And God is One—no partners, no family members, no associates. The oneness of God is where a Muslim life of faith begins.

"And what about so-called fundamentalism?" he asked. He and his audience knew just how often the question comes up. It is the one question bound to come up in any Islam Awareness forum. "That term has nothing to do with Islam whatsoever," Badawi responded. "In Christianity, there are people who have rejected the fruits of science and the critical study of the Bible. They are called fundamentalists. But Islam is not a closed system. For 650 years, Muslim scientists were the brightest, the most predominant scientific thinkers in the world. Islam does not reject the fruits of scientific thinking. Through the process of discrimination—we call it *ijtihad*—Islam is dynamic and is renewed in each century. "

As he spoke, I thought of the colossal intellectual accomplishments of Muslim thinkers and philosophers: Ibn Rushd, whom we know as Averroës, whose commentaries on Aristotle were translated into Latin, and Ibn Sina, whom we know as Avicenna, a physician and a commentator on Plato. In the eleventh and twelfth centuries, they preserved Greek philosophy at a time when Western intellectual life was ebbing. True enough, intellectual life, including philosophy, science, and mathematics, has blazed brightly in the Islamic world. On the other hand, the critical study of the Qur'an is still very controversial, and Muslim scholars who have turned their investigative eye to the study of early versions of the Qur'an have been soundly criticized. I didn't raise my hand to ask Badawi this question, but I imagine his response would be that the revelation of the Holy Qur'an *is* one of Islam's fundamentals. In this sense, as he and many other Muslims would point out, all Muslims are fundamentalists. They take seriously the revelation of the Qur'an. But the term *fundamentalist,* as it resonates in the Christian tradition, does not really suit Muslims at all. It is meant to convey political extremism and fanaticism, but most Muslims are not political extremists or fanatics. They are simply faithful people who live their lives and die their deaths in terms of the word of God they have received.

Then Badawi turned the question on us: "Why is Islam always associated with violence?" he asked. People in this audience could readily recall the stinging impact of the 1994 television film by Steve Emerson called *Jihad in America,* which portrayed American Islamic centers as linked with terrorist elements. They were still sensitive to the image of Islam as the religion of the sword, whether the medieval Saracen galloping across the sands with sword raised or the modern-day terrorist. "*Jihad* cannot be equated with senseless terrorism." Badawi spoke decisively, as one who has confronted this issue over and over in America. "One of the greatest myths is that there is anything in scriptures equivalent to Holy War. I would challenge anyone to find an instance of the term *holy war* in the Qur'an. *Jihad* means exertion, effort, excellence. The Qur'an is described as the tool of *jihad,* 'Make *jihad* with the Qur'an,' but not with the sword. Actual armed *jihad* is permissible under two conditions alone: one is for self-defense, and the other is for fighting against oppression."

Violence is one of the questions that won't go away. Siraj Wahaj was the next speaker. The African-American imam of Masjid al-Taqwa in Brooklyn, New York, has built his reputation on a hard-hitting and warmhearted ethical message. He has put the message into practice by cleaning up his own violent, drug-ridden corner of Brooklyn. He is one of the most dynamic Muslim speakers, carrying his audience along with the vocal modulation of the greatest black preachers. His genial, winning smile can open the heart of even his most piercing critiques. Siraj Wahaj had another response to the dominant media image of Islam as conspiratorial and violent. "This is America. America is built on competition. American businesses spend over $130 billion a year to advertise products," he said. "Don't be naive. America is about the business of competition. So stop whining about how they show us as violent, about what they said in *Jihad in America*. Don't be surprised. You don't expect Pepsi to suddenly start advertising Coke, do you? Go on the offensive. Make yourselves known as you want to be known." Turning the tables on the defensive posture that Muslims too often take, he said, "Look at the Islamic community in America today. We are building mosques, we are building schools, recreational centers. But let's not stop there. We need to build Islamic financial institutions and credit unions. We need to build a television station. Should we have to beg the networks to be able to get on television to defend our faith? No. We should have our own network!"

I left that first Islam Awareness week session with a stack of information flyers and even a few audiotapes of Jamal Badawi and Siraj Wahaj. I had learned how important these events are for the formation of the American Muslim community. Every day these Muslim students are in contexts that require the kind of dialogue modeled and practiced here. As long as they live in American society, where the consciousness of Islam is high, but the knowledge of Islam low, they themselves will be the interpreters of their tradition in daily life—whether they work in law offices, in engineering firms, or on Capitol Hill. Now, at the beginning of the twenty-first century, American Muslims are in the process of doing just what Siraj Wahaj suggested—creating a positive Islamic infrastructure that serves the interest of the community.

THE ROOTS: AFRICAN-AMERICAN ISLAM

Siraj Wahaj is fluent in Arabic and well known to American Muslims from all over the world. He speaks at conventions of the Islamic Society of North America and at strategy sessions of the American Muslim Council, organizations that include the whole spectrum of Muslims. As an African American, however, he would be the first to remind us that Muslim immigrants from Lebanon in the 1890s or Pakistan in the 1990s came to a country where there was already a small Muslim population—a Black Muslim population. The first major movement of Muslims to America came with the slave trade. Some ten million Africans were forcibly brought to North America to be sold as slaves in the eighteenth and nineteenth centuries, and many came from West Africa, which, by this time, had been acquainted with Islam for more than a century. At least 10 percent of these slaves were Muslim, according to Allen Austin, whose research extrapolates from the relatively good port records kept in the port of Charleston.[6] His groundbreaking book, *African Muslims in Antebellum America,* opens an important chapter in the history of America's many religious traditions.

The Muslims from West Africa were as diverse as the West African cultures from which they came—Mandingoes and Fula, Fulbe and Fulani. The French scholar Sylviane Diouf writes, "A large proportion of the Muslims arrived in the New World already literate, reading and writing Arabic and their own languages transcribed in the Arabic alphabet." According to Austin and Diouf, the presence of literate Africans was vexing to those who bought and sold Africans as slaves. Indeed, because of their literacy, they did not fit the white stereotype of the African race as ignorant and uncivilized. White slave owners often did not classify them as black Africans but rather as Arabs. Diouf's analysis is that "it was more acceptable to deny any Africanness to the distinguished Muslims than to recognize that a 'true' African could be intelligent and cultured but enslaved nevertheless."[7] From the standpoint of these African Muslims, however, among whom race consciousness was not high, their captors were classified not as white so much as Christian. Omar ibn Said, in his autobiographical account, speaks of being "sold into the hands of the Christians" and taken across the sea "to a place called Charleston in the Christian language."[8]

The literacy of many of these unwilling Muslim immigrants to America was also dangerous, so clearly did it subvert the sense of intellectual and racial dominance of those who purchased them as slaves. In some cases, however, slave owners clearly recognized and manipulated the literacy of Muslim Africans by making them deputies on their plantations. As Allen Austin put it, "Any assertions of dignity or cultivation had to be either suppressed and thenceforth ignored or, if recognized, manipulated—often with trepidation—to some sort of mutual advantage for servant and master."[9] While we know nothing of a gathered Muslim community, we glean some glimpses of early African Islam in America from the lives of these few individuals. We know some of their names and stories. Ayyub ibn Sulaiman Jallon, for example, was a slave in Maryland, set free in 1732 and given passage home via England. Yarrow Mamout was set free in 1807 and is said to have settled in Washington, D.C., where he lived to well over one hundred years of age. Charles Peale painted Yarrow's portrait in 1819 and wrote of him, "He professes to be a

Mahometan, and is often seen and heard in the streets singing Praises to God."[10] Several more extended narratives give us a glimpse of this important, but understudied, part of America's religious history.

Salih Bilali, for example, was born in 1765 near Timbuktu in what is today the state of Mali. As an enslaved African in America, he worked on the plantation of James Hamilton Couper, serving on his St. Simon's Island plantation from 1816 to 1846. Couper wrote about the remarkable abilities of this slave, whom he called Tom. "I have several times left him for months, in charge of the plantation, without an overseer, and on each occasion, he has conducted the place to my entire satisfaction," Couper wrote.

> He has quickness of apprehension, strong powers of combination and calculation, a sound judgment, a singularly tenacious memory, and what is more rare in a slave, the faculty of forethought. He possesses great veracity and honesty. He is a strict Mahometan; abstains from spirituous liquors, and keeps the various fasts, particularly that of the Rhamadan. He is singularly exempt from all feeling of superstition; and holds in great contempt the African belief in fetishes and evil spirits. He reads Arabic, and has a Koran (which however, I have not seen) in that language, but does not write it.[11]

The loss of literacy was also common, for Salih Bilali had been captured as a teenager and by this time was in his seventies.

Salih Bilali was a friend of another man also named Bilali, owned by Thomas Spalding in Sapelo on the Sea Islands of Georgia. Both men were named for the African Bilal, one of the first Muslims in the circle of the Prophet Muhammad who, because of his strong voice, was the muezzin who called the community to prayer. Bilali gave some of his nineteen children Muslim names, like Fatima, the wife of the Prophet. He is said to have had a Qur'an and a prayer rug, and according to the narrative, he was buried with them.[12] According to this narrative, Bilali spoke French, English, and Arabic, perhaps the reason Spalding singled him out and put him in charge of other slaves. He was noted for his heroism during the War of 1812 and was said to have rescued Sea Islanders from a hurricane in 1824.

A woman from Broughton Island met the aging Bilali and his family in late 1850s and wrote,

> They were tall and well-formed, with good features. They conversed with us in English, but in talking among themselves they

used a foreign tongue that no one else understood. The head of the tribe was a very old man called Bi-la-li, He always wore a cap that resembled a Turkish fez.

She went on to mention that they "worshipped Mahomet" and "held themselves aloof from the others as if they were conscious of their own superiority."[13] Decades later in 1940, the Georgia Writers Project interviewed a woman who knew of "Belali" and his wife, Phoebe, through their children. Their daughters used to tell how Belali and Phoebe would "pray on the bead," using the prayer beads so common in the Muslim world, and were very particular about the time they prayed.

When the sun come up, when it straight over head, and when it set, was the time they pray. They bow to the sun and have a little mat to kneel on. The beads is on a long string. Belali he pull a bead and he say, "Belambi, Hakabara, Mahamadu." Phoebe she say, "Ameen, Ameen."[14]

Omar Ibn Seid was a West African Fula, like Salih Bilali. He was born in 1770 and told in his own words the story of his life and his capture, how he arrived in Charleston and was sold into slavery.

My name is Omar ibn Seid. My birthplace was Fut Tur, between the two rivers. I sought knowledge under the instruction of a Sheikh called Mohammed Seid, my own brother, and Sheikh Soleiman Kembeh, and Sheikh Gabriel Abdal. I continued my studies twenty-five years, and then returned to my home where I remained six years. Then there came to our place a large army, who killed many men, and took me, and brought me to the great sea, and sold me into the hands of the Christians, who bound me and sent me on board a great ship and we sailed upon the great sea a month and a half, when we came to a place called Charleston in the Christian language. There they sold me to a small, weak, and wicked man, called Johnson, a complete infidel, who had no fear of God at all. Now I am a small man, and unable to do hard work so I fled from the hand of Johnson and after a month came to a place called Fayd-il.[15]

Fayd-il was apparently Fayetteville, and Omar Ibn Said recalled how he went into a church to pray, was arrested by someone with a pack of dogs, and was put in a "house from which I could not go out," in other words, a jail. After more than two weeks, he was bought by Jim and John

Owen, who apparently treated him very well. His account is filled with gratitude and respect for the Owen brothers, and during the years he spent in their household he became a Christian. A tangle of tales circulating about him refer to him as an Arabian prince who turns from the "bloodstained Koran" to the Prince of Peace.[16] But in his retrospective account, written in 1831, he tells us about his previous life as a Muslim.

> Before I came to the Christian country, my religion was the religion of Mohammed, the Apostle of God—may God have mercy upon him and give him peace. I walked to the mosque before day-break, washed my face and head and hands and feet. I prayed at noon, prayed in the afternoon, prayed at sunset, prayed in the evening. I gave alms every year, gold, silver, seeds, cattle, sheep, goats, rice, wheat, and barley. I gave tithes of all the above-named things. I went every year to the holy war against the infidels. I went on pilgrimage to Makkah, as all did who were able. My father had six sons and five daughters, and my mother had three sons and one daughter. When I left my country I was thirty-seven years old; I have been in the country of the Christians twenty-four years. Written A.D. 1831.[17]

These remembrances give us the intriguing traces of the lives of America's first Muslims. They give us a sense of how deep our multireligious history really is, and we need to know more of this early Muslim experience. Interestingly, for all the scholarly interest in the slave trade and in the history of Africans in America, few have explored these Muslim roots. We have only glimpses of a life about which we know all too little, like the Muslims on deck praying in Steven Spielberg's film *Amistad* or the glimpse Malcolm X gives us of his grandmother who would set out a mat to kneel when she prayed or the hints we hear from the names of Toni Morrison's Sea Island characters in her novel *Song of Solomon*—Bilaly, Medina, Omar, Muhammat.

THE MIDDLE EAST IN THE MIDWEST

Between the fading traces of old African Islam in mid–nineteenth century and the revival of a new African American Islam in the 1930s, another group of Muslims began arriving in the United States. Immigration from Syria, including much of what we know today as Jordan and Lebanon, began slowly in the 1870s and gained in intensity in the 1890s.

On the whole, these early Middle Eastern immigrants did not strike out for America because of political oppression or dire poverty in the homeland but simply because economic opportunity beckoned. Most intended to return home. When Alixa Naff studied this early Arab American history she noted, "Almost without exception, the pioneers of the first phase and many in the second came with the intention of returning home in no more than two or three years much wealthier and prouder than they came." But in the process of making a living in America, they gradually made a home here as well. As Naff writes, "It was in America, while pursuing their goals, that immigrants became aware of the ideals of freedom, individual liberty, and equality of opportunity—ideals that at first had little relevance to their motivation for emigrating. As the Syrian immigrants became conscious of those ideals, however, they embraced them fervently."[18]

Theirs was a chain migration, in which those who came first and succeeded in America sent money for the next family member or neighbor back home to come. This was the way my own Swedish family came to America two and three generations ago, just about the time these immigrants were arriving from Syria and Lebanon. One of the common means of making a living for the first wave of immigrants from the Middle East was peddling, especially in the rural Midwest where farm families had little access to stores and little time to travel to find the goods they needed. From their packs, peddlers unloaded an enticing spread of ribbons and rosaries, jewelry and buttons, notions, knives, and napkins. A new immigrant often hit the road within a few days of arriving, knowing little English but "Buy sumthin', ma'am." They immediately encountered both the hospitality and the hardship of America. When Naff interviewed those who remembered the pack-peddling days, she concluded, "Peddling must be held to be the major factor in explaining the relatively rapid assimilation of Arabic-speaking immigrants before World War I."[19]

At first, this late-nineteenth- and early-twentieth-century immigration brought many more Christians than Muslims. Syrian Orthodox congregations were established in Worcester, Massachusetts; Fort Wayne, Indiana; and Cedar Rapids, Iowa. About 10 percent of the immigrants were Muslim. While the Sunni population predominates among Muslims in Syria and Lebanon, the immigrants to the U.S. included a relatively higher proportion of Shi'ite Muslims and Druze.[20] Shi'ites, who make up only about 15 percent of Muslims worldwide, hold that the Prophet Muhammad designated his son-in-law Ali and his descendants to be leaders of the community after his death, and the Druze are a small sect of

Shi'ites found primarily in Syria and Lebanon. Sunnis, who make up about 85 percent of Muslims, place authority in the consensus of religious scholars to interpret the Qur'an and the Sunnah (custom) of the Prophet. In the first two decades of this century, we hear of Shi'ites in Fort Dodge, Iowa, Sunnis in Cedar Rapids, Iowa, and a Druze Association in Seattle, Washington. We can look in many places for the beginnings of organized Islam in the U.S., but most of us would not think first of North Dakota.

In three small communities on the windswept plains of North Dakota, small groups of Muslims began to hold Friday prayers in the first years of the 1900s, the first evidence of communal Muslim prayer in the United States. A review of this history in the *Fargo Forum* reports how Syrian peddlers, originally from Damascus, moved into North Dakota from Crookston, Minnesota:

> At first these pioneer Moslems peddled their wares on foot throughout North Dakota, but used horse and buggy when they could afford it. Some of the more successful bargainers were even able to purchase automobiles. Finding North Dakota a good place to live, they soon moved from Crookston and clustered in three localities—the Stanley-Ross area, Rolla-Dunseith, and Genfield-Binford. . . . And when they had saved and borrowed enough money and had learned the rudiments of the language, they became homesteaders or operated small stores. In turn, they taught the newer immigrants the skills of peddling—and so on the cycle—until they were all settled in their new homeland.[21]

In Ross, North Dakota, one of America's first purpose-built mosques was erected in 1920.[22] By 1925 the Muslim population of the Ross-Stanley area was thirty to forty families. The headline from the *Fargo Forum* on August 8, 1937, was "Ross, N.D., Area is Home for Some 50 Mohammedans." But by this time, the numbers were already declining. In the 1920s new immigration had come to a halt, and the forces of assimilation were as strong as the prairie winds of the Great Plains. By 1948 the mosque was no longer in active use and the building, a historic one for Islam in North America, was eventually bulldozed. In 1967 the *Fargo Forum* revisited the history of the community in an article bearing the headline "Time, Americanization Take Harsh Toll on Once-Thriving Moslem Colonies in ND."

> Though the adults were generally accepted into the society of the community, the children received some scorn from their fellow

classmates because of their non-Christian religion and differing practices. Amid Hach . . . recalled how often his children had asked, "Daddy, how come we don't go to church." The reasons were difficult to understand for the young minds. As these children grew to manhood and womanhood, many of them forsook their father's faith and adopted the Christian religion when they married a non-Moslem.[23]

Other early mosques, most in buildings adapted from other uses, sprang up in unlikely places, like Biddeford, Maine, where Albanian immigrants created a space for a mosque as early as 1915. In Highland Park, Michigan, an imam with a brother who was a construction contractor brought the small community together to build a mosque. It was dedicated in 1923 but closed amid internal controversy several years later. Perhaps the oldest mosque still in use is the building in Michigan City, Indiana, which was purchased by the Muslim community in 1925. One part of the building was designated for social events and religious instruction and the other part for prayer.[24]

In the American heartland in Cedar Rapids, Iowa, is a building that is today called the Mother Mosque of North America. Its claim to fame is twofold: it was built from the ground up as a mosque, and the same Islamic community that built it is still thriving today, albeit in a larger building. According to Cedar Rapids old-timers, "This was the first place of worship specifically designated and built as a mosque in North America."[25] Muslim history in Cedar Rapids goes back to 1895 when Hussein Ali Sheronick arrived from Lebanon. He made a living as a traveling peddler until he was able to open a dry goods store in Cedar Rapids in 1900. Other Muslims arrived, also single men who started out as peddlers— Ahmed Sheronick, Abdo Aossey, Hussein Igram, and later his cousin Hassan Igram. Sheronick's store served as home base for many of these pioneers, and the first gatherings for prayer were held in Sheronick's home. By 1914 some forty-five Muslims lived in Cedar Rapids.[26]

By the 1920s the community was settled. The peddling days were over, and the Muslim pioneers had married and were beginning families. Regular prayers rotated among houses, and the community rented a hall for the Eid al-Fitr prayers and celebration at the end of Ramadan and the Eid al-Adha feast during the time of the pilgrimage to Makkah. In 1929 the community had its first imam, and by the early 1930s the Muslims of Cedar Rapids began to plan for a mosque. The fund-raising campaign, as

American as apple pie, began with bake sales and Lebanese dinners for the wider Cedar Rapids community. The first of the annual fund-raising dinners attracted over six hundred ticket buyers. In 1934 the community formed the Rose of Fraternity Lodge, which became the official administrative and fund-raising body for the mosque. In organization, this lodge resembled hundreds of voluntary associations formed by immigrants to protect and promote their culture and, in this case, their religion as well. The stated purpose was "to promote the Arabic-Islamic name in this, their adopted country, and to perpetuate their beautiful and characteristic customs, to keep the Arabic language alive, and to permeate the spirit of the Islamic teachings ... promoting love and devotion among [Muslims] in particular and among all other religious bodies in general."[27] Representatives of the Rose of Fraternity Lodge went from city to city during the Great Depression, appealing to Muslims in Toledo, Chicago, and Detroit for help with the project. Miraculously, they raised enough to build. The groundbreaking took place on March 10, 1935, and the "Moslem Temple" opened on June 16, 1936. This bold effort also required its compromises: through the early years, indeed until the 1950s, the Moslem Temple held its Friday prayers on Thursday nights, since many Muslims were grocery store owners who could not close for business at midday on Friday. Eventually Friday prayers became regularized, but as the community grew Sunday prayers and services came to predominate, coinciding with the work and worship week of most Americans.

There is something heartwarming and thoroughly American about the success story of Cedar Rapids. After the mosque opened in 1936, young Abdullah Igram and Hussein Ali Sheronick were the first American-born Muslims to study the Qur'an there in Arabic. The first designated and registered Muslim cemetery in America opened in Cedar Rapids in 1949; the first Muslim publishing house, Igram Press, was established there in the 1950s. By this time the community also supported a mosque softball team and a women's group. The roots of activism can be found there as well. Abdullah Igram, when he served in World War II, was refused the right to have *Islam* inscribed on his dog tag as his religion but had to settle for *Other*. Igram was determined to secure recognition for Islam in America, and in 1952 he and other Muslims formed the Federation of Islamic Associations (FIA), declaring as their primary purpose to "band together to combat the false and degrading propaganda leveled at them and to present to the American public a true and unadulterated picture of the true Moslem."[28] These early pioneers not only built Iowa's first mosque but also laid claim to the freedom of religious practice that is the real promise of America. For Igram and others, that meant not simply the freedom to practice one's faith quietly, but the freedom to organize and agitate for change when the practicing of one's faith was in some way hindered or obstructed.

The Igram family in Cedar Rapids arrived in the earliest wave of Middle Eastern immigration, which by 1914 had brought about a hundred thousand Arabic-speaking immigrants to the U.S. A second and larger wave began about 1918, bringing Lebanese to the Detroit area, particularly to Dearborn, Michigan, to work in the Ford Motor Company plant, and to Quincy, Massachusetts, to work in the shipyards. After World War II a third period of immigration began, bringing Palestinians displaced from Israel, Egyptians and Iraqis leaving political turmoil at home, and Yugoslavian and Albanian Muslims fleeing communism. The fourth wave began with the changes to immigration law in the mid-1960s and brought educated professionals from throughout the Muslim world, some of whom settled in America to take the kinds of jobs for which they prepared as students and graduate students in American universities.

If Cedar Rapids is Muslim America's hometown, Detroit is surely its urban epicenter. Ironically, it was Henry Ford, who discriminated so blatantly against Jews and blacks, who brought the Muslims to Detroit with the magnetic offer of five dollars a day for work in the new Ford Motor Company. Dearborn was originally the estate of Henry Ford, but eventually the whole of Dearborn was developed to house Ford employees. The Muslim population in those days was small, perhaps only 2 percent of the total, but it put down roots and built mosques and community centers. With each generation of immigrants, Dearborn kept growing. Today, with the post-1965 immigration, over a quarter million Arab Americans live in the metropolitan Detroit area.[29] The largest part of the Muslim population is Lebanese, both old and new immigrants, followed by Iraqis, especially with the new influx following the Gulf War in 1991, Yemenis, and Palestinians. Of the eighty-seven thousand citizens of Dearborn today, about 25 percent are Arabs, most of them Muslims.

Driving down Warren Avenue through the heart of Dearborn, I found myself in what is now called Arabic Town, with groceries, restaurants, bakeries, music, and clothing stores catering to a Middle Eastern clientele. My host in Detroit was Bill Gepford, a minister at Littlefield Presbyterian Church in Dearborn who spent many years in the Middle East. At the time we met in 1996, he was likely the only full-time minister on any American church staff whose primary work was to build bridges between Christians and Muslims. The leafy neighborhood around his Presbyterian church is over half Muslim, and in the greater Detroit area as well he has his work cut out for him. "When the Arab population began to grow around 1976," he explained, "people took all the negative images they had of blacks and just put them wholesale on the Arabs."

We drove to the Islamic Institute of Knowledge a few blocks away, a Shi'ite center located in the heart of the Arab-American business district in a building that had been a bank. During the Gulf War the institute was defaced with anti-Arab graffiti, and people from the Presbyterian church came over to help the Muslim congregation scrub it off. The institute is one of half a dozen Muslim centers in Dearborn. Today in 2001, it has erected a new multimillion dollar mosque and school in the heart of Dearborn. Next we drove to the Islamic Center of America, dubbed the Joy Road Mosque, a Shi'ite mosque whose groundbreaking took place in 1962. The mosque is a hub of community activity—classes for all ages, meals in the dining hall, Thursday evening youth programs with pizza, even a Girl Scout and a Brownie troop.

My first contact with the Joy Road Mosque came through one of my students, Katie, a blond Euro-American convert to Islam whose husband's family lived in the Detroit area. During her summer research stint she stayed with them and visited more than a dozen mosques, including this one. She wrote in her research notes,

> This is the first mosque I was ever in that gave me the feeling of an established congregation. It was very strange for me, because most mosque communities are as new to their neighborhoods as I am to Islam! I was totally surprised at how relaxed these believers are. They have a famous mosque and a big budget. The sermon was fantastic.

Katie also noted something I had not seen before. As people assembled for prayer, they picked up small, flat clay discs made of the soil of Karbala, the sacred place in Iraq where Husayn, the grandson of the Prophet and the leader of the Shi'ite community, was martyred. Here, during the prayer prostration, Muslims touch their foreheads to the very soil where the martyrs died.

After prayers, when Katie introduced herself to the imam, he not only welcomed her but invited her to a barbecue fund-raiser that very night. At the barbecue they celebrated newly returned pilgrims who had gone to Makkah on the Hajj (pilgrimage), and proud parents videotaped children, fresh out of Qur'an classes, who recited surahs. In Boston, Katie's circle of friends were first-generation immigrants, but here in Detroit she found a seasoned community of second- and third-generation Muslims, comfortable with being both Muslim and American.

The fund-raiser Katie attended was part of a long-range effort to build a new mosque. In the past forty years, the community has grown steadily and now counts about two thousand families or ten thousand people among its members. It has outgrown the Joy Road Mosque and is in the process of building a new domed mosque with a prayer room to hold at least a thousand, which will make it one of the largest mosques in North America. This new mosque will also have a full-time school. A single March 1999 fund-raising dinner at Detroit's Hyatt Regency raised three million dollars for the project.[30]

Later that day I left Bill, my Presbyterian guide, and made my way into the southern fringe of Dearborn, near the original Ford plant, where new immigrants, mostly from Yemen and Iraq, have settled. Today this part of Dearborn is about 90 percent Arab American, and in the neighborhood school 98 percent of the children are said to be Arabic-speaking immigrants, mostly Muslim. The largest mosque in the area, the American Muslim Society, is also one of the oldest, dating to 1938. It is a strong, square, utilitarian brick building, like an old armory or school, with a gesture of a dome, a huge prayer hall, a thriving weekend school in the basement, and three basketball courts. I spent two hours that afternoon at the girls' weekend school, discussing everything from dress and dating to college and careers with teenagers, eager to talk and surprisingly willing to include me in the conversation. The adult leader of this teens group is a young woman named Anne, who grew up Methodist and met her Muslim husband at college. They started reading the Qur'an together, she said, and the rest is history. Embracing Islam, she also became an active participant in the community.

I returned to this area the next day to visit ACCESS, the Arab Community Center for Economic and Social Services, one of the nation's most successful advocacy groups for Arab immigrants. Its dozens of pamphlets describe the beginnings: "Back in 1971, amid discussions of discrimination in the auto plants, the grape boycott and issues concerning newly arrived Arab immigrants, a community center was launched in a small storefront on Vernor Highway in Dearborn, Michigan. From that humble, grassroots start, The Arab Community Center for Economic and Social

Services (ACCESS) has become the nation's premier Arab-America service and advocacy agency." Its annual cultural arts program is the largest Arab festival in the United States and brings other Dearborn communities together too—Latino, African, Asian, and Native American.

While the Arab-American identity is strong, Detroit's Muslim community is not defined by Arab identity alone. As an ACCESS activist put it, "Twenty years ago Muslim meant Arab. Now the Muslim Council is accepting and enacting the diversity of Islam—Pakistani, Lebanese, Yemeni, Arab. We are all here."

"All here" also means those of America's indigenous Islam—African-American Islam. Detroit has a special place in the history of America's Black Muslims. As we have seen, Muslims came from Africa on the steady stream of slave ships in the late eighteenth and early nineteenth centuries, and their religious life was largely submerged in America until it resurfaced in the 1930s—right here in Detroit.

AFRICAN-AMERICAN ISLAM
IN THE TWENTIETH CENTURY

The image of young African-American men in suits, white shirts, and bow ties, with impeccable posture, a look of confidence and strength on their faces, has now become familiar to most Americans. They are the members of the Nation of Islam's unarmed and highly disciplined Fruit of Islam, which closes crack houses, conducts drug patrols, and has proven so effective in security that it has been hired by housing authorities in Los Angeles, Chicago, Washington, and New York to provide security patrols for some of urban America's most distressed high-rise projects. Equally important, the self-respect and discipline of these young Muslim men has transformed their lives and given them leverage on some of America's most intractable problems.

The Nation of Islam has captured headlines, positive and negative, in the past twenty years, not least because of the charisma and rhetorical skills, as well as controversial views, of its leader, Louis Farrakhan, who is heir of the movement launched in the 1930s by Elijah Muhammad. But the Nation of Islam is not the largest of America's Black Muslim movements today. By far the majority are the followers of a loose coalition of mosques that follow the son of Elijah Muhammad, W. D. Mohammed, who turned the movement his father had started back from black separatism toward orthodox Sunni Islam.

We could follow many strands as we investigate the black recovery of Islam in twentieth-century America. One began in Newark, New Jersey, in 1913, when a twenty-seven-year-old man named Timothy Drew, renamed Noble Drew Ali, established the Moorish Science Temple of America. It was not orthodox Islam by any means, but Noble Drew Ali was inspired by Islamic ideas, calling urban blacks of America's cities to a sense of dignity and belonging, rooted in what he called their Moorish past, which he also referred to as their Asiatic past. He traveled widely as a young man, and according to the lore surrounding him, the queen of England made him a noble, the sultan of Turkey gave him the name Ali, and the king of Morocco commissioned him to teach the Muslim faith to Americans of African descent.

The *Holy Koran of the Moorish Science Temple of America* is not the Qur'an revealed to Muhammad but is rather an eclectic composite of Christian, Muslim, and Eastern religious traditions. It calls readers to a life of dignity and love:

> Come all ye Asiatics of America and hear the truth abut your nationality and birthrights, because you are not negroes. Learn of your forefathers' ancient and divine Creed. That you will learn to love instead of hate.[31]

Here the call to American blacks is not to deny their racial identity but rather to resist the meanings of that identity in white America, yet the use of the term *Asiatic* to describe black origins falls into yet another, at that time romantic, racial stereotype.

The *Holy Koran* of Noble Drew Ali strongly emphasizes the essential divinity of the human soul, a view far more consonant with the spirituality of India than with either Christianity or Islam. The *Holy Koran* proclaims that Allah is known under many names. "You Brahmans call Him Parabrahm, in Egypt he is Thoth, and Zeus is His name in Greece, Jehovah is His Hebrew name, but everywhere His is the causeless cause, the rootless root from which all things have grown" (10:19).[32] In this Koran, Jesus is said to have studied and taught in India, a view common to the Ahmadiyya movement, which came to America at about the same time.[33]

Noble Drew Ali was the first to realize that a new people reclaiming their past needed a new name. In the Moorish Science Temple, they were not black or Negro but Moorish Americans. The men wore the Turkish fez, the women long dresses. Many took Muslim names. While they did not perform the ritual sequence of kneeling and prostrating in prayer, they did pray facing Makkah. The nationality card given to new members, which they carried, reportedly, with considerable pride, affirmed their Moorish-American heritage and bore, in addition to the crescent of Islam, clasped hands of unity and a statement that the bearer of the card honors all divine prophets, including Jesus, Muhammad, Buddha, and Confucius.[34] Like these prophets, Noble Drew Ali was himself seen to have a divine mission.

Noble Drew Ali died in 1929, amid both mystery and rivalry within the movement. The Moorish Science Temple has continued through the decades since then but has been overshadowed by other African-American Islamic movements. Even today, however, there are a few local Moorish Science Temples and a Chicago headquarters. While the movement was not orthodox Islam, it was the first to recover an awareness of Islam in the struggle for a new black identity.[35]

Recovering an awareness of Islam took another giant step with Wallace D. Fard and, later, his successor, Elijah Muhammad, both of whom apparently associated with the Moorish Science Temple before they launched what would be a new and decisive phase in the recovery of Black Islam.[36] It began in Detroit in the 1930s. Wallace D. Fard, also called Wali Farad or Farrad Muhammad, is a mysterious figure who appeared as a peddler and itinerant evangelist in Detroit in 1930. He was said to be Turkish or perhaps Iranian, but he preached to black urban folk from the Bible and the Qur'an and claimed to have been sent from Makkah to restore blacks to their proper Muslim heritage as members of the "Lost-Found Nation of Islam." In Detroit he established the first Temple of Islam, which became known as Muhammad's Temple No. 1. The two-story red brick building is still standing today on Detroit's Linwood Avenue.

The times were ripe for a new message. The shift in the black population from the South to the urban North had created settlements of disaffected people in search of new identity and suffering from the experience of northern urban racism. In this environment new black identity movements began to grow, including the Moorish-American identity propagated by Noble Drew Ali and the back-to-Africa movement focused on a return to Liberia advocated by Marcus Garvey, who founded the United Negro Improvement Association in 1917. The impact of the Great Depression made the situation of northern cities even worse, and we can well imagine the sense of disillusionment with Christianity and its pretense to a Christian society that the black urban poor must have experienced. It is probably no coincidence that Black Islam began in one of

the cities that already had an established immigrant Arab Islamic population, though little research indicates a direct influence of Detroit's
Muslim immigrants on the incipient Black Muslim movement.

In the climate of anti-immigrant nativism that followed World War I,
racism was on the rise, anti-Semitism was on the rise, and more than a few
Americans were attracted to a new spate of racial theories about the inherent superiority of the blue-eyed "Nordic race." Detroit's own Henry Ford
was one of the most vocal, and he controlled the *Dearborn Herald,* the pages
of which were filled with searing racial rhetoric. Neither Jews nor blacks
were hired at the Ford Motor Company. It is thus hardly surprising to find
Fard in Detroit in the late 1920s turning the claims of blue-eyed superiority upside down, teaching that whites were "blue-eyed devils." In Fard's
racial origins theory, the black man is the "original man," from which
whites are a deviant, weak, hybrid race, created by a misguided scientist
and destined for certain defeat in the apocalyptic confrontation of black
and white. In this view, the nation of America does not include blacks, who
have their own identity, their own nation—the Nation of Islam. Fard's new
movement created cadres of discipline and identity—the Fruit of Islam
corps for young men and the Muslim Girls Training Class for women.

In 1934 Fard passed the mantle of Messenger of Allah to Elijah
Muhammad, his foremost disciple in the new Muslim cause, a man then in
his thirties, born the son of a black Baptist minister in Georgia. Fard disappeared as mysteriously as he had come. Some say he returned to Makkah.
His mysterious departure, like that of Noble Drew Ali, seems to have been
part of his mythic persona. The transition of power after Fard's disappear-
ance was clearly not without contention, for Elijah Muhammad had to leave
Detroit under threat. He eventually established Temple No. 2 in Chicago's
South Side, which became the home base of the Nation of Islam. According
to historian C. Eric Lincoln, "Elijah Muhammad must be credited with the
serious re-introduction of Islam to the United States in modern times, giving it the peculiar mystique, the appeal, and the respect without which it
could not have penetrated the American bastion of Judeo-Christian
democracy."[37]

In building the Nation of Islam, Elijah Muhammad used everything
available to him. He drew on the Bible, which he and the black urban
poor knew well. He introduced the teachings of the Qur'an, which
brought a new and authoritative voice. He drew upon the manuals and
teachings of W. D. Fard, including the teaching of black dignity and the
white man as devil. He adapted Islamic practice to the situation at hand,

for instance, observing Ramadan in December, coinciding with the Christmas season. Perhaps the greatest change was reformulating the confession of faith, the *shahadah,* to affirm: "I believe that there is only one God (Allah) who came in the person of Master Fard, and (Elijah) Muhammad is the Messenger of Allah." This was more than an adaptation, however. For Muslims, this was wholly unorthodox Islam. Mainstream Islam insists that Allah takes no human form whatsoever. The very idea that anything or anyone can be compared with God constitutes heresy in Islam, for God is without peer, without comparison, without form. For orthodox Islam, the final messenger was and is Muhammad, and to speak of Elijah Muhammad as the messenger constituted a clear heresy. But in Detroit in the 1930s, no one was checking, and what attracted urban blacks to the movement was not internationally sanctioned orthodox Islam.

Orthodoxy, after all, has never been the measure of black religion in America. Experience has always won out over official doctrine. As Lincoln put it, "The salient tradition of Black religion has always been the sufficiency of its own insight."[38] Christians in the new black Christian churches had little reason to respect or imitate the so-called orthodoxy or authenticity of the white churches that excluded them. Black Christians developed their own rhythms, forms, structures. For new black Muslims as well, meeting standards of orthodoxy was not their first priority. Decades later, in the 1980s, Louis Farrakhan again responded to the question of orthodoxy in characteristic fashion:

> We believe in Muhammad, the Qur'an, God, the Honorable Elijah Muhammad and his mission and work among us. And now all of a sudden we have to come prove to somebody that we're Muslims. I don't care if none of you believe I'm a Muslim. You are not my judge. Take off the robes of Allah. They don't fit you well![39]

Continuing in this vein in 2000, Minister Farrakhan appointed the first woman, Minister Ava Muhammad, to be a regional representative of the Nation of Islam and to be imam of a mosque in Atlanta. This unprecedented move is yet another way in which Minister Farrakhan follows his own lights, not those of an imposed orthodoxy.

Elijah Muhammad preached not only Islam, but also self-help, hard work, and economic self-reliance. There was almost a Gandhian hue to his views of social transformation: that self-governance begins in one's own life and in one's own neighborhood. Starting small businesses, selling newspapers, and opening credit unions were the economic manifestations. Giving up drugs, alcohol, and smoking became the expressions of personal transformation. This "Black Puritanism" came with a new surname: X. It meant ex-addict or ex-Negro or ex-slave. As scholar Lawrence Mamiya puts it, "It also signified that the new convert to Black Islam was 'undetermined,' no longer the predictable 'Negro' created by the white man."[40]

The idea that blacks constitute a new nation without primary obligation to the America of racism was also integral to the movement. During World War II, Elijah Muhammad and about one hundred other members of the Nation of Islam were imprisoned for resisting the draft. Elijah Muhammad did not permit the bearing of arms, even by the Fruit of Islam, a position that was later challenged by Malcolm X's militancy and insistence on the right of blacks to defend themselves. There was agreement, however, on refusing to participate in the armed forces of a country that denied them equal rights and dignity. This tradition led Cassius Clay, who became Muhammad Ali after his conversion to Islam, to go to prison for refusing to serve in the military in the Vietnam War, saying, "No Vietnamese ever called me a nigger."

The ministry of Malcolm X brought nationwide attention to the Black Muslim movement. During the period from 1952 to 1965, Malcolm was a minister of the Nation of Islam and eventually its national representative, second only to Elijah Muhammad himself. His leadership and energy were responsible for the tremendous growth of the Nation in this period. He was a fine orator and a talented organizer. He was also a real missionary who preached in the streets of Harlem and launched the publication of *Muhammad Speaks,* a newspaper that he required young men in the movement to sell on the streets as part of their mission and ministry.

As is well known from his autobiography, Malcolm Little grew up in Omaha, where no one expected a young black to succeed, even though he was a fine student. His adviser suggested carpentry, not law, as an appropriate ambition. After dropping out of school, Malcolm became a shoeshine boy, a pimp, a pusher, and a small-time thief and eventually ended up in Norfolk State Prison in Massachusetts. There he encountered Islam through the testimony of a fellow prisoner and in 1948 wrote the critical letter that initiated his relationship with Elijah Muhammad. Malcolm turned the next four years in prison into a strenuous tutorial in English literacy and literature and in Islam and its relation to the issues of the day. By the time he was released in 1952, Malcolm X was ready for a lifelong ministry in the Nation. He was made Minister of Temple No. 11

in Boston and eventually of Temple No. 7 in Harlem. He became one of the strongest voices of the 1960s in articulating black power and black pride. He was known for expressing in clear terms the rage and frustration that were, by that time, seething in black urban America.

Malcolm's straight-talking manner eventually brought an end to his meteoric career in the Nation of Islam. He heard rumors about Elijah Muhammad's alleged sexual liaisons with several women and went to the source to confirm it, and when he was convinced it was indeed true, he was deeply upset. At that time, in December of 1963, Elijah Muhammad officially imposed a three-month period of silence on Malcolm X, claiming it was because of impetuous remarks about "chickens coming home to roost" that Malcolm had made at the time of President Kennedy's assassination. But it was clear to Malcolm that the silencing was a reprimand for his brewing critique of Elijah Muhammad.

In 1964 Malcolm X left the Nation of Islam and traveled to the Middle East and Africa, where he came into contact with leading spokesmen for orthodox Sunni Islam. The story of his Hajj, his pilgrimage to Makkah, has gained almost mythic dimensions as it came to symbolize the shift to a new vision of Islam for African Americans—nonracist, non-separatist, and truly universal. He wrote,

> There were tens of thousands of pilgrims from all over the world. They were of all colors, from blue-eyed blondes to black-skinned Africans. But we were all participating in the same ritual, displaying a spirit of unity and brotherhood that my experiences in America had led me to believe never could exist between the white and the non-white.[41]

With a determination to transform the course of American Black Islam toward the mainstream of international Islam, Malcolm returned to the U.S. and launched a new mosque in New York, openly challenging what he now saw as the implicit racism of the Nation of Islam. He was assassinated on February 21, 1965—some say by members or agents of the Nation of Islam, but the case has never been proven.

The vision of a new future for the Black Muslim movement did not die with Malcolm X, however. In the long run, this became the new mainstream of African-American Islam, and it began under the leadership of none other than Elijah Muhammad's own son. When Elijah Muhammad died in 1975, twenty thousand members of the Nation of Islam came together in Chicago for his funeral. There they unanimously chose his son, W. D. Mohammed, as the successor to leadership. Within a year of taking the reins, W. D. Mohammed dissolved the structure of the Nation of Islam that his father had built over thirty years and began to follow Malcolm X down the road toward mainstream orthodox Islam. He turned from theories of black racial superiority to the Islamic foundations of human racial equality. He even welcomed whites into the Muslim family. "There will be no such category as a white Muslim or a black Muslim," he said in a speech a few months after his father's death in Chicago. "All will be Muslims. All children of God."[42]

W. D. Mohammed signaled this transition toward universal orthodox Islam by dropping the term *minister* and taking the name *imam,* as did his clergy. The "temples" were now mosques or "masjids." The observance of Ramadan was brought into accord with the lunar calendar followed by Muslims throughout the world. In 1976 W. D. Mohammed fasted during the recognized month of Ramadan for the first time. He changed *Muhammad Speaks* to the weekly newspaper now published as The *Muslim Journal.* And to emphasize the turn from black separatism to black citizenship, the *Muslim Journal* bears the American flag on its masthead.

The movement has had several names, beginning with The World Community of Al-Islam in the West, then the American Muslim Mission. Then even that name was dropped. "We're just Muslims. Within Islam there is no division," says Mohammed. His words have special force in an American in which Indo-Pakistani Muslims and Arab Muslims are trying, for the first time, to come to know one another as "just Muslims." Imam W. D. Mohammed now has a considerable number of mosques that "follow his leadership," as they put it, but they are independent. A loosely structured national organization of these mosques now calls itself the Muslim American Society, and under its banner African-American Muslims gather in an annual national conference and in workshops on race, jobs, education, and the role of women. Some fifty Sister Clara Muhammad Schools are also operating, named for the wife of Elijah Muhammad who took on her own children's education as a young mother in Detroit and was so instrumental in starting Islamic education as an alternative to public schooling.

At the time Malcolm X was silenced and fell from favor, Louis Farrakhan was appointed national representative of the Nation of Islam. He also succeeded Malcolm X as minister of Temple No. 7 in Harlem, one of the most active centers of the Nation. In many ways, he was a protégé of Malcolm X and came closest to duplicating the charisma and fiery frankness that made Malcolm X one of the most powerful black leaders of his time. Indeed, Malcolm X had been one of those who first moved young Louis Eugene Wolcott, a talented violinist and calypso singer, to become Louis X, a minister of the Nation of Islam.

Louis did not share the turn toward universal orthodox Islam made by Malcolm X and W. D. Mohammed. He did not think Islamic ideals alone were insurance against racism. Indeed, he saw in Islam some of the same hypocrisy and racism that he hated in America. By 1978 Louis Farrakhan had revived a remnant of the old Nation of Islam and become its chief minister. The enemy was still racism. Everywhere in the world, blacks are still at the bottom of the social order, he observed, no matter which religious tradition is prevalent. At a speech in Harlem in 1980, he said,

> If you [orthodox Muslims] are so interested in the Black Man in America, why don't you clean up the ghettoes in Mecca. . . . The ghettoes in the Holy City where the Sudanese and other black African Muslims live are some of the worst I've seen anywhere. . . . I see racism in the Muslim world, clean it up!"[43]

This railing against hypocrisy spared no one, especially Muslims. It became and remained a distinctive note of Farrakhan's rhetoric. I first heard Farrakhan at the 1993 Parliament of the World's Religions in Chicago, where his very presence was enough to lead a major Jewish organization to withdraw from sponsorship. But his speech at the parliament, presented in one of the glittering ballrooms of the Parker House in a session that included the Reverend James Forbes of the Riverside Church in New York, featured a critique wide enough to offend anyone, if one were in the mood to take offense. "Racism has poisoned the bloodstream of religion," he said. "Every one of our communities has had an enlightened one to teach us. But where is our enlightenment? Look around. It looks as if Jesus never walked among us. It looks as if Moses, Muhammad, Buddha, and Confucius never walked among us. The House of Islam is broken into pieces. Where is the enlightenment?" Years earlier when he had described Judaism as a "gutter religion," he had launched a relentless and by now hopeless tangle of accusation and counteraccusation. But it became clear to me that his critique of religion was much broader and included self-criticism of Islam and fellow Muslims. Islam, too, is a gutter religion, he said, as is Christianity and every community of faith that ignores its own noble teachings while people perpetuate injustice.

Today African-American Islam is complex in composition and constitutes over 25 percent, some say as much as 40 percent, of all Muslims in America. Farrakhan and the Nation of Islam still receive most of the headlines but are a small minority in the total picture, with only about ninety affiliated mosques. By contrast, hundreds of mosques follow the less charismatic but more centrist and orthodox leadership of W. D. Mohammed. The world of African-American Islam is dynamic, however, and there have been signs of a milder and more universalistic voice coming from Louis Farrakhan, which some attributed to his recovery from a life-threatening illness and his determination to leave a lasting legacy as a Muslim leader. On the Nation's annual Saviour's Day celebration on February 21, 1999, he was joined on the platform in Chicago by Imam W. D. Mohammed and a range of Muslim leaders from immigrant communities. The widely noted embrace of Imam Mohammed and Farrakhan was amplified by indications from both sides that they would like to resolve their differences and begin walking together on the path of Islam. If so, this chapter in Islam in America will be written in the years ahead.

AMERICA IS PART OF THE MUSLIM WORLD

Labor Day marks America's transition from summer to fall with barbecues, picnics, and weekends at the beach. For many American Muslims, however, Labor Day is convention time, and the huge annual convention of the Islamic Society of North America, ISNA for short, has become a ritual ingathering—part family fair, part conference, and part business. The convention has been held in Cincinnati, Kansas City, and St. Louis, but in recent years the group has outgrown virtually every major convention venue except Chicago. On Labor Day weekend in 1994, between twelve thousand and fourteen thousand Muslims attended, and Chicago mayor Richard Daley proclaimed September 2, 1994, Islam Appreciation Day.

The Islamic Society of North America has its headquarters in Plainfield, Indiana, a town with a water tower and a Main Street like hundreds in Indiana. The modern brick mosque and its extensive office complex are alive with activity—a speaker's bureau, workshops for teachers, and planning for conferences. An extensive publications department produces informational pamphlets on Islam and the *Islamic Horizons* magazine. Matrimonial listings appear on the ISNA Web site, and the society provides information on Muslim marriage certificates and Islamic wills.

Above all, it is a broad spectrum organization designed to serve the needs of Muslims in America and to connect them to one another.

ISNA grew out of the Muslim Student Association organized in the 1960s by what were then international students from South Asia and the Middle East. Now they are middle-aged immigrants, American citizens with families of teenagers and college students of their own. The range of topics they discuss in these annual meetings gives us a quick roster of the concerns of Muslims in America. In Chicago, for example, they discussed Islam and the American judicial system, Islamic banking systems, the coverage of Islam in the media, Islamic weekend and full-time schools, and Islamic political involvement. There were new issues as well, such as the use of the Internet for Islamic networking and information. The theme of the Chicago convention, "Our Youth, Our Family, Our Future," highlighted the tension between assimilation as Americans and the preservation of religious identity as Muslims, a tension that has been the story of immigrants to America for two hundred years. Thousands of Muslim teens attended, some in T-shirts and jeans, some of the girls wearing the head scarf and some not. During their own conference sessions, they engaged in energetic discussion with a few members of their parents' generation on what are called the "controversial and conflicting issues of entertainment and socializing: Who should set limits and how?"

Hosting the meeting of ISNA in Chicago were the Muslims of the greater metropolitan area—some five hundred thousand strong, affiliated with about seventy mosques and Islamic centers. There are old Muslim communities, like the Bosnians who formed an Islamic society in the early part of this century and have built a striking new mosque in suburban Northbrook. There are more recent immigrants, primarily from India and Pakistan, who have converted an old movie theater into the Muslim Community Center, with thriving educational programs and a huge prayer hall where more than a thousand gather weekly under the glittering crystal chandeliers for congregational prayers. In the western suburb of Bridgeview is the Mosque Foundation of Chicago, a complex that includes a mosque and two full-time Islamic schools enrolling some four hundred students in the full range of twelve grades. Some two thousand Muslim families purchased an elementary school in Villa Park in 1983 and transformed it into an Islamic Center and a full-time school up to eighth grade. Across town close to the lake shore stands America's first Islamic University. On the South Side are a dozen active African-American Islamic centers and the nationwide headquarters of both Louis

Farrakhan's Nation of Islam and W. D. Mohammed's Sunni Islamic movement. The spectrum of Chicago's Islam spans the entire world.

The "Muslim world" is not somewhere else; Chicago is part of the Muslim world. In America the Islamic population is conservatively estimated to be about six million and growing. The so called Muslim world can't be limited in our mind's eye to those nations with large Muslim populations from Indonesia, to India, to Iran, to Egypt and across north Africa to Morocco. Today there are mosques in Paris and Lyon, and more Muslims than Protestants in France. Storefront mosques are found in the Netherlands and Sweden and landmark mosques near the Tiber in Rome and in Regent's Park in London. They signal the rise of substantial Muslim communities and the marbling of religious communities old and new in most of the countries of the West.

America's more than 1,400 mosques give a visible testimony to the presence of Islam. Some are storefront and commuter mosques used only for daily and Friday prayers during the workday. A mosque is not a sacred space but a functional space, a place for prayer. It is not consecrated, in contrast to Christian cathedrals or to many of America's Hindu temples, which become, through the process of consecration, the architectural image of the body of God. Nonetheless, the architectural gestures of a mosque, including a dome, the crescent moon, and perhaps a stylized minaret, are often added to a refurbished building. Of the many American mosques that have improvised in this way, I think, for example, of the Islamic Center in Youngstown, Ohio, where a former church structure has been capped with a dome and a façade has been added, with decorative arch motifs over and to either side of the front door.

Spectacular new mosques are adding a new dimension to America's skyline, such as the enormous mosque on 96th and Third in New York designed by Skidmore, Owings, and Merrill; the Islamic Society of Greater Toledo with domes and minarets visible across the cornfields; and the Islamic Center of Cleveland, glistening white at the end of a tree-lined approach road. The Phoenix area has two extraordinary mosques: Masjid Jauhartul is a replica of a mosque in Makkah, with a large court-yard at the center, and in nearby Tempe near Arizona State University is a mosque designed after the Dome of the Rock mosque in Jerusalem—octagonal with a central domed prayer room. Other new, spectacular mosques include the Islamic Center of Virginia in Bon Air near Richmond; Masjid Abu-Bakr Al Siddiq in Metairie, Louisiana; the

Islamic Center of Connecticut in Windsor; and the Pullman Islamic Center in Pullman, Washington.

The post-1965 Muslim immigrants have come in greatest numbers from India and Pakistan, but they have also come from Indonesia, Africa, and the Middle East. The story of Islamic expansion can be told in many American cities. In Houston, the booming oil industry and the space program brought Muslims to town. Today there are over two dozen Islamic centers, ten of which have joined together in the Islamic Society of Greater Houston. Formed in 1968, the ISGH dedicated itself to the dual task of providing for the religious needs of Houston's Muslims and explaining Islam to Houston's non-Muslims. As Houston and its Muslim population have grown, the ISGH divided the sprawling city into five zones and developed a cohesive Islamic plan for the urban environment. The main ISGH mosque now anchors these ten satellite mosques. In every zone, the Islamic centers began in suburban homes, storefronts, or transformed office buildings, and today they are busy building, moving from temporary quarters into new mosques. The Southwest Zone Mosque on Synott Road, for example, is a huge structure of warm terra-cotta colored bricks, with a copper dome and a tall minaret.

In Florida the Muslim community is also growing, with as many as fifteen thousand Muslims in Dade and Broward Counties alone. Masjid Miami was the first community in the area, converting a home into a mosque in 1976 in a largely Hispanic neighborhood near the Miami Airport. Today the two hundred people who attend Friday prayers spill out onto the patio and the lawn. Masjid Miami Gardens began in a former Pentecostal Church and has completed a new mosque in Opa Locka with a prayer room that accommodates five hundred. The Islamic Center of South Florida in Pompano Beach began as a small, largely Palestinian, community and has grown in fifteen years to an ethnically diverse community of more than five hundred, holding its Eid prayers in a local park. Muslims in Fort Pierce hold prayers in a converted Presbyterian Church. All these Muslims in South Florida can locate their friends and their businesses in a Muslim telephone directory and can read area news in the *Muslim Chronicle*.

Each mosque in America has its own story—how it began in makeshift quarters, gradually grew, rented property, moved, purchased a building, perhaps moved again. Here is a thumbnail sketch of a few of these local histories. The Muslims who started the Islamic Center of Mill Valley in California first began holding Friday prayers in the storeroom of a

Travelodge Motel and finally were able to purchase a former Baptist church building for their center. In Denver, the Muslim community first worshiped in a small house converted into a mosque and by the mid-1980's the community was large enough to purchase an elementary school, which it transformed into a mosque complete with dome and minaret. When the Muslim Association of Pennsylvania's Lehigh Valley was formed in 1980, it included thirty families. Today there are more than two hundred, and the community has built a new mosque in Whitehall, Pennsylvania. The long list of American mosques in the Pluralism Project database shows ZIP codes from Alaska to Alabama. The history of American Islam is being written in the stories that unfold at each address. In a way, these are many tellings of a common story new Muslim immigrants forming associations, meeting in homes or garages for Friday prayer, raising money, growing in numbers, buying a building to convert into an Islamic center, and eventually laying plans to build. This story has been repeated hundreds of times in America from the first communities in places like Cedar Rapids, Iowa, to the scores of mosques being built today.

What is the shape and size of the American Muslim population today? In the mid-1990s the Islamic Research Institute found over 1,200 mosques in the United States.[44] Today the number is closer to 1,400. About 80 percent of these mosques were founded in the last twenty-five years. Though each mosque could estimate the number of Muslims regularly attending prayers and the number on its mailing list, mosque affiliation is not an accurate gauge of the Islamic population. Of the some six million American Muslims today, we noted that about 25 to 40 percent are African Americans, and the rest are immigrants, both old and new. There is also a small but growing number of Euro-American converts to Islam.

What seems from a distance a unified tradition is, like all religious traditions, diverse and complex up close. Most American Muslims, and most Muslims in the world, are Sunni. A small percentage, certainly no more than 20 percent, are Shi'ite. The Shi'ites include both Iranian and Iraqi Muslims and are further subdivided to include Ismailis and the sectarian movements of Bohras and Nizaris. In many American communities, there are also mosques of the Ahmadiyyas, founded by a nineteenth-century leader to await the final return of the imam or *mahdi*. There are clearly many streams of Islam, and Muslims themselves have different interpretations of these many streams. The Ismailis and Ahmadiyyas, for example, are often seen as unorthodox by Sunni Muslims, and yet the very meaning of orthodoxy is contested.

Sufism, the interior path of spiritual life, is not a separate sect of Islam, but suffused through the entire tradition. Its form of meditative and ecstatic dance called *dhikr* is increasingly known through traveling performances of the Mevlevi order of "Whirling Dervishes," and its devotional poetry is popular in the West. Indeed the best-selling poet in America is currently Rumi, the thirteenth-century mystic whose breathtaking poetry is translated in multiple popular editions.

There are many Sufi movements in the United States. The Naqshbandi movement looks for leadership to Shaykh Muhammad Nazim al-Haqqani and seeks to build bridges of understanding among many schools of Islamic thought and spread the appreciation of the Sufi way of devotion among non-Muslims as well. The International Association of Sufism also creates a forum of dialogue, publishing a journal called *Sufism, An Inquiry*, and hosting an annual Sufism symposium. Part of the Association is the Sufi Women Organization that brings Sufi women together to advocate for women's rights and justice for women in society and within the Muslim community. Appealing primarily to Euro-Americans is The Sufi Order International founded by in 1910 Hazrat Inayat Khan, who described Sufism as the universal "religion of the heart." Today the worldwide movement, led by his son and successor Pir Vilayat Inayat Khan, has nearly one-hundred centers in the U. S. and sponsors Dances of Universal Peace in dozens of cities.

Americans, at least the vast majority who are not Muslim, not only see Islam as monolithic, but are clearly anxious about Islam. In my experience, many people who ask about the Islamic community want first and foremost to know how large it is. How many Muslims? The truth is, we do not know precisely, but probably about six million. In entering full force into the electoral process in the 2000 election, Muslims themselves used this number to emphasize their potential significance in voting. As important as numbers are, however, they do not carry us very far into understanding Islam. Beyond numbers, what else do we want to know?

UNIVERSAL CALL

Islam is truly universal in its reach and cultural diversity. But the convergence of this diverse family on one soil is the special destiny of American Muslims. New Muslim immigrants come from countries as different from each other as India and Nigeria. Here they encounter Muslims already part of the American scene—the indigenous home-grown Black

Muslim communities and the long-settled Arab-American communities like those in Cedar Rapids and Detroit. Imagine what this transcultural reach means for American Muslims who have grown up in an African-American Muslim community in Columbia, South Carolina, or in a Muslim family that has come to America from Hyderabad in India. Suddenly, their religious community spans the whole world, not just in the imagined worldwide community called the *ummah,* and not just in the once-in-a-lifetime experience of pilgrimage to Makkah, but in the week-to-week life of a local mosque.

The American experience of religious diversity is not new for most Muslim immigrants. After all, in nations like India or Indonesia religious diversity is taken for granted. But the internal cultural diversity within Islam itself is challenging. As my colleague Ali Asani, an Ismaili professor originally from Kenya, put it, "You have all these Muslims from different ethnic and cultural backgrounds coming together here who have never even been in touch with each other. In theory, you know that they exist, but when you encounter them on a day-to-day basis and practice your faith with Muslims who may have a different cultural expression, this is new. I think this is what being Muslim in America means—having to deal with the diversity, the pluralism within Islam itself."[45]

One spring day in 1999, I sat leaning against the wall at the back of the huge prayer hall of the Islamic Center in Santa Clara, California, draped in my head scarf, quietly watching the women in the back section of the hall assemble for Friday prayers. Surveying this array of women, dressed in clothing distinctive to Egypt, Lebanon, Somalia, and India, I thought of the Qur'anic challenge Siraj Wahaj had placed in prayer before the U.S. House of Representatives: that the "nations and tribes" should come to know each other. It is certainly happening here in Santa Clara. I also thought of Malcolm X and his pilgrimage to Makkah in 1964, when his eyes were suddenly opened to a multiracial and multinational community. How amazed Malcolm X would be if he were here today in the Silicon Valley! Here and now in America, the Hajj experience of Islam's unity and diversity is replicated every Friday at *jum'ah* prayers and to a lesser extent at prayers every single day. This hall, which had once been a Hewlett-Packard plant, occupies almost an entire city block in this high-tech industrial zone of Santa Clara. The women's section alone seems to be the size of a basketball court, and the men's section is at least twice that. More than two thousand Muslims gather here for Friday prayers. Clearly Santa Clara, like Chicago, New York, and Los

Angeles, is also part of what we now mean by "the Muslim world." The bottom line is quite clear: Islam is not to be confused with any particular culture and its ways but is a universal path of faith. In the U.S., where Islam is too often identified with the Middle East, Muslims continually remind us, and one another, that "Islam is a universal call. It is not an Arab religion or an eastern or Middle Eastern cult."[46]

Muslims take pride in the universalism of Islam—its insistence on human equality and dignity before God, on the irrelevance of nation and tribe when it comes to walking in the way of God. The Muslim communities of America have been challenged to put Islamic universal ideals into practice as nowhere else on earth. Worldwide, translocal Islam has always been ecumenical, but the very complexity of American Muslim communities has begun to generate ecumenical Islam at the local level as well. Islamic educator Shabbir Mansuri puts its strongly: "If some people lose their identity with India, the language, the customs, they feel they have lost their tradition. But for us as Muslims ethnicity does not matter. In fact, we discourage a South Asian identity or an Arab identity. We discourage connection of ethnicity with identity. I left all that business behind when I left India and came to America. I am an American now."[47]

Some American Muslims go even further in emphasizing the universal *ummah,* the community. I visited with the American-born principal of a full-time Muslim school who contended that even the Sunni-Shi'ite distinction has no future in the long-term development of Islam in America:

> I don't believe in Shi'ah-Sunni. I think it is an aberration for American Islam. Some of the things I say are not popular, but I firmly believe that there is no place for the Sunni-Shi'ah division for Muslims in America. The board of our school is half Sunni, half Shi'ah. Of the two assistant principals, one is Sunni and one is Shi'ah. Whatever happened 1400 years ago in the Middle East, happened then and was significant for a time. We can study it in our Islamic studies and history classes. We can understand it. We can even learn from it. But it is not relevant to the future of Islam in America.[48]

First-generation immigrants rarely go this far, but this educator's views may well indicate a growing commitment to a community that has left some of the scars of ethnicity and sectarianism behind.

Most Muslim observers of the American scene admit that even if the first generation is not as committed to leaving ethnicity and division behind, the second generation will be. It is difficult to reproduce deep ethnic and sectarian identities half a world away from their sources; at least that is what optimists postulate. Hassan Hathout and his colleagues at the Islamic Center of Southern California put it this way:

> Parents who are still torn apart between two cultures, the old and the new, should bear in mind that their children are the fruit of only one culture, the American. This does not mean that Islam is to be compromised or changed. But parents should not confuse ethnic habits and Islamic religion.[49]

When the Friday prayers were completed there in Santa Clara, it was time for the sermon or *khutba*. It began in full-throated Arabic, and I resigned myself to being unable to understand a thing, expecting that the teenage girls and the non-Arabic speaking Muslim women in the back of the prayer hall would share my boredom. Within three or four minutes, however, he shifted to English, and immediately I found myself listening attentively. Taking as his theme the *ummah,* the community, he said, "Allah says you are a single *ummah* and I am your Lord, worship me. That is the big task. Allah will keep us as a single *ummah,* not as many fragmented nations, but we Muslims have to unite. We have to unite. We have to work hard on this one. It is the order of Allah that this *ummah* be a single *ummah,* not many fragmentations."

The idea of creating a single community in Silicon Valley from the cultural diversity of worldwide Islam is truly challenging. It is the challenge of understanding community as the product of diversity rather than the antithesis of it. The American motto *E pluribus unum* came to mind, articulated now in an Islamic key for American Muslims. The pitch of the speaker rose; his voice became more urgent. "The ladder of responsibility goes from ourselves to our family to our society to our nation to our *ummah* to all of life. It begins with ourselves. Unless we establish Islam inside of us, it is not going to be established on our land. Unless we establish Islam in our character, in our manners, on our tongues, and in our thinking, it is not going to be established in our land. That is your duty, my dear sisters and brothers. What are you going to do about it? Are you going to watch soccer games and baseball games and forget about the *ummah,* the Muslim community? Or will your lives contribute to the foundation of the community?"

Creating a framework to bring Muslims together in the public arena has become the agenda of several national Muslim organizations. As Mohammad A. Cheema, then president of the American Muslim Council, put it at a retreat of Muslim leaders in 1994, "Our sluggers are hitting home runs, but the scoreboard is not changing. The only explanation can be that these players are not jelled into a team yet." Creating a team and giving voice to Islam in the public arena, especially in Washington, D.C., has been the agenda of the American Muslim Council since its formation in 1990. In just over a decade, the AMC has become one of the strong consensus-building instruments of America's diverse Muslim community. Midway through the 1990s, Cheema articulated the challenge as building community among Muslims, bridging the "wide gap between the immigrant and indigenous segments." He spoke of a "melting pot" solution to creating a Muslim community. As we will see, by the year 2000, the AMC had created a structure with local and regional chapters and was well on its way to building the team Cheema envisioned.

Through groups like the AMC, the Islamic Society of North America, the Muslim Public Affairs Council, the American Muslim Alliance, and the Islamic Circle of North America, Muslims have begun creating a distinctively American infrastructure. Reaching out and making common cause with one another is a natural extension of the *ummah,* and it is also a natural part of the American alliance-building process.

THE PILLARS OF ISLAM IN AMERICA

The Muslim community is sustained by five pillars of faith observed by Muslims everywhere. *Islam* means "submission" to God, aligning one's life with the path of faith. It comes from the Arabic word *salama,* which means both surrender and peace. It is this same word Muslims use in greeting one another, *salam alaikum,* literally, "peace be with you." The word *Muslim* comes from the same Arabic root and means one who surrenders or submits to what God has made plain. The proper response is not so much "believing" it but responding to it. Islam, in this sense, is not so much a noun but a verb, an action. The five pillars of faith undergird and support the lives of Muslims: the confession of faith, prayer, fasting, charity, and pilgrimage. These are foundational to many religious traditions, but in Islam they are lifted up as obligatory, for they are literally the pillars of a strong house of faith.

The first pillar is the affirmation of the *shahadah:* "There is no God but God, and Muhammad is God's messenger." Speaking these words with true commitment makes one a Muslim. It means bearing witness to the truth of God's oneness and the compelling authority of God's word and making it a reality in one's life. It does not mean that there is no God but Allah, as if Allah were other than what Christians and Jews mean by "God." It means that there is none worthy of worship except God, who is beyond our every description, beyond all our adjectives and names. Even so, virtually every chapter of the Qur'an begins with the *Bismillah,* "In the name of God, the Most Merciful, the Compassionate . . ." The invocation of God as merciful and compassionate is constantly reiterated.

Muhammad is the messenger, the prophet, who received the revelation of the Holy Qur'an and recited it to the people. He did not write it, for he was illiterate. But Muhammad is known as the trustworthy, the honest, messenger of God. Muslims do recognize other messengers, including Moses and Jesus. Indeed, in every place on earth God has spoken to humankind through messengers, but so much has gotten lost, gone awry, and been distorted. To Muhammad the whole of God's intention and message for humankind was once and for all time revealed. For this, Muslims love Muhammad, even revere him, even utter a blessing, "peace be upon him," when they speak his name, but they do not worship him. He is but the bearer of the message of God, and only God is worthy of worship.

For new Muslims, professing the *shahadah* is the act of conversion to Islam. In the early 1990s in Houston, I met a young man named William, an African American in his twenties who described "making *shahadah.*" William was a garage mechanic. He told the story of his conversion to Islam. "The first day I'm here at the garage, I see this guy, one of the mechanics, going over to the grass on the side of the shop to bow down and pray. I couldn't believe it. I had never seen anyone do this at work. Then he came back and got his lunch bag and ate just like the rest of us. That was the beginning for me. We started talking. He said he was in the religion of Al-Islam, and I started going to the *masjid* over on Bellfort, just to see. I thought getting a job was my best chance at life, and I do work hard. But now I say, it is Islam that is my best chance." William's *shahadah* took place at the Houston Masjid of Al-Islam on Bellfort Avenue, an African-American community now following the leadership of W. D. Mohammed. I had met Talib, the imam of that community, at a meeting of the Texas Conference of Churches. Talib was a soft-spoken but powerful man who had been raised a Baptist and had himself made *shahadah* as a Muslim more than forty years ago. In Talib's community, the personal story of African Americans embracing Islam can be told in a hundred voices by old-timers and newcomers.

Karen's conversion story began in a different place: with her own

Christian background and her zeal to witness to Muslims at a community college. I met her in Chicago, where she teaches courses on Islam in an Islamic girls school. She is Caucasian, with a sunny disposition and a warm, open, freckled face and blue eyes. When we talked at her school, she wore a long flowing navy blue dress and a white head scarf. I asked Karen how she became a Muslim. "I grew up Catholic. But when I was in high school, I became a very fervent Baptist, and I used to carry my Bible with me everywhere and find chances to witness to Christ. When I went to DuPage Community College, my Bible went with me. There I met a couple of young Syrian men, and I started to witness to them. They said, 'Listen, we'll read your Bible if you'll read our Qur'an.' So I took them up on it, and I got a Qur'an and some pamphlets on Islam."

Karen decided to transfer to a Bible college in Iowa to prepare herself for a life of mission and witness, especially to Muslims. Her Qur'an went with her to the Bible college, and she kept on reading. "Something happened one week that first semester. I started to wonder, really for the first time ever, if Jesus was *really* God. I went to Bible study prayers that week, and when my turn came to pray, I found that I just wanted to say, 'Dear God,' not 'Dear Jesus.' Wouldn't 'Dear God' be enough? By the time I had said that for a few days, one of my girlfriends came to me and said, 'Listen Karen, I don't know what's going on with you, but God likes it better when we pray in the name of Jesus.' I knew that day I probably wasn't really a Christian. I cried and cried. I called my folks to come and pick me up. I knew I just couldn't stay."

When she returned to her community college, she couldn't find the Syrian students, but she did find some of their friends and some tapes on Islam by Jamal Badawi. "There wasn't much to go on, yet I felt inside that I was probably a Muslim. But I didn't know any Muslims and didn't even know how to pray." She transferred to Southern Illinois University, which she knew many Muslim students attended. "Every week or two, the Muslim Student Association would have a table full of Muslim information and announcements. I always stopped by and picked up a flyer, even though I already had them, but there were only men at the table. One day one of the brothers gave me a piece of paper with the name of a Muslim sister, Sister Becky, and her phone number. It took me weeks to call, and when I finally did, she asked, 'How come you didn't call sooner? I've been expecting you.' So I met her. She was the first Muslim person I ever met to talk with."

Karen made her *shahadah* there at Southern Illinois University, and eventually she met and married a young Muslim computer engineer.

Today she is actively involved in Islamic teaching, called *da'wah.* The word *da'wah* is sometimes translated as "mission" or "call," but she prefers to call it "invitation." "It is a welcoming attitude toward the people you encounter," she said. "The girls here in school learn to speak about their Muslim faith. They will have to do this all their lives—to speak about their faith with confidence, to answer questions from people who don't know anything but Christianity." Karen herself is, of course, a living witness to the importance of *da'wah,* having responded years ago to an invitation to have a look at the Qur'an.

For both William and Karen, becoming a Muslim meant making a simple statement—simple, but the most important statement in the world. "It is not the words that matter," said Imam Talib in Houston. "Anyone can say these words. What it means to become a Muslim and submit yourself to God is to say these words with faith in your heart and to make them the guide of your life." Muslims hear them regularly in the call to prayer, and William and Karen repeat them daily in the context of their prayers:

> *La ilaha illa Allah.*
> *Muhammad rasul Allah.*
> I bear witness that there is no god but God.
> Muhammad is God's messenger.

The second pillar of faith is prayer, *salat.* It was this unselfconscious midday prayer of a co-worker that first caught William's eye and began to turn his face to Islam. *Salat* refers to the prayers offered five times a day—before dawn, at noon, midafternoon, sunset, and night. Every tradition includes some form of prayer and even regular daily cycles of prayer—for the orthodox, for the priests, or for the monastics. But no other tradition has so universally and elegantly ritualized a daily rhythm of prayer. Muslims speak not just of praying every day but of "establishing" prayer as a part of everyday life. In Islamic understanding, our human condition is not so much a matter of original sin but of perpetual forgetfulness. We do forget God and thus fail as well to remember who we are as human beings. To establish prayer in one's life is to stop the daily rush of life and commerce at regular intervals, to collect the mind and will in intention to prayer, and to perform the required prayers.

In places with large Muslim communities, the call to prayer, the *adhan,* can be heard throughout the neighborhood from the minaret:

God is most great. *Allahu Akbar.* God is most great. I witness that there is no God but God; I witness that Muhammad is His messenger. Come to prayer. Come to prosperity. *Allahu Akbar.* There is no God but God.

In the United States, the *adhan* is heard publicly in very few places, but if you pass by the storefront of the Muslim Community Center on Divisadero Street in downtown San Francisco you might hear the *muezzin* come out on the sidewalk to issue the call to prayer, or if you visit the Islamic Center of Washington, D.C., on Embassy Row, you will hear the call broadcast over loudspeakers, at least for community prayers on Friday noon. The first public call to prayer was probably made at the Islamic Center of America, the mosque I visited on Joy Road in Detroit, where Muslims have lived since the first decades of this century. When the community built the present mosque in 1952, they included a minaret also. From the shopping center across the street, from the Episcopal church next door, and from the homes in this Dearborn neighborhood, the sounds of the call to prayer can be heard along with chimes of the church bells.

Most American Muslims, however, do not have the prompting of a public call to prayer, but the hours of prayer are still built into the inner clock of each day. Sometimes prayer times are programmed into their watches or computers and the directions of prayer indicated on special compasses. Living a life structured by prayer is second nature. It is not a burden but a joy. And it is not rigid but flexible. If it is impossible to keep one of the prayers, it can be made up later. The point is not slavish obedience but establishing a rhythm of life in which remembering God has a place. And it makes a difference to know that at virtually every hour of the day there is a worldwide prayer wheel of millions of Muslims, facing Makkah in prayer.

Finding the time for prayer is simply part of daily life for most Muslims. In Los Angeles, in a high-rise downtown office building, a Muslim woman takes time from her lunch hour to find a quiet place in the stockroom for prayer. She wears a long loose skirt, a suit jacket, a scarf. At noon a group of African Americans, working on an educational project in Newark, excuse themselves from the conference table and find a vacant room nearby for prayer. Toward evening, on the grassy bank next to a filling station off the Van Wyck Expressway in Queens, a young man takes out a small prayer mat and unrolls it for evening prayer. At Harvard a college junior with her *hijab* in her backpack ducks into the suite of rooms in the basement of one of the freshman dorms that is used as a prayer room for the Harvard Islamic Society. She pulls the *hijab* over her head, and it falls to her ankles, covering her sweater and jeans. She joins a few others who have stopped for midday prayers. Muslims students keep up an information flow about other places for daily prayers—a little-used library stairwell, an empty classroom, a house common room.

Most of the daily prayer cycle is done individually, but some Muslims come to a mosque for one or more daily prayers, and certainly for noon prayers on Friday. On a regular weekday, several hundred men and a few women gather for midday prayers in the huge prayer hall of the Muslim Community Center, located in a former movie theater in downtown Chicago. The leader calls out the *adhan*. "God is great. *Allahu Akbar*." The group assembles in lines, shoulder to shoulder, and all begin the prayer together—bowing, kneeling, touching the head to the floor, sitting back on the heels, rising again. The women, who line up at the back of the room, would resist any suggestion that this indicates second-class citizenship. After questions about head covering, no question is asked of Muslim women more often than how they experience praying at the back of the prayer hall. It is not the back of the bus, most would insist. "There is no lesser role for women in Islam," one woman at the MCC explains. "We ourselves don't want to be bowing to the ground in front of a row of men while we are praying. It would be embarrassing for us and distracting for them." Among many Muslim women with whom I have raised the question, prayer at the back is simply not an issue. Many would nonetheless prefer the prayer room to be divided down the middle, with men and women praying side by side on opposite sides of the hall. What is problematic, at least for some, is to be relegated to the basement or a separate room altogether and to be cut off from the sense of participation in the whole community.

The direction of Makkah is marked in a mosque by the arch called the *mihrab*. It is not an altar and bears no symbols of the faith. It is simply a marker of orientation, but it does indeed orient the whole community toward a symbolic center as surely as does the cross or the ark of the covenant. Muslims turn toward Makkah, the birthplace of Islam, not because it is a sacred place or because God is especially present there, for God is present everywhere. Rather, this is the place where Abraham worshiped, where Muhammad received the revelation of the Holy Qur'an, and where Muhammad himself worshiped. Centering upon Makkah is the only location-oriented aspect of a worldwide community that has transcended nation and ethnicity. Facing Makkah is not a theological statement but a statement about the nature of a community that is both local and translocal.

In the United States, most buildings refurbished for Islamic prayer are oriented not toward Makkah but rather toward the street or corner on which they sit. In these buildings, the *mihrab* may well be in the corner of the room, and prayer lines will form obliquely on the diagonal. The landmark Islamic Center of New York at 96th Street and Third Avenue in Manhattan, is not square with the intersection but faces into the intersection for just the same reason. Whether the whole building rotates, or whether the congregation within the building rotates, the experience of a mosque reorients those who bow to pray, turning them from the familiar grid of urban streets, from the rush of commerce and traffic to the worldwide circle of prayer facing Makkah. Jerrilyn Dodds of the School of Architecture at City College of New York has done extensive architectural documentation of the mosques of New York City. She quotes a taxi driver from Bangladesh, who put it this way: "At the Masjid, Third Avenue comes to its knees." Dodds comments, "The notion that New York's urban landscape presents a force that must be defied or held at bay by a mosque building or space is one that appears often in interviews with Imams and worshippers."[50] The *mihrab* reminds everyone that they live by a different compass.

While daily prayers are to be said wherever one happens to be, Friday midday prayers, called *jum'ah* prayers, are congregational. Friday is not a Sabbath or day of rest. It is a business day like any other, but it does require a longer break in the routine of work for prayers. One of the first difficulties new Muslims faced in America was finding the acknowledged time and space for these prayers. The early Muslim community in Cedar Rapids, Iowa, was made up of merchants who could not afford to close their shops on Friday, so they moved weekly *jum'ah* prayers to Thursday evening. Getting time off in the middle of working hours for Friday prayers has been difficult for many Muslims in America, and the time is gone when Thursday night was close enough. In 1989, after hard work by the Muslim community, the District of Columbia passed a Religious Accommodation Act, making it explicit that employers in the district, including the government, must allow Muslims time off for *jum'ah* prayers.[51] The subsequent federal guidelines on "Religious Expression in the Federal Workplace" have made attendance at Friday prayers a clear example of the need for workplace accommodation.

Fasting during the month of Ramadan is the third pillar of the House of Islam. It is observed throughout the world, and Greensboro, North

Carolina, is no exception. Dr. Sayid Muhammed Sayeed, Secretary General of the Islamic Society of North America, often tells the story of the year his daughter Najeeba, an American-born Muslim, was a freshman at Guilford College in Greensboro. As Ramadan approached, both Najeeba and her parents were apprehensive about how it would be for her to observe the Ramadan fast far from home and in an overwhelmingly non-Muslim environment. Since she was the only Muslim student at a liberal arts college originally endowed by the Quakers, it promised to be a lonely spiritual regimen. The first day of Ramadan, Najeeba set her alarm clock and rose before dawn to head down to the dormitory kitchen for breakfast. She was surprised and delighted to find a dozen other girls in the dorm ready to join her for this predawn meal. The others went on about their day, having a snack and soda when they felt like it, having lunch or not as they wished. But all of them knew that from sunrise until sunset Najeeba would not eat or drink anything. They also learned firsthand during that Ramadan season that Najeeba would not be alone in her fast. A fifth of the world's population would be observing the Ramadan fast as she did. She missed the evening meals at home during Ramadan, for they always had a special celebratory quality, but the support of her friends, many of whom had not had a Muslim friend before, made the fast of Ramadan easier. Her father and mother were relieved and moved by what had happened.

Fasting is sustained by the community, even though, as in Najeeba's case, the community may not be close at hand. The Ramadan fast is not so much an individual penance or discipline, like the decision of many Christians to give up something for the forty-day period of Lent. It is closer to the Lenten discipline of Russian Orthodox people I have known, in which the whole community gives up eating meat, fish, and eggs for the entire period of Lent. Fasting in Ramadan is not only an individual but a community obligation. Muslims speak of the deep sense of sustenance and energy they feel, realizing that the same fast is being observed throughout the entire Muslim world by nearly a billion people. The fast becomes especially arduous when the month of Ramadan, which moves gradually through the year on a lunar calendar, falls in the summer when the days are hot and the time from sunrise to sunset very long.

People like to be together as they break the fast each day at dusk, taking a glass of water and sharing some dates. The ritual fast breaking, called *iftar,* is followed by evening prayers and then a hearty and festive meal. Gathering for an *iftar* has become one of the ways in which Muslims make their presence in the workplace and in public contexts known during this pivotal time of religious observance. An *iftar* hosted on Capitol Hill has become a tradition for Muslim aides and staffers in the government, and in 1999 Madeleine Albright was the host for an *iftar* that took place at the U.S. State Department, an event that was repeated in 2000.

Muslims experience both the unity and diversity of the American community during Ramadan. "During the month, we often share the evening meal with other Muslims," says Shabbir Mansuri of Los Angeles. "One day last year, for instance, we shared the breaking of the fast with a Bosnian Muslim family in L.A. When we sat down to eat, it was delicious, but it was not my chicken curry. There was a cultural difference there, just as there is with Muslims originally from Turkey or Africa. But as soon as we finished eating, we went into the living room, and the young man in the family led us in prayer. Then the common bond came into being. He led the prayers in the Arabic of the Qur'an that I have known all my life. That's when we feel real community. That's when I felt truly at home."

Charity or almsgiving, *zakat*, is the fourth pillar of Islamic faith. If you were to enter the lobby of the Muslim Community Center in Chicago or the Islamic Center of Southern California in Los Angeles, you would find fliers and information sheets put out by many charitable organizations announcing needs for *zakat*: relief programs in Bosnia, refugees in Somalia, literacy programs in Africa, the Red Crescent disaster relief fund for Turkey. Just as prayer is integral to the life of the community, so is responsibility for the welfare of the whole community. *Zakat* is a form of tithing—a percentage, usually 2.5 percent, of one's entire wealth and assets. This is what one owes to others. As one Muslim graduate student explains, "Unless you pay *zakat* on your income and wealth, all your income and wealth becomes impure, in a sense. One of the meanings of *zakat* is related to purity. *Zakat* is what 'purifies' your wealth for your own use."

Zakat is not really charity, for it is based on the belief that human beings are entitled not to ownership, but only to stewardship of resources. It is not because one is pious that one gives, it is because wealth is really not one's own. It is the same understanding that in Jewish law prohibited harvesting the corners of the field so that the poor may do so and required the forgiveness of all debts at regular intervals. These are reminders that we are not owners but trustees. As one of the many brochures introducing Islam puts it, "This precept teaches that what belongs to the individual also belongs to the community in the ultimate sense."[52]

Zakat cannot be used to build mosques or other Islamic institutions. It is for people, more specifically for Muslims, in need. The categories of people who should receive *zakat* include, according to the Qur'an, poor Muslims, new Muslims, Muslims in bondage, debt, or service to Allah, Muslim travelers, and Muslims who are employed to administer *zakat*. A contribution packet I picked up at one of the mosques in Boston provides a worksheet for calculating one's assets in cash and accounts, gold and silver (including jewelry), and in business accounts. The distributor of *zakat*, in this case, is Care International, which operates an orphan sponsorship program and enables sponsors to specify from which country—from Afghanistan to Tajikistan—they would like to sponsor an orphan.

The obligation to give *zakat* reminds us that Islam has its own distinctive form of economics and economic ethics, and we must not pass by this fact without note. Islam prohibits usury: charging interest on money loaned or paying interest on money borrowed. How Muslims manage their financial affairs, buy homes, even rent cars in a world premised on credit and interest will amaze non-Muslims, most of whom have no idea that the prohibition on interest is part of Islamic faith. Fasting for the whole month of Ramadan may be far easier for non-Muslims to grasp than life without a credit card. Harvard's Islamic Legal Studies Program regularly sponsors conferences on Islamic banking, with hundreds of Muslim participants gathering to discuss the emerging worldwide Islamic banking system that carefully negotiates alternatives to interest-driven banking.[53]

Pilgrimage to Makkah, called the Hajj, is the fifth pillar. It takes place in the month of Dhu al-Hijja, not long after the month of Ramadan. The pilgrimage to Makkah is required of Muslims once in a lifetime, if one is able, both physically and financially, to go. Every Muslim yearns to go, if not this year then next or sometime before one dies. For most Muslims, throughout most of Muslim history, it was a long and risky journey of many months by land or sea. It still is a long journey, even today, though most pilgrims come today by plane to the nearby airport of Jeddah in Saudi Arabia. In 2000, more than two million are estimated to have arrived in Jeddah for the Hajj. As the month of the Hajj approaches, announcements are posted on the walls of mosques and Islamic centers throughout the U.S. Brochures are stacked near the shoe racks at the door of the prayer room, offering the services of a travel agent specializing in Hajj travel. One agency in Fremont, California, advertises round-trip packages from New York to Jeddah and back beginning at $3,895, including the Sheraton Hotel in Medinah, an air-conditioned private tent at Mount Arafat, and four nights of accommodations in Makkah. A Riverside, California, agency starts its tour programs at $2,495.

When I went to Detroit to speak at the local interfaith roundtable, I was seated at lunch next to a woman named Mrs. Siddiqi who had recently returned from the Hajj, her second, and had photographs that showed her and her husband dressed in the plain white garments, called *ihram,* worn by all pilgrims. Their group included Muslims from all over Michigan and Ohio. In their white garments, however, they could have been anyone, rich or poor, doctor or cab driver, American or Syrian. She explained the tremendous impression of unity in faith that this experience left in her heart. "It was the community and our relationship to God that was fore-most in our minds. It was the sense of oneness, the absence of any trace of class, privilege. I have never felt anything like it, hearing those words we said at the beginning of our Hajj journey, 'I have responded to your call. I am here. . . .' It was the most moving experience in my life."

Michael Wolfe, an American convert to Islam and an ABC journal-ist, reported on his journey to Makkah in 1998, also conveying this sense of its profound impact on his life:

> Here I join people from all over the earth, all these human beings drawn together by the call of an idea, by the oneness of God. We have left daily life behind and come to a place hardly belonging to this world, a place filled by the almost tangible presence of God. . . . The duties of the Hajj are symbolic of the story and obligations of Islam. Before prayer, Muslims wash, representing ritual purity. The walk around the Ka'ba—the black stone block in the great mosque—is an expression of our desire to put God at the center of our lives. Pilgrims also make a journey to Mina and to the plain of Arafat, thirteen miles outside of Mecca. Making our way on foot, we trade city streets and buildings for . . . tents and carpets on the sand of the barren plain, giving up our usual comforts, get-ting back to basics. On the plain of Arafat, we perform the central obligation of the pilgrimage, to be here together from noon until sunset. There is no ceremony. We stroll, we pray, we meditate.
>
> The Hajj goes on inside the hearts and thoughts of each of us. This is a rehearsal for that day of judgment. How will we account for our acts? Have I injured anyone? Have I been grate-ful enough for the simple gifts of life, water, food, friends, family and the air I breathe? Before leaving Mecca, we visit the Ka'ba one last time. For most of us, this will be our last glimpse of the shrine. There is an old proverb—before you visit Mecca, it beck-ons you. When you leave it behind, it calls you forever.[54]

At the center of the great mosque of Makkah is the Ka'bah, the cube-shaped structure in which a black stone is embedded, shiny with the touch of millions of pilgrims through hundreds of years. It is said to have been established by Abraham and his son Ishmael, to have fallen into the worship of pagans, and to have been restored by the Prophet as a symbol of God's covenant with humankind. The Prophet cleared the tribal gods out of the Ka'bah, angering the clans of Makkah in his day. Muhammad and his early community adopted the rite of circling the stone, which is the rite most frequently seen in the West—the circular sea of people moving in seeming slow motion.

When all these pilgrims return home, they have the additional name Hajji, one who has been on the Hajj. Driving through the old Muslim neighborhoods of Dearborn, Michigan, after the Hajj, one will see banners stretched out on the porches of bungalow-style homes welcoming the Hajj-returned pilgrims, like the woman I had spoken with at lunch during my visit. The pilgrims are awaited with joy and excitement, for they bring with them the dust and touch of Makkah.

The five pillars make it easy to remember the fundamentals of Islam, whether one is a college student in a class on religion or a Muslim eight-year-old studying at a weekend school in the American suburbs. They must not make our task of understanding Islam too simple, however, for there are many Muslims for whom this structure of life is not the definitive formula for Islamic life. They might not pray five times a day or ever go to the mosque. They might visit the shrines of Muslim saints for blessing and inspiration, or they might learn their grounding in Islam from the women's cultures of their grandmothers and aunts, women who have listened to Qur'anic recitation in their homes, who have taken seriously the notion that there is no priesthood in Islam, who know in their hearts that there are no intermediaries between human beings and God, and whose lives of faith are not at all set by the dictates of Islamic legal tradition.[55]

As in the study of any tradition, our eyes should remain open to the amazing multiplicity of ways of faith, even when we have found some simple and convenient roads of entry into the tradition.

THE NEXT GENERATIONS

"If you lose your children, no number of mosques will help you." These words of Jamal Badawi are repeated in one form or another by Muslims all over America. Speaking at an annual meeting of the Islamic Society of North America, Badawi continued,

> Establishing of Islamic schools, in the environments in which we live, takes precedence over building mosques. You can have a huge, decorative, expensive mosque and lose your children, and end up having no one in the mosque to pray. I have seen it in Australia, where the early Afghan immigrants built mosques like monuments, some of which are now museums. Many of their children have already been lost.[56]

In the squash courts of a gymnasium-turned-mosque in Houston or a mall storefront in Atlanta, young Muslim children are studying Muslim history, learning their Arabic letters, reciting verses of the Qur'an in Arabic, and raising their hands to describe the five pillars of Islam in weekend Islamic schools. On the whole, American Muslims have placed a priority on a solid educational program for young Muslims, even before buying or converting property for a mosque. Every mosque has a weekend school of one sort of another, with programs on Saturdays, Sundays, or both. As Mian Ashraf of the Islamic Center of New England put it, "We have a tendency to take Islam for granted, especially those of us who grew up in an Islamic environment before coming to America. But here you have to work at it. We're scared that we're going to lose our identity. Our kids are going into this melting pot, where they might not be able to maintain their religious values, and we'll lose them."[57]

On a Sunday afternoon in 1993, I parked in the lot at the Islamic Foundation of Chicago, in the Bridgeview area. It was my first visit to this mosque, and as I entered the prayer room I found about seventy-five high school boys seated in the middle of the carpet under the dome. I took a seat at the back of the hall and listened. The speaker was a young journalist from Oaklawn who had grown up in America. He was eloquent, and every ear seemed attentive. "When I was growing up, what did I know of Islam? There was Allah, the Prophet Muhammad. But mostly what we heard as kids was, 'Don't eat pork. Don't date. Don't be like the Americans.' It was all a lists of don'ts. Islam was, for us, a series of stop signs. But this is not enough, this is not Islam. We were ripped off. Islam is more than a no."

I felt I was listening to the Muslim version of some of the great Methodist youth ministers of my teenage years whose passion and commitment had widened and changed my own vision of Christianity. He continued, "When I left home and got a job, when I started to travel, I had to ask myself, 'Who am I?' There is no running away from this question. You have to answer it. You can't run to the military or to college. You have to ask yourself this question," he said, pausing long enough to let it sink in. "I was in Japan, ten thousand miles from home, when I opened up the Qur'an one night, and I asked, 'Am I going to believe this or not? Is this going to be in the least relevant?' And when I look into the Qur'an, I found that there was nothing else that *is* relevant.

"So I want to challenge you. I want you to do two things. First, sit for five minutes with yourself every single night. Ask yourself who you are and who God is. Just five minutes a day. And second, I want you to open this book. Read it, just a verse at a time, a verse a day. I guarantee, it will change you. And you will change the world. The world needs changing too. Two-thirds of the people dying of hunger in the world, in Somalia and Ethiopia, are Muslims. Two-thirds of the world's refugees are Muslims. No one else is going to do this, but we are asked to do it. We are commanded to do what is right and to forbid what is wrong: That is what the Qur'an says."

He fell silent, and a question-and-answer session began. I wondered if I would ever hear anything quite so persuasive at a Hindu youth group in Chicago or at a Buddhist temple. In these traditions there is nothing that resembles the concept of *daw'ah,* the mission-invitation to one's own community and others to follow this path of faith. There are knowledgeable and engaging swamis and monks, to be sure. And there is certainly a deep concern about the younger generation. But the clear focus on Islamic education, taking priority even over the building of mosques, is especially important for the Islamic communities of America.

I was impressed with his articulation of the negative identity young people so often deplore. The leaders of the Islamic Society of Southern California address the issue of young people in unequivocal terms. In a book they have prepared for American Muslim communities, they write,

> One of the most detestable actions that could be conceived is to make coming to the Islamic Center an unpleasant experience to the young people. We hear it time and time again from parents across the country: "Our children hate to come to the Islamic Center." Some parents force their children to go to the Islamic Center. How short-sighted we are! Our children have to be convinced and motivated if we want them to make use of the institutions set up in the name of Islam for the future generations of Islam. This is the United States of America, and everybody knows parental authority ceases to function beyond a certain age.[58]

Islamic youth activities have a high priority at the Los Angeles center. The philosophy is that if the youth do not want to come, something is wrong with the center.

> Our youth group is autonomous and enjoys its own self-govern-ment through an elected board and an elected chairperson from amongst themselves. Not pressured by the elders, the youth find no reason to feel animosity or reservation against them. Many of them find in the center the comfort they lack in their own homes.[59]

The youth group in L.A. does not strictly segregate its activities by sex. It is clear, they say, that the marriage crisis among young Muslims is, in part, because Muslim girls and boys get to know non-Muslims better than Muslims if mosque activities are separate. As the leaders of this mosque see it, segregating Muslim boys and girls simply means that young people arrive at the age of marriage without getting to know other Muslims of the opposite sex at all. The summer camps in the San Bernardino mountains, the weekend conferences in Orange County, the social service activities—all are undertaken by young women and men together. So far, they say, dozens of successful marriages have come from the youth group alone.

Both the Islamic Center of Southern California and the Mosque Foundation at Bridgeview in Chicago are associated with full-time Islamic schools. Across the country, there are more than two hundred full-time Islamic schools, according to the Council of Islamic Schools of North America. A 1998 *New York Times* article reported twenty-three Islamic schools in New York City alone, and more in the planning stage.[60] At Al Noor in Brooklyn, it was reported that the student body was capped at six hundred, and four hundred more had to be turned away. The large Islamic Cultural Center of New York in Manhattan is in the process of building a school in the lot next door that will accommodate a thousand students when it is completed. As Americans debate the question of vouchers for private education, the American Muslim community is keenly involved and interested, for an Islamic education system is clearly in the making.

Dr. Dawud Tauhidi, co-founder and director of Crescent Academy International in the suburbs of Detroit, can give us some insight into the process of founding an Islamic school. He is an American convert to Islam and a Ph.D. candidate in Islamic Studies at the University of Michigan in Ann Arbor. When I spoke with him in Detroit, he described how the school began. "There were a few of us who all had elementary school kids. We wanted our kids to have an education that respected Islamic values and enabled them to become grounded in Islam, so we started a small Islamic school in Ann Arbor. It grew quickly. After two or three years, I realized that we had put our hand on something there's a real need for." Among the goals of the school is "to provide the Muslim students of the USA with an environment where they can practice their Islamic values and where they can find role models for Islamic behavior and attitudes."

After the Ann Arbor school was flourishing, the group bought land in 1988 for another school in a suburb of Detroit. "We thought the most we could scrape together was $500,000. In the end we spent more than $2,500,000." Doors opened in 1991 for kindergarten through fifth grade. By 1995 sixth through ninth grades had been added and plans for a high school were quickly developing. "When we started back in 1985 there were probably fifteen Islamic schools in the country. Now there are about two hundred full-time Islamic schools."

Yellow school buses bearing the name Crescent Academy International were parked in the lot when I arrived on that March morning. In the classrooms, boys in white shirts and girls in plaid jumpers, some with scarves but most without, went about their work. In the second-grade room, the teacher was sitting in slacks on the front table, a scarf wrapped around her head, reading a story to the class, everyone in eager attention except the two who were cleaning the hamster cage. The middle school was housed for the time being in a set of prefabricated buildings next door. The English and the literature classes would be familiar fare in any junior high school, but the Arabic class is also required three times a week, Islamic studies three times a week, and the study of the Qur'an three times a week. Do they study other religions as well? I asked. Tauhidi responded, "We have a hard enough time getting a good curriculum in Islamic studies together. Students have to feel secure about themselves first. Because of the history of the modern Muslim world, most are insecure."

A domed prayer room is part of the new school, with a tall window looking out to the fields, indicating the direction of Makkah. The early afternoon prayer is offered here daily as part of the school day, and, depending upon the time of year, the late afternoon prayer is also included. About one hundred families in the area, for whom this school prayer room is their local mosque, join the children for prayers at noon on Fridays.

The public-private school debate is lively within the Islamic community today in ways that to some extent revisit the earlier experience of both Catholics and Jews in America. Dr. Tauhidi takes his place in a long historical debate on parochial education in the United States when he says, "Muslims have to wake up and realize that they have to take care of their children. As the community gets stronger, we can make a contribution to society. But first the community, including the younger generation, must get stronger." Many Muslims despair of the drugs, the dating, the saturation with entertainment culture that are so much part of the public school experience. These parents establish full-time Islamic schools to create a stronger environment of support for Muslim faith and practice.

But establishing full-time Islamic schools is not without its opponents, even within the Muslim community. A panel on the public-private school debate at the 1993 ISNA convention in Kansas City drew hundreds of participants and elicited strong views. "Will two or three hours of weekend school do it, when seventy hours a week are spent in the non-Islamic environment of the public schools or the TV?" asked Aminah Jundali, the mother of four children. "You put children in school eight hours a day, five days a week, and then you expect them to come out of that with an Islamic personality and Islamic values? That's almost an impossible task."[61] A young high school girl responded in favor of public schooling. "It is even harder for us as girls, because we wear *hijab* to school and we stand out as different. Still, I want to go to the public school, because if we are not there as Muslims, how will other kids ever understand anything about Islam?"

Both sides in the debate realize that it is not an either-or issue. Full-time schools are being established, one after another, year after year. But it is also important to focus on critical issues for Muslims in the public schools. To this end, ISNA published a brochure that is sent by the thousands to public school teachers and administrators. *You've Got a Muslim Child in Your School* spells out some of the basics of Islam and specifies some of the restrictions.[62]

> On behalf of the Islamic Society of North America, the largest organization of Muslims in the United States and Canada, we would like to request that in view of the above teachings of Islam, Muslim students in your school system should not be required to:
> 1. sit next to the opposite sex in the classroom,
> 2. participate in physical education, swimming or dancing classes. Alternative meaningful education activities should be

arranged for them. We urge you to organize physical education and swimming classes separately for boys and girls in accordance with the following guidelines:

    a. Separate classes should be held for boys and girls in a fully covered area.

    b. Only male/female instructors for the respective group.

    c. Special swimming suits which will cover all the private parts of the body down to the knee.

    d. Separate and covered shower facilities for each student.

    3. participate in plays, proms, social parties, picnics, dating, etc. which require free mixing of the two sexes.

    4. participate in any event or activity related to Christmas, Easter, Halloween, or Valentine's Day. All such occasions have religious and social connotations contrary to Islamic faith and teachings.

We also urge you to ensure that the following facilities are available to Muslim students in your school:

    1. They are excused from their classes to attend off-campus special prayers on Fridays (approximately 1:00 to 2:00 P.M.).

    2. They are excused for 15 minutes in the afternoon to offer a special prayer in a designated area on the Campus. This prayer is mandatory for all Muslims and often cannot be offered after the school hours.

    3. All food items containing meat of a pig in any form and shape, as well as alcohol should be clearly labeled in the cafeteria.

    4. At least one properly covered toilet should be available in each men's and women's room.

    5. Muslim students are excused, without penalty of absence, for the two most important festivals of Islam: Eid al-Fitr and Eid al-Adha, in accordance with the lunar calendar.

Such requirements may strike the Muslim student as precisely the list of "don'ts" that constituted the young Chicago journalist's negative experience of Islam when he was a child. Most of what children end up telling their classmates and teachers is what they can't do. For school boards and principals, a brochure like this may be received as a welcome and educational set of guidelines for a new situation. On the other hand, it might be received as an unwarranted intrusion into the secular atmosphere of the school. What is clear, however, is that the church-state issues in public education have changed forever and make the discussion of such issues as school-sponsored prayer, the posting of the Ten Commandments, and the teaching of creation science the arguments of yesterday.

Shabbir Mansuri has pioneered in quite another area: Islamic participation in school curricula. He was an engineer in California when he entered the 1990 debate over the California state guidelines for the teaching of Islamic history and religion in social studies. As he tells the story, his sixth-grade daughter had come home giggling over the portrayal of Muslims at prayer in her school textbook: Bedouins who rubbed their faces in the sand before praying. "Daddy, should we get some sand in the living room?" she said. Mansuri laughed with her but was seriously disturbed by the textbook. Before long, he had organized Muslim participation in textbook hearings. When one text had a unit on Islamic history that began with a picture of a camel, he protested. "I looked at all the other units and the pictures were of people. But with Islam, it's a camel. The human element was completely missing. Why a camel, when most Americans already think of Muslims as remote, and therefore faceless?"

Mansuri founded the Council on Islamic Education and has plunged into the challenge of participation, organizing a wide range of scholars and teachers to work with textbook publishers as they revise social studies and world history texts. The scholars, both Muslim and non-Muslim, took a look at the new textbooks. Finally, the notorious camel was thrown out. "I felt so proud to be an American," he said in a subsequent interview. "That an individual like me, an immigrant, a concerned parent, went through the textbook adoption process and that changes were made because I participated—this is amazing. Nowhere else in the world does this happen." The committee organized by the Council on Islamic Education continues its work. "I'm not interested in just bringing an Islamic perspective, but an academic perspective to all these studies. . . . We are not looking for an ethnocentric curriculum. We want only that schools accurately portray the cultural and racial diversity of our society. . . . We need to participate in a positive way, with a contributory approach. . . . Once you make schools understand that you are part of the solution, not part of the problem, they will listen to you."[63]

HERE TO STAY: CREATING ISLAM IN AMERICA

"I am convinced that the resurgence of Islam will occur in America," said Mian Ashraf, a Boston surgeon and Muslim leader. "That's a big statement to make. Why do I think this is so? Because America is the only country in the world where education is very high. But also, America, to me, is the only place left in this world where you can today stand up and literally say anything you want to say. This is a tremendous opportunity for physical, mental, and emotional growth, and it should be nourished. But in order to take advantage of it, we're going to have to work for it."[64]

Participation and engagement are essential to the texture of real pluralism. American Muslims are engaged in debate about how much to participate in the civic and political life of the country. In Islam the world is seen as divided into Dar al-Islam, the "House of Islam," and Dar al-Kufr, the "House of Unbelief." What these mean is itself a matter of ongoing discussion. Some say Dar al-Islam is a land under Muslim rule and law, while Dar al-Kufr is where Muslims live in a minority, under non-Muslim rule. In these terms, America is not Dar al-Islam. Yet in the view of many Muslims today, any land where Muslims can live safely and freely because the government is committed to religious freedom is a good place for Muslims to dwell. There Muslims can live as if it were Dar al-Islam.[65] Living in this context is not a matter of living in isolated Muslim enclaves but being involved in the society. It is clear that Muslims, however they debate participation among themselves, are increasingly engaged participants in the American pluralist experiment.

Shabbir Mansuri puts the challenge succinctly: "As students and young professionals in the sixties and seventies, we talked about how we would eventually return to India or Pakistan. That's gone now. We're Americans and we're going to be buried here, so we should work within the system and participate in the process." In the past thirty years, America's Muslims have created a multitude of organizations to do just that. We have seen how Shabbir Mansuri's Council on Islamic Education organizes both Muslim and non-Muslim scholars to bring an accurate account of Islam to publishers of textbooks and teachers in public schools, and how the Islamic Society of North America provides a connective web for the concerns of Muslims to be discussed and addressed. The Council on American Islamic Relations monitors the civil rights of Muslims, while the American Muslim Council provides a forum for Muslim voices in the nation's capitol and educates Muslims on participating in the political process. All this is part of a growing American infrastructure enabling Muslims to participate more effectively in political and civil society. The Islamic infrastructure put in place in the past twenty years is by far the most extensive and also the most complex of any of those of the new immigrant religious groups.

Professional societies are active as well—the Association of Muslim Scientists and Engineers, the Association of Muslim Social Scientists, and the Islamic Medical Association of North America, known by the acronym IMANA. The last, based in Downer's Grove, Illinois, is an association of Muslim doctors and medical professionals founded in 1967 to enable them to bring an Islamic perspective to the medical and ethical issues they face in American medicine. IMANA works with the international Red Crescent Society to provide medical emergency teams. It publishes the *Journal of Islamic Medical Ethics,* making clear that the Muslim voice is an important and articulate one on some of today's most gnarled ethical dilemmas.

Islam is here to stay in the United States and will become an increasingly visible part of all our lives. Nothing testifies to this more powerfully than the commitment of American-born Muslims, the so-called second generation, who have taken both their Islamic and American identities seriously and have established their own second-generation institutions. AMILA is an organization of young men and women in the San Francisco Bay Area with precisely this goal. The word *amila* means "work" in Arabic, but it has also become the acronym of an activist network of young Muslims who are fully involved in community and service activities, both for Muslims and for the wider society. *AMILA* means American Muslims Intent on Learning and Activism. They identify as Americans, recognize themselves as part of American society, and want to "contribute to the growth of humanity in America and to be influenced by those aspects of American customs and culture which do not contradict Islam." They are also Muslims; their "moral code and belief system are shaped by Islam." They are dedicated to learning about "both the Islamic outlook and the American reality." As for activism, they say, this "signifies our firm belief that wishes and dreams alone shall get us nowhere. Members of this organization are firmly committed to action."[66] Their activism represents the kind of engagement that is the very fabric of pluralism in a free society. They work regularly at the Loaves and Fishes soup kitchen in San Jose, they are counselors at a Muslim youth camp in Santa Cruz, they sponsor an "Eid for Everyone" gift drive for Muslim children during the month of Ramadan, and they study political and civic issues and are involved in the Muslim Public Affairs Council.

Islam has a long history in the United States but in the past thirty years has expanded exponentially to become one of the most active communities in the new religious landscape of America. As we will see as our story continues, the struggle for Islamic recognition in the American public square has been complicated by stereotypes, discrimination, ignorance, and outright fear. But history cannot be turned back, and America's vibrant new Muslim communities are here to stay. Now more than ever, all Americans need the instructive challenge of the Qur'an: that our differences require us to get to know each other.

NOTES

1. Ali Asani, Pluralism Project interview, 1996.

2. Salam al-Marayati, "Jews, Muslims as Ancient Enemies: A False Paradigm," *Daily News of Los Angeles,* October 10, 1991.

3. Mian Ashraf, Pluralism Project interview, 1996.

4. Webb's speech and some newspaper commentary are published in Richard Hughes Seager, ed., *The Dawn of Religious Pluralism: Voices from the World's Parliament of Religions, 1893* (LaSalle, IL: Open Court Press, 1993), 270–80.

5. Hussein Ahmed Sheronick, "A History of the Cedar Rapids Muslim Community: The Search for an American Identity" (Honors thesis, Coe College, History Department, Cedar Rapids, IA, May 1988), 45.

6. Allen A. Austin, *African Muslims in Antebellum America: A Sourcebook* (New York: Garland Publishing, 1984), 35–36.

7. Sylviane A. Diouf, *Servants of Allah: African Muslims Enslaved in the Americas* (New York: New York University Press, 1998), 99.

8. Austin, *African Muslims in Antebellum America: A Sourcebook,* 465.

9. Austin, *African Muslims in Antebellum America: A Sourcebook,* 20.

10. Austin, *African Muslims in Antebellum America: A Sourcebook,* 70.

11. Austin, *African Muslims in Antebellum America: A Sourcebook,* 321. The document is called "An almost admiring master on his slave: Letter of James Hamilton Couper, Esq."

12. Austin, *African Muslims in Antebellum America: A Sourcebook,* 7.

13. Austin, *African Muslims in Antebellum America: A Sourcebook,* 275.

14. Georgia Writers' Project, *Drums and Shadows,* in Austin, *African Muslims,* 295. Interview with Karie Brown a descendent of Belali.

15. Austin, *African Muslims in Antebellum America: A Sourcebook,* 465.

16. Austin, *African Muslims in Antebellum America: A Sourcebook,* 445.

17. Austin, *African Muslims in Antebellum America: A Sourcebook,* 466.

18. Alixa Naff, *Becoming American: The Early Arab Immigrant Experience* (Carbondale: Southern Illinois University Press, 1985), 13.

19. Naff, *Becoming American: The Early Arab Immigrant Experience,* 1.

20. Naff, *Becoming American: The Early Arab Immigrant Experience,* 85.

21. *Fargo Forum,* December 8, 1967, as cited in Naff, *Becoming American,* 156.

22. Naff, *Becoming American: The Early Arab Immigrant Experience,* 300.

23. *Fargo Forum,* December 8, 1967, as cited in Naff, *Becoming American,* 252.

24. Naff, *Becoming American: The Early Arab Immigrant Experience,* 299–300.

25. William Yahya Aossey, *Journal of Muslim Minority Affairs* 5 (1983–84).

26. Hussein Ahmed Sheronick, "A History of the Cedar Rapids Muslim Community: The Search for an American Identity" (Honors Thesis, History Department, Coe College, Cedar Rapids, IA, May 1988), 28–29.

27. Sheronick, "Muslim Community," 32.

28. Sheronick, "Muslim Community," 40.

29. The estimate was that of ACCESS, the Arab Community Center for Economic and Social Services. A *New York Times* article in 1998 (Keith Bradsher, "Anguish in Biggest Arab-American Community," February 21) said estimates ran from 60,000 to 350,000.

30. George Bullard, "Sacred Places: Islamic Center Looks to Expand New Mosque for 10,000 Faithful," *Detroit News,* December 12, 1998; and George Bullard, "Muslims Raise $3 Million for Mosque: Facility Will Rise in Dearborn, with Room for 1,000," *Detroit News,* March 8, 1999.

31. Noble Drew Ali, *The Holy Koran of the Moorish Science Temple of America* 48:10, as quoted in Yvonne Yazbeck Haddad and Jane Idelman Smith, *Mission to America* (Gainesville: University of Florida Press, 1993), 83.

32. Cited in Haddad and Smith, *Mission to America,* 83.

33. The Ahmadiyya Movement in Islam was established in 1889 in India by Mirza Ghulam Ahmad. He claimed to be the Messiah, or Mandi, of this age, awaited by Muslims, Christians, and others. The missionary movement of his followers is now established in more than 144 countries, including the United States, where there are more than forty branches.

34. Haddad and Smith, *Mission to America,* 87.

35. See C. Eric Lincoln, "The American Muslim Mission," in *The Muslim Community in North America,* ed. E. H. Waugh et al. (Edmonton: University of Alberta Press, 1983), 221.

36. According to the research of Haddad and Smith, both were "reported" to have been members of the Moorish Science Temple. By whom, however, it is not specified. *Mission to America,* 92.

37. Lincoln, "American Muslim Mission," 221.

38. Lincoln, "American Muslim Mission," 226.

39. Mattias Gardell, *In the Name of Elijah Muhammad* (Durham: Duke University Press, 1996), 190–97.

40. Lawrence H. Mamiya, "The Black Muslims as a New Religious Movement," in *Conflict and Cooperation Between Contemporary Religious Groups,* (Chuo Academie Research Institute, Tokyo, 1988), 212.

41. Malcolm X, *The Autobiography of Malcolm X [As told to Alex Haley]* (1964; New York: Ballantine Books, 1973), 340.

42. The speech on June 18, 1975, at McCormick Place in Chicago is cited by Lawrence Mamiya, "Minister Louis Farrakhan and the Final Call," in *Muslim Community,* ed. Waugh et al., 249.

43. Lawrence Mamiya, "Minister Louis Farrakhan," 238.

44. Ihsan Bagby, Islamic Research Institute, Tustin, California.

45. Ali Asani, Pluralism Project interview, 1996.

46. Hassan Hathout, Fathi Osman, and Maher Hathout, *In Fraternity: A Message to Muslims in America* (Los Angeles: Minaret Publishing House, 1989), 27.

47. Shabbir Mansuri, California Social Studies Conference, Santa Clara, CA, 1999.

48. Dawub Tauhidi, personal communication, 1996.

49. Hathout et al., *In Fraternity,* 52–53.

50. Jerrilyn D. Dodds, "NY Masjid," in *Storefront: Art+Architecture,* announcement of photographic exhibit *NY Masjid,* New York, November 23, 1996–January 29, 1997.

51. *AMC Report* 1, no. 1 (Fall 1990).

52. *An Introduction to Islam* (Los Angeles: Islamic Center of Southern California, 1994).

53. There are many resources for Islamic finance on the Web. For instance, Islamic Banking and Finance Network: islamic-finance.net.

54. Michael Wolfe, "An American in Mecca," April 18, 2000. Special to ABC News, available on its Web site: archive.abcnews.go.com/sections/world/hajj1209.

55. I think especially here of the moving account of my colleague Leila Ahmed, who writes of the forms of Islam practiced in her native Egypt, many of which are shaped in the context of lives and communities in which overly doctrinal views of Islam are contradicted by the living variety of Islamic faith and practice. See Leila Ahmed, *A Border Passage* (New York: Farrar, Straus, and Giroux, 1999), 118–29.

56. Jamal Badawi at the ISNA convention in Kansas City, quoted in *Islamic Horizons* (winter 1991), 32.

57. Mian Ashraf, Pluralism Project Interview, 1996.

58. Hathout et al., *In Fraternity,* 51–52.

59. Hathout et al., *In Fraternity,* 56.

60. Susan Sechs, "Muslim Schools in U.S. a Voice for Identity," *New York Times,* November 10, 1998.

61. *Islamic Horizons* (winter 1991), 11.

62. Department of Education, Islamic Society of North America, P.O. Box 38, Plainfield, IN 46168.

63. Shabbir Mansuri, California Social Studies Conference, Santa Clara, CA, 1999.

64. Mian Ashraf, Pluralism Project Interview, 1996.

65. See, for example, Muhammad Khalid Masud, "Being Muslim in a Non-Muslim Polity: Three Alternate Models," *Journal of Muslim Minority Affairs* 10, no. 1 (January 1989): 119–20.

66. See www.amila.org for AMILA's constitution, activities, and projects.

CHAPTER SIX

AFRAID OF OURSELVES

★

"We the people of the United States of America" are now religiously diverse as never before, and some Americans do not like it. For the Fourth of July edition of the *Los Angeles Times* a few years ago, I wrote an op-ed piece on the many places we might find the American flag flying on the holiday—on the grand staircase of the Hsi Lai Buddhist Temple in Hacienda Heights, for example, or next to the blackboard in the fourth-grade classroom of an Islamic school in Orange County. A few weeks later I received a letter from a gentleman in Tampa, Florida, expressing astonishment at my article, which had been syndicated in a Florida newspaper. He was clearly upset by the piece and proffered his own conclusion: "If this is indeed the case, as you have alleged, then I wonder how all these people got here. Now is the time to close the doors. I suggest they go back where they came from." It is clear to me that the religious controversies of the American public square are just beginning.

I have often suspected that many Americans, like the man from Tampa, do not really know how much more complex our "sweet land of liberty" has become. When I read his letter, I thought of the days I had spent in another part of Florida, in the Miami area, visiting with Trinidadi immigrants at a Caribbean Hindu temple set in behind a shopping mall in Oakland Park, then finding my way to an Islamic center in a suburban area of Pompano Beach, and finally heading to a Thai Buddhist temple that translates its name "Temple of the Good Lord" in the flats south of Miami. I had to go looking for these places, as did all of our Pluralism Project researchers. The new religious America did not simply present itself in a coherent group photo. Rather, we made it a point to search out its various expressions. So I often wondered as I drove America's highways from temple to mosque to gurdwara just how many people had any idea that this is all here and what they would think if they did. The man from Tampa gave it a voice. He did not know about all these new neighbors, and when he found out he did not like it. Alas, he is also not alone. The climate of suspicion created by a new spate of American xenophobia has given rise to a thousand stories of insult and insinuation, assault and hatred.

New religious communities keep their stories of trouble within the oral histories of their own communities or in the pages of their local newspapers. The Muslim community of Flint, Michigan, remembers the night everyone ended up with flat tires. They had all come out of the mosque at the close of the Eid-al Fitr celebrations at the end of the month of Ramadan, only to discover, too late, that the parking lot had been strewn with hand-welded triangular spikes. The Hindu community in Kansas City remembers the day a side of beef was hung belligerently on the door of its temple, a clear statement by someone that vegetarian Hindus had no place in a city famous for its red meat. The Hindus of Pittsburgh remember the day that the Hindu temple in Monroeville was desecrated and the word *Leave* written across the altar. And the Sikhs remember that day too, for at that time they shared space in the temple, and their sacred scripture, the Guru Granth Sahab, was torn to bits.

The perpetrators of such harassment surely sense that change is in the air, and they are apprehensive. New people have moved into their neighborhoods about whom they know little except they are "different," and their very difference seems to provide a license for harassment. When President Clinton spoke on the new hate crimes legislation in April of 1999, he said, "Our diversity is a godsend for us, and the world of the twenty-first century. But it is also the potential for the old, haunting demons that are hard to root out of the human spirit." The haunting demons surely include the fear of the foreign and the denigration of the different, whether we speak of race, ethnicity, or religion. The U.S. Department of Justice has started keeping records on hate crimes and has reported a steady rise through the past decade, with hate crimes motivated by race topping the list, followed by those motivated by religion.[1]

About the same time I received the letter from Florida, I bought Peter Brimelow's *Alien Nation,* a collection of statistics and predictive charts that support the alarms voiced by the man from Tampa. Brimelow himself is a British immigrant to the U.S., married to a native-born American. He writes, "There is no precedent for a sovereign country undergoing such a rapid and radical transformation of its ethnic character in the entire history of the world."[2] He compares the cacophony of languages and the diversity of dress at the offices of the Immigration and Naturalization Service to the chaos of Dante's tenth circle of hell. With fearful apprehension he describes the "descent" into the underworld of the New York City subway, teeming with new resident aliens and immigrants. In one graphic chart he describes how the white Anglo-Saxon and European core population is gradually becoming crushed between the "pincers" of the rising Hispanic and Asian immigrant population. Brimelow calls the post-1965 period "America's immigration disaster" and simply advocates the repeal of the 1965 immigration act. Reading his book reminded me of the tenor and tone of the arguments made in the U.S. Congress in the debates over Asian exclusion that stretched through the late nineteenth century.

True enough, America is well on the way to becoming a "minority-majority" country, with the numbers of foreign born higher than at any time in the past century. How we move from being a nation that puts up with what are infelicitously called "aliens" to being a nation that welcomes newcomers of every religion—how we move from being strangers to neighbors—is one of the great challenges of America's new century of religious life. Nothing is more central to most religious traditions than hospitality toward the neighbor, even toward the stranger. But we also know too well that our suspicions of neighbors, nurtured in an environment where walls are many and bridges few, can create the climate in which neighbors become enemies overnight, as we have seen so tragically in multiethnic nations around the world.

A VISIBLE DIFFERENCE

Without question, some Americans are afraid of the changing face of our country. After all, the first response to difference is often suspicion and fear. Fear of the unknown is not so astonishing, especially in a country where we have done so little to make the cultural and religious traditions of the world better known and understood. Although some progress has been made in our public schools in recent years, most of us who are middle-aged know from experience how little we learned about the religious traditions of the world in junior high or high school. When I graduated in the top ten of my class from Bozeman Senior High School, I could not have provided even the most rudimentary account of the fundamentals of Islam or Hinduism, even though these constitute the faith and worldviews of nearly half the world's population. This is not unusual for people of my generation. Most of us simply do not know much about one another, and the images we may have of the strangers among us are transmitted through the shorthand of the media where the extreme too often becomes the norm.

Visible difference is the issue. People of many ideological, political, and religious persuasions may encounter one another without noticing, but when the difference is visible, we do take note. Surely the most visible difference in America's new multiethnic society is race. We are black and white and all the hues of Asia from Korea and Japan to Southeast Asia and South Asia. We are Latino and Hispanic. And we are increasingly multiracial as Latino and Euro-American, Native and African American, Asian and Latino become the components of our own racial *mestizaje*. It is difficult to underestimate just how prominently race figures in the perception of America by immigrants from other parts of the world. As Padma Rangaswamy put it in her book *Namaste America,* a study of Indian immigrants in Chicago, "Indians, because of their race and color, can never achieve total acceptance into a white American society that has race and color bias. It is difficult to envision a period in which race and color have not mattered in American history, or will not matter in the future."[3] This view of America's race consciousness stings on the page, but we must take it seriously if we are to create a multiracial and multireligious society that nurtures a sense of belonging—among all people.

After race, the most visible signal of difference is dress, and this is where religious minorities become visible minorities. Many Muslim women wear *hijab,* either a simple head scarf or a full outer garment. A few even wear a face covering called *nikab.* Muslim men may wear a beard, and Sikh men may wear not only a beard but also a turban wrapped around their uncut hair. Jewish men may wear a yarmulke, or skullcap. Buddhist monks may wear saffron, maroon, black, brown, or gray robes, depending upon their culture of origin. In all these cases looking different may sometimes trigger uneasiness and even fear—the fear that we do not know who "they" are or perhaps that we do not know who "we" are. As Americans, we are literally afraid of ourselves.

Our visible differences are on the rise, not just in the building of mosques and temples, but in the visible presence of people of many religious traditions. And this religious difference often has consequences. Just ask the young Sikh man I sat next to at the *langar* meal in the Fremont gurdwara in California. "You can't show up at a job interview wearing a turban and beard," he said. He was clean-shaven and had a short haircut, but this was the result of having spent five years in the U.S. and having experienced discrimination because of his looks. To some Americans, turbaned Sikhs look like what they imagine snake charmers or genies to be, he said. Others associate the turbaned look with militancy and even terrorism. He found he had no choice but to cut his hair. For observant Sikh women, the visibility of not cutting their hair can also be a burden, as a young woman named Kimpreet recalled when we interviewed her. Kimpreet had grown up in New Jersey, and hers was the only Sikh family in town. She told us, "I was the 'other.' I was the girl with the really, really super long hair who couldn't cut it because of her religion." The thread worn by young Zoroastrians after their *navjote* initiation also elicits this sense of the "other." A Zoroastrian friend confided, "It's very common when young people are in gym class and changing their clothes, someone will come up and say, 'What's that?' If they say, 'This is part of my Zoroastrian custom,' the next line usually is 'Zoro-what?' They want to know what kind of cult is that?"

The presence of Buddhist monks and nuns in America presents another evidence of visible difference. We see fewer and fewer Catholic priests, monks, and nuns on the streets of America these days. In the decades since the Second Vatican Council in the 1960s, most religious orders have moved toward workaday nonreligious dress. Today, however, saffron-robed monks from Laos are visible in Lowell, Massachusetts, and Cambodian monks are found on the back roads of New England. When the Thai immigrant community built the Temple of the Good Lord in the flatlands south of Miami, one of the lay members of the board told a reporter from the *Miami Herald,* "The neighbors didn't know anything about Buddhism. They thought we were a cult."[4] And one of the monks added, "They thought we were Hare Krishnas."

The Hare Krishnas too have had their problems as a visible religious group. For a time, the young men in the order of celibate ascetics moved from their orange renouncers' robes, readily recognizable in the streets of Calcutta, to something that looks more the garb of Christian Franciscans. Though many Krishna devotees today wear ordinary Western dress, on the whole they dress in the dhotis and saris of India, seeing this as a positive way of identifying themselves so that they may be approached by those interested in their spiritual movement

Perhaps the most prominent icons of our new visible religious differences are the Muslim women wearing the head scarf. They are now visible almost everywhere, and every one of them has a story to tell. My friend Mary Lahaj is about my age, and our grandparents came to this country at about the same time, only hers came from Lebanon, whereas mine came from Sweden. Mary and I are both religious and both scholars as well. I am a Methodist and Mary a Muslim. But as third-generation Americans, our experience has been quite different in one respect. I have never experienced the discrimination that Mary has experienced just by being who she is, wearing a head scarf outside the home as part of her faith. Mary describes one incident when she experienced herself as the object of raw fear. She told us, "I was wearing my *hijab* in the toy store Child World, and I was buying some toy guns for my son and his two friends. As I turned the corner this young man about fourteen almost bumped into me. And when he saw me, he just got this awful expression on his face, like he was scared to death. You know, there was just this image of me with my head cover and these toy rifles in my arms, and he looked simply terrified."[5] The guns, of course, fit right into the prejudicial image of Muslims that this fourteen-year-old had already encountered, and then there she was—my friend Mary, the terrorist.

About the time Mary and I met in 1994, an article in the *Minneapolis Star Tribune* told of a woman in full Islamic dress, including a partial face covering, being arrested in the Mall of America for wearing a disguise, which was banned by local ordinance. The police asked her to remove it, but she refused, arguing for the freedom of religious practice. Eventually a settlement was reached, but the issue of the *hijab* persists. A schoolgirl has her scarf pulled off by a classmate, for example, or a white American woman wearing a head scarf in Tukwila, Washington, near Seattle, is accosted and chased through a parking lot by a group of young people yelling, "You Muslim! Go home!"[6] These are stories of harassment and incivility, and at the other end of the scale are stories of civil rights abuses and discrimination, especially in the workplace.

We should remember, however, that both sides experience the instability and fear generated by visible difference. Looking different comes with a price, as America's Amish and Hutterites can testify and as people of racial minorities in the U.S. have experienced. Sister Aminah, a Euro-American Muslim who began wearing the Islamic head cover shortly after her conversion, testifies to this reality. Sister Aminah and I were on a panel together in an open forum of the President's Initiative on Race in June 1998 in Louisville, Kentucky. In her presentation she described the many ways in which she and her family had experienced the barbs of prejudice. "How much discrimination I have myself experienced!" she said. "I was in Oklahoma City after the bombing of the Federal Building, and my son begged me not to wear my head scarf in public. I was frightened, and our whole community was frightened." When she told her story, an African-American man in the audience spoke from the heart in response to her. He said that he had never heard a Muslim woman speak this way, and he had never imagined that Muslims, even Caucasian Muslims, might experience some of the overt discrimination and fear that he himself had lived with all his life.

STEREOTYPES:
THE SCRATCHES ON OUR MINDS

The newsman Walter Lippman spoke of stereotypes as the "pictures in our heads," the sketchy and distorted images created by one group to describe, label, and caricature another. These pictures, shaped by media, reading, and hearsay, inevitably yield images that don't match the human being. They are stereotypes, some romantic and others denigrating. Harold Isaacs's book on American images of Asia first published in the 1950s was entitled *Scratches on Our Minds*. Some of the "scratchings" are not even full-blown images for, as Isaacs concludes, "Vagueness about Asia has been until now the natural condition even of the educated American."[7]

Prejudice is prejudging people and groups on the basis of these images, often half-formed caricatures. As the quip goes, prejudice is "being down on something you're not up on." People "known" through stereotypes do not have the opportunity to tell us who they are. We do not let them get close enough to speak for themselves. We define them in their absence, on the basis of the images already present in our minds. Lata, a Boston Hindu friend, put it this way: "People have a prejudged opinion about you. Just seeing you, they already know who you are, even though they never want to take the time to really know who you are."

Stereotypes and prejudice have a long history in America. European settlers held negative racial stereotypes of the Native peoples and the Africans brought as slaves. We have been practicing our prejudices ever since, for these habits of the heart are very hard to change. Americans of Anglo-Saxon and northern European heritage held demeaning racial, religious, and cultural stereotypes of other European newcomers—especially the Irish, Poles, and Italians. Virtually all Europeans of Christian origin brought with them the bigotry and demeaning stereotypes of Jews they had come to know in Europe. As we have seen, prejudice also shaped

European immigrants' attitudes toward newcomers from Asia—the Chinese and Japanese "yellow peril" and the turbaned Sikh "ragheads."

Even today statistics reveal that the greatest percentage of hate crimes is racially motivated, most against blacks, followed by whites, Hispanics, Asians, and Arabs. But religion is often conflated with race as a marker of the difference that generates fear or hate. An analysis of the politics of hatred, both historically and today, requires that we look at the ways in which religious symbols are manipulated and the ways in which demeaning a religion or defacing its place of worship targets the very soul of a community. The 1996 publication *Hate Crimes Statistics* reveals that most religiously motivated hate crimes are directed at property rather than people. But an American Muslim Council brochure provided to Muslim communities astutely explains, "Drawing graffiti on walls is designed to deface a structure; the same act done to a mosque is meant not only to deface the structure, but also to intimidate and invoke fear within the group."

Religious prejudice takes many forms, and among the most destructive is simply erasing a group's legitimacy as a religion. Anglo-Saxon newcomers to the continent did not see Native Americans as people with a "different" religious tradition but rather as "pagans" with no religion at all. Native peoples are sensitive to this negative image even today. Anne Marshall, a Muscogee Creek Indian and an executive in the United Methodist Church, says, "Our Native traditions are not pagan, they are sacramental. They have allowed our people to survive for five hundred years, no matter what was done to us. But people don't even classify our religion as a religion, along with Hinduism and Islam." Fellow citizens who identify religiously as Pagans also face an uphill climb toward recognition. Most people have no idea about the spiritual ecology of American Paganism, a path that emphasizes humans' intimate dependence upon the Earth and its ecosystems. They know little of Pagan ethics and the principle of the Threefold Return, reminding Pagans that every word and action directed outward, whether for good or ill, whether generous or miserly, will return to them threefold. Instead, people tend to identify Paganism with broad negative strokes, classifying it with Satanism and their worst stereotypes of witchcraft. Other religious communities have also felt the sting of being left out of majority consciousness, like the young Sikh college student who told us, "The thing that really bothered me about stereotyping and discrimination was just the fact that we're not really even recognized as a religion. You're Sikh? How do you spell that? You know, like, I've never heard of this before. I honestly feel I'm not accepted as fully having a religion here."

America's Catholics and Jews experienced not erasure but built-in tension with the vastly dominant Protestant mainstream. Catholics and Jews were pioneers, as we have seen, in dealing with the religious prejudices of America. Anti-Catholic prejudice began in the colonial period with the Puritans, who brought with them the anti-Catholic attitudes of the English Reformation. In the nineteenth century the growth of the American Catholic Church with immigration from Ireland, Italy, and Eastern Europe set in motion a new wave of anti-Catholic sentiment. Catholics were stereotyped as Romanists and Papists and were suspected of being incapable of participating in a Constitutional democracy. In 1834 a Protestant mob burned a Catholic convent school in Charlestown, Massachusetts, and in the 1850s the Know-Nothing party with its virulent anti-Catholic rhetoric rose for a time to the public eye and elected candidates to office. Even during the campaign of John F. Kennedy for president in 1960, more than a hundred years later, the image of the American Catholic as subservient to the authority of the pope and potentially un-American lingered in the minds of some. Kennedy's election was a critical turning point in laying many of these stereotypes to rest.

Anti-Semitism also has a long American history. In colonial America Jews were warned out of town in Boston and after the Revolution were prohibited from voting and holding office in North Carolina and Maryland. The pervasive negative image of Jews was as Christ killers with the traits of Shylock—wicked, greedy, unethical. The climate that permitted overt discrimination against Jews was based on the unquestioned assumption of Christian superiority and Jewish stubbornness and perfidy in rejecting Christ as Savior.

In the first decades of the twentieth century, Christian anti-Judaism gathered up the fears of a society convinced that not only were Jews a blight on Christian America, but they were also gaining too much power. Of the more than sixteen million immigrants who came to the U.S. from 1890 to 1914, just over 10 percent were Jewish.[8] The rising concern about Jewish economic success compounded prejudice and suspicion. I have mentioned, for example, Harvard president Abbott Lawrence Lowell, who in the 1920s proposed a quota system to address the "Jewish problem," noting with alarm that the percentage of Jewish men at Harvard had risen from 6 percent in 1908 to 22 percent in 1922. The faculty rejected the plan but for many decades acquiesced in a de facto limitation on Jewish admissions.

The post–World War I xenophobia, spearheaded by the likes of

Henry Ford, his Dearborn, Michigan, newspaper, the *Dearborn Independent,* and the resurgence of the KKK, linked anti-Catholicism and anti-Semitism. In the 1920s both Jews and Catholics were under attack by the newly reorganized Ku Klux Klan. In the 1930s and early 1940s hate organizations grew, and conspiracy theories about Jewish influence spread like wildfire. Despite reason for common cause, some American Catholics participated in anti-Semitism. Father Charles Coughlin publicly articulated its propaganda through weekly radio programs that reached 3.5 million Americans. In 1939 he and his organization, called the Christian Front, filled Madison Square Garden with more than nineteen thousand people. The arena was draped with banners saying, "Wake Up America! Smash Jewish Communism!" and "Stop Jewish Domination of Christian America!"[9]

The experience of being the object of suspicion and distrust, of changing one's name to avoid being penalized for one's religion, of being called clannish and aloof if they kept to themselves and pushy and power hungry if they claimed a place in the public sphere; the experience of being seen as parasites on the economy if they were in need and taking jobs from others if they were successfully employed—all this is the texture of the immigrant experience pioneered by Jewish Americans. Unfortunately, Sikhs and Muslims, Hindus and Buddhists have now, in different ways, experienced it all for themselves.

The new immigrants of the late twentieth century faced denigrating stereotypes planted in the soil of ignorance and fed by a stream of negative media images. Terms like *Sikh militant* or *Islamic fundamentalist* express a shorthand version of complex political struggles abroad, and they shape in profound ways the mental images people hold of all Sikhs and Muslims. Muslims feel especially vulnerable to the stereotypes that so readily pair the word *Muslim* with *fundamentalist, terrorist,* or *holy war.*

Mary Lahaj, my third-generation Muslim-American friend, told us, "Muslims are stereotyped as terrorists, fanatics. These kinds of labels, I would say, dehumanize the Muslim. This means that you literally don't look at the Muslim as another human being." Mary's words reminded me of the words of Nina Morais more than a century ago. Nina, a Philadelphia-born Sephardic Jew, lamented in 1881 in an article called "Jewish Ostracism in America," "In the popular mind, the Jew is never judged as an individual, but as a specimen of a whole race whose members are identically of the same kind."[10] Being judged as a group, not an individual, erases the human face and is the first step toward the dehumanization that gives rise to hate crimes. At the Islam Awareness Week I attended at Boston University, a Latino Muslim from Los Angeles spoke frankly about the stereotypes he encountered, and not the usual ones that associated Islam with violence. He told us, "When I first embraced Islam, I told my cousin. He said, 'How come your head's not shaved? Where's your pony-tail? Your women wear a red dot, right?' He was unbelievably confused. Ladies and gentlemen, take a deep breath and relax. One of the reasons we are afraid of difference is because we know so little. But how are they going to understand unless we help them understand? I grew up in the USA, Chevrolet, mom and apple pie, and Little League baseball. The problem is most people just don't have an accurate knowledge of Islam!"

Couple a deep negativity toward religious difference with a deep ignorance of other religious traditions, and we have a recipe for prejudice. For example, in 1990 a small item in the *New York Times* caught my eye under the headline "Yoga and the Devil: Issue for Georgia Town."[11] The dateline was Toccoa, Georgia, and apparently officials barred a town-sponsored yoga class "because the relaxation of yoga exercises would open practitioners to the influence of the devil. 'The people who are signed up for the class are just walking into it like cattle to a slaughter,' said a leader of a local group comprised of Baptists, Lutherans, and other Christians." Defenders of the class insisted that the class was only for stretching and relaxing, not for promoting religion. Clearly what to many Americans has been a spiritual practice is perceived as threat in what must be a fairly homogeneous town. The small town of Winter, Wisconsin, was the scene of another such incident. A high school student found the computers of the school district blocked, preventing her from access to information on Wicca, and a member of the school board accused her of being a "devil worshiper" for seeking such information. The district had installed a computer filter system to restrict Internet access to subjects deemed controversial. The student complained, "I tried to look up Buddhism and it was blocked. Then, I tried to look up Wicca and it was blocked. Then, I looked up Christian churches and you could find anything you want."[12] The case attracted nationwide attention, and eventually the school district changed the system before the case reached the courts. But at the civic level, it is yet another example of the potent mixture of fear and ignorance that sparks so many incidents of outright discrimination.

In New Jersey in the late 1980s, the dot, or *bindi,* on the forehead worn by many Hindu women stood for the strangeness of the whole Indian immigrant community in the eyes of a racist group calling themselves the Dot Busters. The attacks had nothing to do with Hinduism as a religion but were directed at all South Asian immigrants. In 1987 in Jersey City, a climate of constant low-level harassment turned to violence. A thirty-year-old Indian immigrant, Navroze Mody, was beaten to death by a gang chanting "Hindu, Hindu!" They conflated race, religion, and culture in one naked cry of hatred.

At that time, the Indian immigrant community was about fifteen thousand strong in Jersey City, and it was part of a much larger Indian community in northern New Jersey. Before the attack in the summer of 1987, a local newspaper had called attention to the rising number of incidents of harassment against South Asians. In response, it received a venomous letter signed by the "Jersey City Dot Busters":

> I hate [Indian people], if you had to live near them you would also. We are an organization called dot busters. We have been around for 2 years. We will go to any extreme to get Indians to move out of Jersey City. If I'm walking down the street and I see a Hindu and the setting is right, I will hit him or her. We plan some of our most extreme attacks such as breaking windows, breaking car windows, and crashing family parties. We use the phone books and look up the name Patel. Have you seen how many of them there are? . . . You said that they will have to start protecting themselves because the police cannot always be there. They will never do anything. They are a week race physically and mentally. We are going to continue our way. We will never be stopped.

The letter was published a month before the death of Navroze Mody. Then, a few weeks later, a young resident in medicine, Dr. Sharan, was assaulted by three young men with baseball bats as he walked home late one night in Jersey City. He was beaten severely and left unconscious with a fractured skull. Sharan was in a coma for a week and suffered severe neurological damage. He recalled that one of the young people yelled, "There's a dothead! Let's get him!" as they set out after him with their bats.

These incidents were a severe blow to the Indian immigrant community and jarred the community into taking political action seriously. A group called Indian Youth Against Racism (IYAR) was formed with a base at Columbia University. The group helped in getting a bill passed in the New Jersey legislature in 1990 that raised the mandatory penalties for "bias crimes." It documented instances of violence against Indians in New Jersey, and it helped implement a series of educational programs on

South Asian cultures for students and faculty at a Jersey City high school. But the attacks have not ceased. In 1991 there were fifty-eight cases of hate crimes against Indians in New Jersey. In 1992 an Indian physician was hit on the head and sprayed with Mace, and an Indian businessman was struck on the head with a bat. In 1998 an Indo-Caribbean man was beaten on the streets of Queens. The Asian American Legal Defense and Education Fund has started tracking incidents and organizing community awareness.[13]

America's Muslims are also targeted solely on the basis of their religion. The image of the violent Muslim was called into play almost immediately when the Murrah Federal Building in Oklahoma City was bombed on April 19, 1995. Muslim families in Oklahoma and all over America felt a backlash of harassment because of the mistaken assumption, broadcast only for a few minutes, that the bombing was linked to "Middle Eastern–looking" men. Across the country, Islamic centers became the targets of drive-by shootings and telephoned bomb threats. Muslim students were assaulted on campus, a fake bomb was thrown at a Muslim day care facility, and individual Muslims reported a great increase in harassment by co-workers and in public. Muslim parents feared for their children's safety and in some cases kept them home from school. On May 19, 1995, the Council on American-Islamic Relations (CAIR), a newly formed Muslim watchdog organization, released a report detailing more than two hundred incidents of anti-Muslim threats, harassment, and property damage reported in the aftermath of the bombing.[14]

What the media failed to report was that in Oklahoma City, Muslim firemen were involved in rescue efforts in the Murrah Building, Muslim doctors worked in the city's emergency rooms, and Muslim organizations donated money and time to the relief effort. Yet a nationally televised memorial service at which President Clinton and Rev. Billy Graham spoke included Catholic and Jewish words of consolation, but nothing from the Muslim community of Oklahoma. This was despite the fact that Muslims had specifically asked to participate because they had been so visibly affected as the focus of blame for the tragedy. Oklahoma City has become a turning point in Muslim consciousness of their vulnerability here in America. It is hard to lay to rest the stereotypes generated over years of negative imaging.

Waking up to the isolation and needs of many of our new neighbors sometimes requires a lightning bolt. Although many Thai Buddhist temples and monasteries are open around the United States, the first time most

Americans had any idea of their presence was on the August morning in 1991 when newspapers across the country carried the story of the murder of nine people—monks, nuns, and laity—at Wat Pronkunarum, a temple in the far suburbs of Phoenix. The investigation of the execution-style murder was long and convoluted, eventually focusing on a disturbed teenager, the son of a Thai mother and an American military father. The murder had virtually nothing to do with religion, except to display in horrible Technicolor the vulnerability of a new Asian community with no civic sources of support. Asian-American groups in Phoenix revealed that they had often been the targets of racial ugliness, facing "a constant low level of harassment that ranged from verbal insults to the throwing of eggs." Swastikas had been painted on the Chinese Christian church and on the wall outside the Japanese American Citizens League.[15] What was clear in the aftermath of the tragedy was how little anyone in Phoenix knew of these new neighbors who had put down roots at the edge of town. As E. J. Montini put it in the *Arizona Republic,*

> Most of the nine people murdered at the Buddhist temple had names we can't pronounce and belong to a religion we don't understand. . . . They lived here, as Americans. Then they died here, as foreigners.[16]

AFRAID OF OUR NEIGHBORS: "NOT IN THIS NEIGHBORHOOD!"

In the summer of 2000 the city council of Palos Heights, a suburb of Chicago, offered prospective buyers $200,000 to walk away from the offer they had made on the Reformed Church building. The prospective buyers were Muslims and planned to convert the space into an Islamic Center. Having grown too large for a nearby mosque, a small group from the mosque, the Al Salam Mosque Foundation, found in the Reformed Church what they thought would be an ideal property. It had been on the market for two years, and they made an offer.

No sooner did the offer become known than a group of city residents demanded that the city council reconsider a long-delayed proposal that the church be converted into a recreation center. The proposal had not made headway because the property had been found to be ill suited for a recreation center. But now citizens showed up by the dozens to add their voice to the discussion. One remarked that the value of his property would go down should a mosque come into the neighborhood. An alderman spoke of Islam as an "upside down" religion, what with its prayers on Friday rather than Sunday. Many insisted the case was not about freedom of religion but about the need for more recreational facilities. The mayor, Dean Koldenhoven, disagreed. He said, "It's a veil of hypocrisy. I see it as an attempt to stop the Muslims from coming into Palos Heights. I don't see it as a real, true need for recreation."[17] Many citizens supported him. One woman rose to say that she would rather raise her children in a community without any recreational facilities than in a community that obscures the truth and disallows freedom of religious expression. The Reformed Church pastor, interviewed on National Public Radio, said, "When, in a village hall meeting, someone stands up and says, quite frankly, 'I don't want these kind of people in our town,' and receives a rousing ovation, that makes me wonder why people say, 'Well, there's nothing with race to do with it.'"[18]

After several heated meetings of the city council, the Muslims accepted the $200,000 offer. Their attorney explained, "Deciding to accept the money and walk away was a tough decision, but [his clients] did not want to be in a place where they were unwanted." The controversy escalated as a quiet Chicago suburb became the focus of national attention. The Al Salam Mosque Foundation filed suit against the town for reneging on an agreement, and Palos Heights residents on both sides felt their community had been given a black eye by the fracas.

Many lessons can be learned from this controversy. First, it is clear that a new immigrant religious community may first encounter its neighbors not over a cup of tea but in a city council or zoning board hearing. Every religious tradition in America has faced zoning boards, but new and struggling religious communities often feel more acutely the sting of this civic scrutiny. Second, while questions of zoning and traffic, and even the need for more recreational space, are real concerns, they also are ways of articulating, in concrete terms, some of the amorphous fears that residents may have about new neighbors. As Mayor Koldenhoven well knew, many of their anxieties were not really about parking, traffic, or other civic interests. They were about change and the problems a new religious community might bring to their neighborhood. I have often told my students and researchers that if you want to know how things are going in the new religious America, go to the zoning boards and city councils. There you will hear how people express their anxieties about the change that is afoot.

"I'm not a prejudiced person. I just don't want this to suddenly start changing the neighborhood."[19] These words of a New Jersey woman could well be the epigram of a chapter on America's zoning controversies. She was reflecting on the conversion of an old Jewish summer camp up the road from her home into a Jain religious retreat center. The truth is, many people simply do not like change, and change is in the American air.

Sometimes the fear of difference comes from the negative association some exclusivist Christians have with anything non-Christian. Although some members of the so-called Christian Right would like to post the Ten Commandments in public buildings and schools, the ethos of the seventh commandment seems not to have sunk in: "Thou shalt not bear false witness against thy neighbor." One might wish that those so keen on cultivating a loftier moral climate would satisfy themselves with a "What Would Jesus Do?" bracelet and use it to contemplate Jesus' attitude toward strangers and neighbors, an attitude of inclusion and welcome.

Unfortunately, the sharp edge of Christian prejudice has been keenly felt by many new religious communities. When Muslims in Edmond, the suburb of Oklahoma City where the University of Oklahoma is located, planned to build a mosque in 1992, a move was made to deny a building permit because, as a Pluralism Project researcher reported, "One of the minister's wives attended the first public hearing and vehemently opposed it. She said, 'The constitution says One nation under God, and that's a Christian God. These people have absolutely no right to be here.'" Word got around about the tenor of the meeting, and concerned Edmond residents visited their existing mosque and started a real relationship with the community. Eventually, the mosque did get the permit. Even so, the words of the minister's wife ring in our ears, for they express a view of a normative Christian America that many still hold, despite our constitutional commitment to religious freedom and despite the facts of our multireligious society.

What will the new building look like? This is a frequent concern. Fitting in with the feel of southern California was the issue in a Sikh gurdwara controversy in San Diego, where the gold domes proposed on the plan were initially rejected by the zoning board. The city council, however, overturned its decision, so the gold domes will rise in San Diego where the approach to the city is now dominated by the landmark Mormon Temple. The Mormons, for their part, have also faced their share of apprehension, especially in building the large landmark temples that house the special rites of the community. In liberal Belmont, Massachusetts, an upper-middle-class suburb of Boston, the size and height of the new Mormon Temple was at issue for several years.

Eventually, Belmont restricted the height of the proposed sixty-seven foot steeple, but litigation on the issue continues. Similarly, the Swaminarayan Hindus of Norwalk, California, met resistance when the planning commission challenged their proposal for a $1.2 million dollar temple. A modified proposal for the temple was approved two years later, after the city demanded the lavish, ornamental exterior be toned down, in keeping with the "Spanish" style of the neighborhood, and reduced the maximum capacity by 50 percent.

The story of Dwarakadish Temple in Sayreville, New Jersey, sums up the building issues new immigrant communities have faced. We visited this temple before in our exploration of Hindu devotion in America, for it is a lively community of Krishna devotees called the Pushti Marga, the Path of Grace. The Hindus of northern New Jersey thought the old YMCA building in Sayreville would be the perfect site for a new temple to Lord Krishna, and they first negotiated to buy the building in May 1992. A year later, however, more than two hundred people packed the planning board meeting—only twenty-five of them New Jersey Hindus who supported the temple. After detailed discussions of how much traffic the temple would generate, the Hindus' plan was rejected by the board, citing issues of traffic and parking. But many at the hearing felt the deeper issue was sheer animosity toward the Hindus. "They only challenged us on traffic, but they were not in favor of having a temple here," concluded one temple member.

The fears of the Hindu community were confirmed when the YMCA building, still standing empty, was sprayed with graffiti. The newspaper *India Abroad* reported, "The mayor of Sayreville, New Jersey, John B. McCormack, says he is 'not taking lightly' anti-Hindu slogans that were painted on the walls of a proposed Hindu temple site. Written on several walls of the building were such expressions as 'Get out Hindoos' and 'KKK.'"[20]

The Hindu temple filed suit in U.S. District Court against the Sayreville Planning Board for "bias and discrimination against Asian Indians and practitioners of the Hindu faith." The Hindus insisted their religious freedom was being denied in the decision of the board to reject their proposal for a temple. As an article in the *New Jersey Law Journal* put it, "The plaintiffs also note that the board cited traffic concerns in denying the permit even though the state's Municipal Land Use Law prohibits use of off-site traffic considerations as a basis for making planning decisions. In addition, the suit alleges that the use of the YMCA as a temple conforms to the borough's zoning regulations and that even the board's chairman recognized that there was no legal basis for denying the trust permission to operate its temple."[21]

The case eventually was settled by mediation between the Hindu community and the planning board. The temple agreed to add more on-site parking, to prohibit on-street parking on its three major holy days, and to make other parking arrangements for those days. A representative of the planning board said, in retrospect, "The main consideration had to do with traffic. There is already a lot of traffic on the street, Washington Road. But the temple was a small part of the traffic problem and should not be asked to bear the burden of correcting an already existing problem."

Finally, the temple opened in 1994. Priests came from India for the occasion. More than three thousand people flocked to the temple opening. The newly renovated building had been painted a pale pink and decorated with thousands of flower garlands for the occasion. Every day since the temple opened, the devoted service of Lord Krishna has brought immigrant Hindu Americans to the temple on Washington Road.

VANDALISM AND HATE CRIMES: TARGETING THE SOUL

When a building is defaced or when a fire is deliberately set, the real target is not property but the people who live there or worship there. Attacks on buildings that are places of worship are attacks by proxy on a community of people, and they are meant to be. Synagogues, black churches, and Native American institutions have a long history of being subjected to the broken windows, graffiti, and attacks of arson that are the signatures of bigots. Religious institutions are often only the most readily visible targets of a much more diffuse animosity. The 1991 publication *Racial and Religious Violence in America: A Chronology* lists 650 pages of acts of violence "perpetrated on the grounds of racial or religious prejudice from the discovery of North America to modern times." Arson was committed at a Hasidic school in Brooklyn in 1982; a synagogue was bombed in Chattanooga, Tennessee in 1984; a synagogue was pipe-bombed in Northbrook, Illinois, in 1985; a black church attacked in Alton, New York, in 1989; a Korean church vandalized in Anaheim, California, in 1990; a black church burned in St. Louis in 1989. And these are just a few of hundreds of incidents as of 1991. The rash of arson attacks on African-American churches in 1995–96 is tragic evidence that such hate crimes continued, seemingly unabated.

As attention focused on the black church fires of the mid-1900s, it became apparent that many Islamic centers had also experienced the devastation of attack and arson. The cumulative ledger of these hate crimes has gradually been assembled. For example, the new mosque in Yuba City, California, was almost finished when it was destroyed by fire on September 1, 1994. The electrical wiring had not yet been installed in the building when it went up in flames, and the sheriff's department determined that the five-alarm fire was an act of arson. The report of the incident that appeared in the *Muslim Journal* expressed the pain the Muslim community experienced:

> The dream of a mosque and an Islamic center for Muslims in the Yuba-Sutter area of California was one that all the local Muslim brothers and sisters held very dear for a long, long time. For now, after the struggle and toil to make that dream a reality, it has been taken back to zero. The brand new nearly-to-open mosque on Tierra Buena Road outside of Yuba City is gone. It burned to the ground late on Thursday night, Sept. 1, 1994. The distinctive dome and minaret of the mosque was left lying in its ashes. Only a wall with pointed arches remained to show the beauty of what once was.[22]

A fact-finding team from the Islamic Circle of North America noted public reactions to the fire. Local media responded supportively with outrage, but the tragedy was ignored by state and national media. The ICNA wrote in its report,

> The national media, which is fueling anti-Muslim sentiments, completely ignored the burning of this beautiful *masjid*. . . . Unfortunately the California governor Pete Wilson, who sits only 50 miles away in Sacramento, was conspicuously silent. Not a message of support, regret, dismay at the seriousness of the attack or the importance of a swift arrest. Not a word on the victimization of this peaceful Muslim community.[23]

The burning of the Yuba City mosque was but one of a number of attacks on American mosques. Some seem to have been provoked by world events, such as the firebombing of the Daar Es Salaam mosque in Houston in 1985. The president of the Islamic Society of Greater Houston speculated at the time that the attackers had acted in retaliation for the taking of forty hostages on TWA flight 847 by Lebanese Shi'ite Muslims. More often, the community has no sense of what might have caused such hostility. Since its founding in 1990, the Council on American-Islamic Relations (CAIR) documents and investigates anti-Islamic incidents, providing a report on its Web site and publicizing action alerts through the Internet and the press. In 1995 alone, CAIR reported the arson of a mosque in High Point, North Carolina, in April, in Springfield, Illinois, in June, and in Greenville, South Carolina, in October. In October, CAIR also reported vandalism and spray-painting at three mosques across the country, including the Islamic center in Flint, Michigan, where Muslims emerged from their prayers at the end of the holy month of Ramadan two years later to find the parking lot strewn with hand-welded iron spikes.

On the night of March 5, 1999, two fires deemed to be arson were set at the mosque in Northeast Minneapolis leaving the structure a complete loss. When Senator Paul Wellstone visited the building the next week, *The Star Tribune* began its story, "Broken glass crunched into the water soaked carpet and the acrid smell of charred wood filled the air as U.S. Senator Paul Wellstone toured the ruins of the Masjid Al Huda with leaders of Minnesota's Mulsim community." Later that spring there was a bomb threat at the Islamic center in Denver, and a huge concrete block was thrown through the window of the Islamic center in the Chicago suburb of Villa Park, shattering the glass. Most of these incidents do not make national news. They are part of the painful history of individual religious communities, but collectively they are also part of our American history as we come to terms with a new multireligious reality.

Hindu communities have also experienced the animosity of vandals. In 1987, for example, the newly built temple in a Houston suburb was attacked, and nearly a hundred of the foot-high ornamental spires on the roof were broken off and smashed on the walkway below. The spires were the work of Hindu craftsmen who had spent many months on temple ornamentation. In 1989 the temple in Troy, Michigan, was attacked on the anniversary of Kristallnacht, the day Nazis vandalized synagogues and smashed the storefront windows of Jewish merchants all over Germany. Now the broken glass of Kristallnacht has also became part of the Hindu community's history in Detroit.

I met Swami Chidanand Saraswati, called Munji, at the Hindu-Jain Temple in Monroeville outside Pittsburgh in 1994. This saffron-robed sage and priest had been one of the leaders of this temple community from the beginning. The Hindu-Jain temple in Monroeville is one of two major Hindu temples in Pittsburgh, along with the Sri Venkateswara

Temple in Penn Hills. When the temple opened it included altars for both Jains and Sikhs. "This is the first Hindu-Jain temple in the world," said Muniji. "But the Gods don't belong to Hinduism or to Jainism. God is not in the church, God is not in the temple, but God is everywhere. That is the true meaning of God's omnipresence."[24]

Muniji recalled the early history of the temple, showing us an article from the *Pittsburgh Post Gazette* from 1983.

> Vandals swinging clubs and hurling paint desecrated the Hindu Temple of Pittsburgh in Monroeville over the weekend, painting obscenities on walls and smashing five statues of sacred deities. Scribbled on the main altar in black paint was the word "Leave." A large religious book called the Granthe, described by Hindu leaders as comparable to the Jewish Torah, was torn to pieces.
>
> Temple Chairman Dr. Prakash Srivastava said it was the worst of several incidents of burglary and vandalism that have plagued the temple in recent years. "This is the act of a fairly extreme group of some sort," said Srivastava. "It really destroyed our temple for the moment." He estimated the damage at $30,000 to $50,000. The marble deities alone cost $20,000, he said.[25]

The Hindu community had suffered the by-now common opposition from neighbors and the zoning board when it tried to build. Unlike the Chicago Muslims in Palos Heights who pulled out, the Hindu community in Pittsburgh had decided to stay. During construction, bullets were fired and stones thrown, but no one could have imagined the smashing of the images of deities, even in their worst nightmares. The people of the temple were deeply shocked by this violence. We will return in the next chapter to Muniji's response to the attack, for it makes clear what every immigrant feels: that they are not merely victims of American prejudice and discrimination, but are initiators and actors in the creation of new communities.

The story of a Cambodian Buddhist community in Portland, Maine, sums up many of the themes we have been reviewing. We don't usually think of Maine as a place of wide religious diversity, but the Catholic Charities and the Refugee Resettlement Center have brought refugees to Portland from Somalia, Bosnia, and Cambodia. A recent look at Portland's public schools reveals that in 1999–2000, 13.8 percent of the students in school had a first language other than English, up from 3.2 percent in 1990–91. One of America's largest Cambodian refugee populations is in the suburbs north of Boston, and by the mid-1980s, the Khmer community had extended up the coast into southern Maine.

Most of the Khmer who came to Portland were farmers in Cambodia who fled the Khmer Rouge terror that began in 1975. In Cambodia they lived in small villages where the central institution was the Buddhist *wat,* where the monks lived and people gathered for worship. By 1984 the eight hundred or so Khmer in Portland established a nonprofit organization called Watt Samaki, "Unity Temple," to raise funds to purchase a building.

The community located a promising site for its new temple—a large, abandoned chicken barn located on five acres some miles west of Portland. The community elders hired a lawyer to research the deed and appropriate variances, and they set up meetings with local churches to introduce themselves and their plan. The meetings went well, so they thought, and the Cambodians submitted a request for a special variance to turn the chicken barn into a "church."

The neighbors, however, were astounded and disturbed and based their objections on local zoning ordinances. More than seventy towns-people showed up for the hearing. The Portland media began covering the story, intensifying the debate in newspaper and on television. The ethos and worldview of the Cambodian Buddhists was not at all suited to such controversy. They did not like the publicity, even the well-intentioned supporters, and they were embarrassed and distraught by the charges of those who opposed them and did not want them as neighbors. New immigrant communities often adapt, not by standing up for their rights through the process of litigation, but by seeking a more harmonious and less combative way. The Cambodians withdrew their application for a zoning variance and forfeited their $1,500 deposit. Meanwhile, a few churches in the area became concerned about the plight of their new neighbors, and donations of over $800 came in to offset the loss.

Six months later the community found a small two-story house in Portland. The local Quaker meeting loaned them $10,000 to help with the down payment, and the gray house was dedicated as the Watt Samaki Buddhist Center. At last the community could pour its energies into creating a Buddha Hall for worship and festivals. Supporting a monk, however, became a huge financial commitment, and after the community's monk left, the small temple remained empty except for weddings, New Year and ancestor festivals, and frequent fund-raisers.

Pluralism Project researcher Julie Canniff tells the story that we already have heard, how in August 1993 Pirun Sen, a leader of the community who was a nurse and former monk, received a call from the Portland police notifying him of vandalism at the Buddhist center.

Electronic equipment had been stolen, but the most sickening sight was the writing on the wall: "Dirty Asian, Chink, Go Home."

A few weeks later, Pirun Sen spoke of his feelings in an interview with Julie Canniff. Fortunately, the media had not discovered the story, he confided, expressing the mixture of shame and rage that victims of violence so often feel about the attacks upon them. "You know our center is not a luxurious place, but we love it, take care of it as our heart and soul. It is the only place that can bring all of us together to love, to care for one another, to pass on the Khmer culture to the youngsters. This is why my tears keep dropping when I talk about vandalism of the Watt Samaki with friends and caring people. These tears are for my people who are the foundation of the Watt Samaki and people who have passed away. It is a small house, but these people reminded me to take care of Watt Samaki as if it were diamond and gold."[26]

The police were not successful in locating the vandals or the stolen equipment, but the neighbors, who up until this time did not know the purpose of the little house, pledged their support and watchful vigilance from then on. But as a result of this tragedy, many members of the community relived the nightmare of the Khmer Rouge and the unspeakable persecution they suffered. Repairing the damaged temple was only part of a much deeper process of repair that needed to take place in the wake of this attack. The community has continued to struggle and now is looking for another piece of land to construct a larger meeting hall where they can hold their New Year festivals, dances, and classes. Despite all the difficulties, this is a community of survivors—first in Cambodia and now in Portland, Maine.

WORKING IT OUT: THE WORKPLACE AND RELIGIOUS PRACTICE

One of the places we most commonly encounter religious difference in America today is the workplace. What religious attire may one wear? A cross? Yarmulke? Head scarf? Turban? Where and when is it appropriate to pray? What facilities do employers need to provide, and what policies do they need to implement? Religious difference is a question not just for theological schools and religious institutions but increasingly for businesses and corporations, offices and factories. These are the places where "we the people" most frequently meet, and how we manage our encounters here might be far more important than how we cope with imaginary encounters in the realm of theologies and beliefs.

The most common workplace issues have traditionally concerned working on the Sabbath, which is Saturday for Jews and Seventh-Day Adventists. Consider the case of a computer operator at a hospital in Fort Smith, Arkansas. Although he is a Seventh-Day Adventist and asked not to work on Saturdays, he was placed on call on Saturdays. When he refused to make himself available on his Sabbath, the hospital fired him. Title VII of the Civil Rights Act of 1964 prohibits discrimination on the basis of race, color, religion, national origin, or sex. In interpreting the act in relation to the religious practices of workers, the employer must try to make "reasonable accommodation" of religious practice, at least as long as it does not impose an "undue hardship" on the employer. In this case, the court ruled that the hospital was in violation of the Civil Rights Act. But just what constitutes "reasonable accommodation" and "undue hardship" is the thorny issue as each case comes forward.

In the past ten years the Equal Employment Opportunity Commission (EEOC), which considers workplace complaints that may violate the Civil Rights Act, has reported a 31 percent rise in complaints of religious discrimination in the workplace. This is not surprising, given the number of new immigrants in the workforce and the range of questions their attire, their holidays, and their religious life bring to the workplace environment. We have already looked at the incivility and prejudice Muslim women wearing the *hijab* may encounter. But sometimes incivility slides up the scale toward discrimination. For example, in 1996 Rose Hamid, a twelve-year veteran flight attendant with U.S. Air, became increasingly serious about her faith in the wake of some health problems and made the decision to wear a head scarf. Her first day at work, she was ordered to take it off because it was not part of the uniform of a flight attendant, and when she refused she was put on unpaid leave. Rose filed a complaint with the Equal Employment Opportunity Commission. What is reasonable accommodation in Rose's case? Rose had modeled different ways in which the colors of her uniform would be duplicated in her scarf, and some would argue that reasonable accommodation would mean allowing some flexibility in the uniform as long as it was readily recognizable. But U.S. Air moved Rose to a job that did not require a uniform and hence put her out of public visibility. The issue was resolved in a slightly different way by Domino's Pizza in 1998. That year, a convert to Islam who showed up at work wearing a head scarf was told by her employer at Domino's, "Unless you take that stupid thing off you have to leave."[27] The employer soon learned his response to her was more than just rude. It was against the law. Here, the Council on American

Islamic Relations called attention to the case. The employers reached what they believed was a reasonable accommodation: wearing the signature Domino's baseball cap over a red and blue head scarf.

Employees wearing *hijab* have brought complaints at such companies as Kmart, J.C. Penney, and Boston Chicken and have requested the accommodation of their head scarves as religiously mandated. The Council on American Islamic Relations (CAIR) has acted as a watchdog agency to help Muslims who are concerned about discrimination and to bring cases like these to public attention. Most of these cases of Islamic dress have been solved out of court, but each involves negotiating the issues of difference anew in each workplace. According to Ibrahim Hooper of CAIR, "Our biggest obstacle has been ignorance on the part of the employers—not prejudice."[28] Even so, the cases continue, and their resolution depends upon a continuous process of complaints and hearings. Perhaps the most widely publicized incident in recent years was the 1999 case involving six Muslim women who were fired from their jobs with a security firm at Dulles Airport because they refused to remove their head scarves at work. Only after filing a complaint with the EEOC was a settlement reached and were the women allowed to work.

Hair and beards have also raised workplace issues. In 1987 a Sikh immigrant, Prabhjot Kohli, who had managed a pharmaceutical company in India before coming to the U.S., was turned down for a job at Domino's Pizza in Baltimore because of his religiously mandated beard. "Domino's wants clean-shaven people," he recalls being told, "and you've got a beard."[29] In this case, wearing the baseball cap was not enough. For Domino's it was a business decision: people prefer to be served pizza by clean-shaven employees. The case went to the Maryland Human Relations Commission and was resolved only after a twelve-year lawsuit. In January 2000 the pizza chain dropped its no-beard policy. In California, Manjit Singh Bhatia, a machinist, was removed from his job at Chevron company because new safety requirements mandated the shaving of facial hair. His beard might prevent him from having an airtight seal when he wore a respirator. Chevron moved him to a different job that did not require a respirator and promised to reinstall him as a machinist if a respirator were developed that he could safely use. For the courts, this was "reasonable accommodation."

Some Muslim men, though not all, choose to keep a neatly trimmed beard, considering it part of their customary religious observance. A discrimination case went to court in New Jersey where members of the Newark police force sued for the right to wear a beard for religious reasons. In a 1999 ruling (*Fraternal Order of Police v. City of Newark*) the U.S. Court of Appeals upheld the right of Muslim members of the Newark police force to wear beards on the job. As we have seen from the Sikh experience, however, workplace decisions on beards have varied. And so too with Muslim men. A bus driver for a New York transit company can now wear a beard, but an employee of one of the major airlines cannot.

Prayer in the workplace is another issue that has gained complexity with the new immigration. A Christian group might gather at 7:15 to pray together before work. A Buddhist meditation group might spend part of its lunch hour in sitting practice. In the spring of 1998 I received a CAIR bulletin with information on three similar cases of workplace prayer accommodation in manufacturing plants around Nashville. Whirlpool Corporation reportedly had refused to allow Muslim employees to offer obligatory prayers on the job. One Muslim employee quit, and the others continued to perform their obligatory midday prayer secretly during bathroom breaks. When CAIR intervened, contacted the managers, and began a dialogue, together they envisioned a solution: the Muslim employees could perhaps customize their coffee breaks so that they could fit an Islamic prayer schedule. Today, Muslim organizations, including CAIR, are taking the initiative in providing the kind of information that might head off the endless round of discrimination cases. They have published a booklet called *An Employer's Guide to Islamic Religious Practices,* detailing what employers might need to know about the obligations of Muslim workers.

Employers today are encountering workplace issues most of us have never even thought about. For example, where do Muslim cab drivers who work the airport routes pray during the long days in line at the airport? In Minneapolis, at last word, they stand outside in a lot, according to Salina Khan of *USA Today.* She wrote, on June 25, 1999,

> Taxi driver Farhad Nezami rolls out his prayer rug, removes his shoes and raises his hands to begin the early afternoon prayer. Nezami's not worshipping in a mosque. He's standing in a lot near the Minneapolis-St. Paul International Airport that about 300 Muslim cab drivers turn into a makeshift prayer hall several times a day. They pray there in rain, snow and sleet because the Metropolitan Airports Commission has repeatedly denied their request for a room for four years.

The case is not clear-cut, and it probably falls more in the realm of civility than legality. But Denver handled a similar case differently. A hundred

Muslim cab drivers there put the question to the Denver Airport authority and received a positive response. Jillian Lloyd of the *Christian Science Monitor* reported, "When the city of Denver moved a glass shelter to its international airport this winter, giving Muslim cabbies a warm place to pray to Allah, it did not merely show government goodwill toward a religious minority. The move highlighted the growing willingness of American employers to provide for their workers' religious needs."[30]

At the federal level, the White House has addressed the complexity that our new religious texture has brought to the workplace. In 1997 it released *Guidelines on Religious Exercise and Religious Expression in the Federal Workplace.* They provide a pathway through some of the issues, generally following one principle: "Agencies shall not restrict personal religious expression by employees in the Federal workplace except where the employee's interest in expression is outweighed by the government's interest in the efficient provision of public services or where the expression intrudes upon the legitimate rights of other employees or creates the appearance, to a reasonable observer, of an official endorsement of religion." For example, employees can keep a Bible or Koran in their desk and read it during breaks. Employees can speak about religion with other employees, just as they may speak about sports or politics. Employees may display religious messages on items of clothing to the same extent as they are permitted to display other messages. A supervisor can post an announcement about an Easter musical service on a bulletin board or can invite co-workers to a daughter's bat mitzvah as long as there is no indication of expectation that the employee will attend. There is a veritable thicket of examples in this nine-page document. It is the first herald of a new day in the workplace.

SEE YOU IN COURT

The American Constitution guarantees that there will be "no establishment" of religion and that the "free exercise" of religion will be protected. As we have seen, these twin principles have guided church-state relations in the United States for the past two hundred years. But the issues have become increasingly complex in a multireligious America, where the church in question may now be the mosque, the Buddhist temple, the Hindu temple, or the Sikh gurdwara. Every religious tradition has its own questions. Can a Muslim schoolteacher wear her head covering on the job as a public school teacher? Can a Sikh student wear the *kirpan,* the symbolic knife required of all initiated Sikhs, to school, or a Sikh worker wear a turban on a hard-hat job, in apparent violation of safety regulations? Should a crèche be displayed in the Christmas season on public property? Can the sanctity of Native lands be protected from road building? Should the taking of peyote by Native Americans be protected as the free exercise of religion? Can a city council pass an ordinance prohibiting the sacrifice of animals by the adherents of the Santería faith?

These difficult questions make clear that one vital arena of America's new pluralism is the courts. Since about 1960, church-state issues in America have been increasingly on court agendas. Just as the "church" is not a single entity in multireligious America, the "state" is multiple too, with zoning boards, city councils, state governments, and the federal government. At all levels, courts hear disputes and offer interpretations of laws and regulations and the constitutional principles that undergird them.

The First Amendment principles of nonestablishment of religion and the free exercise of religion sometimes almost seem to be in tension: the free exercise of religion calling for the protection of religious groups, while the nonestablishment of religion prohibiting any such special treatment. On the "no establishment" side, a landmark Supreme Court decision was made in the case of *Everson v. Board of Education* (1947) in which a school busing program in New Jersey was ruled to be accessible to students going to parochial schools. The Supreme Court's decision was clearly and narrowly defined: the busing program was a "generally available benefit" that should not be denied to children simply because their destination was a religious school. While the court has consistently ruled against state support of private religious schools, in this case, the benefit in question was not to the schools, but to the children. Justice Black wrote, "[T]he First Amendment requires the state to be neutral in its relations with groups of religious believers and non-believers; it does not require the state to be their adversary. State power is no more to be used so as to handicap religions than it is to favor them." The extended logic of this decision was that religious communities should have "equal access" to those benefits that are available to nonreligious communities. In other words, if a high school gymnasium in Bethesda, Maryland, can be used by the Girl Scouts or the Garden Club, its use cannot be denied to a Hindu temple community for its annual fall Diwali festival.

In "free exercise" cases, the *Sherbert v. Verner* decision in 1963 set a precedent that guided religious liberty cases for thirty years. In South Carolina, Adell Sherbert, a Seventh-Day Adventist, was fired from her job because she refused to accept a schedule requiring her to work on

Saturday, her Sabbath, and was then refused state unemployment compensation. In her case, the Supreme Court articulated three questions to guide its decision: Has the religious freedom of a person been infringed or burdened by some government action? If so, is there a "compelling state interest" that would nonetheless justify the government action? Finally, is there any other way the government interest can be satisfied without restricting religious liberty? In sum, religious liberty is the rule; any exception to the rule can be justified only by a "compelling state interest." This form of reasoning came to be called the "balancing test"— balancing state interest against the religious freedom of the individual.

In the Sherbert case, the court ruled that there was no state interest compelling enough to warrant the burden placed upon Sherbert's religious freedom. Similarly, when an Amish community in Wisconsin insisted on withdrawing its children from public schools after the eighth grade and the State of Wisconsin insisted the children comply with compulsory education laws, the Supreme Court applied the three-pronged test and ruled that the religious freedom of the Amish outweighed the state's interest in four years' more compulsory education (*Wisconsin v. Yoder*, 1972).

Beginning in the 1980s, however, a series of Supreme Court rulings gradually weakened the force of the Sherbert balancing test and, in the view of many, weakened the constitutional guarantee of the free exercise of religion. These rulings began to raise disturbing questions about the religious rights of minorities. In the case of *Lyng v. The Northwest Indian Cemetery Protective Association* (1988), the issue was whether the Native Americans' right to preserve intact their sacred sites outweighed the government's right to build roads through Forest Service land. The Yurok, Karok, and Tolowa Indians argued that building a logging road through the land would have "devastating effects" on their religious ways. A lower court acted to prevent the Forest Service from building the road, but the Forest Service appealed to the Supreme Court. In this case, the Supreme Court supported the Forest Service, saying,

> Incidental effects of government programs which may make it more difficult to practice certain religions, but which have no tendency to coerce individuals into acting contrary to their religious beliefs [do not] require government to bring forward a compelling justification for its otherwise lawful actions. . . . However much we might wish that it were otherwise, government simply could not operate if it were required to satisfy every citizen's religious needs and desires. . . . Whatever rights the Indians may

have to the use of the area, however, those rights do not divest the government of its right to use what is, after all, its land.

Here, the balance tipped precipitously in favor of the government, whose policies, just incidentally, compromised Native religious practice.

For the Indians, one of the issues in this and other cases is whether the government recognizes the deeply held religious importance of preserving particular sacred sites undisturbed. A Hopi and Navajo case (*Wilson v. Block*, 1983) questioned whether a ski area could be built on a sacred mountain. The court ruled that the Forest Service had not infringed the religious rights of the Indians because it had not denied them access to the mountain. But the Navajo and Hopi argued that the mountain, the home of the Kachinas—divine messengers—would be desecrated by its commercial development. The court seemed to give little weight to the fact that the Native peoples considered the mountain to be inherently sacred, the very locus of the Divine, and not simply the place where they pray to the Divine. Here, the very nature of Native religious claims for the sanctity of the land seemed to be undermined, or perhaps not even understood, by the court's reasoning.

These and other cases led many to see an increasingly restrictive interpretation of the scope of religious freedom by the Supreme Court. In each case, the government did not have to demonstrate a "compelling interest" in order to restrict religious freedom. And in each case, the government did not have to alter its basic procedures to accommodate a specific religious claim. For example, an Abnaki Indian asked that his daughter, Little Bird of the Snow, be exempt from having to have a Social Security number in order to receive the benefits from the Aid to Families with Dependent Children program (*Bowen v. Roy*, 1986). The father insisted that to assign a number to his daughter would "rob her of her spirit" and interfere with her spiritual growth by making her a number, regulated by the federal government. The court ruled that the First Amendment could not be interpreted to require the government to alter its procedures in this way. Little Bird of the Snow would have to have a Social Security number.

Altering government procedures to accommodate various religious practices was also at stake in the case of *Goldman v. Weinberger* (1986). Dr. Goldman, an Orthodox Jewish psychiatrist serving in the U.S. Air Force, insisted on his right to wear his yarmulke on duty in the hospital, even though Air Force regulations prohibited a uniformed officer from wearing a head covering inside. The Air Force insisted that its code of military discipline requires that it not be continually making exceptions. The court said it would defer to the Air Force's judgment in this matter, which was to say: no yarmulkes.

Friday prayer for a Muslim prisoner was decided along similar lines in the case of *O'Lone v. Estate of Shabazz* (1987). Here, a Muslim prison inmate wanted to return from the work gang at noon for Friday prayers with other Muslims. He was turned down because officials insisted that it would require extra prison security at the work site and the gate in order to bring him back, and the court upheld the prison system's refusal to alter prison practices. In making this ruling, the court also said that a restrictive institution like the prison system had security needs and regulations that would necessarily mean that constitutional rights would not be as broad as those of ordinary citizens.

These increasingly restrictive interpretations of the guarantees of the First Amendment culminated in the controversial 1990 Supreme Court decision about peyote use. In this case (*Employment Division, Department of Human Resources of Oregon v. Smith*, 1990) two members of the Native American church ingested peyote, as is common in the ceremonial life of the church, and were subsequently fired from their jobs for "misconduct." The state of Oregon denied them unemployment compensation because they had been dismissed for the use of peyote, which was classified as an illegal drug. The Supreme Court upheld Oregon's decision, arguing that the state had a "generally applicable" law against drug use. The law did not specifically target the Native American church or any other group, and carving out exceptions to such laws would be impracticable, according to the 5–4 majority of the court. Justice Antonin Scalia argued that to require the government to demonstrate a "compelling state interest" in enforcing generally applicable laws would be "courting anarchy."

The Smith decision thus reversed many years of court precedent, which presumed that religious freedom would be the rule, with any infringement requiring the demonstration of a compelling state interest. Many critics insisted that for the court to refuse to apply the balancing test to "generally applicable laws" would seriously damage the first-amendment protection of religious freedom. The Smith decision, critics argued, would be especially hard on minority religions, since generally applicable laws are passed by the majority. Freedom of religion, on the other hand, is not subject to majority rule. The purpose of the Bill of Rights was precisely to limit the power of the majority in areas of fundamental rights, such as the freedom of conscience and speech.

The Santería Church of the Lukumi Babalu Aye in Hialeah, Florida, was a minority group in danger of losing its freedom of religious practice due to its unpopular and widely misunderstood practice of animal sacrifice. An estimated fifty thousand practitioners of the Afro-Caribbean Santería religion now live in South Florida, and their ceremonial life includes the sacrifice of chickens, pigeons, or other small animals to the *orisha,* their gods. The case that came to the Supreme Court (*Church of the Lukumi Babalu Aye v. City of Hialeah,* 1993) began in 1987 when Ernesto Pichardo, a priest of the Santería religion, purchased a building and a former used car lot to open a place of worship. The city council of Hialeah met to consider the matter, and many voices hostile to Santería were raised. The council passed three ordinances that effectively prohibited animal sacrifice within the city limits. As the city attorney explained, "This community will not tolerate religious practices which are abhorrent to its citizens."

Ernesto Pichardo and his community protested, insisting that the ordinances specifically targeted Santería, as they did not prohibit the killing of animals within city limits for secular reasons but only for religious ones and only, seemingly, for those of the Santería religion. Indeed, the ordinances specifically excluded Jewish kosher slaughter practices. Animals could be killed in butcher shops and restaurants but not in the religious context of Santería. Many quipped that the Church of Lukumi Babalu Aye was being persecuted for killing a few chickens with a prayer, while Frank Perdue and Colonel Sanders kill tens of thousands without one. The question before the Supreme Court was whether the three ordinances passed by the city council were constitutional or whether they violated the constitutional rights of the practitioners of Santería by specifically legislating against their religious practices. The judges unanimously struck down the ordinances, stating that they were not generally applicable laws at all but specifically aimed at the Santería religion. As Justice Anthony M. Kennedy wrote, "Although the practice of animal sacrifice may seem abhorrent to some, 'religious beliefs need not be acceptable, logical, consistent, or comprehensible to others in order to merit First Amendment protection.'"

The Santería case was an easy one, resting on the principle that "government may not enact laws that suppress religious belief or practice." However, many people, including Justice David Souter, were still disquieted about the merits and the precedent of the Smith decision. By this time, legislation called the Religious Freedom Restoration Act had been introduced in Congress precisely to restore the religious freedom many people in public life felt had been eroded with the Smith decision. This act, passed in 1995, stated simply, "The government cannot burden a person's free exercise of religion, even if the burden results from a rule of general applicability, unless the burden is essential to further a compelling governmental interest and is the least restrictive means of furthering that interest." In effect, it reinstituted the balancing test of the Sherbert case, this time in law. The legislation was eventually ruled unconstitutional by the Supreme Court in 1997, in part because it was a legislative maneuver to reestablish a form of judicial reasoning. This, the court believed, was the prerogative of the judiciary.

Questions of religious freedom lie at the heart of some of America's most hotly contested cases. The courts are one site of the encounter and disputation that are endemic to America's new pluralism. They represent the difficult places where we the people do not seem to be able to resolve our differences on our own. Cases involving America's newer religious communities have gradually made their way into the court system and into case law. The willingness to take advantage of access to the courts is itself a signal of the Americanization process.

In California's Livingstone School District, for instance, the schools and the Sikh community arrived at a stand-off on the question of whether three young Khalsa-initiated students would be permitted to attend school wearing the symbolic *kirpan,* a ceremonial dagger that is one of the five sacred symbols of the Sikh faith and is worn by all initiated Sikhs. In 1994 classmates of an eleven-year-old Sikh youngster had spotted his *kirpan* when his shirt slid up on the playground and reported this to the teacher. From the standpoint of the school, policy prohibited carrying weapons, including knives, on the school premises. From the standpoint of the Sikh youngster and his two siblings, the *kirpan* was part of their religious life, a symbol of their historic willingness to stand up for justice, and being required to take it off amounted to an infringement of their religious freedom. The U.S. District court barred the three youngsters from wearing the *kirpan,* and their parents kept them home from school. But when the case came to the Ninth U.S. Circuit Court of Appeals, the court overturned the ruling and required the Livingstone School District to make "all reasonable efforts" to accommodate the religious beliefs and practices of the three Sikh youngsters. According to the ruling, as long as the *kirpans* are small, sewn in the sheath, and not a threat to the safety of other students, the Sikh students must be allowed to wear them to school. Here, the courts were an avenue for working out a genuine dilemma that schools had not before encountered.

In New Jersey the Indo-American Cultural Society also found the court system necessary in order to resolve a community dispute having to do with its annual festival of Navaratri, the "Nine Nights" of the Goddess, observed on a series of weekend nights on the grounds of the Raritan Convention Center in Edison. This fall festival attracted as many as twelve thousand celebrants, and though it was arguably well out of earshot of residential areas, a group of citizens tried to block the festival. A 1995 meeting with the Township Council of Edison revealed a level of overt prejudice that was shocking to the representatives of the Indo-American Cultural Society. The chair of the society wrote to the township council following the meeting,

> We wonder if there is any awareness in Edison of freedoms of assembly and religion. We are immigrants to a democracy that provided the model for the constitution India adopted less than fifty years ago. We wonder how the folk who inspired our struggle against colonialism can arbitrarily dismiss our rights.

The council passed an ordinance aimed at restricting the hours of the festival, permits for the festival were delayed, and the Indo-American Cultural Society responded by seeking an injunction against what it considered the township's unfair ordinance. Eventually, in July of 1996, a district judge upheld the rights of the Indo-American Cultural Society. But all this required the willingness of the Hindus to use the court system. Reflecting on the whole affair, Vivodh Z. J. Anand, a New Jersey human rights advocate, wrote,

> As a New Jersey State Civil Rights Commissioner, I have, since my immigration in 1963 at the height of the American Civil Rights movement, personally struggled for equity. I can report that the courts seem to be the only venue available to resolve vexing communal conflicts. While advocacy groups for a wide spectrum of social issues exist, the onus of resolving issues of religious freedom and rights, and in this case the more complex conflation of religious and racial "otherness," seems to rest only on those who are wronged and whose rights have been compromised.[31]

Anand went on to report that during the entire struggle of the Indian community in New Jersey not a single religious group or community leader reached out to support the Indo-American Cultural Society in its well-publicized case. "In our democracy there is a paucity of institutions to study, educate, arbitrate, and promote the credence of the religious 'other.' Yet for a democracy to flourish, it is imperative that both individuals and groups be enabled to recognize that their own stories may be found in the stories and lives of fellow citizens who may appear dissimilar to themselves."

THE LOTUS TEMPLE ON BIXBY STREET

Thich Chon Thanh, the resident monk at Chua Lien Hoa, has encountered most of what we have reviewed in this chapter, and he managed eventually to negotiate civic and religious conflict in the way Vivodh Anand so ardently envisions. This soft-spoken Vietnamese monk, with shaved head and brown robes, no doubt attracted the stares of the neighbors when he moved into a small ranch-style home on Bixby Street in the late 1980s and made it into a small Buddhist temple. During his first ten years there, he saw the whole gamut of difficulties—from suspicious neighbors to antagonists on the zoning board, the planning commission, and in the code enforcement office of Garden Grove. His story concludes this chapter well and is a good introduction to the next, for Thich Chon Thanh seems to have worked through many obstacles to a new relationship with the community and a new life for his temple.

Pluralism Project researcher Chloe Breyer first called my attention to this temple. She found its legal troubles so interesting that she eventually wrote her senior thesis at Harvard on the temple.[32] Shortly after Chloe's research stint in the summer of 1991, I made my first of what would be many visits to Thich Chon Thanh and the temple on Bixby Street. It looked just like all the other ranch-style homes in this residential neighborhood of Garden Grove: a one-story house, set slightly back from the street, with a two-car garage and a driveway. The driveway was often full of cars, which sometimes spilled into the front yard. The only thing that set the house apart from its neighbors was the Buddhist flag of yellow, red, blue, white, and orange hanging in the living room window.

Inside the front door, however, the resemblance of this house to the houses next door ended. Just inside was a pile of shoes, left by worshipers and guests as they entered the living room, which had been transformed into the Buddha Hall. Against one wall sat an altar bearing the seated image of the Buddha along with offerings of flowers, fruit, candles, and incense. Forming a halo behind the head of the Buddha were multicolored concentric circles of fluorescent lights. Next to the main altar was the family memorial altar, bearing photographs of the beloved dead. Of course, in this Vietnamese community many are remembered—family members lost in the long war in Vietnam, friends and family who died as boat people fleeing Vietnam as the war ended, and the many who have died here in America since arriving as refugees in the period after 1975.

In the small adjoining kitchen, preparations were always being made for a community supper or for a meal, for newcomers to Garden Grove who needed hospitality and a place to stay. The teapot was constantly emptied and filled again. On the back patio were picnic tables and a blackboard set up for meals and for weekly classes. A "meditation walk" wound through the flower beds and bushes of the backyard.

Chua Lien Hoa means "Lotus Flower Temple," named for one of the great Asian symbols of life: the lotus flower, which blossoms beautifully on top of the pond but has its roots in the mud below the waters. This temple was one of dozens of Vietnamese home temples in the Orange County area, serving a total of more than eighty thousand people. Although the temple is considerably transformed today, it was and still is typical of America's Vietnamese temples. Its story reveals both fault lines and bridges in the Vietnamese Buddhist encounter with America. There were tensions in the neighborhood, in city hall, and in the courts, with lawyers arguing on both sides. Finally, from the mud of controversy, a new Lotus Flower Temple was born, right in the spacious backyard of this suburban home.

The Vietnamese practice of combining temple and monastery in one complex contrasts with the American pattern of separating parsonage or rectory from a much larger church. As Nguyen Trong Nho, the lawyer for Chua Lien Hoa, put it, "The nature of Buddhism is to be close to the people. This means that in Vietnam there was a small temple in every village. When you talk about Buddhism, it means a small temple in the middle of a community where a monk is available as a kind of spiritual counselor all of the time. It is this way so that people can come over and talk to someone in the middle of the night if they have some kind of an emergency and a relative dies. The temple has to be small and close to the village—not big and glorious like many Christian churches here."[33]

When Thich Chon Thanh moved to Bixby Street, he was supported by a small group of Buddhists. During the week a few people would come to his temple on a daily basis. On the weekends, the community was considerably larger but still only about sixty or eighty people. Services were held in the temple room. The chanting of scriptures was amplified on the speaker system, classes were held on the patio, and community meals were held in the backyard. But on the three big festival days of the year—the Vietnamese New Year, called Tet, the Buddha's Birthday, and the Vietnamese "Mother's Day," called Vu Lan—there would suddenly be as many as two hundred people at the temple. Funerals and memorials for the dead might also be attended by large crowds.

Soon complaints from the neighborhood began to pour into the police department and the code enforcement office regarding traffic and parking and related matters of nuisance. The loudspeakers in the backyard during the festivals raised just too much noise for some. As one neighbor explained, "It's not like a Catholic church or something where it's just an hour or two. These chants would be going on pretty much most of the day." The city officials discovered that the temple did not have a conditional use permit, so they restricted the number of people who could be present in the temple. But the level of tension continued to rise in the neighborhood.

On the Buddha's Birthday in June 1991, the code enforcement officers arrived during the day-long ceremonies and closed down the temple, sending everyone home. Too many people were present. The same thing had happened at a Vietnamese temple on Magnolia Avenue during the New Year observance, when the temple had been closed as people were praying for the souls of their beloved dead and seeking blessings for the coming year. It was an unhappy omen for those present, a bad way to start the new year. The city of Garden Grove and its new Vietnamese residents were at a standoff on difficult zoning issues. In December 1991 the code enforcement office, acting on behalf of several temple neighbors, asked the California Superior Court for an injunction that would prohibit all activity at the temple on Bixby Street. Rather than issue an injunction, however, the judge placed a cap of twenty-five on the number of persons who could be inside the temple—more than the neighbors wanted yet fewer than the temple thought feasible. The judge also prohibited any form of electric amplification.

In response, Thich Chon Thanh explained that he could not and would not bar a person from the temple because there were already twenty-five people inside. As a religious leader, he could not close the door to anyone who came for worship. When two temporarily homeless Vietnamese refugees came to the temple, he let them live for a time in the garage. For this he was placed on probation. As Thich Chon Thanh said, "As a Buddhist priest I see my duty to everyone to open my door to shelter them when they ask for a shelter, to give them a meal when I have things to eat and they do not."[34] Difficult as they were, the hearings on the injunction began a process of dialogue among the temple, the city, the neighbors, and the code enforcement office.

Some of the neighbors' complaints were matters of nuisance, but there were legal questions as well. According to the city code, a church or religious organization in Garden Grove must be located on a minimum of one acre of land and have a parking space for every three to five seats. But clearly the patterns of temple attendance and use were not like those of a church with an established membership. Indeed, the concept of membership in a temple would have been unfamiliar in Vietnam. The community in Garden Grove included temple regulars plus literally hundreds of other people who would come especially for funerals or festivals.

From an economic standpoint, the monk and his new community could not afford an acre of land in Garden Grove in order to have a temple. Yes, a church like the United Church of Christ a block away down Bixby Street could be built on a whole acre or more of land. But the Vietnamese temple is smaller, and the pattern of temple use was such that only a few times a year would the crowd be unsuitably large. A city official suggested that using an old warehouse or commercial property would avoid problems, but this would alter the structure of Vietnamese Buddhist religious life. Should Thich Chon Thanh and other monks live in a warehouse rather than in a neighborhood? The very term *home temple* was used by city officials, a classification that clearly came from the difficulty of deciding whether these were residences or temples—a dilemma clearly reflecting a more common Judeo-Christian pattern of religious life in which home and temple were separated. In Vietnamese Buddhist culture they were not separated. How would the city cope with assuring religious liberty for people with a new pattern of religious life? How well would our court system work for new religious minorities?[35]

The dialogue was difficult, long, and ultimately fruitful. In the end, Chua Lien Hoa decided to raise money to build a more adequate temple structure on the site. Plans were drawn up for the temple's expansion and were carefully reviewed by both the city and the temple committee. The lot was not quite one acre, but the city agreed that a small temple could be built behind the current ranch-style residence, which would now serve as the monks' quarters and entryway. There was not enough parking, but the front yard was transformed into a parking lot. On festival occasions, the temple could use the parking lot of the United Church of Christ church down the street. Step by step, both the city and the temple made their compromises.

This story has a happy ending. On May 14, 1995, on the day of the Buddha's 2,539th Birthday, the new Lien Hoa Temple was dedicated. It is a small but beautiful temple built in the backyard where the meditation walk used to be. Though it was a Sunday, and Mother's Day at that, the UCC church offered its parking lot to the overflow crowd. The mayor, the chairman of the code enforcement office, the lawyers for both sides, and neighbors were all present, along with hundreds of members of the Buddhist community. The mayor, Paul Brockwater, cut the red ribbon and said, "The Buddha taught harmony to his people, to work with their fellow man. Today, the Buddha would be very happy with the Vietnamese community in Southern California. Congratulations to all of you for putting your temple together and making it a beautiful asset for our community."[36]

Reverend Holland, minister in the United Church of Christ church down the street, said, "As your neighbors, we are delighted to share this community with you. As both Buddhists and Christians, we want to work together for peace and harmony in our neighborhoods. We celebrate the birth of Christ at Christmas, and you celebrate the birth of Buddha today. Both Buddha and Jesus represent for us truth, light, beauty, harmony, and tranquillity. In a world in which there is so much violence and disharmony, I pledge to you that we will work together as spiritual people so that our community can become a place where we can live together in harmony and raise our children."

The Vietnamese lawyer, Mr. Nho, spoke for the whole Buddhist community when he said, "This is a small Buddhist temple, but the dedication of this temple is a giant step forward for the harmony of our neighborhood. It symbolizes one thing that is important for all of us— that people of different backgrounds, of different ethnicity, and of different religious beliefs can live together and resolve our differences in the spirit of understanding." The neighbors had their turn at the microphone as well. One woman put it simply: "Thank you for welcoming me to the temple. I also welcome you to the neighborhood. I am very happy to share neighborhood with you folks." Throughout the festivities, Thich Chon Thanh simply beamed with happiness.

This is one of the hopeful signals of America's new multireligious experiment. Time and again, stories that begin with incidents of hatred or conflict evolve in time into stories of new neighbors who have, in the course of their conflict, learned much more about one another. Distant images have become people with faces, voices, and problems. Strangers, in time, become neighbors. And neighbors, even those who differ from us, become allies in creating our common society.

NOTES

1. William J. Clinton, Remarks in the Roosevelt Room, The White House, April 6, 1999. For hate crimes statistics see the U.S. Department of Justice FBI Web site: www.fbi.gov/ucr/hatecm.htm#bias.

2. Peter Brimelow, *Alien Nation: Common Sense About America's Immigration Disaster* (New York: Random House, 1995), 57 .

3. Padma Rangaswamy, *Namaste America* (University Park, PA: The Pennsylvania State University Press, 2000), 333.

4. Peggy Landers, "Answer to a Prayer: Buddhists Break Ground on Controversial Temple," *The Miami Herald,* June 12, 1995.

5. Mary Lahaj, Pluralism Project interview, 1996.

6. Marc Ramirez, "Islam on the Rise—Muslim in America," *Seattle Times,* January 24, 1999.

7. Harold Isaacs, 1958, *Scratches on Our Minds: American Images of China and India* (Armonk, New York: M. E. Sharpe, Inc. 1980), 37.

8. Leonard Dinnerstein, *Antisemitism in America* (New York: Oxford University Press, 1994), 58.

9. Dinnerstein, *Antisemitism,* 122.

10. Cited in Dinnerstein, *Antisemitism,* 41.

11. "Yoga and the Devil: Issue for Georgia Town," *New York Times,* September 7, 1990.

12. Doug Grow, "Wisconsin Teen Victorious in Her Free-Speech Fight," *Minneapolis Star Tribune,* March 31, 1999.

13. Their reports include a wide range of incidents: a Pakistani family's home spray-painted with satanic phrases; a Sikh youth taunted on a school bus and beaten by fellow students in Union City, California, in 1997; an Indo-Caribbean man beaten with bats by young men in the streets of Queens, New York, in 1998. See also the India Abroad Center for Political Awareness; phone: (202) 289-3654.

14. This report of the Council on American-Islamic Relations (CAIR) was published in *The Minaret,* a monthly magazine of the Islamic Center of Southern California, in June 1995 (43). The 200 incidents reported in the aftermath of the bombing compares with the 119 such incidents reported during all of 1991, the year of the Gulf War.

15. *New York Times,* August 13, 1991.

16. E. J. Montini, "Monks Lived in Valley, Died as Aliens," *Arizona Republic,* August 29, 1991.

17. Transcript of *Morning Edition,* National Public Radio, June 30, 2000.

18. Transcript of *Morning Edition,* National Public Radio, July 30, 2000.

19. *Newark Star Ledger,* August 12, 1996.

20. *India Abroad,* May 28, 1993.

21. *New Jersey Law Journal,* December 20, 1993.

22. Saleem Shah Khan, "Faith Survives Devastating Fire," *Muslim Journal,* September 30, 1994.

23. Islamic Circle of North America, "Report on Yuba City," 1994.

24. Swami Chidanand Saraswati, Pluralism Project interview, 1992.

25 Jim Gallagher, "Vandals Toss Paint, Smash Holy Statues in Hindu Temple," *Pittsburgh Post Gazette,* February 8, 1983.

26. Julie Canniff, "The Story of Watt Samaki," Pluralism Project Research, 1993.

27. Katherine Roth, "God on the Job," *Working Woman,* February 1998, 65.

28. Salina Khan, "Employers Adjust to Muslim Customs," *USA Today,* June 25, 1999.

29. David Lauter, "Who Lays Down the Law: God or Your Boss?" *Charlotte Observer,* November 30, 1997.

30. Jillian Lloyd, "Religious Practices vs. Work Demands," *Christian Science Monitor,* December 31, 1998.

31. Vivodh Anand, with Farhana Rahman, Lisa Ramos, and Rebecca Flores, "Edison's Navaratri: A Report of Religious Conflict in the Community" (unpublished paper presented at the Pluralism Project Conference, Cambridge, MA, November 1999).

32. Chloe Breyer published a synopsis of her 1992 honors thesis as "Religious Liberty in Law and Practice: Vietnamese Home Temples and the First Amendment," *Journal of Church and State* 35 (Spring 1993): 367–401. The story of Chua Lien Hoa is told, in part, in the WGBH film *Becoming the Buddha in L.A.,* directed by Michael Camerini. As chief academic adviser for the film, I took part in our research there over the course of several months in 1992.

33. Nguyen Trong Nho, interview with Chloe Breyer, July 5, 1991, cited in "Religious Liberty," 377.

34. Declaration of Thich Chon Thanh in opposing application for a preliminary injunction, California Supreme Court, case no. 673449 (1991).

35. Chloe Breyer, in "Religious Liberty," showed how the "balancing test" of *Sherbert v. Verner* would protect a religious minority by asking about the beliefs and practices of a particular religious tradition and whether there would be a compelling state interest in burdening this religious practice. The Smith decision, however, requires the court only to apply a "strict neutrality" test, establishing that the generally applicable law did not target any particular religious tradition or practice.

36. The citations from the ceremonies are from the video made of the occasion by Chua Lien Hoa.

CHAPTER SEVEN

BRIDGE BUILDING: A NEW MULTIRELIGIOUS AMERICA

★

Bridges are the lifelines of a society on the move. They enable us to cross the deepest gorges and widest rivers, linking the two sides with a flow of traffic. This final chapter investigates the evidence of bridge building in the new religious landscape of America. In what ways are we flinging soaring spans of steel across the differences, creating a new infrastructure for a society in which religious difference is just part of the traffic of a creative democracy? From the Brooklyn Bridge to the Golden Gate, civic and religious bridge building is our greatest challenge today. Without bridges and traffic, we will allow ourselves to be fragmented into a multitude of separate religious, ethnic, and cultural enclaves.

Many political scientists, of course, remind us that the most successful multireligious states have been those ruled by the iron fist of strong imperial or authoritarian regimes. Witness the way in which the Soviet Union held together the diversities of ethnicity and religion, all of which began to unravel with the loss of authoritarian central power. Where tolerance is the imperial policy, tolerance will prevail, whether or not bridges are built. But in a democracy, tolerance cannot be imposed, and at the same time we cannot retreat into an enclave mentality in which newcomers are forever foreigners. We need energetic bridge builders to create a truly pluralistic society. A complex society, as ours now is, depends on an infrastructure of communication. In the United States, the climate of tolerance and the engagement of pluralism emerge not from an authoritarian central regime, but from a democratic experiment as an immigrant nation, a nation in which, at our best, we are motivated by ideals and principles.

The vitality of religion in America has astonished observers from Alexis de Tocqueville to the present. While the state is religiously neutral, he noted, the peoples of the United States form a multitude of religious associations. Freedom of religion spins forth into American civil society ever new religious communities and associations. For immigrants these associations today, as in earlier eras of immigration, enable people to solidify their sense of ethnic, cultural, or religious identity while providing a base for participating in the wider society.

At the local level we see temple associations and Islamic societies and at the national and regional level groups like the American Buddhist Congress, the American Muslim Council, the Federation of Zoroastrians in North America, and the Jain Associations in North America. These are entirely voluntary associations. Some people participate, some don't. And as in previous eras of immigration, these religious associations provide for immigrants one of their first training grounds in participatory democracy. After all, "religions" are, in the view of the Internal Revenue Service, nonprofit corporations, and they must have boards of directors and elections, membership lists, and accountability. The arguments, the power moves, and the fragmentation so legendary in the governing bodies of new American temples, mosques, and gurdwaras are often stressful and disconcerting. But it also comes with the territory of America's way of giving official nonprofit status to religious communities. The positive side is that religious communities are precisely the places where new immigrants gain their feet and practice the arts of internal democracy. Long before they stand for election to the school board, they will stand for election in the governing body of the Hindu temple. Long before they enter the fray of local and state politics, they argue fiercely about their internal Sikh, Hindu, and Muslim politics. In his book *What It Means to Be an American,* Michael Walzer reminds us that American citizens acquire political competence first of all within their ethnic, cultural, and religious associations. In this way, civil society is the seedbed of democratic politics.

In their religious associations, new immigrants not only negotiate differences with one another, they also inevitably encounter people of very different religious commitments, including the dominant majority, in this case Christian and, to some extent, secular. Whatever else immigrants may dream of finding in the U.S., the one thing they will find, virtually everywhere, is people different from themselves. Our differences are not localized by geographical zones, though regions and states do have different mixes of difference. Ours is a land of what Walzer calls "dispersed differences."[1] As we have seen in the previous chapter, some of these encounters with difference are full of fear, conflict, and tension. Some display the ragged edges of prejudice and stereotype, and some result in acts of insult and injury, vandalism and violence. On the whole, however, I would venture that the experience of immigrant religious communities is not bigotry and prejudice but a rough-hewn tolerance, combined with a kind of laissez-faire ignorance and individualism that enables people to live and let live. Even so, much work in bridge building remains if we are to create a positive pluralism that builds upon our differences rather than ignores them.

Despite incidents of harassment and violence, people in every religious community also tell us that the most serious threat to their life and longevity in the U.S. is not from harassing outsiders but from disaffected and disaffiliated insiders. Secular society gives immigrants a much-yearned-for freedom, and for some this is freedom *from* religion and an opportunity to shed identities they do not wish to have as dominant and all-encompassing. Generational issues also surface, as first-generation immigrants seek to preserve a religious culture they brought from home, while their children want to be "American," sometimes even juxtaposing American with Hindu, Sikh, or Buddhist identities. I remember the words of a thirteen-year-old at the Lien Hoa Temple in California. "I want to be an American, not a Buddhist," he said. I tried to explain that he could be both, but clearly in his own head, these were two very much opposed identities. My colleagues Mary Waters and Marcelo Suarez-Orozco here at Harvard confirm in their studies of immigrant identity and ethnicity that for most young second-generation immigrants, *American* still describes someone else's identity, not their own. Can one be Vietnamese, Buddhist, *and* American? Of course, I would respond. But the process of developing multiple and strong identities is unclear, and both Waters and Suarez-Orozco point out that the study of immigrant children is just beginning.

As this Vietnamese teenager grows up, he might describe himself simply as an American, leaving the rest behind. Or he may discover that there are many ways of "being American" that do not involve the erasure of other identities. He might describe himself as a Vietnamese American, with the Buddhist component of his Vietnamese identity very much in the background except in times of crisis. He might describe himself as a Buddhist American and bring these two identities, along with his professional and family identities, into his participation in public and civic life.

Or he might choose to be a Buddhist at home and an American on the job and in the streets, in other words to sustain separate worlds and maintain religious identity as private. Or he might move into American society as an individual, with shifting but relatively weak attachment to any community identity, whether Buddhist, Vietnamese, or American.

All this forces us to ask, as we do in every generation, what it means to be an American. For some, at least at the outset, America is virtually identical with American popular culture, entertainment, sports, and values—with both the negative and positive charge that these may have. One can almost hear the Vietnamese Buddhist or Egyptian Muslim parent warning their children about the dangers of becoming "Americans." But obviously, being American is much deeper than this, as anyone who lives here long enough will, and must, discover. It is a place that allows them the freedom to grow and become someone new, nourished by old roots, not merely transplanted but cross-pollinated by the breezes of freedom. What it means to be American is constantly being expressed in new ways as the fabric of America's peoples changes.

We have already heard some of the voices of new Americans as they articulate the consonance of American ideals with their own faith. Buddhists have found the individual responsibility and the pioneering spirit of American life to be consonant with the spiritual pioneers, the bodhisattvas, the freedom seekers of their own tradition. Jains have stressed the importance of their ancient doctrine of *anekantavada,* the manyness of perspectives on Truth, for the project of pluralism. Hindus have found in America's diversity good soil for the built-in theological diversity of their own tradition, and Muslims have found the constitutional values of religious freedom, human equality, and justice to be supportive of Islamic life. An orthodox Jewish scholar in Boston summed up his experience of America in a way that the others might also agree with: "What America means to an Orthodox Jew is that after centuries of being persecuted precisely because of the way he looks and he eats, he is for the first time in a place where it is perfectly all right for him to wear a black coat and to talk Yiddish, and to teach his children the *aleph-beth* before he teaches them the alphabet. He appreciates it, because America gives him a chance to be himself without losing his humanity."[2]

Bharati Mukherjee, one of America's great immigrant writers of the 1990s, describes herself not as an Indian American but as a regular American of complex multiple identities, just like everyone else here. "You see for me, America is an idea. It is a stage for transformation. I felt when I came to Iowa City from Calcutta that suddenly I could be a new person. . . . Suddenly I found myself in a country where—theoretically, anyway—merit counts, where I could choose to discard that part of my history that I want, and invent a whole new history for myself." The interviewer was Bill Moyers, who went on to ask her, "What is the difference between an expatriate and an immigrant?" Her response flags for us a disposition of the heart that is important as we think about the new "we" in American life.

"An expatriate is someone who is nourished by the old world, whose psychic life is still totally attached to the discarded world thousands of miles away. An immigrant is someone who in psychological, social, psychic ways has made herself or himself over in the new world. Who's accepting the new world as her own." It is more than asking the individualistic economic question, she said. "It is more than asking, What part of the pie is for me? Rather, we should be asking, What kind of America do we want?" This, of course, is the project of pluralism in America, taking the "America" question not as someone else's but as our own.[3]

In these terms, Dr. Havanpola Ratanasara was an immigrant, not an expatriate. For twenty-five years he moved confidently around Los Angeles, his adopted home, in the saffron robes of a Sri Lankan Buddhist monk. His community was, in its narrowest sense, a Sri Lankan monastery and temple, Dharmavijaya Buddhist Vihara on Crenshaw Boulevard, but the circles of his acquaintance and identity widened from there. Dr. Ratanasara was a founding member of the International Buddhist Meditation Center, with programs of Buddhist studies and meditation involving practitioners from across the traditions. He was also a founding member of the Buddhist Sangha Council of Southern California, bringing monks and Buddhist leaders together from the whole spectrum of Buddhist Los Angeles, Asian and native-born American. In his widest circle, he was a founding member of the Interreligious Council of Southern California, one of the oldest and most successful urban interfaith councils in the nation. This avuncular, good-hearted Buddhist leader was somehow born to the American project, constantly networking and involved in voluntary associations. When he died on May 26, 2000, at the age of eighty, the photographs of his life, his cremation, and his funeral were posted on Buddhist Web sites, an indicator of just how far he had traveled with the dynamic pace of the world from his roots in rural Sri Lanka.

Traditional as he was in some respects, Dr. Ratanasara advised Buddhist immigrants to take part in American society and contribute to

American culture. "Go camping," he wrote in an open letter to the Buddhist community. "Visit the many spectacular national parks around the country." He encouraged Buddhists to observe the popular holidays. "Americans as a people celebrate several major religious holidays regardless of their own personal beliefs." So he encouraged Buddhists to look on the celebration of Christmas as the Birth of Peace and to exchange gifts. As for Thanksgiving, "This is not a religious holiday, but a custom started when the first American immigrants, the English pilgrims, celebrated and gave thanks for their life in the New World." His only caveat: avoid being involved in the mass slaughter of turkeys, but have your own feasts of thanksgiving.

Shabbir Mansuri, founder of the Council on Islamic Education, has found his niche as an American by participating actively in the give and take of school curricular issues. "America is not perfect, no. But we have a system that is the most unique system in the world, and it is important to recognize the open system we have here. When I say I am an American, I mean this as a religious matter. Sustenance is given me from this land, not from India. My accountability is as an American. It is a religious matter. When I called home to ask my father about Hindu-Muslim troubles and riots in India in 1992, he said I should be concerned about the riots in LA. What was I doing to help in that situation?"

SEQUELS AND SILVER LININGS

Many stories of vandalism and violence, like the ones we told in the last chapter, have a sequel: the story of new beginnings and new bridges of understanding and cooperation built across the lines of religious differ-ence. We can see these sequels as the silver linings behind the dark storm clouds of civic turbulence. In the long run, these sequels may be more prognostic of our life together than the stormy stories. For example, when the Lao Buddhist temple on the fringes of Rockford, Illinois, was sprayed with rifle fire and then had a pipe bomb land in the front yard, the response from the Rockford Urban Ministries was strong, fast, and visible. Stanley Campbell, a United Methodist minister and director of the Urban Ministries, called his colleagues, called the monks at the temple, and called a press conference to make clear that the religious communities of Rockford welcomed the Lao Buddhists. As Campbell put it, "The media did its job. The lead story on every television channel was 'Christians Welcome Buddhists.' Every media outlet had images of Christian minis-ters with Buddhist monks in front of the image of the Buddha. Our message," he said, "was clear: 'We as Christians surround this building with love and welcome it to the community.'" He said, "To this day, the Buddhists associate with Rockford's Interfaith Council. They helped raise money when the Muslim Community Center was defaced and donated money to fix broken windows at the Jewish temple."[4]

In 1993 I met Nancy Ali, an active member of the Islamic Foundation in Villa Park, a mosque and school in DuPage County west of Chicago. She had grown up as a Christian and became a Muslim in midlife when she married a Muslim man. When we met, Nancy was speaking at a workshop session on interreligious relations during the Parliament of the World's Religions in Chicago about the reasons for her community's involvement in the DuPage Interfaith Network. "Every time there was an uproar in the Middle East or a plane hijacking, paint would be thrown on our cars while we were inside praying or there would be graffiti on the building," she said. The response of the Villa Park Muslim community was to become more proactive. They joined the DuPage Interfaith Network. As Nancy put it, "We wanted to participate in the interfaith network because we felt we were not doing justice to the people we lived among in order to dispel their misunderstanding of Islam."

Now and then, problems still come up in the Villa Park community. In May of 1999 huge chunks of concrete were used to shatter windows of the newly completed $3.6 million mosque. The largest, a concrete block weighing some fifty pounds, was found in the foyer amid shards of glass. According to one of the community leaders, Abdul Hameed Dogar, the mosque had been the target of several attacks in recent months. In the fall of 1998 several windows of the mosque were broken with rocks. One night a few weeks earlier, he said, people stood outside the mosque, screamed, and threw stones while hundreds of worshipers prayed inside. But the attack in May was "the worst we've ever had," he said.

Once again, however, the response to this violence brought people together. A group of people from across the spectrum of Chicago's religious communities came to Villa Park that May to show their solidarity and their joint outrage at such hate crimes. The Muslims recalled what Muhammad had done when there was a dispute about who should carry a sacred stone from a flooded house of worship: they placed it on a sheet and all of them carried it together. In this Chicago suburb, people of many faiths expressed their common cause by carrying the block out together. Hamid A. Hai, a Chicago physician and a member of the board of directors of the Islamic Foundation, remarked, "It takes all of us together to move a stone, and it takes us all to fight religious bigotry and hate."[5] A photograph of the inter-faith group sweeping up the broken glass together was published in the *Chicago Sun-Times*. A representative of Chicago's Board of Rabbis said, "For sixty-five years we have stood amid broken glass, painted swastikas. It has to stop. When evil is on the march, it must be confronted."[6]

In Springfield, Massachusetts, a Methodist minister's first visit to the new mosque was prompted by a headline in the newspaper, "Rocks Thrown at West Side Mosque." In the few months after the new mosque had opened in 1992, it had been pelted with stones on several occasions and eighteen windows had been broken. In March of 1992, young mis-creants showered one of the Muslim leaders with stones as he arrived at the mosque for evening prayers during the month of Ramadan. The Springfield newspaper found out about these incidents and published the story.[7] For many who read the article, it was the first they knew of the Springfield mosque and its troubles. The president of the Springfield Council of Churches called the mosque, called the television station, and brought people from the churches to visit. A local rabbi came forward on television and said that whenever there is a crime of hatred, Jews must speak out forcefully. For the Christians, Jews, and Muslims of Springfield, the rock-throwing incident at the mosque created a new climate of con-cern and new interfaith relationships, and for all Springfield it created a new level of civic awareness. One of the mosque leaders, Kitam G. Khatak, wrote an open letter saying, "Most negative actions probably do have some positive results coming from them. I cannot express how grateful and overwhelmed I am by the support our community has received from the people of West Springfield, Springfield, and the sur-rounding towns. We have received multiple telephone calls from people of different walks of life who were disgusted with this incident."[8]

We have told the story of the vandalism in Pittsburgh, with the smashed images of the Hindu deities. Here too an ugly attack sparked a new level of communication. "It hurt. It hurt people very much," said Swami Chidanand Saraswati, affectionately called Muniji, the spiritual leader of the temple, when he spoke with a Pluralism Project researcher in the early 1990s. Deciding how to react to the violent attack was diffi-cult. Muniji took the lead in a conciliatory approach. "After the vandal-ism, I told the people in the temple, It doesn't matter. It is the duty of religion to tolerate. It happens, you know. There are bad people every-where, in every religion. It is really just fear based upon lack of under-standing. What is our duty? Our duty is not to react."

Under Muniji's leadership, the temple community took a friendly offensive. They posted a Help Wanted sign in front of the temple and hired two teenagers from the neighborhood to cut the lawn. They started yoga and meditation classes at the temple and advertised among people in the community. People from the neighborhood started coming for these classes. When Christmas came around, Muniji sent a letter of friendship, with flowers and a fruit basket, to every family in the neighborhood. Now it is a custom at the temple to send something to the neighbors at both Christmas and Easter. "People started to get to know us and discovered we're not so different. We are not alligators or something to be afraid of." Swami Chidanad's strategy was not responding as a victim but reaching out proactively as a neighbor. It takes courage to take this kind of initiative. But in doing so, the chasms opened by hate crimes can become the sites of new bridge building.

Jewish Americans have had a lot of experience in the strategies of responding to hate crimes and know what it means to speak up forcefully against bigotry and hatred wherever and to whomever it occurs. Interestingly, other religious communities in our new multireligious America have modeled their own watchdog agencies on groups like the Anti-Defamation League, which keeps a watchful eye on discrimination against Jewish people and has extended its watchfulness to other communities as well. Most of the new national Muslim organizations, for example, now have some action-alert network for reporting and responding to discrimination and hate crimes. The most focused is the Council on American Islamic Relations (CAIR). Among Hindus, there is the newly formed American Hindus Against Defamation (AHAD), and for Sikhs there is the Sikh Mediawatch and Resources Taskforce (SMART). The Sikhs described their mission this way: "Our aim is to build bridges of understanding, to help foster greater social harmony and acquaintance of Sikhs as an integral, active part of the wonderfully diverse American community. We believe the Sikh American community has an important contribution to make to all aspects of society, and that this will be promoted by accurate media coverage." Wiccans have their own civil liberties organization, like the Witches League for Public Awareness and the Lady Liberty League. All these groups keep an eye on incidents involving members of their own community. But keeping an eye out for one another is still all too rare. The story of Sacramento's synagogues is one of those rare stories.

In the early morning of June 18, 1999, three synagogues were burned in Sacramento, California. B'nai Israel, said to be the oldest congregation west of the Mississippi, now over one hundred fifty years old, lost its library of more than five thousand books. Knesset Torah Israel sustained fire and smoke damage, and Congregation Beth Shalom was damaged by water from the sprinkler system that discharged when the fire was set. Anti-Semitic flyers left near the synagogues contained allegations about the negative impact of Jews and the "Jewsmedia," blaming Jews for the war in Kosovo and the NATO bombing of Belgrade.[9]

In the days following the Sacramento incident, I received a widely circulated e-mail from a longtime member of Congregation B'nai Israel, Alan Canton. He described his feelings as he phoned members of the congregation in disbelief, and the story he tells begins with "we" in the sense of we who are Jewish. But it is a story of discovering a much wider sense of "we" in the aftermath of this violence.

> We talked about how this could happen in America. What have we done? Why do they still hate us so much? Aren't we good members of the community? We volunteer for local services and donate funds to civic causes. All we ask is to be allowed to worship the way we wish and to be allowed to keep our culture alive in our own homes and temples. . . . And on one night, in my hometown, they firebombed three of our temples. Not in New York or L.A. But here.

The Sacramento story made all the national newspapers and elicited a top-level response. Andrew Cuomo, secretary of the Department of Housing and Urban Development, promised federal loan guarantees for helping to restore the buildings. "Let's make a clear sign that this act has not dissuaded us, this act has not torn us apart, but if anything, has brought us together and energized us." Cuomo went on to say that we "must repair the bonds between us as Americans, just as we must repair the building. And frankly, it is sometimes more difficult to repair the bond because that deals with our hearts and minds, rather than just repairing bricks and mortar."[10]

There is a sequel to this story of hatred, however. It does not erase the story but provides another narrative of response. One of the first groups to speak out about the Sacramento bombing was the Muslim Public Affairs Council (MPAC), based in Los Angeles and Washington, D.C. On June 21, 1999, MPAC released the following statement:

> The Muslim Public Affairs Council (MPAC) condemns the arson attacks against three Jewish synagogues in Sacramento last

Friday, 18 June. "People of all faiths must band together to reject
the intolerance demonstrated by this violent act," said Dr. Maher
Hathout, Senior Advisor to the Muslim Public Affairs Council.

The Council expressed its solidarity with major Jewish organizations in Los Angeles today to reaffirm and fortify dialogue
and cooperation. "It is astounding that in this modern era of
mass communications, we still see the ugly face of hate and misunderstanding," said Dr. Hathout.

All too often in the case of hate crimes, the religious watchdog agencies that bring such incidents to light speak for their own tradition. In
this case, predictably, the Anti-Defamation League spoke swiftly, clearly,
and publicly. Less predictable was the response of Dr. Hathout and
MPAC. The Northern California Methodist Conference, which was
having a conference in Sacramento at the time of the attacks, also
expressed solidarity." For many Jews, this was not business as usual. Alan
Canton tells the story:

> We heard . . . that our weekly Friday Sabbath service would be
> held in the 2000 seat Community Theater. I wasn't going to go
> at first. . . . However I thought that someone should be there to
> "stand up" to the terrorists who would attempt to rend and
> destroy us. Even though it was announced that everyone was
> invited, I figured that there would be 150 or 250 people there,
> enough to fill up a few rows in the huge theater, which has two
> balconies. When I arrived, I was totally surprised. Eighteen
> hundred people from all over our community—Jews, Catholics,
> Buddhists, Hare Krishnas, and members from every sect of the
> Protestant community were there. . . . Never have I seen such
> an outpouring of grief and concern from the community—for
> Jews.

He went on to describe the Methodists, circulating by the hundreds
through the gathering in the community theater. The Reverend Faith
Whitmore stood during the service and spoke on their behalf.

> She reached into her suit coat and took out a piece of paper. "I
> want you to know that this afternoon we took a special offering
> of our members to help you rebuild your temple and we want you
> to have this check for six thousand dollars." For two seconds
> there was absolute dead quiet. We were astounded. Did we hear
> this correctly? Christians are going to do this? On the third

second, the hall shook with thunderous applause, and then people broke into tears.

Standing forth publicly and audibly for one another in times of trial is critical in the emerging world of interreligious relations. It is not such a difficult thing to do, but we do not do it often enough. In the end, it amounts to the most basic act of communication: hearing the pain or hardship of another community and signaling back that you have heard it and are with them.

One final story has become known by its simple slogan: Not in Our Town! It is the story of a civic revolution of awakening in my home state of Montana. On December 7, 1993, a sporting equipment store in Billings, Montana, sent a message on its huge billboard to all who passed on the busy street: "Not in Our Town! No hate. No violence. Peace on Earth." Five days earlier a cinder block had been thrown through the window of a Jewish home displaying a menorah for Hanukkah. It had shattered the glass all over the bedroom of the five-year-old son of Brian Schnitzer, a doctor in family practice, and Tammie Schnitzer, a convert to Judaism. There are only about one hundred Jews in Billings, with a population of over eighty thousand. But as this city prepared for Christmas, the open display of anti-Semitism was a wake-up call for everyone.

This was not the first evidence of a growing climate of hate crimes. Ku Klux Klan literature saying "Jews Out!" "Take Back America!" appeared in the fall of 1992. In September of 1993 a painted swastika was nailed to the door of the small yellow house that serves as the Beth Aaron Synagogue. In the Beth Aaron cemetery, gravestones were pushed over. In November a beer bottle was thrown through the door at the home of Uri Barnea, the Jewish director of the Billings Symphony. These were all single acts of bigotry that one would just as soon forget, but they accumulated. There were no arrests, no suspects. Of course "skinheads" and "neo-Nazis" could be identified in the area. But the problem of prejudice is wider and deeper: for the most part prejudice lives undetected within the minds of seemingly ordinary people. It may not incite a hate crime, but it leads people to silently tolerate these small incidents of hatred. Yet each public expression of hatred makes the next bolder. So when the cinder block landed on Isaac Schnitzer's bed, Billings could no longer ignore this chain of events.

At first some in the police department urged the Schnitzers to remove the menorah as a public indicator of Jewish identity. But Billings had another response. Margaret MacDonald of the Montana Association

of Churches got her United Church of Christ congregation to put menorahs in their own windows—real ones, if they could find them in Billings,
and cutouts if they couldn't. The idea caught on. The *Billings Gazette*
printed a cutout menorah for readers to place in their own windows. For
the first time in its hundred-year history on the Montana prairie, Billings
was decorated for Hanukkah. No one knows just how many homes displayed menorahs. Estimates ran between three and ten thousand. Even at
the minimum end of the spectrum, it was a lot for a city the size of
Billings. On the Sabbath, Friday, December 10, more than one hundred
fifty people turned out for a candlelight vigil, across from Beth Aaron
Synagogue. Billings Central Catholic High School wished "Happy
Hanukkah to our Jewish Friends" on its marquee.

Goodwill aside, that was not the end of the violence. The very night
of the vigil, gunfire shattered windows at Billings Central High School,
and a few days later six more homes displaying menorahs had broken
windows. The solidarity and outrage with which the Billings community
responded was heartening. Some likened it to the response of the king of
Denmark when the Nazi army forced Jews to wear a Star of David on
their person. The king and hundreds of other Danes courageously wore
the star themselves. The public outrage in Billings was swift. "Not in Our
Town! No Hate. No Violence."

Since then, according to Margaret MacDonald of the Montana
Association of Churches, "there have been a few swastikas painted here
and there, but when it happens it is instantly and widely publicized." The
local supermarket carries menorahs now in December—many more than
the small Jewish population would warrant. The display of menorahs has
become a Billings tradition for those in the churches and in the human
rights network. And since Hanukkah of 1993, Christian-Jewish dialogue
has flowered. The United Church of Christ has sponsored a Christian-
Jewish dialogue family camp in the summer. The Montana Synod of the
Evangelical Lutheran Church of America and the Montana Association
of Jewish Communities have entered into a partnership of intentional
dialogue and relationship and have taken a joint trip to the Holy Land.

The problem of hatred and scapegoating is wider and more insidious
than the relation of Christians and Jews. The Montana Association of
Churches has launched a statewide program, Christian Witness for
Humanity, to educate people in the churches about the dangers of the white
supremacist "theology" underlying the hate movement. This so-called
Christian identity theology sees an "inherent evil" embodied in Jews, in

people of color, and in institutions such as the United Nations and even the U.S. government. According to the Montana Association of Churches, this Nazi-influenced theology of the skinheads, the Ku Klux Klan, and the white supremacist militia movement must be named and combated. As Margaret MacDonald puts it, "Our struggle has shifted from Billings alone to much broader statewide issues such as the scapegoating of the hate movement. The struggle continues and is more difficult than ever. "

It should not surprise us that the gaping chasms that open when a community's life is torn by violence become the occasions for bridge build-ing. On the whole, Americans may be a people of laissez-faire tolerance, but when that ethos is violated, we realize that it cannot be taken for granted. A whole new range of social dramas has emerged in which we enact the creation of a new multireligious society. The truth is, Americans have a deep ethos of neighborliness and do not like to see it violated.

NEXT-DOOR NEIGHBORS: MUSLIMS AND METHODISTS

On April 18, 1993, St. Paul's United Methodist Church and the Islamic Society of the East Bay in Fremont, California, broke ground together for a new church and a new mosque, to be built side by side. Six hundred people were there, including the mayor of Fremont. The two communities mingled in an atmosphere of celebration and took turns at the shovel. They named the new frontage road that enters their property Peace Terrace.

That April day they also dedicated the signs that would front the street on their property for months to come: Future Home of St. Paul United Methodist Church and Future Home of Islamic Center and Masjid. The message was a strong and clear witness to passersby that something new in the religious landscape of Fremont was being created here. Eventually, the dome and minaret and the church steeple, side by side, would convey in brick and stone the message of these signs: Muslims and Christians as next-door neighbors. This is one of America's hearten-ing stories of bridge building.

Both the Methodists and Muslims were looking for land before they met each other. This parcel of land between Interstate 880 and a resi-dential neighborhood stood vacant. As Lynn Shinn, chair of the building committee at St. Paul's, recalls, "Someone in the planning department suggested that they change the zoning for this parcel and put in a conve-nience store. The neighbors were notified and they got together and protested. They said this was institutional open space and they wanted the city to build a park. But the city had no money for a park. So the planning department said to the neighborhood, 'We'll give you a year. See if you can figure out how we can make this a park.'"

Lynn recounted the story to us with pleasure. "I was watching this in the newspaper, so I called the Homeowners Association and the Parks and Recreation Department. What if the city were to sell part of it to a church and then use the proceeds to build a park?" Eventually, this was what happened. In 1987 the city held an auction to sell two parcels of 2.1 acres to nonprofit corporations. At the auction the Methodists and the Muslims bought the two parcels of land and suddenly became neighbors, even before they knew each other. "We met at the time of the bidding," said Nihal Kahn of the Islamic Society of the East Bay. "All the people decided it was a great idea. We want to set an example for the world."

"Some people were a bit uptight," said Syed Mahmood, one of the leaders of the Islamic center. "The reason, I would probably say, is they did not know much about us. A lot of times we live in the community and don't even know who lives next door. So we made an effort to reach out to the community, to let them know who we are." In this part of the East Bay, the Muslim community is composed predominantly of immigrants from India and Pakistan, with a smaller number of Muslims of Arab, Southeast Asian, and Afghani origin. The Islamic Society of the East Bay was established only in 1985. The group grew rapidly with new immigration and rented a place for prayers. The space was adequate for daily prayers, but it was too small for Friday prayers or for Eid celebrations in a community that had grown to more than three thousand families.

St. Paul's United Methodist Church has its own diversity, with as many Filipinos as there are Caucasians, and with a significant number of Hispanic and African American members as well. St. Paul's had also grown from a core of committed people to a vibrant church community. Its minister at the time of the groundbreaking was the Reverend Ardith Allread. She said, "Long before I was here, this congregation had been open to interfaith dialogue. We have become more aware of our common heritage with Muslims and of the need for a witness: that people of different faiths and cultures can not only work together, but live together."

From the beginning, the two communities became one in relation to city hall. "Every time we have to go to the city, we go together. We are working as a group. Now we are part of a team," said Syed Mahmood. The Muslims may have been surprised to have the building committee of the

Methodists headed by a woman, but Lynn Shinn, a business supervisor, was the boss on the Methodist side. She said, "We agreed early on that 'united we stand, divided we fall.' In front of the guys at city hall, we're going to be locked elbow to elbow." And so they were. Their first issue was parking. By sharing parking, each could build a bigger facility. Getting to know each other began not by discussing their faith as such, but by planning the landscaping, the outdoor lighting, and the common parking that the communities would share. The agreement between them, with its complex set of easements, was signed on May 31, 1991. Lynn Shinn recalled the signing. "The city of Fremont has married us, for better or for worse, till death do us part. Actually, not even death would do it. The agreement requires that anyone who might buy the property in the future has to agree to this set of easements!"

As the foundations were laid and the two houses of worship began to rise on the property, the Methodists and Muslims worked together on planting and landscaping. Syed Mahmood explained, "It's a good experience for all of us, the Christian and the Muslim community, to prove that yes, we can live together, we can respect each other, and we can take care of each other's needs. We have no choice now. We have to live together in order to have a good and happy environment." Cooperation in working together has, so far, been a success, but real interaction between the two communities will take time. Although the Methodists moved in first, both communities have been busy with the immediate issues of building. On our most recent visit, the Methodist minister, Blake Busick, told us, "I wish we were doing more with activities and joint ventures, but that is just going to take time, because they are just now getting to the point that they are going to start focusing on more than just their building." The Muslims have used the flexible space of the Methodist sanctuary for some of their classes, and the Methodists have visited in the mosque for special events.

In the second phase of construction, the Muslims are building a full-time Islamic school on the site, so the construction continues. In our most recent discussion with Lynn Shinn, she told us how a reporter from the local paper called and asked whether the Methodists were frustrated about the slower progress of the Islamic construction process. "I asked this reporter, 'Do you have any idea what is going on? Do you know how large this building is? Do you know what a mortgage is? Well, the Muslims don't have one. We are green with envy. It is amazing to do what they're doing, and it's all paid for. Their religion will not allow them to borrow money. And they don't have a hierarchy to loan them money."

Both the Methodists and Muslims discovered that the city of Fremont was able to learn from this new challenge. Lynn Shinn told us, "Until virtually yesterday, the city was in the habit of referring to 'churches' in its official statements. If you want to build a 'church,' you have to do this and that. Since we've come along, the city says a 'religious facility' has to do this and that. There are many of us in Fremont now. Churches and synagogues, of course. But now there's a Buddhist temple, a Hindu temple, and a Sikh gurdwara." As Syed Mahmood put it, "The city of Fremont has been very supportive, very cooperative. They actually thanked us for choosing Fremont to build an Islamic center. They see Peace Terrace as being a landmark for Fremont."

The Methodists and the Muslims have different days of worship. Friday noon prayers are the largest for the Muslim community. Sundays, of course, are the main days of worship for the Methodists. For the weekend school of the Muslims and the Sunday school of the Methodists, the communities may even share facilities. "If we ever have the end of Ramadan and Christmas on the same day, we'll have to have valet parking!" said Lynn Shinn as the project was beginning. "And we'll say, 'What a great day!'" As it turned out, Ramadan and Christmas did indeed overlap in 1999 and 2000, and the evening prayers and fast breaking at the end of the day in Ramadan coincided with Christmas Eve services. The parking lot was filled to capacity as Muslims parked for prayers. But Lynn had a solution, at least for this time. "I brought a load of rocks in and we parked here in the field. This was all we did, but it was a major accomplishment, getting us all in."

We have followed the progress of these neighbors for nearly ten years now. Their story, and the story of America's pluralism, is being written, year after year. The years and decades ahead will tell the tale of what a difference it makes to both communities and to the city of Fremont that the Methodists and Muslims share Peace Terrace. In many places in the United States, as we have seen, the proximity of new religious neighbors is striking. Churches and mosques, synagogues, temples, and gurdwaras stand within a stone's throw of one another. More often than not, no stones are thrown. But are there corridors of communication? Bridges of relationship? The potential is real, but interactive engagement of pluralism is just beginning.

PROCLAMATIONS AND PARADES IN
A NEW RELIGIOUS AMERICA

In March of 1999 I went to the opening of the new Durga Temple in Fairfax County, Virginia. The Pluralism Project had followed the development of the temple for some time, from viewing the site to looking at plans and photographs when Ellie Pierce, our senior researcher at the Pluralism Project, visited in 1998. At the time the temple was completed, it was estimated that sixty to seventy thousand Hindu immigrants lived in Fairfax County, more than double the number counted in the 1990 census.[12]

I parked over a mile away in a school parking lot from which shuttle buses were plying the road to the temple. The on-site parking, sufficient for several hundred, was not nearly adequate for the thousands who attended the grand opening. The crowds approaching the temple reminded me of my many visits to pilgrimage temples in India. The doorway of the large temple sanctuary was piled high on either side, not with Indian sandals, but with the Reeboks and Nikes of a new generation of Hindu Americans. I left my Rockport pumps in the pile and joined the crowd that was settling down on the carpeted floor of the sanctuary for the program. As proud parents sat cross-legged on the floor, children competed in reciting Sanskrit hymns in praise of Ganesha, Durga, and Shiva. Those who had steered the community through the building process were thanked and given the honor of receiving the first blessings of the Goddess. Everyone was in a festive mood, snapping photographs and taking home videos.

The part of the program that set me to thinking, however, was the role that Katherine K. Hanley, chair of the Fairfax County Board of Supervisors, played in the ceremonies. She read a declaration on behalf of the board declaring the week of March 21 to 28 "Durga Temple Celebration Week." The declaration began:

> Fairfax, Virginia, is a county where citizens proudly welcome, maintain and blend in the rich and wonderful culture of ethnic diversity, and where all work together in the spirit of friendship and cooperation to positively influence our society. . . . This date marks the inauguration of the first Hindu Temple in Northern Virginia and the first Durga Shrine in the United States of America; and Fairfax County is pleased to join in increased public awareness and community involvement in the celebration of the Durga Temple. We congratulate the members of the Indo-American community on their achievement on this joyous occasion.

This is, of course, a ritual statement of the sort that town councils routinely prepare, but as we assess the changing contours of public life, it strikes me that these are not insignificant ritual occasions. A public official or her assistant has to decide what to say when a Durga temple opens. She needs to find out, to begin with, who Durga is and think about what it means to the county that Durga is now here. That morning, she too arrived and greeted her hosts, left her shoes at the door of the temple, and received a garland of marigolds around her neck. She may be a Christian or a wholly secular person, but she had to negotiate the etiquette of the honor offerings presented to her by the priest on behalf of the Goddess Durga. Should she partake? Eat the sweets, the bananas, offered to the Goddess? I do not know how Katherine Hanley experienced her role that morning as she officially received the Goddess into Fairfax County, but there is no question in my mind that these enactments have a significance quite beyond the merely ceremonial. And beyond whatever it may have meant to the county as a whole, the morning at the Durga Temple surely reshaped Hanley's view of the Hindu tradition.

Part of our task, then, is to observe the many ways in which a public acknowledgment of America's new religious diversity is becoming more visible and frequent. A public ceremonial discourse about a new multireligious America is beginning to take shape. It might be U.S. Representative Nancy Pelosi and Oakland Mayor Jerry Brown participating in the inaugural ceremonies of a new Jain temple in Milpitas, California, or it might be a city council member in Savannah drafting an appreciative declaration on the role of Islam in the history of the city. It might be Ohio governor Bob Taft proclaiming "Khalsa Sikh Day" in Ohio on April 14, 1999, in honor of the three hundredth anniversary of the Khalsa, the brotherhood and sisterhood of initiated Sikhs, members of a religious tradition dating to the sixteenth-century teacher, Guru Nanak, in North India. It might be Governor Jane Hull of Arizona issuing a proclamation for the Buddha's Birthday in May of 2000. No matter who undertakes them, these are not easy assignments. One must say something sensible about the values of the Jain community, the contribution of Muslims to Savannah's life, the significance of the Khalsa for Sikh Americans, and the meaning of the Buddha's birth. These are far from perfunctory tasks, for they are the stretching exercises of a new multireligious nation.

I don't know how it first came about that the month of Ramadan was officially declared in Kansas. It is likely a Muslim community or organization raised the question in the governor's office, as has certainly been the case in state and local governments across the United States. However it happened, Governor Bill Graves of Kansas proclaimed the month of Ramadan in Kansas in 1997. The proclamation itself is an education for non-Muslim Kansans and an articulation of the rationale for a public square that recognizes religious diversity:

> Whereas, The people of the State of Kansas observe many tradi-
> tions of faith; and
>
> Whereas, Each community of faith deserves the recognition,
> respect, and protection of all others; and
>
> Whereas, The citizens of the Muslim faith are sincere and
> proud Americans serving their communities in many capacities;
> and
>
> Whereas, The period of January 10 to February 9, 1997, is
> the holy month of Ramadan in the Islamic calendar; and
>
> Whereas, Muslims observe this month by fasting from sun-
> rise to sunset in order to remind themselves that others hunger,
> and to relieve the hunger of others, to practice discipline through
> self-denial, to nurture family relationships, and to strengthen
> commitment to God; and
>
> Whereas Muslims also commemorate this month of Rama-
> dan by recalling the first revelations of the Qur'an by God to the
> Prophet Mohammed over 1,400 years ago; and
>
> Whereas, Observing the month of Ramadan is one of the
> Five Pillars of Islam; and
>
> Whereas, Many citizens of the State of Kansas are not
> acquainted with the meaning of Ramadan to their Muslim
> neighbors;
>
> Now, therefore, I, Bill Graves, Governor of the State of
> Kansas, do hereby proclaim the month January 10 to February 9,
> 1997, a month of special assistance to the needy, in the spirit of
> Ramadan, and call upon citizens of the State of Kansas to recog-
> nize the dedication and service of Muslims as an important part
> of the fabric of religious pluralism which enriches us all.

I do not know how many people read this proclamation. Was it printed in every newspaper? Or did it disappear into the great plains of the official business of the state of Kansas?

For the most part, alas, we don't pay a bit of attention to official proclamations or city council resolutions. Most of us don't know about them at all unless we are part of the group being recognized. Nonetheless, statements like the Kansas proclamation of Ramadan provide an important grassroots index of the changes that are taking place in America. Were such a statement widely distributed, it could not help but raise the consciousness of Kansans about the Muslim presence in their state. And it must surely have raised the consciousness of the governor or the governor's staff. In a place where one might imagine diversity to have a bad name, Governor Graves called for the celebration of it all in his subsequent 1999 inaugural address. "We are a diverse state," he said. "We are diverse in geography, in culture, in race, in creed and in philosophies. We should celebrate that diversity and ensure that Kansans live in a state where all are treated with fairness and where a common-sense balance directs the process of governance."

Tracking the single, incremental, official landmarks of positive change is as important as tracking the single, incremental incidents of hatred. In this public record, we begin to assemble a richer and more comprehensive picture of who we all are. When Imam Siraj Wahaj opened a session of the U.S. House of Representatives with a prayer on June 25, 1991, or when Hillary Clinton welcomed Muslims to the White House on Eid al-Fitr in 1996, or when the first Muslim chaplain was appointed to the New York City Police Department in 1999, or when both the Republicans and Democrats made a place for a Muslim to offer a prayer at their summer conventions in 2000, or when President Clinton first issued a public proclamation of the Hindu festival of Diwali in the fall of 2000, we the people were photographed, so to speak, in the process of becoming new. As Hillary Rodham Clinton put it on that Eid day in 1996, "This celebration is an American event. We are a nation of immigrants who have long drawn on our diverse religious traditions and faiths for the strength and courage that make America great."[13]

Parades and public festivals are also American events, and they too begin to yield a new portrait of who "we" are. In America's parades, communities present themselves in the streets of the city. An India Day parade in New York City might include an enormous representation of the Goddess Kali, the Divine Mother both in life and death, moving slowly down the canyons of Manhattan skyscrapers. It might also include members of the Vishva Hindu Parishad proclaiming a worldwide Hindu revival, while South Asian lesbian and gay activists celebrate the freedom to be themselves and ardent young protesters stand on the sidewalks to decry the intolerance within the Indo-American community. The Festival of India in Fremont, California, also displays the vibrancy and diversity of

Indian Americans. In August 2000 more than fifteen thousand people lined the streets of Fremont as floats showed off India's regional cultures from Gujarat to Orissa. Perhaps the Bengali float, "Bridging the Gap," made the clearest statement, showing the Golden Gate Bridge linking America with a fishing hut in Bengal. During the 1999 celebration of the three hundredth year of the Sikh Khalsa, the Sikh Day Parade down Broadway in New York included a float of the Golden Temple in Amritsar, while in Washington, D.C., twenty-five thousand Sikhs marched along Constitution Avenue from the Lincoln Memorial to the Capitol. Downtown Los Angeles saw a procession of another ten thousand Sikhs.[14]

One of the most striking parades is the Muslim World Day Parade in New York City. While the parade route may vary, this public procession has claimed a place in the New York calendar since 1986. In 1991, for example, it began at the corner of Lexington and Thirty-third Street, where large sheets of plastic were spread out at the intersection for prayers.[15] A makeshift mosque oriented toward Makkah was created right there on the pavement, with the prayer lines facing one corner of the intersection. Following the community prayers, the parade proceeded down Thirty-third Street, with banners bearing quotations from the Qur'an, floats representing the Ka'bah in Makkah and the Dome of the Rock in Jerusalem, and marchers representing Muslim organizations from throughout the country.

MILITARY MILESTONES

The U.S. military has also seen many landmark changes in the past few years as America has come to terms with a growing religious diversity. Remember that in World War II, the Muslims and Buddhists who served in our armed forces were not even permitted the inscription of their faith on their identification dog tags. They were identified as "other." Today, however, the "other" has a name, and a voice, and a space in America. In 1996 the first Muslim chaplain was sworn into the corps of navy chaplains. M. Malak Abd al-Muta' Ali Noel Jr. finished a master's degree at the University of Chicago as part of his qualifications to be the navy's first Muslim chaplain. By the year 2000, there were nine Muslim chaplains. Now the armed forces are working with an Islamic institution in Leesburg, Virginia, to provide a place where Muslim chaplains can gain accreditation. The official seal of the chaplains' corps has changed too, modified to include the crescent along with the cross and Star of David.

In January 1999 Muslims held an observance of the Night of Power at the U.S. Pentagon. The Night of Power, Laylat al-Qadr, is the night toward the end of the fasting month of Ramadan when Muslims observe the holy event of the revelation of the Qur'an. Perhaps no acreage in the U.S. is more associated with military power than the land occupied by the Pentagon, but the gathering here had to do with a very different kind of power, that of divine revelation. Deputy Secretary of Defense Dr. John J. Hamre was asked to speak, and he began by expressing the "tremendous honor" this was for him. "I am a Lutheran in my own religious background and not a Muslim," he said, "so I cannot fully appreciate how important this Night of Power is for all of you. But I can understand why this Night of Power is deeply important to you, because I am a religious person myself." He went on to quote the opening lines of the Constitution, "We the people of the United States . . . " which express ideals and fundamental values of liberty, justice, equality, and opportunity. These ideals, he concluded, are "grounded in our shared community of faith."[16]

In his remarks at the Pentagon, the deputy secretary recalled the difficult history of Muslim presence in the U.S. military. He recalled that not until 1998 was the first military mosque opened, in Virginia at the Norfolk Naval Base. "I heard the story about what it took to establish a mosque in the naval base in Norfolk, where Muslims had no place to worship until just a few years ago. Through those fights—large and small—our men and women are being faithful to the ideal expressed in our Constitution, recognizing the religious freedom and rights of our own soldiers, sailors, airmen, and Marines. It is the same ideal expressed in the Holy Koran: 'O mankind, I created you from a single pair and made you into nations and tribes that ye may know each other, not that ye may despise each other.'"

Knowing each other is not necessarily easy, even, perhaps especially, in the tight quarters of a military base. During the winter of 1996, a chaplain from the U.S. Air Force called the Pluralism Project to talk about the challenges of chaplaincy in a multireligious air force. He was interested in using parts of our CD-ROM, *On Common Ground: World Religions in America,* as an educational tool on military bases. He had seen firsthand the changing religious composition of America and confessed that the armed forces needed the kind of informational and educational resources that would help them address this rapidly changing situation.

In the course of working with this air force chaplain, I became increasingly aware of the special no-nonsense support for religious pluralism that is unique to the military. A manual prepared by the

Department of Defense puts the obligation of the armed forces succinctly:

> The military chaplaincy is perhaps the most critical point at
> which the interests of religion and those of public institutions
> intersect. Schools may need prayer, but they can educate without
> it. Christmas and Hanukkah can be publicly celebrated without
> creches or menorahs on the courthouse lawn. But the Armed
> Forces are unique institutions, maintained for a unique purpose
> under unique conditions, and the constitutional right of service
> men and women to engage in the free exercise of their religion
> cannot be provided without a chaplaincy. Here religion and a
> major public institution come inexorably and necessarily togeth-
> er. But there are problems in bringing them together that have
> never previously been faced.[17]

Probably the most controversial issue the military has faced has to do
not with Islamic religious practice but with the accrediting of Wiccan
chaplains. At Fort Hood, Texas, the nation's largest military base, the Fort
Hood Open Circle became the focus of a nationally publicized controversy when it became known that the Wiccan group was meeting on the
base and had been given a campsite for its gatherings. Its high priestess,
Marcy Palmer, from the Sacred Well Congregation of San Antonio, had
impeccable credentials. She had been in the military police and had been
named soldier of the year. Even so, U.S. Representative Bob Barr, a
Georgia Republican, was outraged by the news. "Please stop this nonsense
now," he demanded. "What's next? Will armored divisions be forced to
travel with sacrificial animals for Satanic rituals? Will Rastafarians
demand the inclusion of ritualistic marijuana cigarettes in their rations?"[18]

Captain Russ Gunter of the Armed Forces Chaplains Board spoke of
the controversy at a Pluralism Project symposium in 1999. "We facilitate
the free exercise of religion to all people in the military," he said. "We
don't minister only to people who wear our label." He explained that all
requests for religious accommodation are adjudicated by the commanding officer, and in this case the commanding officer stood firm on religious accommodation for the Wiccans and the Department of Defense
backed him up. Captain Gunter explained, "There have been Wiccans
accommodated in their religious needs for over twenty years in the military. This was not the first time a Wiccan group has operated on a military base. It was the first time there was a media article about it. I tell you,

my phone rang for six weeks after the article appeared, and the answer I gave each time was very simple: The Department of Defense does not evaluate, judge, or officially sanction any religious faith. It is not up to us to judge religions or to make a list of denominations or religious groups that are officially acceptable. It is up to us to ask what is the religious need of the member. That's the important thing." Captain Gunter recalled a typical phone call, this one from a Roman Catholic woman who asked, "Are you telling me that the Department of Defense recognizes Wicca?" I responded to her, "It may come as a shock to you, madam, that the Department of Defense does not recognize the Roman Catholic Church." Recognizing religious traditions in any evaluative sense is not the business of military chaplaincy. Providing for the practice of religion is, and every chaplain needs to be prepared to see to the needs of the men and women at his or her base.

So Wiccans too have the right to have "Wicca" engraved on their dog tags as their religious preference and have won the right to wear Pentagrams. High priestesses now lead circles from Fort Polk, Louisiana, to Fort Wainwright, Alaska, and the spring equinox and the full moon are observed by members of the armed forces from Okinawa to Florida. The *Washington Post* reporter who broke the Fort Hood story summed it up this way: "Far from clashing cultures, the Wiccans and the military coexist cheerfully. . . . To the Army, the Wiccans are part of a proud tradition, proof that 'people with different religious beliefs are all working together successfully.'"[19]

PARTICIPATING IN PUBLIC LIFE

In June 2000 I attended the annual convention of the American Muslim Council in Washington, D.C. In the hotel conference center, the council hosted three days of presentations and discussions on issues of Muslim participation in American public and political life. It was not like the huge Labor Day conventions of the Islamic Society of North America, fifteen thousand strong, with forums, families, and festivities. Rather, this was the focused gathering of Muslim activists who are involved, locally and nationally, in American public life. The conference center was filled with tables on political issues, such as the AMC campaign to register voters for the 2000 election. I had visited the AMC offices in downtown Washington before, but this was the first time I had come as an observer to the convention.

The first person I met was Josefina Ahmad, a Muslim woman, from Portland, Oregon. It was her first time too, and she had come as a representative of the AMC chapter in Portland, which had formed just ten months earlier. Born in the Philippines, she had lived in Portland for twenty-six years. Now, she said, Muslims in Oregon were beginning to be heard. "This year, the governor of Oregon met with Muslims for the first time. We were invited to a bring-your-own lunch in the governor's office. And this year, the *Daily Oregonian* staff has met with Muslims on a regular basis, and we have been discussing issues Muslims are concerned about, which issues should be in the paper." Sister Josefina was one of several speakers on the topic of starting an AMC chapter in their area.

Dr. Khalid J. Qazi, from the Western New York chapter in Buffalo, presented the strategies of the AMC in Buffalo. "We have to be able to say in one sound bite what we are about. Our sound bite was the 'Empowerment of American Muslims.' That's what we're about. There are ninety-three county boards in our county. We want to find people who are willing and qualified to sit on these boards. We can't be congressmen all at once, but we can be councilmen and councilwomen. Now, for the first time, we have two Muslim commissioners in city government: an assistant commissioner of the Equal Employment Opportunities Commission and an assistant commissioner of Youth Services."

The discussion session was a lively exercise in grassroots politics. One speaker took the microphone and said, "The key point is that the American political system is accessible, and we should be bold enough to enter it." Another spoke of the importance of outreach programs in the community, "The AMC can't be known in our communities if we aren't doing any programs in and for the community. We need to make our presence felt, whether in interfaith activities or civic activities." An African-American Muslim from Alabama took the mike and announced that he was currently a candidate for mayor of the city of Selma. A representative of the group on Long Island described the "candidates' nights" that his mosque sponsored, inviting candidates from both parties to the Islamic center to speak about the issues.

From an American standpoint, the menu was heartening fare. And it was not limited to old-guard members of the immigrant generation. Second-generation Muslims made their own contribution. One had been an intern at the White House, another in the Justice Department, another was a Texas delegate to the Democratic National Convention. An entire group of young interns were part of the Muslim Student Network summer program, living together in an old house near the Capitol and spending their days as interns on the Hill. They made time every day for prayer and discussion. Former interns, graduates of this program, now had jobs as staffers in Congress. One young woman was now the senior legislative counsel for a congressman, and her advice was strong and clear. "Politics is more open here than anywhere in the world," she said, "But we have to make sure we are not hypocritical in the way we deal with issues. That means we have to acknowledge problems, say with issues of justice, in some countries in the Muslim world, as well as in our own. And we also have to get over our extreme suspicion. Just because something happens that is adverse to our community does not mean people are sitting in a room somewhere and saying, How can we be mean to the Muslims. It's just not like that." And she had one more piece of advice to the young interns there—and to the activists of her parents' generation. "We can disagree. Even among ourselves, we can disagree on many issues. But we don't walk away from a disagreement." Later, over supper, I spoke with Mrs. Iffat Qureshi, the pioneer in Muslim summer camps in California who is now the godmother, so to speak, of the young interns program in Washington. "Kids growing up in this country are our best ambassadors." Having heard the whole range of the afternoon's speakers, I couldn't agree more heartily.

Pluralism requires two-way traffic. Yes, Muslims are increasingly recognized in American public discourse, in city council pronouncements, and in the snapshots at the White House that are part of our political iconography. But more than this, Muslims increasingly participate in American public life. Participation is, after all, the critical element in the construction of a pluralist, democratic society. As I sat and took notes on the panels that weekend in Washington, I thought often of the ways in which the imam at the Islamic Center in Quincy, Talal Eid, would urge his congregation toward participation in American society, something about which many new immigrants were very hesitant. "As Muslims living in North America," he had said on the previous Eid al-Fitr day, "we have the moral responsibility to present Islam and to contribute to the success of this country. We Muslims should be in front of the march, leading, rather than simply reacting to events."

Participation of newcomers is not always readily embraced by old-timers, especially if it begins to open new territory and involve the renegotiation of influence and power. This became clear in the summer of 1999 when Congressman Richard Gephardt nominated Los Angeles Muslim activist Salam Al-Marayati, executive director of the Muslim

Public Affairs Council, to the National Commission on Terrorism. A Muslim who had grown up in the U.S., Salam is part of a progressive new generation of American Muslim leaders. His nomination seemed an astute and wise one. The Muslim Public Affairs Council under his leadership had spoken forcefully on the subject of terrorism, condemning acts of terrorism associated in any way with Islam. For example, in August 1998 when the U.S. embassy in Nairobi was bombed, Al-Marayati wrote in an op-ed piece in the *Los Angeles Times,* "Like Christianity and Judaism, Islam has no room for terrorism."[20]

The story of Salam Al-Marayati's nomination made the national news, however, only when it was withdrawn. On Saturday, July 10, 1999, the *New York Times* carried the story, "Muslims Denounce Gephardt for Withdrawing a Nominee." We learned from reporter Laurie Goodstein, "Since he made the appointment in June, Mr. Gephardt, a Missouri Democrat, had been severely criticized by Jewish organizations that portrayed Mr. Al-Marayati as a terrorist sympathizer cloaked in a moderate's guise." In the same article, a representative of the American Jewish Committee was quoted as saying that, of course, Muslims deserve a place at the table, but "this table is not just any table." The accusations focused on statements Al-Marayati had made that were critical of the state of Israel, though well within the spectrum of general American opinion, and offered what critics deemed a sympathetic explanation of the sources of terrorism, an interpretation that Salam Al-Marayati denied, pointing to his long record of work against terrorism and violence. After his nomination was withdrawn, the ten-member commission to review national strategy for preventing and responding to terrorism had no Muslim member and, more important, no member deeply knowledgeable about the Muslim world, including the part of the Muslim world that is now America.

Muslims across the country were discouraged by this development. A coalition of American Muslim and Arab-American organizations wrote, "We hoped that Mr. Al-Marayati's appointment might mark a turning point for our communities, inasmuch as it would represent a sign of inclusion and recognition of the role that American Muslims and Arab Americans should rightfully play in the shaping of critical policy issues." They were also concerned, however, about the negative impact this would have, not only on Muslims, but also on American democracy and pluralism. "Exclusion of any group from the national discourse is contrary to America's values and detrimental to its national and international

interests."[21] Some charged that the Jewish voices blocking the appointment amounted to a new form of McCarthyism.[22]

Some of this discouragement was repeated in the 2000 election season, when campaign contributions of prominent Muslims were returned,
both by Hillary Rodham Clinton and by George W. Bush, because these
contributors were accused of supporting the radical Islamic group
Hamas. Even more offensive, however, was New York Representative
Rick Lazio's accusation that these contributions amounted to "blood
money" and his use of what many called anti-Muslim baiting in his New
York campaign for the U.S. Senate. A national coalition of religious leaders represented by the Interfaith Alliance responded in strong terms:

> For too long, Muslims in America have been excluded from par-
> ticipating in civic dialogue on public policy matters because of
> negative and erroneous stereotypes. Indeed, if working with
> Muslims makes one vulnerable to the allegation of working with
> terrorist sympathizers, civic leaders will be less likely to engage
> members of the Muslim faith community. The accusations and
> activities in New York perpetuating stereotypes about Muslims
> are receiving national attention and contribute to a national
> paranoia about the intentions and activities of Muslim leaders in
> communities across our nation.[23]

Despite the turbulence of these incidents, the 2000 election marked
a major turning point in Muslim politics in the United States. Muslims
really were, perhaps for the first time, actively involved. Muslim delegates
attended especially the Democratic convention, and Muslim leaders met
with both candidates as the campaign heated up. Muslims were watching
the debates and heard one of their key issues explicitly mentioned by
George W. Bush: the issue of secret evidence used to detain suspects
without public charges made. Muslims were publicly outraged at the allegations and the anti-Muslim baiting, but tumult and disappointment
aside, there is no doubt Muslims were involved in this election.

It is not as easy to follow the increased participation of Hindus and
Buddhists in American public life. This is largely because these traditions
have not developed an infrastructure for doing so and probably will not
because their forms of organization are inherently less structured. They
do not tend to identify as a single religious community, with common
interests that would lead to position taking, lobbying, and activism. This

does not mean Hindu and Buddhist communities are not involved but rather that they are not involved explicitly as Hindus and Buddhists.

American Hindus, for example, tend to define their public participation through their Indian-American identity and not specifically as Hindus. Yash Agarwal, who in 1996 challenged twelve-term Republican incumbent Benjamin Gilman in New York's Twentieth District and gained a remarkable 38 percent of the vote, spoke just to this point at a Harvard forum. "I was born of South Asian parents, I am a lover of curries, and I'm glad I'm a Hindu, but that doesn't define me. We need also to break from our past." It would be unusual to see a movement organizing Hindus as such to vote, to lobby, or to discuss American political issues, and that fact tells us a great deal about the nature of the Hindu tradition, its domestic and temple-focused activities, and its tremendous diversity. Nonetheless, political awareness is on the rise among immigrants from India. The India Abroad Center for Political Awareness maintains a Washington office and sponsors a summer internship program on Capitol Hill for young Indian Americans. It does not have a religious element, but it does bring young Hindus, Jains, Sikhs, Muslims, and, no doubt, ardent young secularists into the sphere of public life as Indian Americans.

In a recent issue of *India Abroad,* an immigration attorney commented on how Indian Americans are increasingly moving from the status of green card holders to that of citizens. One of the reasons, he thought, was the increasing zest for political participation on the part of Indian Americans. This seems to be what Gopal Khanna, an Indian-American Minnesota businessman and Republican activist, affirmed in an interview in *India Today:* "Many of us have been smitten by the bug of political participation. We are also becoming aware that we cannot meaningfully participate in American politics unless we are citizens—and vote." In the 1996 elections a twenty-seven-year-old Democrat, a graduate of St. Olaf College and the University of Minnesota Law School, Satveer Chaudhary, won a seat in the state House of Representatives and, in 2000, in the Senate, the first Asian American to be elected to state office in Minnesota. In Hollywood, Texas, Bala K. Srivinas, called Beekay, served for many years as city councilman and then mayor. "America is a culture in evolution," Yash Agarwal said. "It has evolved. It is evolving." Clearly Hindu Americans are evolving too, and part of that evolution is the beginnings of political involvement in the life of the United States but not under an explicitly Hindu banner.

Participation cannot be gauged in political terms alone, however. Voluntarism rises with the sense of involvement in the life of a community that extends beyond one's own identity group. The Hindu Students Council at the University of Michigan maintains a section of the highway outside Ann Arbor, picking up litter on its part of the road, just like the Rotary Club or the Garden Club. A Sikh gurdwara in Florida holds periodic blood drives for the American Red Cross. A Hindu temple in New Jersey sponsors a free walk-in health clinic one weekend a month. A Buddhist community in western Massachusetts sponsors an annual peace walk sixty miles from its hilltop temple to Springfield, where they join African Americans in commemorating the end of slavery in Juneteenth celebrations. Along the way, they beat a drum and chant the Lotus Sutra and gather a crowd on each town green to hold a public speak-out on racism. All of this is part of the move toward participating in the issues that shape the nation.

Many of America's new Buddhists point to "engaged Buddhism" as an index of the public consequences of personal transformation. Far from being a private path toward enlightenment, socially engaged Buddhism stems from the seed of the bodhisattva vow: to save not only oneself, but all sentient beings. So engaged Buddhists are involved in all kinds of movements: Joan Halifax at Upaya in Santa Fe, New Mexico, has dedicated her Buddhist work to hospice care, being with the dying. Bo Lozoff in North Carolina is part of a growing movement of prison ministry, bringing the Buddhist practice of freedom and inner transformation to those in prison.

We have already met Bernard Tetsugen Glassman Roshi, from the Zen Center of New York, who launched a successful commercial bakery in Yonkers as a community development venture. For the non-Buddhist unemployed he provided training, skills, and jobs, and for Buddhist practitioners, baking became another zendo, where the arts of moment-to-moment attention could be refined. Although zazen sitting was still important, Greyston became a living laboratory for the "work-practice" that Glassman sees as key to making Zen a part of ordinary life.

To address homelessness, the Greyston Family Inn purchased an abandoned building and converted it into eighteen apartments for homeless families. The Greyston Builders was formed for training and jobs in construction. A former convent on property high above the Hudson River was purchased and converted into Maitri House, a residence for people with AIDS, and the House of One People, an interfaith meeting place where people of different religious traditions are able to meet together to grapple with the racial, cultural, and religious divisiveness of society. When Glassman finally left New York to work on developing the Zen

Peacemaker Order, he left a distinctive style of Zen, adapted to the social consciousness of American voluntarism. A teacher, says Glassman, is "a thief who steals our preconceptions." Glassman surely steals the preconceptions of anyone who thinks of Zen as sitting in silence in a beautiful, leafy retreat.

Engaged Buddhism has learned much from Asian activist teachers such as Sulak Sivaraksha, the Thai founder of the International Network of Engaged Buddhists, and Thich Nhat Hanh, who told his monks forty years ago in Vietnam that they could not choose between meditating and helping the war-shocked suffering people at their door: they had to do both. Both the Fo Kuang Buddhism of the Taiwanese teacher Hsing Yün and the Soka Gakkai International of Daisaku Ikeda also emphasize this-worldly involvement in social and civic affairs. But by far the most vocal proponents of engaged Buddhism in the United States are the American-born Buddhist activists of groups like the Buddhist Peace Fellowship and the Zen Peacemaker Order. The Buddhist Peace Fellowship is at the forefront of peacemaking and environmental movements, building on a deep awareness of human interrelatedness and the web of being that connects all humankind with the ecological system. It remains to be seen how much this vision of Buddhist responsibility will touch and influence immigrant Buddhist communities.

THE PARLIAMENT OF RELIGIONS

Imagine, against this burgeoning multireligious background, the 1993 Parliament of the World's Religions in Chicago, convened to celebrate the one hundredth anniversary of the 1893 parliament. Over seven thousand people gathered from every religious tradition imaginable, from all over the world, and, more surprisingly, from all over America. The 1893 parliament, held as part of the Chicago World's Fair, was the first interfaith event ever to be convened in America. It had been organized by American Christians, Reform Jews, and Unitarians, all seized with the idea that an era of universalism in religion was dawning. Indeed, the parliament was dubbed the "morning star of the twentieth century." Ten thousand invitations were sent out all over the world, and an astonishing panoply of religious leaders appeared. We have met some of them in these pages, such as the Hindu Swami Vivekananda from India and the Buddhist reformer Dharmapala from Sri Lanka, who came to Chicago from halfway around the world.

One hundred years later, cities like Chicago were part of an increasingly global village that had seen unprecedented currents of immigration, the development of transnational movements, and the creation of increasingly cosmopolitan urban areas. As planning for the 1993 centennial began, the Chicago-based planners realized that "the basic elements of a parliament are already here. We just don't know each other and we rarely talk together."[24] They set out to change that, and people of the world's religions in Chicago began to get to know each other. As the months passed, they formed fourteen "host committees," including a Hindu host committee, a Buddhist one, a Muslim one, a Zoroastrian one, and so forth, each charged with arrangements for an international delegation. While one hundred years earlier delegates from these traditions had been the guests of the parliament, now Chicago-based immigrants were the hosts.

The 1993 parliament was much more than a public gathering of international religious leaders. Indeed, the most striking thing about it was that it marked, for the first time, the public manifestation of America's own religious plurality. It was the coming out, so to speak, of a new religious America that would have been inconceivable one hundred, or even thirty, years ago. One hundred years ago, the strains of "Praise God from Whom All Blessings Flow" filled the hall during the opening ceremonies. But in 1993 the procession entered the hall to the polyphonic chanting, the cymbals, and the drums of the Drepung Loseling Tibetan Monks, invoking the forces of goodness.

During the opening ceremonies, I flattened myself against the wall as the procession moved into the great ballroom of the Palmer House. I was lucky to find standing room at all. Each delegate in the procession wore a large-print name badge, and I watched a new religious reality pass before my eyes. This was in the early 1990s, and even I had not seen such a manifestation of our diversity. The saffron-robed Buddhist monks who led the procession came not only from Thailand but from temples in Los Angeles, West Virginia, and suburban Chicago. The red-turbaned Jains were from Elmhurst, Illinois, and Cypress, California; the Zoroastrians came from Houston and Hinsdale, Illinois. The Hindu delegation included, along with prominent swamis from India, scores of Hindus from Baltimore, Minneapolis, and Pittsburgh. There were Muslims from Jordan and Indonesia, but many more were from Lombard, Northbrook, and Skokie in the Chicago suburbs. Ranks of Sikhs came from the Sikh Religious Society of Chicago and the Richmond Hill gurdwara in Queens. Of course, Protestant ministers and Catholic priests and cardinals attended from across the spectrum of Christian communities, and Jewish scholars and rabbis passed by also, although relatively fewer, as the opening ceremonies were held on the Sabbath. And then I saw all the people who had not attended the parliament at all one hundred years ago: Taoists from the Fung Loy Kok Institute of Taoism in Denver, who would lead tai chi and chi kong exercises each morning during the coming week, representatives of the Covenant of the Goddess and Wicca, who would spend their sessions that week explaining their traditions to audiences of sympathizers and skeptics. A Baha'i youth, part Yaqui and part Apache, wore fringed leggings, a feathered headdress, and a band of jet black paint across his eyes. He was part of the most multiracial of all delegations, those of the Baha'i faith, whose North American landmark temple was just north of downtown Chicago in Wilmette.

Finally, representatives of the many Native peoples of the Americas—Navajo and Crow, Lakota and Ojibway—took the stage to offer a blessing of the four directions, the opening ritual act of the parliament. Recalling that one hundred years ago America's Native peoples had not been invited at all, except as curiosities on the exhibition grounds of the world's fair, Burton Pretty On Top, a Crow from Montana, said, "One hundred years ago we were not present because we were not invited." Recently, he had climbed into the Big Horn Mountains in Montana. "I fasted without food and water. I did this, my brothers and sisters, not for me, but for you. I love you."

The message of the parliament of 1993, from beginning to end, and ritually enacted in dizzying proportions, was, "Here we all are." And this message was indeed a remarkable one. In a day when global gatherings and international meetings are increasingly commonplace, the most remarkable thing about the 1993 parliament was the fact that it was also local. It grew from the soil of today's Chicago and from the new reality of the American Midwest. If not a single delegate had come across the Pacific or Atlantic, the magnitude and diversity of the 1993 parliament would have remained virtually intact.

During the parliament, an Assembly of the World's Religious Leaders met for three afternoons in a large hall of the Art Institute of Chicago. The hall was set up, not as an auditorium, but in tables of eight, as if for a dinner party. Each table was set with the name cards of the participants, and around each table for two hours each afternoon, we were to discuss the "Global Ethic," proposed by the council and its drafter, the theologian Hans Küng. At one table the Sikh guru Yogi Bhajan sat between the

Reverend James Forbes of Riverside Church in New York and Azizah al-Hibri, a feminist Muslim law professor. Across the table were Louis Farrakhan, the Korean Zen master Samu Sunim, and the Crow leader Burton Pretty On Top. At another table sat the Dalai Lama, with Theodore Hesburgh from Notre Dame University, and Mehervan Singh of the Sikh community in Singapore. At my table were Hans Küng himself, the Jewish feminist theologian Susannah Heschel, and the Islamic philosopher Seyyed Hossein Nasr. Our discussion was rich and energetic. We disagreed, of course, over the religious basis for ethical directives such as not killing. We might cite the Qur'an or the Ten Commandments or Jesus' Sermon on the Mount; Hindus and Jains might speak of the divine soul within or the bad karma that would accrue from taking a life. The point of our discussion was not to gloss over the differences but to ask whether out of these differences a common standard of action might still be possible and a global sense of accountability for action might be achieved. In the end, the Global Ethic was signed, an enunciation of principles so basic they seemed too little, but so profound that if people truly adhered to them, the world would never be the same.

One hundred years earlier, when the parliament opened, a replica of America's Liberty Bell tolled ten times for each of the great religions present. Swami Vivekananda said, "May it be the death knell of fanaticism." But, as we know, in the twentieth century fanaticism did not die. One hundred years earlier, the chairman opened the first session saying, "Henceforth, the religions of the world will make war not on each other, but on the giant evils that afflict humankind." But, as we know, in the twentieth century wars continued apace, and religions continued to supply fuel for the strife. One hundred years earlier, a Jewish speaker, Rabbi Emil Hirsch, said, "The day of national religion is past; the God of the universe speaks to all mankind." And yet to the very end of the twentieth century, the alliance of religion and nationalism continued to challenge and vex many parts of the world. One hundred years earlier, Charles Bonney set forth the purpose of the colloquy as "to inquire what light each tradition might afford the other." And that challenge remains too, as people seek to know how the light of truth, as they see it, illumines the lives of neighbors of other faiths.

For me, the tables of eight became yet another image of the kind of encounter that is ours from now on as Americans. In addition to building our bridges, we will have to find the "tables" where we might articulate our faith and our commitments sincerely and without illusions about our differences. It is not a matter of finding common faith that is acceptable to all, watering down one's own faith so it will be palatable to someone of another faith. Far from it. It is, rather, a matter of engaging the diverse faiths in the challenges of building a society of neighbors rather than strangers. It is a matter of finding the tables in our civic, public, and private lives where we can meet.

AMERICA'S INTERFAITH MOVEMENT

One thing the parliament of 1993 made crystal clear: interfaith understanding is not simply a global matter today but a local matter—in Chicago and in every other major city in the United States. The interfaith agenda, in all its complexity, is now America's agenda. Religious diversity here in America is a reality. It is here to stay. It is not going to disappear. So how can we make the most of our diversity in the service of our communities? This is the question. Over the past ten years the interfaith movement, with all its vivid variety, has gained extraordinary momentum all over the United States.

Who would have imagined that Columbia, South Carolina, would be the home of a vibrant interfaith coalition bringing Hindus, Muslims, Baha'is, Christians, Jews, Unitarians, and Buddhists together for dinner and dialogue? A local Columbia newspaper reporter challenged her readers this way:

> Maybe you're the sort of person who believes your religion to be true and any deviation from it to be false. You would rather not know about anyone else's beliefs because they might weaken yours. If so, Partners in Dialogue is not for you. But if you have even a glimmer of interest in what other people believe, this you should know: People are meeting regularly in the Midlands to talk about God and Humanity and how we mortals figure into this wonderful and wicked world.[25]

When I arrived in Columbia in February of 1996, I was taken to the home of the Dr. and Mrs. Sinha, a Hindu couple hosting a dinner for representatives of all of Columbia's religious traditions, the core group of Partners in Dialogue. I had not been to Columbia since my days at Smith College in the 1960s when I had participated in a student exchange with Benedict College in Columbia and spent a week living, for the first time in my life, in a completely African-American environment. Just as

Columbia had been a revelation to me in 1965, so was it a new experience for me thirty years later. After dinner, along with Muslim, Hindu, Sikh, and Presbyterian dinner guests, I took off my shoes and stepped into the part of the Sinha's family room where the home shrine was located. Mrs. Arunima Sinha explained each of the deities, each of the photographs of religious teachers. She spoke of the prayer life of the Sinha household, how they would gather here before work and at the end of the day. Here I was in the heart of Dixie, feeling as at home as I might feel in the heart of Delhi. My stereotypes were falling fast.

In the next few days, as the guest of Partners in Dialogue, I learned more about the faces of Columbia, South Carolina, than I imagined possible. In addition to participating in their annual conference, I visited the newly completed Hindu temple and an old, established African-American mosque. I heard from young people who had organized an interfaith youth group. Some of the people there were experiencing their own internal dialogues. One woman described herself as an Irish Catholic married to a Muslim, raising her children as Muslim but also influenced by Hinduism. When she had a severe back problem, her physician, a Chinese chiropractor, suggested she take up the form of Hindu yoga called hatha yoga. Rather than dwell on differences, she confessed, "I am filled with the joy of these confluences."

Reflecting on the whole experience, Nancy Songer from the Baha'i community wrote,

> Picture a Hindu woman in a sari, a Muslim woman—her hair and arms covered by her garment—a Jewish man, a black Christian man, and a white Christian woman in a business suit. Now picture them seated around a table in a Jewish synagogue. They're eating food each has brought to the occasion, and they're smiling and frowning, talking and listening, earnestly. They are members of the Partners in Dialogue interfaith group, and they're sharing with each other something that is very close to their hearts—their religious beliefs. And when they part, there are warm farewells and sincere smiles and "I'll see you next time."[26]

Since 1992 the Partners in Dialogue program has provided a place for people of many faiths to meet and discuss such topics as "Life After Death in Our Religions," "Myths and Facts About Our Respective Religions," and "Women's Roles and Status in Our Religions." When the group began in 1992, it planned to celebrate the one hundredth anniversary of the 1893 World's Parliament of Religions. But after the 1993 centennial, the group continued. Partners organized worship open houses for communities to visit one another's places of worship and participate as guests in one another's services. They organized potluck dinners and evening discussion groups. They formed educational teams to provide help for public school teachers on holidays and holy days, and they offered themselves as interreligious panels to churches and synagogues. In 1998 Columbia hosted the national meeting of the North American Interfaith Network (NAIN), bringing representatives of interfaith councils together from all over the United States and Canada.

Partners in Dialogue is one of hundreds of new instruments of interfaith relationship that are bringing an entirely new discourse to the public square. This is not advocacy for the agenda of a single religious community but the combined advocacy and energy of many. Each of these councils has its own origins and distinctive shape. Partners in Dialogue is unique because of its relationship to the Religion Department of the University of South Carolina. In most cases, a council of churches has expanded to include clergy or representatives of other religious traditions at the table. For example, the Lincoln, Nebraska, Council of Churches became the Lincoln Interfaith Council in 1989 when members of the Jewish, Buddhist, Native American, and Baha'i communities joined. These moves are not always without controversy. When the Buddhists joined the Boulder, Colorado, Interfaith Council in the 1980s, it precipitated heated discussion among the members. So too in Woburn, Massachusetts, just a few years ago when the new Hindu community in town was proposed for membership. New Buddhist and Hindu members usually evoke a positive consensus, but you can count on controversy with communities thought of as "new religious movements," such as Scientologists or members of the Unification Church. Here in Boston, the International Society for Krishna Consciousness, the neo-pagan Earth Spirit Community, and the Scientologists are regular and active participants in the Boston Clergy and Religious Leaders Group for Interfaith in Dialogue, but their presence in many of America's interfaith councils would be extremely controversial. Each interfaith initiative has to decide, sooner or later, who should be at the table and on what basis. And each has to think carefully about who is excluded and why.

The logo of the InterFaith Conference of Metropolitan Washington, D.C., is an open book, and the description of the qualifications of groups for membership include having a recognized scripture and a monotheistic belief structure. The conference began in 1978 with Protestants, Catholics, Jews, and Muslims, all the usual "people of the book." But when the Hindus applied for membership, the organization's policy was a real challenge. Hindus have a great variety of scriptures and are not, in the common Western view, monotheistic. Undaunted, the Hindus formed the United Hindu-Jain Temples of Metropolitan Washington and wrote an application focusing on the oneness of the many gods and the preeminence of the Bhagavad Gita as the Hindu scripture. In the age-old assimilative pattern, they had to shape their self-presentation to the established pattern of the dominant majority. Interestingly, the varieties of Buddhists in the Washington, D.C., area still have not found a way to participate.

Over the years, Washington's InterFaith Conference has dedicated itself to public education and action on issues of concern to people of all religious traditions—AIDS, drugs and violence, hunger, homelessness, gun control, and racial and ethnic polarization. Its most successful public event is its annual interfaith concert in which cantors and muezzins, Korean church choirs and Yiddish folk singers, Presbyterian bell ringers and Hindu *bhajan* singers all participate in a service of sacred music. Both the work and the music build relationships, and over the years these relationships have made a difference. Following the Hebron massacre in March of 1994, the InterFaith Conference proved the importance of these networks of trust. Within the week, it was able to sponsor an interfaith service at the Muslim Community Center in Silver Spring, where one of the speakers was the chair of Washington's Board of Rabbis. Without a fifteen-year history of interfaith cooperation, this would have been unthinkable. Having such bridges of trust in place is essential, for when the water rises it is often too late to create them. The Reverend Clark Lobenstine, director of the InterFaith Conference, explained, "In the charged atmosphere following a crisis like Hebron there is no time to build trust. Both the rabbi who spoke and the Muslim Community Center told me they simply had to trust the fact that they trusted the InterFaith Conference."

In Dallas the Religious Communities Task Force was launched because the two hundred schools of the Dallas Independent School District needed them. Students speaking seventy languages and practicing dozens of religious traditions posed a challenge for the school district. In addition to Protestants, Catholics, and Jews, the task force included the Cambodian Buddhist Association, the Baha'i community, the International Society for Krishna Consciousness, the Lao Buddhist Temple, the Dallas Hindu Association, the Islamic Association of North Texas, the

Sikh Study Group, the Jain Society, and the Vietnamese Buddhist Association. One of its first tasks was to compose a reference sheet for teachers and administrators, detailing for each religious tradition the medical restrictions, special diet or foods, particular dress or clothing, observances or rituals during school hours, and possible absences due to high holy days. This quick reference guide notes, for example, that Hindu students "may have a paint-like mark on the forehead from morning worship, usually done with family at home." Hare Krishna male students "may have a small tail of hair at back of the head." Some Jewish boys "may wear a skull cap and/or a fringed undergarment under their shirts." Muslims may not receive injections during Ramadan. Jain students are not only strict vegetarians but also do not eat root plants. As the Dallas interfaith group demonstrates, in no place are the challenges of a new religious America felt more immediately than in the schools.

The Interfaith Association of Central Ohio was sparked by a historic event: the summit meeting between President Ronald Reagan and Soviet Premier Mikhail Gorbachev in 1985. As hosts of the summit, the religious leaders of five faiths in Columbus, Ohio, planned an interfaith service to pray for peace. It attracted more than six hundred people and marked the beginning of the Interfaith Association, a group that now includes Baha'is, Buddhists, Christians, Hindus, Jews, Muslims, and Sikhs. Not surprisingly, cognizance of international events often spurs us to reach out to people of different faiths. During the war in the Persian Gulf, for example, there was a burst of local bridge building as many Jews and Christians discovered for the first time the mosques in their own cities. Beginning with interfaith services to pray for peace, new alliances of Jews, Christians, and Muslims came into being.

America's largest shopping mall, the Mall of America in Minneapolis, receives nearly forty million visitors a year, and it has an interfaith council all its own. America's suburbs have been called the "interfaith frontier," for they include a burgeoning multireligious population but lack a Main Street, a discernible public square. Except, of course, the mall. The Mall Area Religious Council (MARC) wants to capitalize on the magnetic power of the mall. It says it hopes to provide a spiritual presence in the mall, to embody the values of understanding, community, dignity, respect, and peace, and to provide opportunities for interfaith dialogue, study, and conversation between people of differing cultures and traditions. A spokesman for the council, John Chell, says, "There cannot be peace in the world until there is growing harmony and understanding among people of

world religions, beginning in local communities. The people in our neighborhoods are often ahead of the religious leadership in desiring practical
opportunities for dialogue and understanding of their neighbors' faith and
world religions. People of all faiths working together significantly will be a
major goal and task of religion in the twenty-first century. The market-
place will become a consequential arena for this development through
interfaith ministries such as the Mall Area Religious Council—MARC."[27]

Along with newcomers like the interreligious council of the Mall of
America, the interfaith terrain also includes old pioneers, like the
Interreligious Council of Southern California. It is one of America's
oldest councils, dating back to 1969, when it began as a Catholic, Jewish,
and Protestant organization. Now it includes Baha'i, Buddhist, Greek
Orthodox, Muslim, Sikh, and Hindu representatives as well. It has worked
for the appointment of a Buddhist chaplain in the state senate and
backed Sikh men in their fight to serve as police officers in Los Angeles
while wearing the required beard and turban. When the Hsi Lai
Buddhist temple in Hacienda Heights was stalled in five years of zoning
battles, the Interreligious Council came to their aid. It helped Los
Angeles Muslims and Thai Buddhists in zoning battles as well. Over the
years, the religious leaders of the council have come to know one another
personally. Roman Catholic Monsignor Royale M. Vadakin, one of the
founders, insists that its strength lies in this network of relationships.
"You cannot institutionalize trust and friendship," he said. The channels
of communication forged by friendship are brought powerfully to bear on
issues as they arise in southern California. In the wake of the L.A. riots of
1992, it was the Interreligious Council that was able to organize a massive
"Hands Across L.A." demonstration, bringing people of all religious and
cultural communities together to form a human chain, joining hands for
more than ten miles across the broken heart of central Los Angeles.

The statements of purpose crafted by these new organizations
amount to new community visions. They are, in a sense, village versions
of a global ethic. The women and men who provide the energy for the
interfaith movement are the dreamers and visionaries of a multireligious
society, and the words they have forged make heartening reading. In
Columbus, Ohio, the council pledges "to create an interreligious community based on understanding, friendship, and trust" and "to educate
members and the general public about the practices and beliefs of different faith traditions." The InterFaith Conference in Washington, D.C.,
speaks of "enabling diverse religious leaders to speak with a unified moral

voice on racial and ethnic polarization, death penalty, drugs and violence, AIDS, church-state relationships, infant mortality and other issues." The Madison Area Interfaith Network in Wisconsin states that it is "founded on the belief that all religious groups have the individual's and society's best interest at heart and work toward a more perfect union of humankind and higher forces; that these groups should not compete, but work together for better human relations." It insists that most prejudice stems from ignorance and that "knowledge and understanding will be the cornerstone of a positive society in the next century." The Marin Interfaith Council north of San Francisco declares, "Without understanding, differences create fear. With understanding, differences enrich life." Of course, the task of translating these visions into a new set of community relations is tested on a regular basis in local controversies and as worldwide controversies make their impact felt locally.

America's college campuses have also become primary sites for new dynamic forms of religious life, especially in the multitude of private schools that were founded by Christian denominations. Gone are the days when the white-steepled Protestant church at the edge of the campus could suffice as a campus ministry center. Even adding the Catholic Student Center and the Hillel Center simply does not provide adequate coverage for the diversity of religious traditions that are now present among students on every major American campus. The last decade has seen campus ministry programs scrambling to assess the new situation and design alternative forms of chaplaincy. Wellesley College was one of the first to decenter the Protestant chaplain and create the post of dean of religious life to preside over a multireligious campus ministry and a student Multi-Faith Council. When Diana Chapman Walsh was inaugurated as president of Wellesley in 1994, the official celebration included prayers in seven languages by Baha'i, Christian, Hindu, Jewish, Muslim, and Native American students. The event was one of the first collegewide services planned by the student Multi-Faith Council. The Reverend Victor Kanzanjian, dean of religious life, explained the concept. "We do not believe in offering a universalized program where people's particular experience is replaced by some kind of common language which primarily seeks not to offend. We are, rather, encouraging people to speak in their own voices and explore in depth a particular religious tradition or spiritual path. This allows us to then explore together that which we also hold in common."

Wellesley's Multi-Faith Chaplaincy has been called "a spiritual revolution on campus," and this spiritual revolution is happening on campuses all across America. At Chapman University in California, the new Wallace All-Faiths Chapel has made interfaith dialogue a cornerstone of its ministry. Originally a Disciples of Christ college, Chapman University believes that "a person can be deeply committed to and passionate about his or her faith, and yet respect and even hope to learn from those who believe differently." The All Faiths Chapel creates the space on campus for this to happen. Similarly, in Baltimore at Johns Hopkins University, the new Bunting-Myerhoff Interfaith and Community Service Center, opened in the spring of 1999, provides a home for Baha'is, Buddhists, Baptists, Muslims, Hindus, and Jews to hold services, plan events, and meet one another.

SPIRITUAL DIALOGUE

While people of many faiths may share social and civic agendas that bring them together in the public square, sometimes for heated discussion and debate, they also recognize the common thirst for deep springs of spiritual wisdom and practice. The most energetic and significant spiritual dialogue in recent years has surely been the Christian-Buddhist dialogue and to some degree the Jewish-Buddhist dialogue as well. It would be impossible to count the number of Christians and Jews who have been involved in various forms of Buddhist meditation practice in the past three decades. For some, and I include myself here, it has enriched their religious lives as Christians, while for others, sometimes referred to as "new Buddhists," it has become the center of their religious lives. The Christian-Buddhist or Jewish-Buddhist dialogue may take place between two people or within a single person. There is profuse evidence of this spiritual dialogue in virtually every city in America, but let me tell you about a single event that gives us a sense of the new frontiers that are being explored.

Gethsemani Abbey, the Benedictine Trappist monastery in the "knobs" of Kentucky, was the home of the influential Trappist monk Thomas Merton, whose books on spiritual life made him just about the best-known Christian monk of the twentieth century. In the 1950s and 1960s, from his hermitage at Gethsemani, Merton became a spiritual traveler, corresponding and meeting with Buddhist monks and writers. In 1968 he left the abbey for the first time in decades and traveled to Asia, where he met the Dalai Lama and in Thailand met an untimely death, accidentally electrocuted in his hotel room.

Merton would have smiled his characteristic broad smile to see the chapter room of Gethsemani Abbey in late July of 1996. There on the facing benches where the Trappist monks have gathered for nearly one hundred fifty years sat a congregation of Buddhist and Christian monks and nuns for a week of exchange and discussion. It was what Merton once called "the dialogue of those who have kept their silences." This spiritual dialogue was sponsored by Monastic Interreligious Dialogue, a network of monks and nuns throughout the United States who, with the blessing of the Vatican, have dedicated themselves to a series of intermonastic exchanges with Tibetan and Japanese Zen Buddhists. I had been something of a token Protestant on the Board of MID and was happy to be included in this meeting. As a college student, I had corresponded with Merton and hoped to meet him someday at Gethsemani. I was deeply upset by Merton's death in 1968, and until the summer of 1996 I never made it to Gethsemani.

This was the first time Buddhists had ever sat in the chapter room at Gethsemani, and it was no ordinary congregation of Buddhists. The Dalai Lama, who had met with Merton at Dharamasala in 1968, led the delegation. As he entered the chapter room, he always bowed especially deeply to the Venerable Mahaghosananda, patriarch of the Cambodian Buddhist community, often called the "Gandhi of Cambodia." Others in the room came from the spectrum of world Buddhism today—from Burma, Thailand, Sri Lanka, Korea, Taiwan, Japan, and the United States.

In the rich landscape of interfaith dialogue this was a historic meeting. Never before, in the U.S. or anywhere, had such a diverse gathering of monastic Buddhists and Christians taken place. Carefully prepared presentations on the practice of prayer and meditation and the stages of spiritual development were given by those who have themselves maintained a prayer practice or a meditation discipline. Those who spoke, spoke from experience.

In Thomas Merton's journal, which he kept on that fateful trip to Asia, he dreamed of the circumstances of such an encounter. "The exchange must take place under monastic conditions of quiet, tranquility, sobriety, leisureliness, reverence, meditation, and cloistered peace."[28] Merton struggled with monastic renewal, and it is clear that he thought the traditions of Asia, especially Buddhism, would play an important role in that renewal. However, much about the Buddhist community that gathered in Kentucky would have surprised Merton. Many of those present, though Asian by birth, were now leaders of substantial new immigrant communities—an immigration that had not yet become visible in Merton's last days. Here at Gethsemani were monks like the Venerable Chuen Phangcham of Wat Dhammaram in Chicago and nuns like the Venerable Yi-Fa of the Hsi Lai

Temple in Hacienda Heights, California. The flourishing of homegrown American Buddhism also would have surprised and fascinated Merton. When Merton left for Asia, Joseph Goldstein was still a Peace Corps volunteer in Thailand, and Sharon Salzberg was a twenty-year-old studying with the Vipassana meditation master Goenka in India. Seated now in the chapter room amid monks from Asia, Joseph and Sharon represented the first flower of America's Buddhism, now the resident teachers of the largest meditation center in America, the Insight Meditation Society in Barre, Massachusetts. While theirs is a full-time vocation of teaching and practice, they are not monastics, and they speak for the distinctive turn toward lay leadership in American Buddhist communities.

"Practice" was one thing everyone in the room had in common, the common realization that it all begins by cultivating the ground of one's own life. Again and again, the topic turned to a question American Buddhist Judith Simmer Brown raised on the first day, "How do those of you who are Christians work with anger? How does your practice address the arising of anger?" Both Buddhists and Christians agreed that it is all too easy to "practice" the habits of mind we know well: impatience, blame, anger, self-deception, pride. But what are the specific ways in which one can begin to turn from these habits of mind and develop new ones?

The Dalai Lama described to us a form of meditation practice in which we were to visualize the suffering of a person one has encountered. By beginning to grasp the suffering of another, one's own heart may begin to open to compassion. His words resonated strongly for those whose spiritual schooling had been Christian. Steering into the heart of suffering is central, though in very different ways, to both Christianity and Buddhism.

With a smile as sublime as many imagined that of the Buddha to be, the Cambodian Mahaghosananda responded to any question about Cambodia's anguish with the insistent words of the Dhammapada, "Hatred can never be overcome by hatred, but only by the power of love." Then Mahaghosananda, who had experienced the Killing Fields of Cambodia, and the Dalai Lama who had fled Tibet, listened attentively to Brother Armand Vieilleux from the Cistercian order in Rome, who had recently gone to Algeria to retrieve the headless bodies of the monks of the community of Our Lady of Atlas, slain and beheaded by Algerian rebels. Brother Armand read out the words written by Dom Christian shortly before his throat was slit, words addressed to those he knew would kill him. They are words of thanksgiving for the blessings of his life with the Muslim people of Algeria, "And also you, the friend of my final moment, who would not be aware of what you were doing. And yes, I also say this 'Thank you' to you, in whom I see the face of God." The sense of communion between Christian and Buddhist monastics here ran deep. Religious communities, even monastic communities, may have many differences, but in the depths of spiritual life, there are simply no borders.

A NOT-SO-RANDOM ACT OF KINDNESS

Today the interdependence of the world in which we live is mirrored in localities all over the world. The global is mirrored in the local. Our economies and our political fortunes are interdependent. Our search for solutions to the environmental crisis, the AIDS crisis, or the crisis of growing economic disparity reminds us perpetually of our interdependence, of the simple, inescapable fact that none of us can go it alone, not anymore. Our religious traditions and communities of faith are also interdependent. The very visions we strive for and the dreams we dream cannot be tackled alone, for there is no such thing as alone, not anymore. And yet, our communities of faith are still way behind banks, business, and telecommunications in learning how to relate to one another globally and locally; our religious communities still lag behind in what the Indian philosopher Radhakrishnan called "the supreme task of our generation," which is "to give a soul to our growing world-consciousness."[29]

Both the global and the local dimensions of this task were very much on my mind on August 27, 2000, the day the Millennium Peace Summit of Religious Leaders convened at the United Nations. As I sat in the U.N. General Assembly through an hours-long litany of prayers from around the world—far too many prayers in my view—my mind was on a local drama underway in Boston. That morning, the *Boston Globe* had announced encouragingly, "A Not-So-Random Act of Kindness: Vietnamese in Roslindale Invite Vandals to a Picnic." It was about the response of a temple community I knew well, Temple Vietnam in Roslindale, to a growing number of vandalism attacks. The temple is located in a mixed African-American, Caribbean, and Latino area, at the end of a tree-lined, dead-end residential street, in a building that was formerly a mechanic's garage, then a day-care center. I had visited the temple several times over the past few years. It is the oldest of Boston's three Vietnamese Buddhist temples, and its leaders, Dr. and Mrs. Chi Nguyen, are dedicated to community building among the first-generation Vietnamese immigrants and their American-born children. It is a wholly unprepossessing cinderblock structure, but a fringe of flowers inside the chain-link fence makes it clear that this is a place people love, and a graceful seven-foot-tall white image of Kuan Yin, the female bodhisattva of compassion, stood welcoming near the front door. Across the tracks is the Archdale public housing project.

In March the trouble had started. Some kids had started throwing rocks at Kuan Yin and had taken a chunk out of her shoulder. A few weeks later, they broke into a toolshed on the property, got hold of an ax, and smashed the image of the bodhisattva to bits. Then they broke a skylight and tried to break into the sanctuary. Inquiring around the Archdale projects, the police investigators found those responsible—a fifteen-year-old troublemaker and some other boys from the neighborhood. But after considerable discussion, the temple community did not want to press charges. In a spirit of compassion, they wanted to reach out to the surrounding community and bring people together. Their response to the crime was to schedule a community cleanup and cookout for September 9 and invite the people in the surrounding neighborhood, including the boys who had been responsible. As Dr. Chi Nguyen, known to everyone as Dr. Chi, put it, "We believe that small acts of kindness can have a big impact. You sow a small seed, and maybe it will grow into beautiful flowers." Captain William Parlon of the Boston police commented, "They want to demonstrate kindness and compassion to people they feel are misguided."[30]

Back in Boston, I found that Dr. Chi had written to Boston's Mayor Menino and asked for his support and help in putting together the neighborhood event. A planning committee had been formed, including people from the mayor's office, the Boston Police Department, the Healthy Roslindale Coalition, the Sacred Heart Parish a few blocks away, and the Archdale housing project. The spirit of the Vietnamese community was contagious. They had stuffed neighborhood mailboxes with a flyer that read "Neighbors Together" and invited everyone to "Come Join Your Neighbors." The day would begin with coffee and doughnuts at Temple Vietnam, include a three-hour neighborhood cleanup, and end with a cookout and a tour of Temple Vietnam. The flyer was translated into Vietnamese, Spanish, and Haitian Creole.

When September 9 came, I drove over to Roslindale for the cleanup and cookout. People joined in from all over the community. A group of four nuns from the Sisters of St. Joseph of Boston spent the morning filling trash bags in a vacant lot, side by side with young people from the housing project, citizens from the Healthy Roslindale Coalition, and members of the Temple Vietnam congregation—all wearing palm-leaf hats in the midday sun, the graceful pointed hats we associate so readily with images of the rice fields in Southeast Asia. The state representative, Liz Malia, spent the morning there. "We did more than we thought we'd do. These streets look a lot better," she said. "But the real work was the connection we made with each other."

The real work *was* the connection: the vandals were there too. The ringleader, a handsome young man named Angelo, wore a Vietnamese palm-leaf hat and worked for three hours on the cleanup. Dr. Chi told me how he had met Angelo that morning, introduced by a police officer. "I embraced him and told him he was welcome here," said Dr. Chi. "I told him, 'You're famous now, and so I have a job for you.' Angelo looked very nervous, and then I said, 'Your name is Angelo, so I would like you to be our temple angel-guardian. You should watch out for us, and protect us like a guardian angel.'" Everyone at the cookout that day seemed to know that Angelo was the culprit, but in a strange way, Angelo was also a hero. Having entered a community whose sanctity he had violated, he was nonetheless the center of positive attention in a way that may well have been new for him.

By the time I met Angelo after the cookout, he was in the temple. The temple tour was over, and the open, carpeted sanctuary was filled with neighborhood children, rolling and roughhousing in their stocking feet. Angelo flipped one of his younger protégés onto the floor in a wrestling move, and then his attention was arrested by a Vietnamese man who stood before the altar, his palms pressed together in prayer. Angelo rose to his feet and quietly approached the altar behind the praying man. When the man's prayers were concluded and he turned to leave, Angelo stepped forward, grinned, and stretched out his hand to shake the hand of this new neighbor. When we began to talk, I asked Angelo how he had felt when he got up this morning and came over here to the temple to meet these people for the first time. "I felt pretty nervous," he admitted. "But if I had known before what they were like, what I know now, I would never have done it."

Making themselves better known to their neighbors was also a lesson for the Vietnamese Buddhist community. Over the nine years they had worshiped there, the Buddhists had been admittedly reticent. "We are a quiet people," said Dr. Chi. "We did not want to be seen as aggressive or imposing our belief on anyone." But the vandalism inspired a new initiative in letting people know who they are. In the weeks before the cleanup and picnic, they prepared a brochure about the temple to distribute in the Roslindale community. It begins, "We are your neighbors at Roslindale's Temple Vietnam on Bradeen Street. We would like to introduce ourselves." It tells the neighbors a bit about Buddhism, the Buddha, and this temple community, and it invites neighbors to annual celebrations and Sunday services.

Dr. Chi and many of the members of Temple Vietnam are followers of the Vietnamese monk Thich Nhat Hanh, whose writings on the practice of mindfulness meditation in everyday life have attracted spiritual seekers the world over. Violence is rooted in suffering, and only kindness can begin to touch the suffering in another. The flyer includes a brief statement of this deeply held view: "The central teaching in Buddhism is that by learning to live lives of loving-kindness and moderation, we can heal much suffering in the world—both our own and that of all other beings." Looking to the future, the image of the Kuan Yin will be replaced with a new marble image now on order from Vietnam, and one of the sisters told me that her Catholic parish is taking a special offering to help with the new image. The seeds of kindness sown by the Buddhists of Roslindale have already begun to sprout.

NEW IMAGINED COMMUNITIES

America's religious diversity is here to stay, and the most interesting and important phase of our nation's history lies ahead. The very principles on which America was founded will be tested for their strength and vision in the new religious America. And the opportunity to create a positive multireligious society out of the fabric of a democracy, without the chauvinism and religious triumphalism that have marred human history, is now ours.

Some would argue that our religious minorities are numerically small, at least compared to the full 281 million Americans. All told, they may account for less than 10 percent of the population. But the news of this new century is that they are here, and in numbers significant enough to make an imprint on every city in America. Numbers do not matter. Our founders did not bequeath to us a nation based on majority rule in matters of religion, but a nation based on free exercise of religion for all people. This legacy comes to us more than two hundred years later as a gift, the value of which those who packaged it for us could scarcely have imagined.

Working from their own religious principles, the founders had sense enough to see that religious freedom was part and parcel of who we are as human beings, created to be free. They had vision enough to see that whoever arrogates to oneself or one's community full truth and authority in matters of religion is usurping the authority that, they believed, was God's alone. They constructed, in effect, a theology of religious freedom and constitutional democracy in which even their own faith would have no pride of place. They could have given no greater gift to the multireligious society that is ours now, in the twenty-first century. Those who want prayer in school classrooms, the Ten Commandments posted on public buildings, or the Christmas crèche displayed at city hall will need to look again at the value and meaning of this gift. The twin principles of religious freedom and nonestablishment provide the guidelines for something far more valuable than a Christian or Judeo-Christian nation. They provide the guidelines for a multireligious nation, the likes of which the world has rarely seen. The presence of new neighbors of other faiths in America has made crystal clear both the strength of these twin principles and the need to reaffirm them again and again.

The relationship and interdependence of religious communities is now enacted in both local and global sites—Hindus and Christians in India and Indianapolis, Muslims and Jews in the Midwest and the Middle East, Vietnamese Buddhists and their Christian neighbors in a rundown neighborhood of Roslindale. The stories of interreligious encounter remind us that religions are not fixed entities but dynamic movements, as people of all faiths struggle to address brand new questions about such problems as AIDS, the degradation of the environment, the rising tide of youth violence, and the presence and vitality of other communities of faith. These stories of interreligious encounter also remind us that our religious traditions are multivocal, that no one speaks for the whole, that we argue within our traditions about some of our deepest values, and that newfound alliances may be made across the political and religious spectrum. These stories of encounter also remind us that our religious traditions are constantly influencing one another. Christians encounter the faith of new Sikh or Hindu neighbors and rethink what it means to speak of God's universal providence. A Lutheran undersecretary of defense finds himself addressing Muslims at the Pentagon on the holiest night of the Muslim year. Jews in Sacramento find new allies in Christian and Muslim neighbors in the wake of synagogue burnings. Christians in Roslindale find themselves moved by the spirit of forgiveness they find in their Vietnamese Buddhist neighbors.

Benedict Anderson, in *Imagined Communities,* investigates the ways in which nations imagine themselves. Even when citizens do not know one another, he writes, "in the minds of each lives the image of their communion."[31] For a nation like the United States to imagine itself anew as a multireligious nation is, for most of us, our deepest challenge. It means being able to imagine in our mind's eye the mosque in Toledo and the Hindu temple in Nashville as we think of America. It means including in our image of "we the people" the Muslim members of the armed forces, the Hindus of Fairfax County, the Sikhs of Cleveland, and the Buddhists of Roslindale. And for new immigrants, it means including themselves in their own mental image of America.

The story of the new religious America is an unfinished story, with both national and global implications. The chapters of the story are still being written in cities and towns all over the country. Whether the vibrant new religious diversity that is now part and parcel of the United States will, in the years ahead, bring us together or tear us apart depends greatly on whether we are able to imagine our national community anew. And the fate of a vibrant pluralism in the U.S. will have an important impact on the fate of religious pluralism worldwide. The ongoing argument over who "we" are—as religious people, as a nation, and as a global community—is one in which all of us, ready or not, will participate.

NOTES

1. Michael Walzer, *What It Means to Be an American: Essays of the American Experience* (New York: Marsilio Publishers, 1992).

2. Rabbi Arnold Weder, *Pluralism Project Interview,* 1996.

3. Bharati Mukherjee, Public Television interview with Bill Moyers. Many of the ideas she also expresses in "American Dreamer," *Mother Jones,* January-February, 1997.

4. Stanley Campbell, "Prayers, Not Firebombs," *Response* (The official publication of the United Methodist Women) 32, no. 10 (November 2000): 19. The saga of this temple in Rockford is also recorded in a superb documentary film, *Blue Collar and Buddha,* produced by Katin Johnston and Taggart Siegel.

5. Arthur J. Pais, "Inter-Religious Group Cleans Up a Vandalized Mosque in Chicago," www.rediff.com/news/1999/may/25us4.html.

6. *Chicago Sun-Times,* May 24, 1999.

7. Ray Kelly, "Rocks Thrown at West Side Mosque," *Springfield Union-News,* March 26, 1992.

8. Kitam G. Khatak, "Islamic Society Official Deplores Vandalism at Mosque," Letter to the Editor, *Sunday Republican,* May 3, 1992.

9. *Los Angeles Times,* June 19, 1999. The crime was later alleged to be linked to members of a group called the World Church of the Creator, which has engaged in persistent verbal rhetoric on the dangers of racial and religious minorities in the U.S.

10. *San Francisco Chronicle,* June 23, 1999.

11. *Los Angeles Times,* June 20, 1999.

12. *Washington Post,* Religion section, March 20, 1999.

13. "Muslims Join Clintons to Celebrate Eid-ul-Fitr," *The Minaret* (March 1996).

14. Sukhjit Purewal, "Dev Anand Grand Marshal at Fremont, Calif. Parade," *India Abroad,* August 18, 2000; *Washington Post,* April 11, 1999; *Los Angeles Times,* April 10, 1999.

15. See Susan Slyomovics, "The Muslim World Day Parade and 'Storefront' Mosques of New York City," in *Making Muslim Space in North America and Europe,* ed. Barbara Metcalf (Berkeley: University of California Press, 1996), 204–16.

16. The speech is available on-line at the U.S. Department of Defense Website: www.defenselink.mil/speeches/1999/c19990115-depsecdef.html.

17. U. S. Department of Defense, *The Churches and The Chaplaincy* (Washington: U.S. Government Printing Office, 1998), 121.

18. Hanna Rosin, "An Army Controversy: Should the Witches Be Welcome?" *Washington Post,* June 8, 1999.

19. Hanna Rosin, "An Army Controversy: Should the Witches Be Welcome?" *Washington Post,* June 8, 1999.

20. *Los Angeles Times,* August 13, 1998.

21. The statement was published on the Website of The Muslim Public Affairs Council (www.mpac.org).

22. Omar Ricci, "Al-Marayati Should Have Remained Nominee: McCarthyism Tactics Apparently Still Alive, Well in U.S. Congress," *Daily News of Los Angeles,* July 16, 1999.

23. "National InterFaith Religious Leader Denounces Anti-Muslim Religion Baiting in New York Senate Race." News release of statement by the Rev. Dr. C. Welton Gaddy, executive director of the InterFaith Alliance. (http://www.inter-faithalliance.org/newsroom/press/001031.html).

24. Ron Kidd, one of the Parliament organizers, personal communication, September 1993.

25. Jennifer Graham, *The State,* February 7, 1993.

26. Nancy Songer, "Partners in Dialogue Aid Religious Understanding," *The State,* February 7, 1993.

27. John M. Chell, Mall Area Religious Council (http://www.fas.harvard.edu/~pluralism/affiliates/portratit.html).

28. Naomi Burton, Patrick Hart, and James Laughlin, eds. *The Asian Journals of Thomas Merton* (New York: New Directions Books, 1973), 313.

29. S. Radhakrishnan. *Eastern Religions and Western Thought* (New York: Oxford University Press, 1959), vii–viii.

30. Ric Kahn, "A Not-So-Random Act of Kindness: Vietnamese in Roslindale Invite Vandals to a Picnic," *Boston Globe,* August 27, 2000.

31. Benedict Anderson, *Imagined Communities* (London: Verso, 1983), 6.

BIBLIOGRAPHY

Abdalati, Hammudah. *Islam in Focus*. Indianapolis: American Trust Publications, 1975.

Abdul-Rauf, Muhammad. *History of the Islamic Center*. Washington D.C.: Islamic Center, 1978.

Abe, Masao, ed. *A Zen Life: D.T. Suzuki Remembered*. New York: Weatherhill, 1986.

Abraham, Nabeel and Andrew Shyrock, eds. *Arab Detroit: From Margin to Mainstream*. Detroit: Wayne State University Press, 2000.

Abraham, Sameer Y. and Nabeel Abraham, eds. *The Arab World and Arab-Americans: Understanding a Neglected Minority*. Detroit: Wayne State University, Center for Urban Studies, 1981.

Adler, Margot. *Drawing Down the Moon*. Boston: Beacon Press, 1986. (Revised and expanded edition).

Agarwal, Priya. *Passage From India: Post 1965 Indian Immigrants and Their Children*. Palos Verdes, CA: Yuvati Publications, 1991.

Ahlstrom, Sydney E. *Religious History of the American People*. New Haven: Yale University Press, 1972.

Albanese, Catherine L. *America, Religions and Religion*. Belmont, CA: Wadsworth Pub. Co., 1981.

Arrington, Leonard J. and Davis Bittons. *The Mormon Experience: A History of the Latter-day Saints*. New York: 1979.

Austin, A.D. *African Muslims in Antebellum America: Transatlantic Stories and Spiritual Struggles*. New York: Routledge, 1997.

———. *African Muslims in Antebellum America: A Sourcebook*. New York: Garland, 1984.

———. *African Muslims in the New World: A Sourcebook for Cultural Historians*. Boston: Garland, 1981.

Barboza, Steven. *American Jihad: Islam after Malcolm X*. New York: Doubleday, 1994.

Barrows, John Henry, ed. *The World's Parliament of Religions*. 2 Vols. Chicago: The Parliament Publishing Company, 1893.

Bartlett, John Russell, ed. *Letters of Roger Williams, 1632–1682.* Rhode Island: Narragansett Club, 1874, Vol. 6.

Bellah, Robert. *The Broken Covenant: American Civil Religion in Time of Trial.* New York: Seabury Press, 1975.

Beversluis, Joel D., ed. *A Sourcebook for the Community of Religions.* Chicago: Council for a Parliament of the World's Religions, 1993; Revised and enlarged, 2000.

Blavatsky, Helena P. *The Key To Theosophy.* London: The Theosophical Publishing Society, 1893.

Bloom, Allan. *The Closing of the American Mind.* New York: Simon and Schuster, 1987.

Boorstein, Sylvia. *It's Easier Than You Think: The Buddhist Way to Happiness.* San Francisco: HarperSanFrancisco, 1995.

———. *That's Funny, You Don't Look Buddhist: On Being a Faithful Jew and a Passionate Buddhist.* San Francisco: HarperSanFrancisco, 1997.

Boucher, Sandy. *Turning the Wheel: American Women Creating the New Buddhism.* San Francisco: Harper & Row, 1988.

Braybrooke, Marcus. *Pilgrimage of Hope: One Hundred Years of Global Interfaith Discovery.* Trinity Press, 1992.

Breitman, George. *The Last Year of Malcolm X.* New York: Schocken, 1968.

———, ed. *Malcolm X Speaks: Selected Speeches and Statements.* New York: Pathfinder, 1989.

Breyer, Chloe. "Religious Liberty in Law and Practice: Vietnamese Home Temples in California and the First Amendment." *Journal of Church and State,* Vol. 35, Spring 1993.

Brimelow, Peter. *Alien Nation: Common Sense About America's Immigration Disaster.* New York: Random House, 1985.

Bromley, David and Larry Shinn. *Krishna Consciousness in the West.* Lewisburg, PA: Bucknell University Press, 1989.

Bryan, William L. *Montana's Indians: Yesterday and Today.* Helena: American and World Geographic Publishing, 1996.

Burke, Mary Louise. *Swami Vivekananda in America: New Discoveries.* Calcutta: Advaita Ashrama, 1966.

Canniff, Julie Ann. "Cambodian Buddhism in Portland, Maine." Pluralism Project Research, 1993.

———. "Step by Step: A Field Study of Cambodian Religion and Culture in Portland Maine." Pluralism Project Research, 1993.

Carter, Stephen L. *The Culture of Disbelief.* New York: Basic Books, 1993.

Centennial Publication Committee, ed. *A Grateful Past, A Promising Future: Honpa Hongwanji Mission of Hawaii 100 Year History 1899–1989.* Honolulu: Honpa Hongwanji Mission of Hawaii, 1989.

Chandler, Stuart. "A Directory of Chinese Buddhist Organizations in the United States." Pluralism Project Research, 1991.

———. "The Hsi Lai Temple, Hacienda Heights, California," and "A Survey of Chinese Buddhist Temples in the U.S." Pluralism Project Research, 1992.

Chen, Jack. *The Chinese of America.* San Fransisco: Harper & Row Publishers, 1980.

Chodren, Pema. *The Wisdom of No Escape.* Boston: Shambhala, 1991.

Coble, Christopher. "A Wreath, a Prayer, and a Shovel of Dirt: Three Case-Studies of Religious Pluralism in the Greater Boston Area." Pluralism Project Research, 1992.

———. "Interfaith Activity at the Local Level." Pluralism Project Research, 1993.

———. "'The Clock Can Never Be Turned Back!' The Formation and Growth of Interfaith Groups in the Greater Boston Area." Pluralism Project Research, 1991.

Connors, Eugene T. *Religion and the Schools: Significant Court Decisions in the 1980's.* Bloomington, IN: Phi Delta Kappa Educational Foundation, 1988.

Council on Islamic Education. *Teaching About Islam and Muslims in the Public School Classroom: A Handbook for Educators,* 3rd. edition. Fountain Valley, CA: Council on Islamic Education, 1995.

Cox, Harvey. *Fire From Heaven: The Rise of Pentecostal Spirituality and the Reshaping of Religion in the Twenty-first Century.* Reading, MA: Addison-Welsey, 1995.

———. *Turning East.* New York: Simon and Schuster, 1977.

Dalai Lama. *The Good Heart: A Buddhist Perspective on the Teachings of Jesus.* Boston: Wisdom Publications, 1996.

Dasgupta, Sathi S. *On the Trail of an Uncertain Dream: Indian Immigrant Experience in America.* New York: AMS Press, 1989.

Dasgupta, Shamita Das, ed. *A Patchwork Shawl: Chronicles of South Asian Women in America.* New Brunswick, NJ: Rutgers University Press, 1998.

Deloria, Vine, Jr. *Behind the Trail of Broken Treaties.* New York: Delacorte Press, 1984.

———. *Custer Died for Your Sins.* New York: Avon Books, 1970.

Deloria, Vine, Jr. and Clifford M. Lytle. *The Nations Within: The Past and Future of American Indian Sovereignty.* New York: Pantheon Books, 1984.

Dinnerstein, Leonard. *Anti-Semitism in America.* Oxford: Oxford University Press, 1994.

Diouf, Sylviane A. *Servants of Allah: African Muslims Enslaved in the Americas.* New York: New York University Press, 1998.

Eck, Diana L. *Darsan: Seeing the Divine Image in India.* New York: Columbia University Press, 1995.

———. *Encountering God: A Spiritual Journey from Bozeman to Banaras.* Boston: Beacon Press, 1993.

———. "New Age Hinduism in America," in Nathan and Sulochana Glazer, eds. *Conflicting Images: India and the United States.* Glenndale, MD: Riverdale, 1990.

——— and Elinor J. Pierce, eds. *World Religions in Boston,* 4th edition. Cambridge: The Pluralism Project, 2000.

Eddy, Mary Baker. *Science and Health, with Key to the Scriptures.* Boston: Joseph Armstrong Publishing, 1904.

Elferdink, Claudia. "Rock Throwers at the Mosque." Pluralism Project Research, 1994.

Ellwood Jr., Robert S. *Alternative Altars.* Chicago: University of Chicago Press, 1979.

Epps, Archie. *Malcolm X: Speeches at Harvard.* New York: Paragon, 1991.

Esposito, John L. Islam. *The Straight Path.* New York: Oxford University Press, 1988.

Farber, Don and Rick Fields. *Taking Refuge in L.A.: Life in a Vietnamese Buddhist Temple.* New York: Aperture Books, 1987.

Feingold, Henry. *Zion in America: The Jewish Experience from Colonial Times to the Present.* New York: Hippocrene, 1974.

Fenton, John Y. *Transplanting Religious Traditions: Asian Indians in America.* New York: Praeger, 1988.

Fields, Rick. *How the Swans Came to the Lake: A Narrative History of Buddhism in America.* (1981) 3rd edition. Boston: Shambhala, 1992.

Fisher, Maxine P. *The Indians of New York City.* New Delhi: Heritage Publishers, 1980.

Flowers, Ronald. B. *That Godless Court? Supreme Court Decisions on Church-State Relationships.* Louisville: Westminster John Knox Press, 1994.

Freeman, James M. *Changing Identities: Vietnamese Americans, 1975–1995.* Boston: Allyn and Bacon, 1995.

French, Harold W. *The Swan's Wide Waters: Ramakrishna and Western Culture.* Port Washington, NY: Kennikat Press, 1974.

Friedman, Lenore. *Meetings with Remarkable Women.* Boston: Shambhala, 1987.

Gandhi, Rajanikant Suresh. *Locals and Cosmopolitans of Little India: A Sociological Study of the Indian Community at Minnesota U.S.A.* Bombay, India: Popular Prakashan, 1974.

Garber, Marjorie and Rebecca L Walkowitz, eds. *One Nation Under God?* New York: Routledge, 1999.

Gaustad, Edwin S. *A Documentary History of Religion in America* (2 Volumes). Grand Rapids: Wm. B. Eerdmans Publishing Co., 1982.

Giago, Tim, ed. *The American Indian and the Media.* Minneapolis: Lerner Publications, 1991.

Glazer, Nathan. *American Judaism.* Second Edition, Revised with a New Introduction. Chicago: University of Chicago Press, 1972.

———. *Ethnicity: Theory and Experience.* Cambridge: Harvard University Press, 1980.

———. "Is Assimilation Dead?" Annals, AAPSS, 530, November 1993.

———. *We Are All Multiculturalists Now.* Cambridge: Harvard University Press, 1997.

Glazer, Nathan and Daniel Patrick Moynihan. *Beyond the Melting Pot: The Negroes, Puerto Ricans, Jews, Italians and Irish of New York City.* Cambridge: MIT Press, 1963.

Gleason, Philip. "American Identity and Americanization." In Stephen Thernstrom, ed. *The Harvard Encyclopedia of American Ethnic Groups.* Cambridge: Harvard University Press, 1980.

———. "The Melting Pot: Symbol of Fusion or Confusion?" *American Quarterly,* Spring, 1964.

———. *Speaking of Diversity: Language and Ethnicity in Twentieth Century America.* Baltimore: Johns Hopkins University Press, 1992.

Glick, Rachel. "Hope and Conflict in a New World: The Zoroastrians of America." Pluralism Project Research, 1992.

Goldstein, Joseph and Jack Kornfield. *Seeking the Heart of Wisdom.* Boston: Shambala Books, 1986.

Goldstein, Joseph. *Transforming the Mind, Healing the World.* New York: Paulist Press, 1994.

Gordon, Milton. "Models of Pluralism: The New American Dilemma," *Annals of the American Academy of Political and Social Science* 454, March 1981.

Guillermo, Artemio R. *Churches Aflame: Asian Americans and United Methodism.* Nashville: Abingdon Press, 1991.

Hackett, David G. *Religion and American Culture, A Reader.* New York: Routledge, 1995.

Haddad, Yvonne Yazbeck and A. T. Lummis. *Islamic Values in the United States: A Comparative Study.* New York: Oxford University Press, 1987.

Haddad, Yvonne Yazbeck. "A Century of Islam in America." Washington: Islamic Affairs Programs, Middle East Institute, 1986, reprinted 1987.

———, ed. *The Muslims of America.* Oxford: Oxford University Press, 1991.

Haddad, Yvonne Yazbeck and Jane Idleman Smith. *Mission to America: Five Islamic Sectarian Communities in North America.* Gainesville: University Press of Florida, 1993.

Haddad, Yvonne Yazbeck and John L. Esposito. *Muslims on the Americanization Path?* Oxford: Oxford University Press, 2000.

Hallberg, Gerald N. "Bellingham, Washington's Anti-Hindu Riots," *Journal of the West.* 12 (January 1973), 163–75.

———. "Muslims in America: A Select Bibliography," *Muslim World.* 76 (1986), 93–122.

Handlin, Oscar. *Boston's Immigrants: A Study in Acculturation.* Cambridge: Harvard University Press, 1979.

Handy, Robert. *A Christian America: Protestant Hopes and Historical Realities.* 2nd ed. New York: University Press, 1984.

Haneef, Suzanne. *What Everyone Should Know about Islam and Muslims.* Des Plaines, IL: Library of Islam, 1993.

Hathout, Hassan. *Reading the Muslim Mind.* Los Angeles: Minaret Publishing House, 1995.

Hathout, Hassan, Fathi Osman, and Maher Hathout. *In Fraternity: A Message to Muslims in America.* Los Angeles: Minaret Publishing House, 1989.

Hawley, John Stratton and Gurinder Singh Mann. *Studying the Sikhs: Issues for North America.* Albany: State University of New York Press, 1993.

Hay, Stephen N. "Rabindranath Tagore in America," *American Quarterly.* 14 (Fall 1962).

Heng Sure and Heng Ch'an. *With One Heart, Bowing to the City of 10,000 Buddhas: Records of Heng Sure and Heng Ch'an.* San Francisco: Sino-American Buddhist Association, 1977.

Herberg, Will. *Protestant, Catholic, Jew.* Chicago: University of Chicago Press, 1983.

Hertzberg, Arthur. *The Jews in America, Four Centuries of an Uneasy Encounter: A History.* New York: Simon and Schuster, 1989.

Hibbets, Maria. "The Interfaith Conference of Metropolitan Washington: A Case-Study of the Boundaries of Interreligious Dialogue." Pluralism Project Research, 1993.

Hotchkiss, Brian D., ed. *Buddhism in America: Proceedings of the First Buddhism in America Conference.* Boston: Charles E. Tuttle Co., 1998.

Hunter, James Davison. *The Culture Wars.* New York: Basic Books, 1991.

Hunter, James Davison and Os Guiness. *Articles of Faith, Aritcles of Peace: The Religious Liberty Clauses and the American Public Philosophy.* Washington, D.C. The Brookings Institution, 1990.

Hutchison, William R., ed. *Between the Times: the Travail of the Protestant Establishment in America 1900–1960.* Cambridge: Cambridge University Press, 1989.

———. *The Modernist Impulse in American Protestantism.* Cambridge: Harvard University Press, 1976.

Israel Zangwill. *The Melting Pot: Drama in Four Acts.* New York: The Macmillan Company, 1911.

Jackson, Carl T. *The Oriental Religions and American Thought: Nineteenth-Century Explorations.* Westport, CT.: Greenwood Press, 1981.

———. *Vedanta for the West: The Ramakrishna Movements in the United States.* Bloomington: Indiana University Press, 1994.

Jain Digest. Cypress, CA: Federation of Jain Associations in North America.

Jefferson, Thomas. "An Act for Establishing Religious Freedom," in Henry S. Randall, *The Life of Thomas Jefferson in Three Volumes.* New York: Derby and Jackson, 1858, Vol. I.

Jensen, Joan M. "Apartheid: Pacific Coast Style," *Pacific Historical Review.* 38 (August 1969).

———. "East Indians" in Stephan Thernstrom, *The Harvard Encyclopedia of American Ethnic Groups.* Cambridge: Harvard University Press, 1980.

————. *Passage From India: Asian Immigrants in North America.* New Haven: Yale University Press, 1988.

Juergensmeyer, Mark. and N. Gerald Barrier, eds. *Sikh Studies: Comparative Perspectives on a Changing Tradition.* Berkeley: Berkeley Religious Studies Series, 1979.

Kallen, Horace. "Democracy Versus the Melting Pot," *The Nation,* Vol. 100. February 18 and 25, 1915.

Kamenetz, Rodger. *The Jew in the Lotus: A Poet's Rediscovery of Jewish Identity in Buddhist India.* San Francisco: HarperSanFrancisco, 1995.

Kapleau, Phillip. *Three Pillars of Zen.* New York and Tokyo: John Weatherhill, Inc., 1965.

Kennedy, Rudy Jo Reeves. "Single or Triple Melting Pot? Intermarriage Trends in New Haven, 1870–1950." *American Journal of Sociology* 58, July 1952.

Khema, Ayya. *When the Iron Eagle Flies: Buddhism for the West.* London: Penguin Books, 1991.

Kitano, Harry. *The Japanese Americans.* New York: Chelsea House Publishers, 1987.

Knitter, Paul. *No Other Name? A Critical Survey of Christian Attitudes Toward the World Religions.* Maryknoll: Orbis Books, 1985.

Kosmin, Barry A. and Seymour P. Lachman. *One Nation Under God: Religion in Contemporary American Society.* New York: Harmony Books, 1993.

Kramnick, Isaac and R. Laurence Moore. *The Godless Constitution.* New York: W. W. Norton, 1997.

Laderman, Gary, ed. *Religions of Atlanta: Religious Diversity in the Centennial Olympic City.* Atlanta: Scholars Press, 1996.

Layman, Emma McCloy. *Buddhism in America.* Chicago: Nelson-Hall, 1976.

Leonard, Karen Isaksen. *Making Ethnic Choices: California's Punjabi Mexican Americans.* Philadelphia: Temple University Press, 1992.

Levinson, David and Melvin Ember. *American Immigrant Cultures: Builders of a Nation.* Vols. I and II. New York: Simon and Schuster Macmillan, 1997.

Lieblich, Julia. "When the Muslims Came to Milton: A Case Study." Pluralism Project Research Seminar, 1992.

Lincoln, C. Eric. *The Black Muslims in America.* Boston: The Beacon Press, 1961.

Lindberg, Richard. *Ethnic Chicago.* Lincolnwood, IL: Passport Books, 1995.

Linder, Eileen W. *Yearbook of American and Canadian Churches 2000.* Nashville: Abingdon Press, 2000.

Madison, James. "A Memorial and Remonstrance of the Religious Rights of Man," in *Letters and Other Writings of James Madison.* Vol. 1., 1867,

Mahagosananda, with Jane Sharada Mahoney and Philip Edmonds, eds. *Step by Step.* Berkeley: Parallax Press, 1992.

Malcom X, with Alex Haley. *The Autobiography of Malcolm X.* New York: Ballantine Books, 1973.

Mamiya, L.H. "The Black Muslims as a new religious movement: their evolution and implications for the study of religion in a pluralistic society." In *Conflict and Cooperation Between Contemporary Religious Groups.* Tokyo: Chuo Academic Research Institute, 1988.

———. "From Black Muslim to Bilalian: the Evolution of a Movement," *Journal of the Scientific Study of Religion.* 21 (1982), 138–52.

———. "Minister Louis Farrakhan and the Final Call" in *The Muslim Community in North America,* Earle Waugh, et. al. eds. Edmonton: University of Alberta Press, 1983.

Mangiafico, Luciano. *Contemporary American Immigrants: Patterns of Filipino, Korean and Chinese Settlement in the U.S.* New York: Praeger Books, 1988.

Marty, Martin E. *The One and the Many: America's Struggle for the Common Good.* Cambridge: Harvard University Press, 1997.

McCloud, Aminah Beverly. *African American Islam.* New York: Routledge, 1995.

Mehdi, Beverlee Turner, ed. *The Arabs in America, 1492–1977: A Chronology and Fact Book.* Dobbs Ferry, NY: Oceana Publications, 1978.

Melton, J. Gordon. *Religious Bodies in the United States: A Directory.* New York: Garland Publishing, 1992.

Mitchell, Donald W. and James Wiseman, O.S.B., eds. *The Gethsemani Encounter.* New York: Continuum, 1997.

Mohammed, Warith Deen. *An African American Genesis.* Illinois: MACA Publications, 1986.

Mohammed, Imam W. D. *Al-Islam, Unity and Leadership.* Chicago: U.W. Mohammed, 1991.

Montero, Darrel. *Vietnamese Americans: Patterns of Resettlement and Socioeconomic Adaptation in the United States.* Colorado: Westview Press, 1979.

Moore, R., Laurence. *Religious Outsiders and the Making of Americans.* NY: Oxford University Press, 1986.

Morreale, Don, ed. *Buddhist America: Centers, Retreats, Practice.* Santa Fe, NM: John Muir Publications, 1988.

———. , ed. *The Complete Guide to Buddhist America.* Boston: Shambhala, 1998.

Muck, Terry. *Those Other Religions in Your Neighborhood: Loving your neighbor when you don't know how.* Grand Rapids: Zondervan Publishing, 1992.

Munekata, Ryo, ed. *Buddhist Churches of America: 75 Year History.* Vol. 1. Chicago: Nobart, Inc., 1974.

Murray, John Courtney. *We Hold These Truths: Catholic Reflections on the American Proposition.* [1960] Kansas City: Sheed and Ward, 1988.

Naff, Alixa. *Becoming American: The Early Arab Immigrant Experience.* Carbondale: Southern Illinois Univeristy Press, 1985.

Nee, Victor G., and Brett de Bary. *Longtime Californ': A Documentary Study of an American Chinatown.* New York: Pantheon Books, 1973.

Nelson, Elva. *A Bird's-Eye View: Vivekananda and his Swamis in Boston and Vicinity.* Boston: Ramakrishna Vedanta Society, 1992.

Neuhaus, Richard John. *The Naked Public Sqaure: Religion and Democracy in America.* Grand Rapids: William B. Eerdmans, 1984.

Nhat Hanh, Thich. *Love in Action: Writings on Nonviolent Social Change.* Berkeley, CA: Parallax Press, 1993.

———. *The Miracle of Mindfulness.* Boston: Beacon Press, 1975.

Noley, Homer. *First White Frost: Native Americans and United Methodism.* Nashville: Abingdon Press, 1991.

Noll, Mark A. *A History of Christianity in the United States and Canada.* Grand Rapids: William B. Eerdmans Publishing, 1992.

Noll, Mark A. et. al. *The Search for Christian America.* Colorado Springs: Helmers & Howard, 1989.

Novak, Michael. *The Rise of the Unmeltable Ethnics: Politics and Culture in the Seventies.* New York: Macmillan Co., 1973.

Nu'man, Fareed H. *The Muslim Population in the United States.* Washington D.C.: The American Muslim Council, 1992.

Oleksa, Michael. *Orthodox Alaska.* Crestwood, NY: St. Vladimir's Seminary Press, 1992.

Oren, Dan A. *Joining the Club: A History of Jews and Yale.* New Haven: Yale University Press, 1985.

Orsi, Robert Anthony. *The Madonna of 115th Street: Faith and Community in Italian Harlem, 1880–1950.* New York: Yale University Press, 1985.

Prebish, Charles S. *American Buddhism.* North Scituate, MA.: Duxbury Press, 1979.

———. *Luminous Passage: The Practice and Study of Buddhism in America.* Berkeley: University of California Press, 1999.

Prebish, Charles S. and Kenneth K. Tanaka. *The Faces of Buddhism in America.* Berkeley: University of California Press, 1999.

Prothero, Steven. *The White Buddhist: The Asian Odyssey of Henry Steel Olcott.* Bloomington: Indiana University Press, 1996.

Queen, Christopher S., ed. *Engaged Buddhism in the West.* Boston: Wisdom Publications, 2000.

Ramaswamy, Sunita and Sundar. *Vedic Heritage Teaching Program* (3 Vols.) Saylorsburg, PA: Arsha Vidya Gurukulam.

Rangaswamy, Padma. *Namaste America.* University Park, PA: The Pennsylvania State University Press, 2000.

Ravitch, Diane. "Multiculturalism yes, Particularism no (in study of Western Culture)." *Chronicle of Higher Education.* 37:44. October 24, 1990.

Richardson, E. Allen. *East Comes West.* New York: Pilgrim Press, 1985.

———. *Strangers in This Land: Pluralism and the Response to Diversity in the United States.* New York: Pilgrim Press, 1988.

Robins, Thomas and Dick Anthony, eds. *In Gods We Trust: New Patterns of Religious Pluralism in America.* New Brunswick, NJ: Transaction Books, 1981.

Rochford, E. B. *Hare Krishna in America.* New Brunswick: Rutgers University Press, 1985.

Rose, Peter I. *Tempest-Tost: Race, Immigration, and the Dilemmas of Diversity.* New York: Oxford University Press, 1997.

Rosenblatt, Roger. "Their Finest Hour." *New York Times Magazine,* July 3, 1994.

Rosovsky, Nitza. *The Jewish Experience at Harvard and Radcliffe.* Cambridge: Harvard University Press, 1986.

Rutledge, Paul. *The Role of Religion in Ethnic Self-Identity: A Vietnamese Community.* Lanham, MD: University Press of America, 1985.

Sadlowski, Caroline. "Writing Whose Religion Back into History? The Secular Study of Religion in California Public Schools." Harvard College A.B. Thesis (Comparative Study of Religion), 1993.

Saran, Parmatma. *The Asian Indian Experience in the United States.* Cambridge: Schenkman Publishing Co., Inc., 1985.

Saran, Parmatma, and Edwin Eames, eds. *The New Ethnics: Asian Indians in the United States.* Foreword by Nathan Glazer. New York: Praeger Publishers, 1980.

Sarna, Jonathan D., ed. *The Jews of Boston.* Boston: American Jewish Historical Society, 1996.

Schlesinger, Arthur M. Jr. *The Disuniting of America: Reflections on a Multicultural Society.* New York: Norton, 1991.

Schreiber-Cohn, Sally. "A Word-Portrait: The Sufi Order Founded by Hazrat Inayat Khan in 1910." Pluralism Project Research Seminar, 1993.

Seager, Richard Hughes. *Buddhism in America.* New York: Columbia University Press, 1999.

———, ed. *The Dawn of Religious Pluralism.* Chicago: Open Court Press, 1992.

———. *The World's Parliament of Religions.* Indianapolis: Indiana University Press, 1995.

Seeling, Holly. "Authority and Transmission in the American Jain Tradition." Pluralism Project Research, 1991.

———. "The Jain Tradition in America: Centers, Organizations, and Temples." Pluralism Project Research, 1991.

Seung Sahn. *Only Don't Know: The Teaching Letters of Zen Master Seung Sahn.* Cumberland, RI: Primary Point Press, 1985.

Shah, Vikram V., ed. *Jain Heritage—Then, Now, and Forever: Pratishtha Mahotsav Souvenir.* Bartlett, IL: Jain Society of Metropolitan Chicago, 1993.

Shen, C. T. *Mayflower II: On the Buddhist Voyage to Liberation.* Taipei: Torch of Wisdom Publishing House, 1983.

Shipps, Jan. *Mormonism: The Story of a New Religious Tradition.* Urbana: University of Illinois Press, 1984.

Sowell, Thomas. *Ethnic America: A History.* New York: Basic Books, 1981.

St. John de Crevecoeur, J. Hector. *Letters From an American Farmer.* London: Thomas Davies, 1782.

Stavans, Ilan. *The Hispanic Condition: Reflections on Culture and Identity in America.* New York: HarperCollins, 1995.

Stockman, Robert. *The Baha'i Faith in America.* (Vol. 1, 1892–1900), Wilmette, IL: Baha'i Publishing Trusts, 1985.

Strong, Josiah. *Our Country: Its Possible Future and Its Present Crisis.* New York: The Baker and Taylor Company, 1891.

Suzuki, Shunryu. *Zen Mind, Beginner's Mind.* New York: Weatherhill, 1970.

Takaki, Ronald. *Strangers from a Different Shore: A History of Asian Americans.* Boston: Little, Brown and Company, 1989.

Taylor, Charles and Amy Gutman. *Multiculturalism and "The Politics of Recognition."* Princeton: Princeton University Press, 1992.

Tejomayananda, Swami. *Hindu Culture: An Introduction.* Piercy, CA: Chinmaya Publications, 1993.

Thernstrom, Stephan, ed. *Harvard Encyclopedia of American Ethnic Groups.* Cambridge: Harvard University Press, 1980.

Thomas, Wendell Marshall. *Hinduism Invades America.* New York: Beacon Press, Inc., 1930.

Tocqueville, Alexis de. *Democracy in America.* Translated by George Lawrence. Garden City: Doubleday, 1969.

Tsai, Shih-Shan Henry. *The Chinese Experience in America.* Bloomington: Indiana University Press, 1986.

Tuck, Donald. *Buddhist Churches of America: Jodo Shinshu.* Lewiston, NY: Edwin Mellen Press, Studies in American Religion, Vol. 28, 1987.

Turner, Richard Brent. *Islam in the African-American Experience.* Indianapolis: Indiana University Press, 1997.

Tweed, Thomas A. *The American Encounter with Buddhism 1844–1912.* Bloomington: Indiana University Press, 1992.

Tweed, Thomas A. and Stephen Prothero, eds. *Asian Religion in America: A Documentary History.* New York: Oxford University Press, 1999.

Tworkov, Helen. *Zen in America: Profiles of Five Teachers.* San Francisco: North Point Press, 1989.

Vecsey, Christopher, ed. *Handbook of American Indian Religious Freedom.* New York: Crossroads Publishing, 1991.

———. *Imagine Ourselves Richly: Mythic Narratives of North American Indians.* New York: HarperCollins Publishers, 1991.

Versluis, Arthur. *American Transcendentalism and Asian Religions.* Oxford: Oxford University Press, 1993.

Villafane, Eldin. *The Liberating Spirit: Toward an Hispanic American Pentecostal Social Ethic.* Grand Rapids: William B. Eerdmans Publishing, 1993.

Viswanathan, Ed. *Am I a Hindu? The Hinduism Primer.* San Francisco: Halo Books, 1992.

Vivekananda Vedanta Society. *Vedanta in Chicago: Golden Jubilee Souvenir.* Chicago: Vivekananda Vedanta Society, 1981.

Vivekananda, Swami. *Raja Yoga.* New York: Ramakrishna-Vivekananda Center, 1973.

Walzer, Michael. *On Toleration.* New Haven: Yale University Press, 1997.

Walzer, Michael. *What it Means to Be an American: Essays on the American Experience.* New York: Marsilio, 1992.

Waters, Mary. *Ethnic Options: Choosing Identities in America.* Berkeley: University of California Press, 1990.

Waugh, Earle H. "The Imam in the New World: Models and Modifications," in *Transitions and Transformations in the History of Religions.* Edited by F.E. Reynolds. Leiden: E. J. Brill, 1980.

Waugh, Earle W. and R. B. Quereshi, eds. *Muslim Families in North America.* Edmonton: University of Alberta Press, 1991.

Waugh, Earle W. et al. *The Muslim Community in North America.* Edmonton: University of Alberta Press, 1983.

Webb, Mohammad Alexander Russell. *Islam in America: A Brief Statement of Mohammedanism and an Outline of American Islamic Progaganda.* New York: Oriental Publishing, 1893.

Williams, Duncan R. and Christopher S. Queen. *American Buddhism: Methods and Findings in Recent Scholarship.* Surrey: Curzon, 1999.

Williams, Peter W. *America's Religions: Traditions and Cultures.* New York: Macmillan Press, 1990.

Williams, Raymond Brady. *Religions of Immigrants from India and Pakistan: New Threads in the American Tapestry.* Cambridge: Cambridge University Press, 1988.

Wilson, John F, ed. *Church and State in America: A Bibliographical Guide.* New York: Greenwood Press, 1986.

Wilson, John F. and Donald L. Drakeman, eds. *Church and State in American History: The Burden of Religious Pluralism.* Boston: Beacon Press, 1987.

Wind, James P. and James W. Lewis, *American Congregations* (2 Volumes). Chicago: University of Chicago Press, 1994.

Yogananda, Paramahansa. *Autobiography of a Yogi.* Los Angeles: Self-Realization Fellowship, 1946.

———. *Scientific Healing Affirmations.* Los Angeles: Self-Realization Fellowship, 1958.

Yoo, David K, ed. *New Spiritual Homes: Religion and Asian Americans.* Honolulu: University of Hawaii, 1999.

Ziolkowski, Eric J., ed. *A Museum of Faiths: Histories and Legacies of the 1893 World's Parliament of Religions.* Atlanta: Scholar's Press, 1993.

INDEX

★

DATE DUE

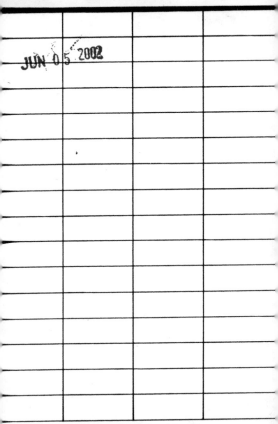

JUN 05 2002